# WITHOUT GETTING KILLED OR CAUGHT

*John and Robin Dickson Series in Texas Music*
Sponsored by the Center for Texas Music History
Texas State University–San Marcos
Gary Hartman, General Editor

# Without Getting Killed or Caught

## The Life and Music of Guy Clark

TAMARA SAVIANO

TEXAS A&M UNIVERSITY PRESS • COLLEGE STATION

This paper meets the requirements
of ANSI/NISO Z39.48-1992 (Permanence of Paper).
Binding materials have been chosen for durability.
Manufactured in the United States of America

LIBRARY OF CONGRESS CATALOGING-IN-PUBLICATION DATA

Names: Saviano, Tamara, author.

Title: Without getting killed or caught: the life and music of Guy Clark /
   Tamara Saviano.

Other titles: John and Robin Dickson series in Texas music.

Description: First edition. | College Station: Texas A&M University Press,
   [2016] | Series: John and Robin Dickson series in Texas music | Includes
   bibliographical references and index.

Identifiers: LCCN 2016009105 (print) | LCCN 2016010392 (ebook) |
   ISBN 9781623494544 (cloth: alk. paper) | ISBN 9781623494551 (ebook)

Subjects: LCSH: Clark, Guy. | Country musicians—United States—Biography.

Classification: LCC ML420.C5364 S38 2016 (print) | LCC ML420.C5364 (ebook) |
   DDC 782.421642092—dc23

LC record available at http://lccn.loc.gov/2016009105

Cover photo courtesy of Jim McGuire Photography.

**For the late Chet Flippo:**

*trailblazer, advocate, mentor, friend*

# CONTENTS

# PREFACE

The first time I heard a Guy Clark song was on my dad's turntable at our home in Milwaukee, Wisconsin. It was Guy's first album, *Old No. 1*. Dad's friend Rudy brought a stack of LPs over to our house. As they debated the worth of Memphis soul versus southern rock, I sat on the floor and planted my ear against the speaker. The lyric sleeve floated on my lap as I tried to listen and read at the same time. I wanted to know everything about the songs that blared out of the box, the vivid four-minute short stories about exotic people and locations.

Who was Rita Ballou and what was a slow Uvalde shuffle? "She's a rawhide rope and velvet mixture, walkin' talkin' Texas texture" was the best line I'd heard in my fourteen years. And that was just the first song. "Words and Music by Guy Clark" was clearly printed beneath each song title on the white paper sleeve. I know for sure this was the first time I understood that an artist had written the songs, and it was the beginning of my love affair with songwriters. At the end of my first listening session (I turned it over for side B, turned it back to side A, and had listened to it three times through before Dad and Rudy even noticed), "She Ain't Goin' Nowhere" was my new theme song, and I could pretty much recite all the lyrics to the other nine tracks. I bought my own copy of *Old No. 1* before the week was out.

The first time I laid eyes on Guy Clark was twenty years later. By now I lived in Nashville and worked as a music journalist at *Country Weekly* magazine. *Dublin Blues* was new, and I went over to Asylum Records to pick up a copy. As I stood at the reception desk, the big glass door opened behind me. I felt his presence before I turned around to steal a look. "Hello, Guy," the receptionist greeted him. "You can go on back." Guy was an imposing figure, tall and solid, with size 14 shoes holding up his six-three frame, hair thick and tousled, and an unlit cigarette between his fingers. It was then, my first-ever glimpse of Guy, that I noticed the striking, oval, turquoise ring flash from his right hand. I stared at Guy's stick-straight posture as he strolled confidently across the reception lobby and disappeared into the cavern of the hallway.

The first real time I spent with Guy was five years later, in April 2000. I was now the managing editor at *Country Music* magazine. During my tenure at *Country Music*, Guy's friend Lee Roy Parnell and I planned to write a book about Texas music. That book never came to fruition, but it did lead me to Guy. Lee Roy, his girlfriend Donna, Guy, Susanna (Guy's wife), and I sat in Guy's workshop for nine hours on a rainy Saturday while the tape recorder ran and I asked questions. The sweet scent of wet grass and spring rain wafted through open windows and mixed with a heady aroma of coffee, cigarettes, marijuana, whiskey, and fresh wood shavings.

Guy's workshop is in the basement of his home on Stoneway Close, a narrow, tree-lined, dead-end street tucked between Knob Road and White Bridge Road on the west side of Nashville. The house itself is unremarkable, but Guy's workshop is a cozy refuge. The floor is covered with sheets of thick particleboard. Two workbenches—one for writing songs and one for building guitars—flank the small room.

An eerie Townes Van Zandt stares from a portrait above the band saw next to the scarred workbench where Guy writes the songs that make all the other Nashville songwriters jealous. A rack of cassette tapes fills the entire wall behind Guy's rolling desk chair. There are hundreds of cassettes. Many of the labels are too faded to read, but I make out a few: "Townes, Cactus Club 1991," "Better Days sessions," and "Demos March 4," are noted in Guy's careful printing on the spines.

On the opposite wall, Guy's antique woodcarving tools hang on a pegboard next to the second workbench, the one where he builds acoustic guitars made of rosewood—an art he's practiced since he lived in Houston in the early 1960s. A blueprint for a Flamenco guitar is taped next to an open window, which faces the lush, green backyard.

The songwriting workbench is littered with graph paper and #2 pencils, Guy's preferred writing materials. The centerpiece is a cluster of rolling papers, a canister of Peter Stokkebye 1882 Danish import tobacco, a Ziploc bag of pot, and a heavy round pottery ashtray ringed with ceramic skulls and roses, a gift from his friend Emmylou Harris.

Watching Guy hand-roll tobacco cigarettes and marijuana joints is now old hat, but that first day I was hypnotized at the way his slender fingers—topped with acrylic nails to aid his guitar picking—methodically dipped into his tobacco can, removed just the right amount of the dried leaves and rolled a perfect cigarette. Guy rarely looked down at what his hands were doing and held up his end of the conversation with ease. I don't think I ever looked up at Guy because I couldn't take my eyes off the movement of his hands and the extraordinary turquoise ring.

The transcript of that first interview contains all the usual Guy Clark stories and quotes that anyone who knows anything about Guy has heard or read over the years. All these years later I ask myself how it is that we did not cover any new ground in nine hours.

The first time (okay, the only time) I got drunk and high with Guy was in September 2002. Earlier that year, Sugar Hill Records had hired me to write the media materials for Guy's album The Dark. Once again I met Guy in his basement workshop, peppered him with questions, and watched him work his magic with rolling papers. The Dark was released the week of the Americana Music Conference, and Sugar Hill hosted a small dinner for Guy on the patio of Sunset Grill in Nashville's Hillsboro Village. I sat next to Guy, who wore an old blue shirt and a black vest. He was a gallant dinner partner. My wine glass was never empty, he asked what I wanted to eat and placed my order with the waitress, and he stood when I excused myself to go to the restroom. Although Guy tried to exhale it away from me, I was happy to whiff his secondhand smoke. After dinner a group of us went into the bar for drinks. One thing led to another, and before I knew it I was heading to the club 12th and Porter with Guy to see a show.

The Americana community is small and close-knit, and Guy and I knew many people at the club. A group gathered around us at the bar.

"What are you having, Tamara?"

"Whatever you're having, Guy."

"Want to go outside and get high, Tamara?"

"Sure, Guy. I'd love to."

I drank what Guy drank (numerous glasses of wine and a few short tumblers of Bailey's Irish Cream on the rocks) and smoked what Guy smoked (we shared a few joints with a few friends). It was just another night for Guy. It took me a week to recover.

The first time I worked with Guy was in 2006. Dualtone Records hired me to head up the publicity campaign for Guy's album *Workbench Songs*. Guy was diagnosed with lymphoma that year. He showed up for a planning meeting wearing a cowboy hat to cover the barren scalp that once nurtured his full head of hair. Before he arrived, the Dualtone staff bumbled around the office. They dashed off in all directions to make fresh coffee, photocopy the marketing plan, and move chairs around the conference table so Guy had a comfortable place to sit. Most of them hadn't spent much time with Guy, and I found it amusing that he intimidated them. Although I didn't know Guy well at the time, he had always struck me as a man with a soft heart, contrary to his tough guy image. His song lyrics supported my notion, from "Desperados Waiting for a Train," "Randall Knife," "Coat from the Cold," "Old Friends," "Stuff That Works," and "Dublin Blues," just to name a few.

We had a great press campaign with *Workbench Songs*, which culminated with a Grammy nomination. Dualtone hired me again to work *Somedays the Song Writes You* in 2009, which was also nominated for a Grammy. Meanwhile, during this time, my Austin friends Gary and Francine Hartman took me to lunch at the Texas Chili Parlor so I could see the place that inspired "Dublin Blues." Gary, the director of the Center for Texas Music History at Texas State University in San Marcos, asked me if I would ever consider writing a book about Guy. "I would love to write a book about Guy," I said. "But he would never go for it, and I wouldn't do it without him." The words of Guy's "Exposé," on *Workbench Songs*, ran through my head:

> Now when you write your exposé
> Don't kiss and tell it all
> No one likes a tattletale writin' on the wall
> Don't go talkin' out of school
> 'Cause you know you got no call
> If you can't say something nice
> Don't say anything at all.

But the idea of a book appealed to me and stuck. I was too chicken to ask Guy outright, so I sent a proposal to his manager, Keith Case. Within a few hours, Keith called me and told me that Guy was in. I'll never forget that conversation.

"Really?" I didn't believe it.

"Yes," Keith said. "Guy says he'll do it."

"I better go over and talk to him about it in person," I said. I still did not believe it.

Keith laughed. "Go ahead. Talk to him about it."

So I did. I sat in my usual spot in front of Guy's workbench and watched him hand-roll his cigarettes and joints, still unable to take my eyes off of the turquoise ring.

"Guy, are you sure you're up for this?" I asked. "I want you to spend hours and hours with me and let me interview you about your life. I want you to introduce me to your family and friends and cowriters and colleagues and anyone who is important to your story and tell them to speak honestly with me. Then I'm going to write the book. And you can't read it until it's published."

Guy took a long toke off his joint, held it, and exhaled—unfazed. "Sounds fair to me, Tamara," he said.

And so it began. In late 2008, I began interviewing Guy on the record, with this book in mind. Between Guy's health problems and a setback of my

own, we got off track in 2009. In 2010 and 2011, Shawn Camp and I copro-
duced *This One's For Him: A Tribute to Guy Clark*. It's a double-CD set with thirty-
three artists singing thirty Guy Clark songs. It interfered with my research
time but I think the book became richer for it.

I traipsed around Texas with and without Guy several times in 2010, 2011,
and 2012, listening to stories of his youth—his early years spent in the hard-
scrabble West Texas plains and coming-of-age years on the sun-baked Gulf
Coast beaches in Rockport. I accompanied Guy and Verlon Thompson to
concerts at cool venues including the Old Quarter in Galveston, the Paramount Theatre in Austin, another Paramount Theatre in Abilene, Gruene
Hall in New Braunfels, Poor David's Pub in Dallas, and the Rockport Music
Festival near the same beach where Guy used to water ski in the mornings
before his high school classes started.

Watching Guy perform night after night took me back to the time I met
him—the day I interviewed him for nine hours without coming away with
any new information. And I came to understand why Guy told the same stories in interviews over and over and year after year. Like the tales he spins on
stage at every concert, they are part of the fabric of Guy's life as a performer.

Take "L.A. Freeway." If you are reading this book, you likely know the
story. Guy and Susanna lived in Los Angeles for a short time. On the way
home from a gig late one night Guy said: "If I could just get off of this L.A.
Freeway without getting killed or caught." He realized there was a song
there and wrote the line on a burger sack with Susanna's eyebrow pencil.
At his live shows, after he sings most of the song, Guy tells the story of the
garage apartment he and Susanna shared in Long Beach as he continues to
strum the pretty melody.

"Susanna and I used to live in this little apartment out in Los Angeles-
damn-California" Guy starts. "Pretty weird place." He pauses. "The weird-
est thing about this particular little hovel was the landlord. He was one of
those guys who'd come home from work every day, go out to the garage
and make his own bullets. Nice thing about it, however, was right outside the front window was the prettiest grapefruit tree you'd seen in your
whole life. Ah, the grapefruit were sweet." Guy pauses, sighs, shrugs, and

bends his words in all the right places to convince the audience to stay with the story. "One morning I awoke to the sound of this landlord outside the front window with an ax, chopping down the grapefruit tree. So I went outside—very carefully. I said, 'Man, what are you doing?' He said, 'Guy, this damned old grapefruit tree, it's been here thirty or forty years, I guess. It's gotten so big and the roots spread out so far it's starting to crack my concrete patio.'" Then Guy breaks into song again and brings the story to a close: "Pack up all your dishes, make note of all good wishes, say goodbye to the landlord for me, the sumbitch has always bored me—" The crowd erupts in applause every time.

Long before I began working on this book I knew his repertoire, had read countless press clips, and spent enough time around Guy to know that he does not like to talk about himself. I pushed on with the knowledge that I could back out if Guy didn't give me anything.

From the first interview, Guy surprised me. The moment I turned on the recorder, Guy opened his mouth and spilled stories that many of his closest friends hadn't heard. He ventured down roads I never believed he would, not tiptoeing around the thorns but barreling right into them, scratches and cuts be damned. I spent three hours with Guy that first day. On my way home, I stopped at Kroger to get a few groceries and wandered through the aisles in a daze—I had a bit of a contact high from breathing in marijuana smoke but mostly I was dizzy with the possibilities that now stretched before me.

Now I want to take you on that journey, down the same roads I traveled, and tell you Guy's story the way I came to know it. Of course, there are hundreds of stories that are not included because otherwise the book would be ten thousand pages long. I wrote the book I wanted to write and chose to focus on three themes: Guy's influence as a songwriter, his recording career, and the fascinating relationship between Guy, Susanna, and Townes. That said, buckle up. It's a hell of a ride.

Tamara Saviano
Nashville, Tennessee
September 15, 2015

# ACKNOWLEDGMENTS

Most importantly, I am grateful to Guy Clark for agreeing to this magical journey. When Guy and I began to discuss the book he said, "I'm not out to rewrite the truth." He opened the door for me to find that truth and allowed me to talk with his friends, family, and colleagues as much as I wanted or needed to understand the full spectrum of his incredible life. Guy spent many hours with me beginning in 2008 and never ducked the painful parts of his life or tried to pretty up his image. It was difficult for me to make decisions about what should go in the book, yet Guy and I never discussed it. He left it to me to follow my own instincts on what was appropriate.

There are hundreds of ways one can approach writing a biography of this breadth and scope. I hope I have conveyed how important Guy is as an artist as well as shed some light on how his lifestyle and relationships fed his artistry. For every story, I found at least one additional source to confirm Guy's side. If Guy and Susanna Clark told me the same story separately, I felt comfortable writing it as their truth. Any mistakes in the manuscript are mine.

Hundreds of people helped me write this book by taking the time to speak with me, assist me with research, transcribe interviews, boost my confidence when it flagged, and reaffirm that Guy's story needed to be written. Each of them played a crucial role and it would take another book to name and thank all of them.

Rodney Crowell's importance to this book cannot be overstated. When I started, Rodney said: "If you want to write honestly about Guy and Susanna, you need to go to the dark side." Rodney took me there, with dignity, grace, and a deep love for Guy and Susanna.

Sorting out Guy's childhood years would have been impossible without his sisters, Caroline Dugan and Jan Clark. The happiest surprise of this project is the friendship that unfolded between Caro, Jan, and me. They took me in, shared the family archives, and told me stories about ancestors, grandparents, and parents. The book may have an end, but Caro and Jan will be my lifelong friends. What a gift.

Another sweet friendship unfolded with Susanna's niece, Sherri Talley. I waited for a year after Susanna's death to contact Sherri, and once we met, I felt like I found insight into Susanna and her family that no one else could have provided. Sherri and I also shared a traumatic and dramatic day with Guy, which bonds us forever.

Louise O'Connor shared insightful raw transcripts from her interviews with Guy, Townes Van Zandt, Susanna, and Guy's family and friends that she conducted in 1990 and 1991. Those transcripts, especially the intimate conversations with Susanna, are pure gold, and I am thankful and honored that Louise chose to share them for this book.

Robert Earl Hardy, Bill DeYoung, and Joe Specht also shared interviews with Guy, Susanna, and others. The generosity of my fellow journalists extends to Grant Alden, Brian T. Atkinson, Deb Barnes, Bill Bentley, Peter Blackstock, Peter Cooper, Don Cusic, the late Chet Flippo, Peter Guralnick, Craig Havighurst, William Hedgepeth, Taylor Holliday, Lynne Margolis, Alanna Nash, John Spong,and Michael Streissguth, all who lifted me up when I needed it most.

Guy's friends Jim McGuire, Verlon Thompson, and Shawn Camp became my good friends along the way. McGuire spent many hours poring through photos for me. All of them allowed me to interview them time and time again. Shawn, Verlon, and I worked together on the tribute album. Most of all, I just had the honor of hanging out with these three amazing men.

I am indebted to my Austin friends Joe and Sharon Ely, Connie Nelson, Bart Knaggs, and Jack Ingram for jumping in (always on short notice) to help in too many ways to list. You know why I love you. Thank you, thank you, thank you.

Enormous thanks to Gary Hartman from the Center for Texas Music History and his lovely wife, Francine; my editors with Texas A&M University Press, Thom Lemmons, Katie Duelm, and freelancer Chris Dodge; Pam Tubridy-Baucom, Dayton Duncan, Katy Haas, Julie Dunfey, and the folks at Florentine Films; Louisa McCune and Dixie Clements at the Kirkpatrick

Foundation; and David Murrah, Janie White and JoAnn Morgan at the Aransas County (Texas) Historical Society.

Thanks to Joe Ables, Terry and Jo Harvey Allen, Claire Armbruster, John Beiter, Matthew Bell, Alison Booth, Rob Bleetstein, Michael Brovsky, Keith Case, Rosanne Cash, Claudia Church, Travis and Krista Clark, Kay Clary, Donald and Kathryn Counts, Dub Cornett, John and Robin Dickson, Richard Dobson, Steve Earle, Harold Eggers, Ramblin' Jack Elliott, Jenni Finlay, Rosie Flores, Radney Foster, James Richard Fox, Joe Galante, Bonnie Garner, Mary Gauthier, Vince Gill, Jimmie Dale Gilmore, Holly Gleason, John Grady, Jon Grimson, Jen Gunderman, Jeff Hanna, Cyndi Hoelzle, Cindy Howell, Lisa and Gene Oltz, Crow Johnson, Christopher Joyce, Robert Earl Keen, Demetria Kalodimos, April Kimble, Carl Kornmeyer, Kris and Lisa Kristofferson, Rick Lambert, Brennen Leigh, Richard Leigh, Craig Leon, Ken Levitan, Mike Lipskin, Fran Lohr, John Lomax III, John Nova Lomax, Lyle Lovett, Noel McKay, James McMurtry, Paul Milosevich, Buddy Mondlock, Ashley Monroe, Elyse Moore, Al Moss, Jay Newberg, Gary Nicholson, Tim O'Brien, Kerry O'Neil, K. T. Oslin, Gary Overton, Wendy Pearl, Richard Pells, Gretchen Peters, Barry Poss, Mickey Raphael, Dave Rawlings, Abbey Road, Scott Robinson, Don Sanders, Darrell Scott, Richard Skanse, Susan Slocum, Connie Smith, Carl Snyder, Joe Specht, Jon Randall Stewart, Keith Sykes, Wendy Thessen, Liz Thiels, Tasha Thomas, J. T. Van Zandt, Ben Vaughn, Kurt Vitolo, Jerry Jeff and Susan Walker, Kelcy Warren, Gillian Welch, Kathi Whitley, Minor Wilson, and Will Wynn. I'm sure I'm leaving someone out.

Nothing is possible without my husband, best friend, and partner Paul Whitfield. Baby, you are the sun, the moon, and the stars. I love you.

# Prologue

Nashville, Tennessee
November, 1971

Guy Clark and Susanna Talley eased into Nashville on a rainy November night in 1971. Guy had driven his rusted junker of a Volkswagen bus from Houston to Los Angeles back to Houston and now to Tennessee. It was loaded with everything they owned: a few clothes and dishes, a guitar, Susanna's paintings, and all the tools and parts needed to fix the damn thing if it broke down in the desert. For once there was a little money in Guy's wallet. He had just signed his first publishing deal as a songwriter. The beat-up leather also held a scrap from a burger sack with a partial lyric that read: "If I could just get off of this L.A. Freeway without getting killed or caught."

Guy often says that Nashville in the '70s was like Paris in the '20s. And if that is the case, Guy and Susanna were the F. Scott and Zelda Fitzgerald of Nashville. Married in 1972, the Clarks would come to shape the folk and singer-songwriter scene in Music City much like the Fitzgeralds fashioned the jazz age.

By the time Guy and Susanna arrived in Tennessee, Willie Nelson had moved back to Austin and banded the hippies and rednecks together with his rowdy mix of country and rock 'n' roll. Kris Kristofferson's star skyrocketed in Hollywood, and Waylon Jennings had just begun to record his album *Ladies Love Outlaws*.

Earlier that year Janis Joplin's hit with Kristofferson's "Me and Bobby McGee" and Sammi Smith's version of "Help Me Make It Through the Night" were at the top of the *Billboard* Hot 100 Chart. Kristofferson graced the cover of *Look* magazine's country music special with the headline: "Kris Kristofferson, First Superstar of the New Country Music." Only a year before, in the fall of 1970, a stoned Kristofferson stumbled on his way to the stage to accept the Country Music Association Song of the Year award for "Sunday Morning Coming Down," and this year, an African American, Charley Pride, won Entertainer of the Year.

Mickey Newbury, the only person Guy knew in Nashville, had just released the album *San Francisco Mabel Joy*, and Jerry Lee Lewis had taken Mickey's song "She Even Woke Me Up to Say Goodbye" to number two. Tom T. Hall had recently topped the chart with "The Year Clayton Delaney Died."

There was a new Music City brewing underground. Outlaw songwriters were bubbling up into the mainstream, and Guy was about to become a lion in this modern breed of Nashville cat.

"Writers like Mickey, Kristofferson, and Roger Miller were writing really good songs," Guy said. "They proved that the audience is a lot hipper than the music business gives them credit for. I wanted to write songs, and Nashville seemed the best place to do it."

Now—just weeks after Guy's thirtieth birthday—Guy and Susanna were here, in Nashville, determined to start a new life together.

On their first night in Music City, they checked into a seedy motel on Dickerson Pike, an area known for drug dealers and prostitutes. They stayed for a night or two until money ran low and then hightailed it out to Old Hickory Lake to crash on Newbury's houseboat for a few weeks. By Christmas, Guy had found a small, cheap house for rent in East Nashville at 1307 Chapel Avenue, and they moved into their first Nashville home.

No one could predict then how Guy and Susanna would transform the lives of songwriters, singers, and artists, weaving threads in a tapestry that would grow in size and strength, an influence that would blanket all of American roots music, stretching to Texas and beyond. No one then realized that they would leave an indelible mark on generations to come.

To understand, one must start at the beginning.

# PART ONE

# The Beginning

# Monahans

Novelist Larry McMurtry once said that Odessa, Texas, is the worst town on earth. Guy Charles Clark was born just thirty-five miles southwest of Odessa near the Sandhills State Park in Monahans. Driving to Monahans from Interstate 10 near Fort Stockton the view is all blue sky draped over dry brown scrub brush. Telephone poles march along the endless asphalt on the highway, and oil well derricks dot the landscape. There is a stark beauty to the desolation yet it feels as lonely as the end of the earth.

On September 20, 2011, my research assistant and I pull into the parking lot of the town's nicest hotel, the Best Western. From Austin, we have driven west nearly four hundred miles through the godforsaken desert to get to the middle of nowhere. Welcome to West Texas.

The hotel parking lot is crawling with oil workers wearing red coveralls with Halliburton patches sewed on them. There is an oil boom in Monahans for the first time in many decades. We check in at the front desk and ask for a recommendation for a restaurant with a decent wine list. There is no wine or liquor by the glass here, we're told. Pizza Hut and the local Mexican restaurant serve beer, and that's it.

More than eighty years after Guy's grandmother Rossie ran her black-market liquor business in her small café, Clark's Lunch, one still can't get a drink. We settle for salad and a potato at the brightly lit Bar H Steakhouse on Stockton Avenue.

Although bleak and monochromatic, there is something irresistible about Monahans. It still feels like the Old West here, and one can easily recognize how the town and its characters, including Guy's own family, so profoundly influenced the narratives of songs including "Desperados Waiting for a Train," "New Cut Road," "Texas 1947," "Rita Ballou," "Lone Star Hotel," and "Crystelle."

"Texas has always had that distinct valor," Guy says. "You know, it's where Davy Crockett and Sam Houston went from Tennessee. People from all over the South hammered signs on their doors that said G.T.T., Gone to Texas. Whenever someone would go bust or had enough of where they were living, they'd put a sign on the door and head to Texas. Romantic notions about Texas have been going on since Coronado and the seven cities of gold. It's hardscrabble land, but it has that independent spirit about it. In first grade, all school kids in Texas [would] get a comic book that's covered like a Texas flag with drawings and cartoons of the history of Texas, and you'd carry that book with you everywhere."

Monahans, in the center of the Permian Basin, got its start as the place where wood- and coal-burning trains stopped to get water after New York Irishman John Thomas Monahan dug a well in 1881 for the railroad-building crews. Comanche, Mescalero Apache, and Lipan Apache Indians once roamed the region around the extraordinary white sand hills, spread out between the great Staked Plain and the Pecos River. The water source came to be called Monahan's Well. The locals installed a pump station and two enormous water tanks shortly after the Texas and Pacific Railway was completed to Sierra Blanca. A depot made from an old boxcar came later.

The post office officially adopted the name Monahans in 1891. By 1905, the Monahans population reached eighty-nine. Ranchers and farmers made up the industry of Ward County until the West Texans found rich oil pools beneath the hard ground in the mid 1920s. Oil surged from newly discovered fields, and it needed to be stored somewhere until it could be shipped to the refinery. The Shell Oil Company built a million-barrel tank on eighty acres in 1928, at a cost of more than a quarter-million dollars, but the tank was only filled once before the town abandoned the project. The tank leaked. Taxes went up. And the Great Depression struck like a gusher.

With a pretty face, a warm demeanor, and a prosthetic leg, Rossie Clark was a tough broad. By the time she was thirty years old in 1926, she had endured a brutal childhood amputation on the family's kitchen table and a taxing life as a single mother in the hot West Texas dust bowl. During Prohibition, which began in 1920, Rossie hid her illicit whiskey outside the back of Clark's Lunch in a rusty water meter box buried in the sand. Legend has it that the hard-nosed local sheriff, Irby Dyer, had a soft spot for Rossie. Dyer had a dependable reputation for busting bootleggers and bank robbers, but most of the time he kept his deputies away from Rossie and turned a blind eye to her undercover liquor business. Although there was that time Rossie served pitchers of gin and whiskey at a local dance. Dyer and his deputies raided the party, and as Rossie was pouring the liquor down the sink with running water, Dyer attempted to plug up the sink to keep the evidence. Rossie fought him off, and they both ended up drenched in whiskey and water. In the end, there was no proof for the beleaguered sheriff to use.

It couldn't have been easy to be a single mother and business owner during the early years of a pioneer town, but Rossie didn't complain and did what she had to do. She was twenty-two when her only child, Ellis Leon, was born in 1918. Rossie raised Ellis with little help from her estranged husband. Frank Clark called himself a pharmacist, and the 1930 census lists him as the proprietor of a drug store, but the people around Monahans considered Frank to be a drug dealer and a drunken fool.

Jan Clark, Guy's sister, remembers:

Frank was caught bootlegging, and they sentenced him to prison in Fort Worth. Rossie went back to their place and knew where he kept those bottles. He was supposed to have eight pint bottles, and there were only seven. In Rossie's own words, "The son of a bitch drank one." So she sold the remaining bottles and began her own bootlegging career. When it came time for Frank to get out of prison, Rossie went to Fort Worth to pick him up. He didn't show up for three days because he went off with friends to get drunk. That was the end of it as far as she was concerned. He would drift through town once in a while, and she'd give him money, but they divorced and never lived together again.

Rossie carried on with her illicit liquor business and raised Ellis alone. By the time President Roosevelt established the New Deal in 1933, Ellis was

Guy's paternal grandparents, Frank and Rossie Clark, 1920s, Monahans, Texas. Courtesy Clark family archives

a freshman in high school and Rossie had moved up to innkeeper, taking over the well-known Lone Star Hotel, which she bought from Mr. and Mrs. J. H. Hicks.

· · · · · ·

Rossie Jenkins Clark was born in 1896 to Henry W. Jenkins and Nancy Caroline Burgess on a farm near Wise County, Texas. The family moved north to Oklahoma Territory in 1900. Rossie recalls her family's life in *Wagon Tracks—Washita County Heritage, 1892–1976*, a book published by the Washita County (Oklahoma) History Committee:

Upon learning land could be bought cheaply in Cheyenne Country, in 1900 Dad took the four older children: Willa Mae, Ada, Alda Irene and Mahota, and traveled by covered wagon to buy a 160 acre homestead 12 miles south of Cordell and 8 miles east of Rocky.

This property, we later learned, had sold for a shotgun and $30 cash. The only improvement on the farm was a one-room dugout where we lived. Our mother was in poor health and came later by train with the two younger children. . . .

Shortly after their arrival, Dad built a one-room frame cabin, and, until a well could be dug, water was hauled from a neighbor. . . .

Dad bought cows, hogs and chickens, and by spring we had plenty of garden vegetables. The only groceries we had to buy were staples such as sugar, flour, meal, and coffee. The coffee was purchased green and Mother roasted and ground it. How well we remember that old coffee mill and the churn. We kids developed strong arms from those two instruments of torture. At times we were convinced there would be no butter in that milk.

The frontier battered many families, and Rossie's family was no exception. In 1906, Rossie's sister Mahota died at fourteen after falling ill with diphtheria. The following year, eleven-year-old Rossie picked up a splinter running through a cornfield. The wound became infected and developed gangrene. The local doctor amputated Rossie's leg twice—first below the knee and then above the knee after the disease spread—operating on the family's kitchen table.

Frank Clark (*wearing dark vest and tie in center of the room*), paternal grandfather of Guy Clark, in his pharmacy, Monahans, Texas, during Prohibition. Courtesy Clark family archives

Losing a leg didn't slow Rossie down. She dusted herself off, made many friends, helped to raise her young siblings, attended college, and taught elementary school before she married Frank Clark, a handsome rascal she met at a party. Together, they moved to Monahans where Frank promised to find work. Although little is known about Frank Clark now, a note he sent to Rossie on December 5, 1928, shows that, at least back then, he loved his wife and son. Rossie was in Oklahoma for her mother's funeral when Frank sent a telegram to the CR Highway Filling Station in Clinton, Oklahoma. It reads: "So far away but heart and mind are with you. Frank and Leon."

In May 1937, Rossie Clark moved the Lone Star Hotel from the corner of Sealy and Water to a new building at the corner of Fourth and Guadalupe S.W. and renamed it the Clark Hotel. The long shotgun hotel had thirteen rooms for rent and small living quarters for the family.

As Rossie was building her business at the Clark Hotel, Ellis studied journalism at the University of Oklahoma and became a charter member of the Delta Chi fraternity. Although he had been a C student in high school English, Ellis graduated with a Bachelor of Arts degree in journalism in 1939. After graduation he was employed briefly in the hotel industry in Oklahoma City and Dallas. Eventually, Ellis returned to Monahans, worked at a gas station, and helped his mother at the hotel.

At a party in Oklahoma City, Ellis met Pearle Frances Greene, a waitress and amateur actress four years his junior from Hugo, Oklahoma. Known by her middle name, Frances was a dark-haired beauty with a penchant for drama and adventure. Her wide-set eyes, a consequence of Paget's disease, a bone growth disorder, only added to her appeal. Frances was the daughter of US commissioner William Nelson Greene and his wife Hazel Bonner Greene. (Commissioners were precursors of today's federal magistrates.)

Much like Rossie Clark, Guy's maternal grandmother Hazel was a strong woman. She was born in 1885 to Robert Sanford Bonner and Nancy Chandler, whose families were prominent in Allen County, Kentucky.

In 1894, Robert and Nancy Bonner packed up their five children, all under the age of thirteen, and moved to San Antonio, Texas. Guy's grandmother Hazel wrote to Guy's cousin in 1965: "The doctors in Franklin, Kentucky, told my father that he would have to go to a warm, dry climate if he wanted to live at all. We know he had chronic bronchitis and one doctor told him

Rossie Clark, proprietor of the Clark Hotel in Monahans and paternal grandmother of Guy Clark. Courtesy Clark family archives

he was tubercular. He and Ma operated a restaurant and he ordered lots of fish and oysters from Chesapeake Bay. The constant handling of the iced fish and oysters kept his throat in a state of inflammation."

The Bonners sold the restaurant and shipped a sewing machine, feather beds, pillows, and Nancy's handmade "crazy quilts" to San Antonio. Made with irregular pieces of silk and satin and stitched together with Zephyr yarn, a wool-silk blend, the quilts would be sold or traded for food. They boarded the Louisville and Nashville Railroad train and rode two days and two nights to San Antonio. The train cars were loaded onto a barge to cross the Mississippi.

When the family arrived, they stayed with a local restaurant owner, Mrs. Ingram, until Robert Bonner found a small restaurant to purchase on Soledad Street. The adobe restaurant had living quarters in the back. A trap door in the floor led to an underground passageway linked to buildings a block away, believed to be troop quarters left over from the Texas Revolution. In

Ellis Clark stands in front of his mother's hotel in Monahans, Texas. Courtesy Clark family archives

a room upstairs from the restaurant, the family found trunks and boxes containing swords, hats, flags, uniforms, and other military items. But the Bonners stayed only a few months in San Antonio, presumably selling the restaurant as quickly as they'd purchased it. In the spring of 1895, Robert acquired a couple of horse-drawn wagons, loaded up the family and bare necessities, and drove north. They stopped for a time in New Braunfels and then San Marcos and Austin. By the fall, the Bonner family joined workers at the Holtzclaw farm near the San Gabriel and Little rivers between Rockdale and Cameron in Milam County. The family stayed on the Holtzclaw plantation for a year with more than a dozen other worker-tenant families. Every weekend the Holtzclaws hosted a dance for everyone on the farm. The Bonner kids learned the polka, waltz, and schottische dances. The old musicians taught youngsters Coleman and Susan to play the fiddle.

By the end of the decade, the Bonners had settled in Old Doakesville, Indian Territory, Oklahoma, where Robert studied to become a doctor and

The Robert Sanford Bonner family. Dr. Robert Sanford Bonner (*in back with beard*) with his wife Nancy and children. Guy's maternal grandmother, Hazel Bonner, is first from left in front row. Guy's uncle Coleman Bonner (subject of Guy's song "New Cut Road") is second from right in first row. Courtesy Clark family archives

opened a practice to tend to the townspeople. Dr. Bonner died in May of 1928, leaving behind his wife, three daughters (including Guy's grandmother Hazel), and his son, Coleman, who did not attend the funeral because he couldn't be located. Ten years later, on May 7, 1938, Coleman Bonner died after a fall from a train. The *Texarkana Gazette* reported:

> Killed as he fell from a fast Texas and Pacific freight train, a transient, identified as Robert Coleman Bonner was buried in Wooten Springs Cemetery late Friday. He was killed in the fall 300 yards south of the Sulphur station crossing near the boundary of Bowie County about 6am Friday. As he fell across the track he was decapitated and badly mangled. Papers found on the mangled body showed him to be a resident of Houston and his name was learned from a social security card. . . . Parts of his body were scattered along the tracks, several feet from his torso. Hurled by the force of the train, Bonner's head was found 20 feet from his torso. A hand was found 50 feet in another direction.

Coleman Bonner's gruesome death happened three years before his great-nephew's birth, but Hazel captivated young Guy's imagination with stories about Uncle Coleman and his fiddle playing.

Hazel Bonner Greene's appointment as the first female US commissioner for the Eastern District of Oklahoma began shortly before her husband, William Greene, died in 1926. The *Daily Oklahoman* ran a cartoon that riffed on Hazel's ruthless treatment of bootleggers. The headline read: *Fort Towson Woman Made U.S. Commissioner by Judge Williams: She Hits Bootleggers Hard.* While Guy's paternal grandmother Rossie was making her living selling moonshine, his maternal grandmother made it her mission to put whiskey peddlers in jail.

Greene's death left Hazel as a single mother to four-year-old Frances. Years later, after Hazel married W. E. Martin, sixteen-year-old Frances moved to Monahans to live with her aunt and uncle and finish high school.

. . . . . .

The early courtship between Ellis Clark and Frances Greene was partially long distance as Frances traveled back and forth between Monahans and Oklahoma to spend time with her family. In 1940, Frances enrolled in a summer drama school at Baylor University in Waco, Texas. By fall Ellis had a straight reporting job with the *Monahans News*. Ellis quit his journalism job for a civil service position at the Monahans post office shortly before he and Frances married on January 12, 1941 at Carlsbad Caverns, New Mexico. They returned to Monahans and lived at the Clark Hotel.

Ellis and Frances's first child, Guy Charles Clark, was born at Rehmeyer Hospital in Monahans on the night of November 6, 1941, weighing 8 pounds, 13 ounces. He was hardly an hour old when Rossie's redheaded hairdresser friend Crystelle accompanied Ellis to the nursery window to look at the new baby. The legend has it that Crystelle and her boyfriend Jelly were gangsters from up north. Jelly was said to have embezzled cash from the Mafia, and the couple had escaped to Texas to hide. Locals dug holes all over Crystelle and Jelly's property looking for buried treasure.

"Crystelle was a real character," Frances Clark told historian Louise O'Connor in 1994. "She was the number one bootlegger in Abilene for years. She got caught, and the judge told her she had to leave town. So she decided to go to El Paso to go to beauty school. She hitched a ride, and first ride she got went to Monahans. It was night, and she started looking for a place to stay and ended up at Ellis's mother's hotel. She made Ellis promise to take her to see the baby the minute he was born. When Ellis came to get her he told her all the way to the hospital how pretty the baby was. It was the prettiest baby you ever saw. When they got to the hospital Ellis took another look at Guy and said 'Well, Crys, I guess he isn't very pretty, but he's smart.' She told that story to anybody who would listen as long as she lived."

"Crystelle was this redhead and just fawned over me when my mother and grandmother would go to her to get their hair done," Guy says. "I was too young to understand, but she was probably a pretty good party girl. I remember seeing her days before she died, I was just seven or eight years old. She was living in the back of this bar out on the highway in a little nine-by-twelve room, bedridden on a cot with the smell of death hanging in the air."

Guy's parents didn't have much time to celebrate the arrival of their first child. Just before eight o'clock on the morning of December 7, only a month after Guy's birth, hundreds of Japanese fighter planes attacked the US naval base at Pearl Harbor, Hawaii, near Honolulu. Within a week, the United States had finally joined World War II, more than two years into the conflict.

Guy's maternal grandmother, Hazel Bonner Greene, with her husband William and son Charles, 1913. Courtesy Clark family archives

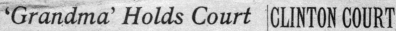

# NDLE 23 MILES NEARE

## 'Grandma' Holds Court

- MRS. HAZEL BONNER GREENE -

365 DAYS IN THE JUG!

IN OFFICE ONLY 3 MONTHS BUT "BATTING" CLOSE TO 1000

---

### Fort Towson Woman Made U. S. Commissioner By Judge Williams; She Hits Bootleggers Hard.

HUGO, June 6.—(Special.)—Southeastern Oklahoma bootleggers, who are haled before the new United States commissioner here are simply "outta luck."

The reason is simple. The new commissioner is a woman—and who ever won an argument with a woman? Besides that "Her Honor" doesn't like liquor, and "she doesn't mean maybe."

Appointed United States commissioner to succeed her husband, W. N. Greene, who resigned on account of ill health, Mrs. Hazel Bonner Greene, of Fort Towson, is one of the few women, and perhaps the only grandmother, in the United States to occupy such a position.

If the public doubted the wisdom of Judge R. L. Williams' unusual act in naming a housewife, the mother of four children, a United States commissioner, that doubt already has been dispelled. Although she has held office hardly three months, she has "batted close to 1,000 percent," as most of the de-

has practiced medicine continuously for twenty-five years.

When she was 10 years old the family moved to San Antonio, Texas. A few years later they toured Texas on account of Doctor Bonner's ill health, later moving to Shreveport, La. In 1900 the family moved to old Doaksville, near the present site of Fort Towson.

The following year she was married to Frank Self, a cattle man and she and her husband lived on a ranch a few miles from the present site of Spencerville, in the northeastern part of what is now Choctaw county.

Recalling the years spent on the ranch, Mrs. Greene says that she cannot remember a single instance of anyone getting drunk then. Long before the Volstead act was dreamed of, she says, folks in that immediate vicinity didn't take so strongly to alcoholic edrinks.

She does remember that back in 1900 at Doaksville, there was considerable drinking. She recalled one instance of a man riding several times on horseback to have wounds dressed after being stabbed. He returned to Doaksville a few hours later, "all lit up," and rode down the street, shooting into every house where he thought his assailant might be hidden.

---

## CLINTON COURT GETS NEW TEST

### Move to Uphold Validity Of Superior Bench Is Made At Statehouse.

Validity of the superior court of Clinton, which has been a subject of controversy in the state supreme court for six months, and now operating with W. T. Keen as judge without pay, under an opinion of the attorney general, is attack again.

Appeal from the judgment of the case of W. R. Gilchrist against Forrest L. Strong, Bert Meacham, attorney for Gilchrist, attacks the acts of the court, and the case is brought to the supreme court. A. J. Welch, Clinton, lawyer, will seek to uphold the validity of the superior court.

When the court declared the acts of the court void several months ago, it was held that the court was valid, but the acts of the judge improper. Then Governor Trapp appointed Judge Kern to serve without pay. Clinton business men have fought vigorously for the court, since Arapaho, the county seat, is several miles from the town, which is the largest in Custer county.

A previous story published in The Oklahoman on this test case was erroneous in that it named Welch as the attorney who brought the attack. Welch has been fighting for the superior court since its inauguration several months ago.

## Trapp Is To Speak At Bridge Opening

NOWATA, June 6.—(Special.—Governor Trapp is scheduled as the principal speaker at the opening of the new Coodys Bluff bridge over the Verdigris river which be celebrated with an old-fashioned basket picnic Monday. The new bridge is part of the $1,000,000 road building program in this county. Other speakers on the program will include members of the state highway commission, federal road men, and members of the Nowata chamber of commerce under whose auspices the celebration is being staged.

A program of entertainment has been planned for the occasion, the business houses of Nowata closing for the occasion.

## Preparations Made

---

A news article about Guy's maternal grandmother Hazel Bonner Greene. She was the US commissioner for the state of Oklahoma and promised to put bootleggers out of business during Prohibition. Courtesy Clark family archives

Guy's mother,
Frances Greene
Clark, circa 1940.
Courtesy Clark
family archives

The Clark Hotel was now a well-established residence for oil wildcatters and bomber pilots. Pyote Air Force Base, nicknamed the Rattlesnake Bomber Base, was fifteen miles from Monahans. During the first five years of Guy's life, the hotel was filled with young pilots on the way to the war or back from it. In the summer of 1942, Ellis relinquished his two-thousand-dollar-a-year job at the Monahans post office and joined the army, enlisting at Fort Bliss, El Paso. More than sixteen million Americans went off to fight what became known as "the Good War," widely viewed as a struggle against the evil empires of Germany and Japan. Their sons and daughters, the war babies, were left to be raised by mothers and grandmothers and aunts, the same women who took over the men's work in factories and on farms. After basic training, Ellis started at the Field Artillery Replacement Training Center in Fort Sill, Oklahoma, where he worked as a drill sergeant.

# *The Fifty-first Summer Session*

PAT M. NEFF
*President*

*Baylor University*
*Waco, Texas*

E. N. JONES
*Dean*

FIRST TERM: June 5 to July 9 - - SECOND TERM: July 10 to August 17
1940

Faculty and Student body of Baylor High School Speech Institute, 1939. 1. President Pat M. Neff, 2. Frank Speaight, Celebrated English Actor, 3. Sara Lowrey, Chairman of Department of Speech, 4. Glenn R. Capp, Director of Forensics, 5. James Barton, Director of Dramatics and Radio.

## SCHOOL OF SPEECH
*First Term: June 5 to July 9 - Second Term: July 10 to August 17*

## SPEECH INSTITUTE FOR HIGH SCHOOL STUDENTS
*June 17 to June 28*

## SOUTHWEST SUMMER THEATRE
*June 5 to August 17*

Baylor Speech Courses continue throughout both terms. The Summer Theater and the Speech Institute for High School Students are added advantages for the Summer Session.

Frances Greene (*second row, sixth from left*) attends the Southwest Summer Theater program at Baylor University in 1940. Courtesy Clark family archives

Guy Charles Clark was born November 6, 1941, at Rehmeyer Hospital in Monahans, Texas. Courtesy Clark family archives

Ellis and Frances Clark with infant Guy in 1942. Courtesy Clark family archives

The fiery redhead Crystelle (last name unknown) was a dear friend of Guy's grandmother Rossie. She was the inspiration for Guy's song "Crystelle" from his 1981 album *The South Coast of Texas*. Courtesy Clark family archives

From there, Ellis was stationed as a gunnery sergeant at Fort Rucker, Alabama. "He was teaching people to use these big machine guns, and his ears got damaged," Jan Clark remembers. "So they picked him up and put him in intelligence."

Staff Sergeant Ellis Clark then moved to Hawaii as a member of the 98th Division Artillery and, with the exception of a couple of short leaves, spent nearly four years away from home. In one of the extraordinary collection of letters documenting their courtship and early married life, Ellis wrote to his wife:

When I decided to join the Army, I was very patriotic and wanted to do my part. I still want to do my part but I'm not so patriotic anymore. The Army takes all the patriotism out of a man. Only civilians can be patriotic. In its stead the Army gives a man hardness and coarseness that is necessary to win wars. You never hear a soldier talk about what he wants to do for his country, except, maybe, in a weak moment. Instead you hear about beer, whiskey, women and how tough a man thinks he is.

While her husband was gone, Guy's fanciful mother, Frances, volunteered at the Pyote Air Force base USO and dreamed of Hollywood stardom. She acted in the Monahans version of the Ayn Rand stage play *Night of January 16th*, playing the part of Karen Andre, the mistress, on trial for killing her lover and boss. Frances and her acting teacher, J'Nevelyn Terrell, talked of going to California together to make it in the movies, but Rossie managed to talk Frances out of leaving. Frances relented, and she and Guy stayed at the Clark Hotel with Rossie and her wildcatter boyfriend, Jack Prigg. Jack was fifty-five years old when Guy was born in 1941.

"Jack was a great painter of pictures and teller of stories, but, of course, you never know whether to believe him or not. He thought it was the funniest thing in the world to tell somebody a big one and they'd believe it," Frances Clark told Louise O'Connor. "From the time I got Guy home from

Elsie Jackson "Jack" Prigg, the subject of "Desperados Waiting for a Train" and an important figure in young Guy's life. Courtesy Clark family archives

the hospital Jack would come in to see him every day. Here's this little scrap lying in his crib looking around and Jack leaning over, petting him, grabbing his toes. 'Well, hello, little Jack.'

"The first time Guy went out with Jack was the day we had to register for sugar rationing at the very first of the war. Ellis's mother [Rossie] and I came back to the hotel, and Jack and Guy were gone. She was about to have a fit. When they finally came back, she was just raising hell with Jack. 'Where have you been with the baby?' Jack said, 'Well, I wanted him to see the drilling rig.' What he wanted to do was to take Guy out there and show him off to the crew. Jack Prigg was the nearest thing to a grandfather my children ever had."

Frances spent many nights away from the hotel at the USO in Pyote. Ellis wrote to his wife from Camp Rucker, Alabama, in November 1943:

> The new USO should be just about ready to move into. I would like to be there to see it when it is all fixed up. It will really be something. However, I still think that the main attraction at the USO is my wife. I am jealous of the men stationed at Pyote, because they can see you every night and I see you only every few months. It really shouldn't be that way because I love you much more than anyone else and I would give anything to be stationed that close to you. I guess I am foolish not to take my discharge and come home and do my best to make you happy, but you know how I am when it comes to the Army. I can't say as I like this life particularly, but I feel that I should do something more for my country than buy bonds.

In two letters the following month, Ellis wrote to Frances and asked for a knife for Christmas. He'd heard from his army buddies about Randall Made Knives. Soldiers from all over the country wrote letters addressed to "Knife Man, Orlando, Florida" to tell Bo Randall how much they relied on the knives for man-to-man combat. Everyone wanted one, including Ellis.

"This was strange to me," Frances Clark told O'Connor. "He never even carried a pocket knife yet wanted this special knife. He gave me the address and stock number to order that knife for him. Well, the thing cost like $50 or $60, which was a bunch of money at that time. I got the damned thing for him, fussing the whole time. I was protesting. But he got the knife."

In the same letters, Ellis again implored Frances to stay home at night:

> One thing I'd like to ask you if I have the right, and that is I wish you
> wouldn't go out at night after you get off work. I know you don't have
> a whole lot of recreation, but I like to know that you are home with Guy
> at night. I know you don't go out on dates, but if you happen to be seen
> in the company of other men it might cause people to talk and I don't
> want anyone to ever say anything derogatory about you. . . . I'll always
> love you and tonight I worship you.

With Guy's father away and Frances doing her own thing, it's not a stretch
to say that Rossie and Jack pretty much raised Guy for the first few years
of his life. He loved both of them. He called his grandmother "Mimi." Jack
and Mimi doted on Guy.

"Jack took it upon himself to take Guy for haircuts and all that kind of
stuff," Frances Clark told O'Connor. "He took him to the barbershop and

Jack Prigg worked as a wildcatter in his younger years and then for Gulf Oil in
Monahans, Texas. Courtesy Clark family archives

Evening tour at the oil rig. *Left to right* (names from back of photo print) "Jiggs Hurst's son-in-law, Hardy, McGraw the Driller, Buddy Williams (Drunken Barber), and Ellis Clark." Circa 1940. Courtesy Clark family archives

the cowboy movies, and we had this nice little park with a wading pool for children. That was my favorite story. Guy and Jack would go out and be gone for two or three hours. One day it got to be autumn, and Guy told me they went to the pool. I said, 'Well, wasn't it a little cool? What would you do at the pool today?' Guy said, 'I sit up front and drink a Coke and Jack and Swede go in the back. They don't let me go in the back.' Jack was taking Guy to the pool hall!"

"Jack was the male figure in my young life," Guy says. "He drilled oil wells all over the world—the first wells in Iraq and Iran in the '20s, in South America, Columbia, and Venezuela. Jack ended up in West Texas working for Gulf Oil. He was a driller and a tool pusher for the driller, which is the guy that runs the oil drill. One time I was with Jack when an oil well was blowing out. They struck oil and it blew the racking board right out—a real gusher. I remember standing next to that rig watching it happen, oil splattering everywhere and the smell, and Jack's running around in every direction. To me, as a kid, he was a real desperado, the real deal."

Jack Prigg holds his little buddy Guy Clark in Monahans, Texas, circa 1942. Courtesy Clark family archives

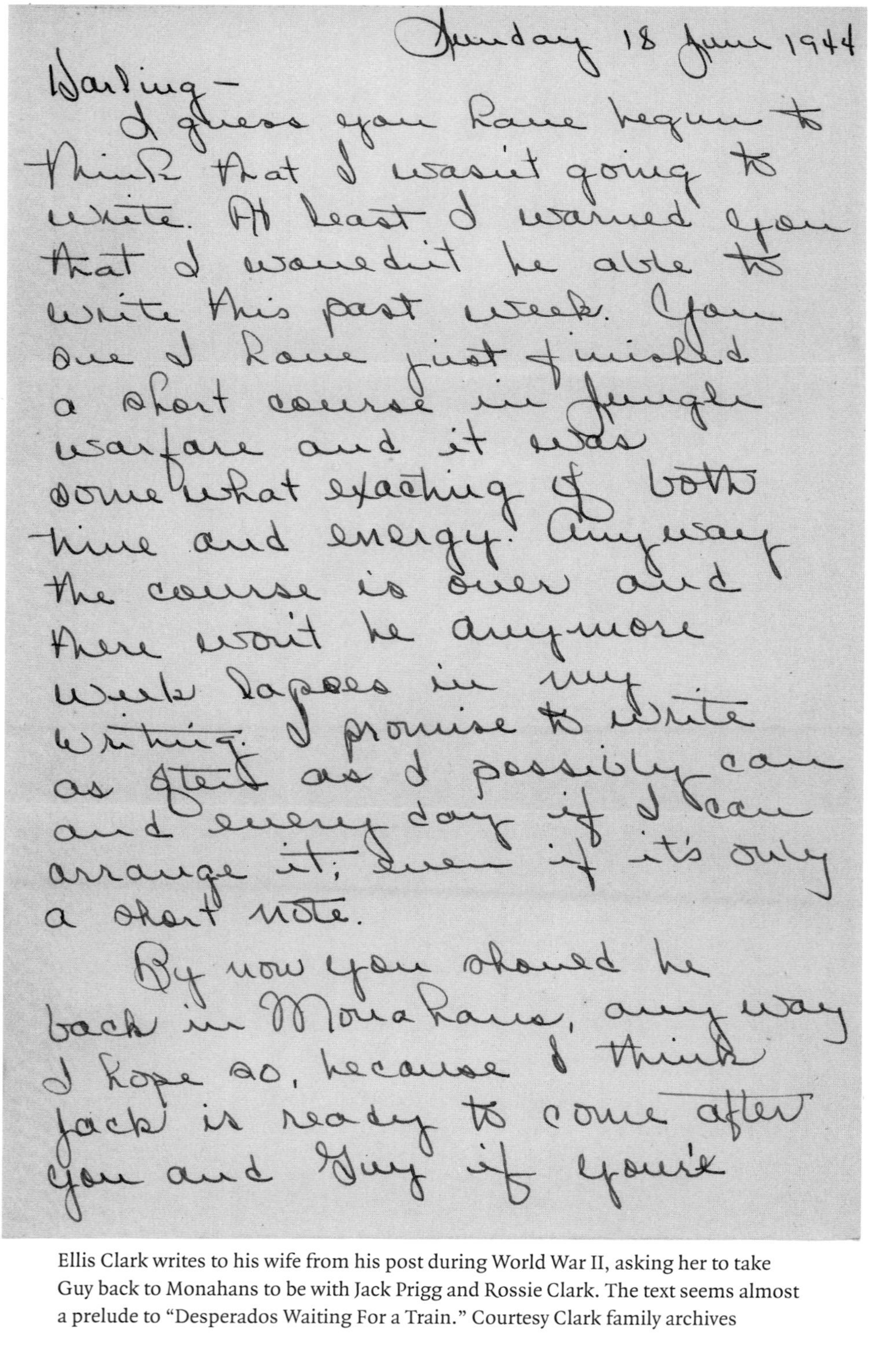

Sunday 18 June 1944

Darling—

I guess you have begun to think that I wasn't going to write. At least I warned you that I wouldn't be able to write this past week. You see I have just finished a short course in jungle warfare and it was somewhat exacting of both time and energy. Anyway the course is over and there won't be anymore week lapses in my writing. I promise to write as often as I possibly can and every day if I can arrange it, even if it's only a short note.

By now you should be back in Monahans, anyway I hope so, because I think Jack is ready to come after you and Guy if you're

Ellis Clark writes to his wife from his post during World War II, asking her to take Guy back to Monahans to be with Jack Prigg and Rossie Clark. The text seems almost a prelude to "Desperados Waiting For a Train." Courtesy Clark family archives

not already home. He
definitely does not like
for Guy to be very far
away. I can just see
him and Guy taking
a stroll down main street
engrossed in a
conversation about nothing.
Only I wish it were
Guy and me. Funny how
you think about things
like that. I guess it's
better if I don't.

I hope you squared me
with your Mother about
not writing to her. You know
how I am about writing.
I know I should write her,
and I will one of these
days, but right now I
can't think of anything
to write.

As a matter of fact I
should have written Dad
a letter, seeing as I have
only written one in the
eight or ten years. I'd to

Guy's younger sisters, Caroline and Janis (known as Caro and Jan), loved Prigg too.

"He was a big man, rotund and bald," Jan says. "He was taciturn and a big presence. Caro and I would sneak up to Jack's room, and he had naked ladies on the calendar. They were calendars put out for the oil rigs—showing their fannies, nothing [fully] nude. The Vargas pin-up girls. Very normal for the time, but you didn't hang it on your kitchen wall. Jack would take us anywhere. He'd give us money. He loved us. Jack is the one who bought us our first bicycles and indulged us."

On June 18, 1944, from his station at the 98th Division Artillery in Oahu, Guy's father Ellis wrote a letter to his wife, who had taken Guy to visit her family in Oklahoma:

"By now you should be back in Monahans. I hope so because I think Jack is ready to come after you and Guy if you're not already home. He definitely does not like for Guy to be very far away. I can just see Jack and Guy taking a stroll down Main Street engrossed in a conversation about nothing."

In another letter dated June 27, Ellis wrote:

Your last letter arrived several days ago and you still make no mention of when you are returning to Monahans. I hope you do plan to go back as Mother and Jack are raising hell about Guy. I guess they think no one can take care of him like they can. However, I am quite sure he is in good hands as long as you are around. I am wondering if you have ever worked up nerve enough to tell Jack that there is going to be another addition to our family circle. Maybe you can console him with the statement that it will be named after him. I want that very much, you know. I am looking forward to seeing a little girl running around the house when I come home.

Guy's sister, Caroline Ellis Clark, was born Christmas Eve that year. But Ellis and Frances weren't finished having kids just yet.

Shortly after the United States dropped atomic bombs on Hiroshima and Nagasaki in August 1945, Japan surrendered, and World War II ended after more than six bloody years. Ellis returned to his wife and children in Monahans. He got his job back at the post office, and the family left the hotel and moved into a house Frances had remodeled at 1300 Water Street. Ellis and Frances joined a monthly supper club with several other couples in town. When it was Frances's turn to host the supper, she served caviar. "I think she wanted to bring us some culture," said supper club member Glen Ratliff. "None of us liked it, but that was Frances for you. She was a caviar woman."

When Ellis and Frances's third child was born, on June 21, 1947, she was named Janis Jackson Clark in honor of Jack Prigg. It was the same summer the streamline train came through Monahans. "I remember everybody getting excited, getting packed into the car and driving down to the depot and standing around waiting for this train," Guy says. "My best friend was Jerry Kittrell, and his dad, Jack, worked at the depot. Old man Wileman was a crusty old guy who was the best checker player in Monahans. He ran the used furniture store in town, and people were always sitting in the back of

Guy wears his Hopalong Cassidy shirt for this early school photo. Courtesy Clark family archives

Rossie Clark, owner of Clark Hotel, with her grandchildren Guy, Janis, and Caroline, circa 1948. Courtesy Clark family archives

his store playing checkers and dominos. Dominos is like the state game in Texas. Every beer joint you walk into has square tables with chalk. The tables are made of chalkboard so you can write the dominos score in the corner, and they have a little rail around the edges to keep your dominos from falling off." Guy later wrote about Jack Kittrell, old man Wileman, and the streamline train in his autobiographical song "Texas 1947."

Many years later, Guy would also write another song about Monahans. Although it would never be recorded, the words bring the town to life:

Highway 80 cross the Texas sand
Makes a little stop called Monahans

*An old Texas and Pacific Railroad depot*
*And 'bout twice a year, they have a rodeo*
*My grandmother ran a cheap hotel*
*It was eight bucks a week and you know damn well*
*That it was nothin' but roughneck and truck drivin' fools*
*And no women in your room was the only rule.*

In September 1949, Guy started the second grade at Jack Edwards Elementary School. His second-grade report card shows all satisfactory grades in reading, spelling, language, arithmetic, fine arts, and writing. His teacher, Louise Hayes, noted that Guy showed significant talent in music, "singing well in chorus, listening to good music, [with] growth in response to rhythm, ability to match tones, singing alone and knowing the meaning of symbols."

Music was part of his life in summertime too. West Texas families, the Clarks included, spent many a summer night at Garner State Park, on the Frio River in Uvalde County on the southwestern edge of the Edwards Plateau in the Balcones Canyonlands. "The dances at Garner Pavilion were rites of passage," Guy says. "Cowgirls and cowboys dancing outside under the moonlight."

It may have seemed to Guy and his sisters that the wide-open spaces of West Texas would remain their home forever. Ellis Clark, however, had other plans.

## CHAPTER TWO

# The South Coast of Texas

It's June 9, 2011. Verlon Thompson is behind the wheel of a brand-new black Cadillac. Guy Clark rides shotgun and smokes a freshly rolled cigarette, indifferent to the red "no smoking" symbols sprinkled across the dashboard of the rental car. I'm stretched out in the backseat. We've been on the road for nearly seven hours, driving from Baton Rouge on our way to Rockport, Texas. We are almost there. Guy takes a deep breath. "My blood pressure drops a bit when I get back home to Texas," he says.

As the car turns onto Fulton Beach Road, soybean and cotton fields give way to palm trees and sand, quaint beachside inns, and shrimp boats in the harbor. A hot wind blows from the Gulf of Mexico. Guy rolls down the car window and points out the dramatically sculpted live oak trees, permanently bent from the wind. "People come from all over the world to see these trees. Japanese artists like to paint them because they resemble bonsai."

Guy nods toward the water. "Down the road a bit is a ski basin. Four or five of us guys would get up early in the morning and go water skiing before school. We'd be dressed for school and stand on the sandy slope. The boat comes around and leaves a big slack in the line and hits it. As the line tightens up, you just step onto the ski. We'd never even get wet."

Rockport, named for the rock ledge foundation of its shore, spans the Live Oak Peninsula thirty miles northeast of Corpus Christi on Texas Highway 35. The town is anchored by barrier islands, which sustain the Aransas National Wildlife Refuge, and is surrounded by the waters of Aransas and Copano Bays. Whooping cranes, pelicans, egrets, and herons make their home on the coastal hideaway. Since the nineteenth century they've shared the land with fishermen, townspeople, and well-heeled snowbirds. A city sign reads "Rockport-Fulton: Charm of the Texas Coast."

It's easy to see why Ellis Clark picked Rockport as the place to raise his young family after he finished law school. The sleepy fishing village on the south coast of Texas is a far cry from the heat and dust of West Texas where Ellis was raised and Guy spent his early years. The first time Ellis came to Rockport, he spotted a dog lying on a road that split around a windswept oak tree. He said to his family: "A town where they build roads around the trees and a dog can safely lie on the street is the place I want to live."

It's been more than a decade since Guy's last visit to Rockport. The town has grown since Frandolig Island in Aransas Bay was built into Key Allegro Isle. A mud flat once used by fishermen and duck hunters is now the site of million-dollar homes and affluent tourists. Even country star George Strait escapes to Key Allegro when he needs a break.

Guy is here this weekend to play the Rockport Music Festival on Fulton Beach, which is just a mile down the road from the former site of the Shack, a thatch-roofed, beach-themed, indoor-outdoor joint where Guy, his high school friend Carl Snyder, and Guy's father's law partner Lola Bonner played acoustic guitars and sang for the customers.

We pull into the palm-tree-lined parking lot at the Inn at Fulton Harbor just as Guy's longtime friend and fellow songwriter Gary Nicholson walks through the lobby door with Delbert McClinton, also in town to play the festival. There are big smiles all around and greetings of "Hey, man, how're you doing?" among Guy, Verlon, Gary, and Delbert. Sally, the desk clerk at the inn and an old classmate from high school, greets Guy and checks him into the VIP suite. We cross the street for dinner at Charlotte Plummer's Seafare Restaurant, and the staff and diners call out "Welcome home, Guy!"

Guy moved with his family to Rockport-Fulton as a sixth grader in March 1954. His sisters, Caro and Jan, still keep a house in Rockport. It's not the family home on Fourth Street in Fulton where Guy spent his last two years of high school but a small home purchased for Guy's grandmother Rossie when she retired and moved from Monahans after Jack Prigg's death in 1970. After Guy's father and Rossie died, Guy's mother moved to the house on

North Austin Street. The Clark family archives—a trove of photos, family letters, and other documents —remain there.

I spend a day with Caro and Jan, sorting through everything. Before Guy and I return for dinner with the family, Jan drives me back to the hotel, her car weighted with papers and photos for me to catalog later. This jackpot includes the love letters Ellis wrote to Frances, showing perspective no one alive could reveal. Magic. In many of the missives, Ellis promises to give Frances a better life after he returns from the war.

"Ellis already had his undergrad degree when we married," Frances told Louise O'Connor in 1993. "Eleven years, three kids, and a war later, he wakes up one day and says, 'If I'm ever going back to school, I've got to go now. They've got this GI Bill and I want to get a law degree.' Well, I didn't know he wanted a law degree. That was a new one on me. He kept hearing about the new school in Houston, the University of Houston. It was quite small and that pleased him."

With the GI Bill and some cash borrowed from Jack Prigg, Ellis Clark signed up for law school. The family lived in student housing on the university campus during the school year. One of Guy's chores included rolling two packs of cigarettes for his father each morning with an old Bugler cigarette roller. The children attended Houston's Lantrip Elementary School, and Frances worked as a secretary to the dean of the university's college of pharmacy. Each summer, they returned to the Clark Hotel in Monahans and lived with Rossie and Jack.

Ellis gained his license to practice law from the Supreme Court of Texas in 1952 on Guy's eleventh birthday. The same month, Guy's father was honored for achieving the highest bar exam score in Texas history. He graduated from law school the following June.

"After my father got out of law school, he opened a little practice in Pasadena, Texas," Guy says. "Had his law office there for less than a year. Every weekend, or every time he had time, we'd just drive around Texas looking for a new place. He just didn't want to raise a family in Houston. There was a place in the Hill Country he really liked, but they didn't need a lawyer. He was looking for a small town. Finally, we came upon Rockport. It's very small, 2,500 population in the winter, [and] that would double in the summer because of tourists. There was another, older lawyer there who was getting ready to retire. They worked out some kind of deal."

Ellis Clark makes the highest score on
Texas Bar exam. Courtesy Clark family
archives

Ellis L. Clark, University of Houston law student who
made the highest grades on the October Bar examinations,
gets rewarded by his wife. Interested watchers are his
mother, Mrs. Rossie Clark of Monahans, and his three
children, Guy, Janis and Caroline.

In March 1954, Ellis Clark opened his law practice next to the post office
and rented a house at the intersection of Victoria and Ruby Streets across
from Little Bay in Rockport. The Clark family settled into the routine of small-
town life on the Texas coast. For some reason, the Rockport years seem to
get lost in the larger story of Guy Clark. His early songs "Desperados Waiting for a Train," "Texas 1947," and "Lone Star Hotel" paint a vivid portrait of
life in West Texas. Over the years, people have become so attached to those
images, and Guy has talked about them in interview after interview. It's easy
to see how Rockport could become almost a footnote to Guy's young life.
Yet this beach town is where Guy came of age.

"It was a small shrimping and fishing village, a tourist resort. It was just a
picturesque little spot. That's why my father picked it," Guy says. "It was far
out. We lived just a couple of blocks from the beach. When we first moved
there, coming from West Texas, all I wanted to do was fish. I must've fished
every day for six months."

Life on the south coast of Texas was idyllic. The postwar years were a
time of prosperity and *Leave It to Beaver* wholesomeness. Guy was a clean-cut,
all-American boy from a solid, middle-class family. Ellis and Frances Clark
ascended to positions of influence in the community as they built the legal
practice at 312 North Live Oak Street in downtown Rockport. Ellis joined

the Lions Club and cooked for its annual Fourth of July barbecue party. He gave law advice to the local fishermen in exchange for the day's catch and advised local officials on legal matters.

Frances hosted extravagant parties, loved doing it, and invited everyone. She cared deeply about appearances, craved attention, and longed for respect and admiration. To Frances, raising enlightened and accomplished children with good manners was paramount. She immersed herself in arts and culture and encouraged the children to do the same. "We had lots of books and talked about art a lot. We were given art lessons," Caroline says. "Mother painted, not well, but she did a lot of nice stuff. We were brought up to do art in the same way we learned to pour tea and wear white gloves and hats. . . . We were enrolled in elocution lessons and took ballroom dancing classes."

"My mother was very smart. She didn't have a college degree, but she worked the *New York Times* crossword puzzle every morning, completely in ink," Guy says. "She was my father's legal secretary. I'm sure she could've passed the bar exam and had a law degree. She had gone to drama school

Main Street in Rockport, Texas, the year Guy Clark moved to town, 1954. Courtesy Clark family archives

The Ellis Clark family moved to Rockport in 1954. *Left to right:* Guy, Ellis, Jan, Frances, Caroline. Courtesy Clark family archives

at Baylor University and was always involved in putting on pageants and plays. She thought it was so cool to know when to wear white gloves and when not to. . . . We always had a copy of the Emily Post etiquette book."

"We did a lot of reading out loud to each other," Jan Clark says. "We all loved to read. We encouraged each other's initiatives. I remember when I had to make a poster for Fire Prevention Week. Guy helped me, and Mother and Daddy made comments, and everybody came up with slogans and stuff. I'm sure Guy gave me my slogan, which was 'Public Enemy Number One.' I got a prize for it."

Frances was also a good cook. Jan says, "My mother cooked very simple, plain food during the week for us, but she enjoyed entertaining and liked to surprise people with her food. She liked to have people over and would make pizza when Rockport didn't know what pizza was. She made them from scratch. She was famous for the chicken and dumplings she served

when district court was in session. The judges and all the defense and pros-
ecuting attorneys would come out one day that week for her chicken and
dumplings, especially when there were visiting judges from San Antonio."

Sadie Hawkins Day was a big deal to the kids in Rockport. The annual
folk event, based on Al Capp's comic strip Li'l *Abner*, fell the first Saturday
of every November right around Guy's birthday. The town newspaper, the
*Rockport Pilot*, reported on Guy's thirteenth birthday party, under the headline "Ellis Clarks Entertain in Honor of Son's Birthday":

> November 11, 1954
> Mr. and Mrs. Ellis L. Clark assisted by Mr. and Mrs. N. F. Jackson
> entertained a group of young people on their son Guy's 13th birthday,
> Saturday November 6, which was also Sadie Hawkins day. This latter
> fact set the motif for the whole party, which was held at Goose Island
> State Park concession hall. Walls of the building were decorated with
> charcoal sketches of Dog Patch characters; the supper table was covered
> with gingham cloth, and lighted by kerosene lamps, Dog Patch style.
> The cake was made in the shape of Mammy Yokum's log cabin and
> decorated with figures of some of the funny strip characters.

Guy celebrated his fourteenth birthday with a Sadie Hawkins party, too, and
wrote the invitation and program:

> Offishal Notise
> Sadie Hawkins Day
> Saturday November 5
> Dog Patch's Goose Island State Park
> All Bachelors Gotta Risk Their Life's in the Race!!
>
> Program
>
> 6:30 p.m. Mammy Yokum's Everlastin' Hot Dogs, Kickapoo Joy Juice
> and Schmoos. (Natcherly Free)
>
> 7:15 p.m. Booty Contest—We gotta find the Bootifulest Bachelor and
> Handsomest Gal in Dogpatch for which a special prize has bin invented

and will be presented by Senator Phineas P. Phoghorn. Gals, wear yo best Dogpatch GLAD RAGS and Bachelors wear yo best Dogpatch SAD RAGS. (No outlanders or tourists allowed).

7:30 p.m. THE RACE. RULES: Bachelors won't be allowed the use of Triple Whammies, Track Shoes, Waterwings or Jet Propulsion!!! Gals kin ketch as ketch kin

8:00 p.m. Marryin' Sam will be on hand to perform Eight Dollah Weddings, fo Foah Dollahs (fo them as has bin caught, natcherly). A Weddin' Party Dance will foller the ceremonies an' last 'til 10:30.

Writ by Hand
Signed
Guy Clark (Only 14 years old)

Mary Lucille Jackson was Guy's first girlfriend and first love. Her family owned the Jackson Seafood Company. In emails to writer Joe Specht in September of 2004, Mary Lucille wrote: "When we went in costume to the Sadie Hawkins parties he, of course, always went as Li'l Abner. Since I was never the Daisy Mae type, I played the role of Moonbeam McSwine."

Guy escorted Mary Lucille to his birthday parties and other town events, and they were regulars at local hangouts Mary's Malt Shop and the Beach Club, known as "the Patio" in downtown Rockport. Guy wasn't at the Patio the day a young Buddy Holly and his band stopped in on the way from Corpus Christi to ask if they could set up and play for tips; they needed to raise gas money to get to their next gig in Houston.

Truly a small-town paper, the *Rockport Pilot* reported the comings and goings of the Clark family. It noted the Clarks hosted a New Year's Day party in 1958 for 150 guests, to show off their new home at 305 Fourth Street in Fulton. The same year, Guy read poetry at an invitational speech tournament and won a science fair prize for his hydrogen generator according to the *Pilot*.

Guy also joined the Explorers Club and the Boy Scouts. Guy took his father's Randall knife on a camping trip, and he and Victor Torres took turns throwing the knife at a tree. "Victor broke the knife," Guy says. "He threw it,

SADIE    HAWKINS    DAY

SATURDAY NOVEMBER 5

DOGPATCH'S GOOSE ISLAND PARK

ALL BACHELOR'S GOTTA RISK THEIR LIFE'S IN THE RACE!!

— PROGRAM —

6:30 P. M.    Mammy Yokum's Everlastin Hot Dogs,
Kickapoo Joy Juice and Schmoos.
(Natcherly Free)

7:15 P. M.    Booty Contest – We gotta find the Bootifulest
Bachelor and Handsomest Gal in Dogpatch for which
a special prize has bin invented and will be presented by Senator Phineas P. Phoghorn. Gals, wear
yo best Dogpatch GLAD RAGS and Bachelors wear yo
best Dogpatch SAD RAGS. (No outlanders or tourists
allowed)

7:30 P. M.    THE RACE

RULES: Bachelors won't be allowed the use
of Triple Whammies, Track Shoes,
Waterwings or Jet Propulsion!!!!

Gals kin ketch as ketch kin.

8:00 P. M.    Marryin' Sam will be on hand to perform Eight
Dollah Weddings, fo Foah Dollahs (fo them as has
bin caught, natcherly)

A Weddin' Party Dance will foller the ceremonies
an' last 'til 10:30.

Writ by Hand

Signed                        GUY CLARK
                                  (Only 14 Yars Old)

His ( X ) Mark

Guy wrote the "Offishal Notise" for his Sadie Hawkins–themed fourteenth birthday party. Courtesy Clark family archives

then I threw it, then he said 'let me try it one more time'—and that's when it broke off. I cut the tip out of the tree after it got stuck. I always took the blame for it." Victor Torres remembers being in Boy Scout Troup 49 with Guy, but he doesn't specifically recall throwing the knife. "It could have happened," he admitted. "It seems like something I would do." Both Caro and Jan Clark agree that it was Victor who broke the tip off the knife, but they kept the secret from their parents for many years. It's not surprising that Guy would take the blame for it, however. Ellis and Frances instilled in their children a sense of integrity. Guy was accountable for the knife and he would take responsibility for whatever happened to it.

When Sputnik orbited the earth on October 4, 1957, Guy and his classmates watched from a pep rally in downtown Rockport. Right after his sixteenth birthday, Guy joined the Fulton Volunteer Fire Department. And all the Clark kids participated in the Christmas pageant at church.

Guy blossomed into a leader, was popular with his classmates, and strived to be the best in all that he pursued. As captain and center, Guy led the football team. He played guard in basketball and ran the hundred-yard dash and threw discus in track and field. He presided over the junior class as president, acted in school plays, and took piano lessons from Tilly Fry. Guy also illustrated section pages for the yearbook with quoted passages from poems by Henry Wadsworth Longfellow, George Wither, and Walt Whitman.

"He was very smart and talented, a very good artist," says high school friend Carl Snyder. He was always drawing things. He did all the posters in high school. I have a banjo he had drawn flowers on. I had a slalom ski, and Guy wrote my nickname, Snatch, at the top of it in beautiful script and colors. Hell, Guy was good at anything he ever did."

Dave Segler coached Guy in football (his nickname on the team was Clerk), basketball, and track. "He was a perfectionist. He wasn't overly talented in athletics, but whatever he did he wanted to do well," Segler told Louise O'Connor. "For example, in football he was our offensive center. He was a good blocker because he chose to pride himself in doing the job and blocking. Sometimes he got there late, but he carried out and did the best job he could. When we got into basketball we demanded that our people do certain things and do them well in order to gain the success you need to have. He was a good rebounder even though he couldn't jump very well.

Guy with his first love, Mary Lucille Jackson, during a country club dance in Rockport, circa 1956. Courtesy Clark family archives

In Guy's sophomore year of high school, the Clark family moved into this house on Fourth Street in Fulton. On New Year's Day, 1958, they hosted 150 people for an open house. Courtesy Clark family archives

He positioned himself and anticipated where things were going to happen and what was going to happen."

During a subsequent trip to Rockport, I had lunch at Mac's Barbecue restaurant with some of Guy's former teammates from the Aransas High School football team: Jimmie Ankel, Billy Boy Johnson, Charles (Pokey) LeBlanc, Buddy Ayers, and James Richard Fox. This group remembers Guy as a solid football player and a Goody Two-shoes, not cool enough to hang out with them outside of football practice. Guy jokingly remembers those teammates as ne'er-do-wells. "Guy always admired the heavy-drinking dudes and the hell-raisers, but he never did it," Carl Snyder says.

Although his parents were heavy drinkers, Guy hadn't discovered alcohol yet and limited his consumption to a few beers now and then. He and Carl did get themselves into trouble throwing beer bottles one night in Aransas Pass. "We were having fun and kicking around, smarting off and throwing beer bottles in the air and letting them crash on the street," Carl says. "Of course, this was at two or three o'clock in the morning. So the cops came around the corner and chased us down. Ellis had to come and bail us out of jail."

In his junior year, Guy was elected vice president of Explorers Post 49 and led the "Trouble Shooters" committee, which built a rifle range four miles south of town. On weekends he worked as a guide at the Port Bay Club.

The Aransas County (Texas) High School freshman class officers in front of Mary's Malt Shop in downtown Rockport. *Left to right*: Hays Warden (vice president), Mary Martha Shivers (secretary), Mike Johnson (president), Mary Lucille Jackson (reporter), Guy Clark (treasurer), circa 1956. Courtesy Clark family archives

Guy Clark illustrated the section breaks for the Aransas County High School annual, 1957. Courtesy Clark family archives

"Rockport always had that tourist element, rich guys coming down to hunt and fish," Guy says. "One of my jobs was taking rich guys duck hunting. By the time I got out of high school, I killed everything that I need to kill in my life. I haven't hunted since then."

Philip Baldwin taught Guy woodworking and general drafting in high school. "The first project we had in woodworking was a little book rack," Baldwin told O'Connor. "Anybody could build it and some of them built it better than others. But Guy wanted his to be fantastic. When he'd bring it up to be graded I'd get my T-square out and check to see if it was square. He'd look at it and go, 'Well, let me take it back and do a little more work on it,' then he'd bring it back and say 'Let me take it back one more time and work on it a little bit more.' That went on for a week before he finally turned it in. He was a perfectionist."

"Some of my first memories are of being given a pocketknife and a whet-stone and the slats of wooden fruit boxes," Guy says. "We made our own toys. A dagger or something. It just always came naturally to me. There's just something about the feeling of a sharp blade and wood that is just unique. The sensation is something I really enjoy. I've always been able to do that."

Carving toys is one thing, but it was the experience of working in Rob Roy Rice's shipyard that would leave an indelible print on Guy's life as a songwriter and guitar builder. Rice had owned the place since World War II, when the shipyard built mine sweepers and big wooden PT boats. The shipyard held machinery from the 1930s—giant band saws, planers, and industrial woodworking equipment. The seventy-year-old Rice had been trying to sell his business since 1957; he wanted to avoid making expensive repairs to the old equipment and wished to retire. It was a good thing for Guy that Rice was unable to sell, as it gave Guy three summers to work for Rice, scrubbing algae from the bottom of shrimp boats and helping the carpenters.

"It influenced me as much as anything I've been through in my life," Guy says. "I really got on with the carpenters. Boats are built square with the world and watching them build a seventy-to-eighty-foot wooden shrimp boat out of the water was fascinating to me."

In the fall of 1958, Ellis took on a young law partner named Lola Bonner. She had graduated from the University of Texas law school in June and opened a practice in Rockport to be near her sister. Lola was statuesque and elegant,

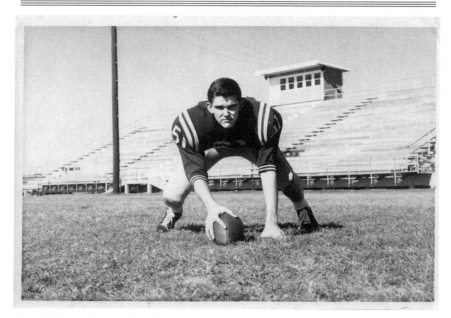

Guy Clark (*number* 51) played center and was captain of the Aransas County High
School Pirates football team. He also played basketball and threw discus in track.
Courtesy Clark family archives

six feet tall, with dark hair and piercing eyes, and she was always dressed to
the nines. She was also a lesbian, but in those days it wasn't talked about,
and Lola was quiet about her private life. At a party at the Clark home, Lola
played flamenco guitar and sang Mexican songs. Guy had never seen anything like it, and he was hooked. It was the beginning of a beautiful friendship that had a profound impact on Guy's life.

Lola took Guy to gatherings at George and Gloria Hill's beach house
on Water Street, where her friends would pass the guitar around and trade
songs. "I was just captivated by it," Guy says. "Hondo Crouch, the founder
of Luckenbach, was there, along with his sister. She lived in Rockport. There
were rich doctors and lawyers from the Hill Country and Houston. They
were singing mostly old cowboy songs. It was far-out. After that I went and
bought a Mexican guitar and asked Lola to show me how to play it. I was
hungry."

Guy learned his first chords on the guitar in the garage apartment that Lola
rented from Dean Steele at 1109 North Broadway. Across from Little Bay and

with plenty of natural light through a long bank of windows, one could see Lola's décor, which included a jawbone of a donkey, a guitar, castanets, and maracas. Her most prized possession was a hi-fi and a collection of Mexican records. Guy asked Lola to show him everything she knew about playing the guitar. Then he'd go home, practice until his fingers bled, and come back for more. The first songs he learned from Lola were Mexican folk songs, which he sang in Spanish.

"I was delighted to show him my very limited skills," Lola Bonner told O'Connor in 1991. "It was definitely the Mexican flair with a touch of flamenco. I would walk through some Mexican rhythms with him because they are unique. It was rhythms principally of the right hand. Most people work on the left hand and chording. I did all right hand, the uniqueness of the various rhythms and beats. I think that is probably what intrigued Guy about the guitar."

When Lola heard that Spanish classical guitarist Andrés Segovia planned to perform at Jones Hall at the University of St. Thomas in Houston, she

The harbor in Rockport where Guy worked at Rob Roy Rice's shipyard during his high school years. Courtesy Clark family archives

Lola Bonner, law partner of Ellis Clark, taught Guy Clark how to play flamenco guitar in 1958. Courtesy Lola Bonner family

secured tickets and took her protégé to the concert. Guy was thrilled to see what one guitar player could do with six strings.

"That was the highlight of my life, to see Segovia play," Guy says. "That was the first influence I had, those nylon string and flamenco guitars and Mexican music. I mean, I still remember it. It was like a three-hundred-seat amphitheater with perfect acoustics and no sound system. He [sits] down on the chair, tunes his guitar, gets up, walks off the stage, and the house is just quiet. You hear this little click and the blower system goes off. I've done the same thing to get rid of that white noise. He comes back, tunes again.

At one point it was so stuffy in there because we're in Houston, and the air conditioner was off. One guy coughed in the back, and Segovia just stopped, threw up his hands and scowled at the audience. Went back and finished what he was doing."

"Of course, we were absolutely spellbound," Lola Bonner told writer Joe Specht in 2004. "I remember Guy was really hooked from that point on. We never did get to see Sabicas together. Sabicas was the flamenco guitarist for Carmen Amaya, the flamenco dancer. At that time, she was the counterpart to José Greco. Sabicas was just so outstanding. I followed him. If he was going to be anywhere within the state confines of Texas, I was going to be there. Same thing with José Greco, but Guy and I never got to see them together. Although we did get to see a flamenco guitarist at Texas A&I in Kingsville one weekend. We had some good times together."

Once Guy began playing the guitar, he would play for anyone who would sit and listen. The Kingston Trio had a big radio hit with "Tom Dooley," a folk song about the murder of a North Carolina woman in 1866. Guy and Carl Snyder started digging into folk music: Woody Guthrie, Ramblin' Jack Elliott, and their favorite, Lead Belly, who popularized "Rock Island Line." The two friends bought Goya guitars together at a Corpus Christi music store.

"Guy's had pearl inlay," Carl says. "We'd buy Black Diamond strings at the drugstore in Rockport and cut our fingers to hell on those things."

Lola, Guy, and Carl Snyder sometimes played during the Saturday pig roasts at the Shack, the beach joint owned by family friend Jim "Peg Leg" Furlong. While Guy's parents hung out drinking with their friends, the trio entertained the customers.

"Peg Leg's was an in place to go," Jan Clark says. "It had concrete floors. It had a patio out front that was just gravel. There were the local drunks and fishermen who stopped in for beers, and then there was the crowd of rich tourists who showed up to slum."

Furlong had a soft spot for Guy and gave him a banjo that had belonged to his father. William Harrison Furlong had been a Texas Ranger and friend to Pancho Villa during the Mexican Revolution, and Jim Furlong had inherited his father's lust for adventure. He had lost his leg to gangrene, which had set in during his attempt to sail across the Atlantic. His prosthesis was a wooden

Guy and Carl Snyder play songs on the patio at Jim "Peg Leg" Furlong's joint, the Shack, on Fulton Beach Road, circa 1959. Courtesy Clark family archives

leg to which he affixed a bottle opener. It made it easier to carry trays of beer around to customers—he would pop the bottles open on his leg.

The Clark family tradition of reading poetry around the kitchen table each evening shaped Guy as a songwriter. Being a poet is part of Guy's DNA. The fifteenth-century English poet John Skelton is an ancestor. Skelton was a poet laureate at Cambridge and Oxford. He became a tutor to Prince Henry and rose to court poet when the prince ascended to the throne as Henry VIII. Skelton wrote at a time when English pronunciation was changing, and his peers and the mainstream often misunderstood his wit and satire. His work didn't fit in with the popular poetry of the era.

Guy's favorite poets were Robert Frost, who wrote about the life and landscape of New England; Stephen Vincent Benet, whose Pulitzer Prize–winning poem "John Brown's Body" knitted historical and fictional characters to chronicle incidents from the Civil War; Robert Service, who illustrated life in the Yukon; and Vachel Lindsey, whose dramatic delivery in public readings could be likened to that of a modern-day troubadour like Guy.

As vice president of the National Honor Society and member of student council, Guy had many opportunities to cultivate his speaking skills. During the Cotton Club Variety Show, Guy and Mary Lucille narrated a piece about Argentina and demonstrated the tango. Guy read at the Future Homemakers of America Sweetheart Banquet and gave a speech at the First Presbyterian Church's fellowship induction with the theme "Why to do one's best when the world is going to hell."

In April 1959, the Aransas County High School junior class presented the play *Our Hearts Were Young and Gay* for two nights. Guy played the father, Otis Skinner, a part made famous by actor Charlie Ruggles in the 1944 film of the same name. English teacher Martha Ballou directed the play. She was Guy's favorite teacher, and he would later borrow her name for his song "Rita Ballou."

The following month, the junior-senior prom was held at the Live Oak Country Club. Mary Lucille led the decoration committee. The theme was "Beneath the Sea," and the room was adorned with images of King Neptune, mermaids, a shell chariot, and seahorses. Guy, as junior class president, performed a monologue titled "Rom and Julie," a contemporary take on Romeo and Juliet.

During Guy's high school years, Elvis Presley, Connie Francis, the Everly Brothers, Ricky Nelson, Jerry Lee Lewis, Dion and the Belmonts, Bobby Darin, Frankie Avalon, Paul Anka, and the Platters were mainstays on the music charts. "I remember some guy had a set of speakers in the trunk of his car on wires, and we'd pull into an empty gas station at night," Guy says. "He'd turn the radio on and it'd come out of the speakers, and we'd dance on the concrete." Yet the first records Guy bought were by jazz trumpeter Louis Armstrong and the folkie Kingston Trio. This new rock 'n' roll wasn't his thing and never would be.

Guy's senior year ended with a luau at Sunset Lake, where he taught his pal Dale Barnard's girlfriend Juliette Tawil how to water-ski, and a concert at school where he and Carl Snyder harmonized on "Rock Island Line."

"I did the narration part before the song, and then Guy came in on the guitar, and we did the verses and the choruses after that. It was great. The whole audience went crazy," Carl says. "That was my first taste of show-biz. I was just hooked from then on. It put us on to the girls. That's what

we were both after. From then on out, we both knew we were going to play
music on stage."

In May of 1960 Guy graduated from Aransas County High School in a
class with fewer than fifty students. He was awarded a National Science
Foundation grant for summer study at M. D. Anderson Hospital in Houston, where he worked with cancer researchers.

"It was really cool because I was a science nerd," Guy says. "I worked
with this crazy scientist who built an electron spray gun to irradiate cancer
cells. He would mix up a batch of cancer cells, spray them with his gun,
then put them in a petri dish for a day or so and count the cells that lived
depending on how much radiation he shot them with. He was the classic
weird scientist."

It was time to get serious about what he was going to do with his life.
Guy's parents expected him to use his experience at M. D. Anderson to go
to college and make something of himself. "Guy could do any damn thing
he wanted to do. Anything he put his mind to do," Frances Clark told Louise
O'Connor in 1993. "He gets this National Science Foundation award to go
and work at M. D. Anderson in Houston for the summer. Well, that makes
us think he's got something on the ball."

Carl Snyder (left) and Guy Clark on Rockport Beach, circa 1959. Many mornings the
boys would water ski before school. Courtesy Carl Snyder collection

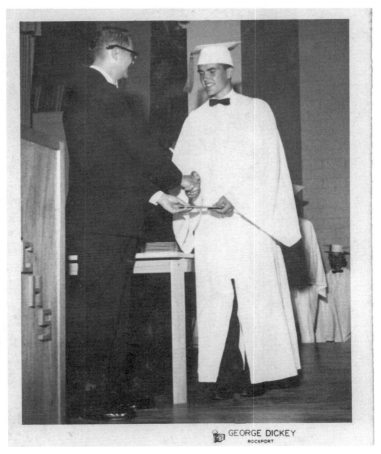

GEORGE DICKEY
ROCKPORT

Guy Clark graduates from Aransas County High School in May 1960.
Courtesy Clark family archives

Without a better plan, Guy packed his guitar and moved seventy miles
down the road to Kingsville. Together with Carl Snyder and some of the other
guys, he enrolled in the Texas College of Arts and Industries. He studied
chemistry, trigonometry, algebra, and geometry, all part of a plan to get an
education that could lead him to medicine or engineering. He didn't care
much for school, though, and his grades were mostly Bs and Cs. He was still
playing music on the side. At Texas A&I, Guy met a girl named Cookie Pop.
"Cookie was from one of those Czechoslovakian families that still spoke
Czech at home," Guy says. "She grew up in San Antonio. Her brother had a

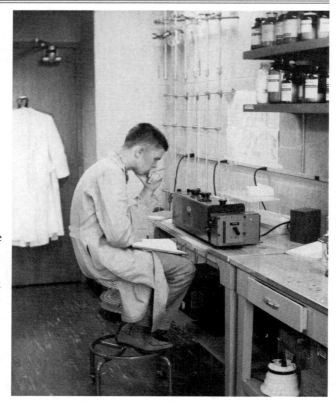

Guy was awarded
a National Science
Foundation grant
for summer study
at M. D. Anderson
Hospital in
Houston in 1960.
He worked in the
cancer research
department.
Courtesy Clark
family archives

scholarship to play football at A&I, and Cookie was a cheerleader. She was really smart and pretty."

In November, Ellis was elected Aransas County attorney, and a youthful, handsome Catholic named John Fitzgerald Kennedy beat Richard Nixon to become president of the United States in one of the closest elections in US history. His running mate was Texan senator Lyndon Johnson. "It was a big deal," Guy says. "Kennedy was appealing to my generation. He made it seem like anything was possible."

The "anything possible" for Guy was music. Although he still didn't think seriously about doing it for a living, Guy played guitar and sang any time he had the chance. On December 3, 1960, Guy and Carl reunited on stage to perform "Rock Island Line" at the A&I Freshman Follies program. When Guy returned to Rockport for the holidays, he told his parents he didn't want to go back to school.

"He decided he was so smart, that those professors didn't know any-thing," Frances Clark told O'Connor. "To quote him: 'They were all so Mickey Mouse.'"

Guy didn't give a shit about college, but to please his parents he reluc-tantly returned to Texas A&I for the spring semester in 1961.

It would not last. The times were changing, and Guy Clark was changing along with them.

## CHAPTER THREE

# Kennedy, Hurricane Carla, and the Peace Corps

On January 20, 1961, John F. Kennedy stood on an inaugural platform next to the Capitol in Washington, DC. Heavy snow had fallen the night before. It was bitter cold as Kennedy placed his bare hand on a Bible and solemnly swore to faithfully execute the office of president of the United States. In a powerful speech, Kennedy proclaimed that the torch had been passed to a new generation of Americans.

Guy Clark pondered this as he frittered away his time at Texas A&I and wondered what to do with his life. During the Christmas holiday in Rockport, Mary Lucille had asked him to come to Austin with her so they might tend to their relationship and perhaps eventually get married. Guy declined. He was not ready for commitment and wasn't especially interested in continuing his education at A&I either. He dropped geometry, failed mechanical and heating, and barely pulled a C average in chemistry. More and more he realized that he didn't belong there.

Guy did show promise in writing and composition, no surprise considering his success in high school with poetry readings, drama, and debate. Guy loved the power of words on a page, but his parents wanted him to do more with his brain. Writing and music was all well and good as a hobby, but doctors and lawyers and engineers made a real living. Ellis and Frances Clark expected Guy to be successful, and their definition of success meant financial security and a prestigious job title.

"We wanted him to have an education and then he could do all the music he wanted to as a hobby," Frances Clark told Louise O'Connor in December

1993. "A career in music wasn't what we expected of him. It was all right to play, fool with it, and entertain yourself or even other people on occasion, but we thought the music business was grimy. He had a lot on the ball and could be anything he wanted to be."

Guy finished his semester at A&I and headed to Austin for the summer. He enrolled in the University of Texas summer study program and took classes in English, American literature, life drawing and philosophy. This was more his style than math and science, and he loved everything about Austin.

Rabble-rouser students at UT-Austin were an integral part of the civil rights movement escalating at universities across the country. UT students initiated biracial lunch counter sit-ins around campus. When that didn't work to desegregate restaurants, they launched a protest march and instigated a rating system, giving restaurants open to all a "Steer Here" designation. They handed out printed cards to restaurant workers that read: "I will continue to patronize this establishment if it is integrated." By the time Guy Clark arrived in Austin, the students had targeted movie theaters and were an unmistakable force in changing the way the establishment treated minorities.

It would be another decade before Austin became famous for its live music scene. Kenneth Threadgill's beer joint attracted guitar-toting folkies and beatniks on Wednesday and Friday nights, but it would be another year before Janis Joplin became a fixture at the college bar. In Nashville, Willie Nelson had just scored his first Top 10 country hit on Liberty Records with "Touch Me."

After a summer spent studying the arts and wandering around the liberal city of Austin, Guy could not bring himself to return to A&I. He returned to Rockport in August and moved back in with his family. Through his father, Guy met a former navy pilot from Fort Lauderdale. The pilot owned a wooden sailboat, the *Silhouette*, and talked about starting a charter business, but first the boat needed a lot of work. The promise of a job on the charter was enough to convince Guy to work for nothing, and Guy and the pilot's son toiled on the boat for weeks. Then Hurricane Carla smashed into Rockport on September 11, 1961.

An old shrimper had taught Guy how to tie the boat to the dock with enough slack to allow it to move with the eight-foot tides. With high winds forecast, Guy and his partner retreated to the cabin to ride out the storm, surrounded by other shrimp boats in the harbor. During Carla's relentless pummeling, a metal crew boat broke loose and repeatedly pounded the *Silhouette*'s stern. The mainstay on the mast snapped, and the steel cable whipped around in the wind. The boys caught the mainstay and retied it, only to have it break away again and again. Winds of 175 miles per hour bumped Carla to a Category 5 hurricane and made her the fiercest storm to make landfall on the Texas coast in the twentieth century. Although the sailboat was saved from complete destruction, by the time Carla was finished the damage was severe, and Guy's dream of sailing ended soon after.

Guy turned his experience into song years later when he wrote "Blowin' Like a Bandit":

> *'Cause out there in the Gulf*
> *The wind is blowin' like a bandit*
> *And I'm talkin' 'bout a hurricane*
> *And your riggin' will not stand it.*

On September 11, 1961, Hurricane Carla smashed into Rockport Harbor. One of Carla's casualties was a sailboat Guy had spent all summer repairing. Courtesy Clark family archives

Guy tired of working for nothing, and his parents urged him to go back to school. In January 1962, Guy enrolled at Del Mar College in Corpus Christi. He registered for physics, biology and the one class that interested him, American literature.

He moved into a fun-loving apartment building across the street from campus and bonded with the bohemians who lived there. School was a drag, and music jams and barbecues on the roof became part of Guy's day-to-day life. He reconnected with the girl from Ingleside who had dated his high school pal. Juliette Tawil was a music major at Del Mar and determined to play guitar. Guy was happy to take her on as a pupil.

He sat Juliette down in front of a record player and taught her to recognize the chords. The first record he played was the Kingston Trio's "The Seine." When Bob Dylan's self-titled album debuted in March, Guy played it for Juliette.

"He made me listen to every word," Juliette says. "Dylan's imagery was hard to adjust to, but Guy would rant, 'Listen to this part! Wow! Oh, man!' He was totally taken by Dylan." Many years later, in 2011, Bob Dylan would be taken by Guy and list Guy Clark as one of his favorite songwriters.

In 1962, Guy was a great deal more interested in Dylan and the new folk revival than his school curriculum. He barely passed the semester and left Del Mar that May with no plans to return. He drifted between Rockport and his grandmother's hotel in Monahans throughout the summer, but his parents persuaded him to register for fall classes at the University of Houston. Houston was a happening place in 1962 as NASA was building its manned spacecraft center twenty-five miles south of town. The citizens of Houston welcomed the Mercury astronauts and their families with a grand parade on July 4, and, at Rice University in September, President Kennedy gave a rousing speech about the space race.

When Guy arrived in Houston, he moved in with his high school pal Carl Snyder. He landed a part-time job at a bookstore, rarely attended his classes and instead spent a lot of time reading the beatnik writers Kerouac, Ferlinghetti, and Ginsberg. Guy dragged Carl down to Bucho's Purple Onion to listen to poets read and play bongos. By the middle of the semester and after the drama of the Cuban missile crisis, he was over school. President Kennedy had called for students to serve their country by moving to isolated, far-off, third-world countries to develop agricultural, economic, and educational programs. That sounded pretty good to Guy, who sent his transcripts to Kennedy's new Peace Corps.

Guy's application was accepted, and he left for Peace Corps training at Camp Radley, Puerto Rico, in February 1963. First, however, he stopped in New York City for Peace Corps meetings and a visit with Juliette, who had moved there the previous year. Together they wrote a postcard to his parents:

Hello there!
    I am dictating this card to Juliette Baby. She is very cooperative. I am leaving for Puerto Rico Monday morning at 5:30. Having a good time. How is everyone!? Juliette says "Hi!" Will write more later (I don't see how he will. I had to twist his arm to send you this little card!)
Love,
Guy

More than a month later, Guy wrote to his family from Dexter Hall at the St. Paul campus of the University of Minnesota. He was on the next leg of his Peace Corps training and wanted to catch them up on everything.

Dear Family,
    Well, I finally got around to writing. I really don't know where to start, everythings been happening so fast. . . .
    We flew to San Juan, Puerto Rico, where we had a brief orientation at the airport, followed by a 60-mile bus trip to an area on the island called Rio Abajo. From the bottom of a fairly good sized mountain we were taken in vans to the camp, which is located at the top of the mountain. More orientation. The island is really beautiful. . . . The training at Puerto is divided into 3 major categories: trekking (hiking), rock climbing, and water survival. The first trek we took was a map trek. Six of us were given a contour map and a compass and were to follow a trail marked on the map through the mountains. . . . The second trek was called an identification trek. We were simply led along one of the trails by a staff member and shown all edible and non-edible plants, what to use to start a fire when it has been raining, and what to look out for in the way of scorpions, centipedes, tarantulas, etc.

# Peace Corps Job Attracts Area Youth

**Caller-Times News Service**

ROCKPORT — Guy Charles Clark, son of Mr. and Mrs. Ellis Clark, left last week for New York to report for duty in the Peace Corps and ultimate assignment in India.

Clark is the first South Texan to report for active duty in the Peace Corps. Nicky Jo Huestis of Taft was selected for duty in June, 1961, but is now on reserve while he completes his pre-medical training at the University of Texas.

Clark graduated from Aransas County High School in 1960 and was a junior student at the University of Houston when selected for Peace Corps duty. He is scheduled to leave New York Monday for a month of camp training at Camp Radley, Puerto Rico, followed by three months of intensive training at the University of Minnesota at St. Paul. Clark will leave for his overseas station in Punjab on June 5.

Clark thinks his work assignment will be either in youth work, small industries or athletic training.

Mathematics and sciences were his strong studies in high school

**GUY CHARLES CLARK**
**. . . headed for India**

and upon graduation in Rockport he was awarded the National Science Foundation grant for summer study in the M. D. Anderson Hospital where he worked with research physicists.

Clark is an accomplished folk-singer and plays several musical instruments, including the guitar and banjo. Art, along with cooking, is another of his hobbies and he works in oils, pastels and charcoal.

Mrs. Clark rates Guy as a "very good cook." This hobby cost him his membership in the Fulton Volunteer Fire Department when he once fell asleep while an oven-full of English muffins were cooking and set the family home on fire.

The *Rockport Pilot* reports on Guy Clark joining the Peace Corps in 1963. Courtesy Clark family archives

The third trek was an all-day overnight trek on which we were led out and dropped off at different spots. We made camp, spent the night and went back to Camp Radley the next day. . . .

The fourth trek was, I must admit, quite an experience. This was called the 4½ day trek. The group of 6 that I was with was taken to the top of the highest mountain in Puerto Rico, called Cerro de Punto, and dropped. Our route back to camp was about 65 miles. We each had 3 boxes of C-rations, poncho, blanket, canteen, pack board and anything else we felt like carrying (which wasn't much). We had a contour map and a compass and 4½ days to get back to camp. . . . We set some sort of record for speed because we made the trek in about 3 or 3½ days. . . .

I suppose rock climbing was the thing I came to enjoy the most. . . . There are two basic parts to the program: climbing and repelling [sic] (coming down a mountainside in a special harness being in control of your own rate of descent.) . . . I climbed a cliff that had never been climbed. It took me an hour and 15 minutes. I can't ever remember having been that tired and only traveled 80 ft. The most fun in climbing is repelling. We repelled the side of a large dam called Dos Bocas Dam, which is about 110 ft. That was a ball! . . .

The people in the mountains of Puerto Rico are unbelievably friendly. They live an extremely simple life but are very happy.

Enclosed is a picture of the group that I went on the 4½ day trek with. It was taken on top of Cerro de Punta, the highest mountain in Puerto Rico.

Guy spent a couple of months at the University of Minnesota. He was to be stationed in India but never made it. "I was having too much fun and not studying enough," Guy says. "I couldn't really get into [it] because of the language. I already spoke Spanish pretty much. Why would they send me to India? I could've easily learned Spanish. Anyway, I didn't go."

After renting a car and driving back to Texas, Guy stayed with Mimi and Jack Prigg in Monahans for the summer and returned to the University of Houston for the fall semester. He took a few classes, worked at the bookstore, and shared an apartment with his high school friend Carl Snyder. At night, Guy and Carl played guitar and sang at the folk joints.

On November 22, 1963, President Kennedy was assassinated in Dallas. The president who had inspired Guy to join the Peace Corps, who stood for his generation, was gone. It changed everything.

"There's a big reflecting pond at the University of Houston and a big circular and wide sidewalk all around it," Guy remembers.

I was walking around that long pathway, and coming towards me real slowly is a guy with a transistor radio. He walked by and I heard the

Guy and his group stop during a four-day trek to take a photo at the top of Cerro de Punta, the highest mountain in Puerto Rico. *Left to right:* Bruce Collard, Desmond McCullough, Terry Clayton, Guy Clark, Larry Merlo, Tom Waltz, Roger Banks, and Jim Mayhugh. Courtesy Guy Clark

news on his radio. I stumbled a little bit but we both kept walking. I went to the office of this assistant dean who was kind of hip. Maybe it had to do with [a] newspaper or some underground rag. Anyway, went straight to her office and they were all real political, you know, and we were all just in tears. From that day on, it's just like, "Fuck you guys. You shot my president, man."

I've always been really put off by politics, and it started with the church. I was a teenager going to the youth thing, and there's a cool youth counselor everybody liked. Well, one afternoon they were going to elect deacons. "Taking nominations from the floor; we're electing two deacons." Somebody nominates somebody, and it hits me. I raise my hand. "I want to nominate so and so, the youth counselor." There's like this gasp. All those nominations were picked before that meeting by the existing deacons behind closed doors. They all knew who was going to be elected. The fact that I had the audacity to raise my hand and nominate somebody who I thought would do a good job and represent me, it was just like "You can't do that. You're too young." It was so black and white. I was so offended by it. I thought I was contributing. I thought I was grown up. Should have known. After Kennedy was killed, that's when I quit politics. I've often said I don't want a politician in my living room.

After Kennedy's death, Guy gave up college for good. He didn't care about getting a formal education. He didn't want to be a doctor, engineer, or lawyer. Guy Clark wanted to be a folksinger, and he was going to figure out a way to do just that.

## CHAPTER FOUR

# Houston

The mid-1960s marked a period of upheaval in the country, and Houston, Texas, was no exception. The war babies, the generation born during World War II, appeared as architects of the countercul-ture, with new ideas and philosophies. Many of them, including Guy Clark, struggled between the idealized version of America cultivated by parents and the new reality: fighting for civil rights and rebelling against the war in Vietnam. Kennedy was dead, and men all over the United States were burn-ing their draft cards. In Houston, the Montrose district became a center for the burgeoning counterculture movement, and folksingers joined the scene.

Rent was cheap in Montrose, which made it an excellent choice for bohe-mians, beatniks, and junkies, along with local college students. The neigh-borhood had an undercurrent of good vibes for idealists and dreamers: Mon-trose had been the place where author William Sydney Porter (O. Henry) lived in 1895 while writing a column for the *Houston Post*. Tycoon Howard Hughes spent his teenage years at 3921 Yoakum Street, a house built for his family in 1918. Leading man Clark Gable stayed at a bungalow at 411 Hyde Park Boulevard while acting with the Laskin Brothers Stock Company in the 1920s. And future president Lyndon Baines Johnson boarded at 435 Haw-thorne Street while teaching public speaking at Sam Houston High School in 1930.

"Montrose is pretty close to town. It was a beautiful neighborhood filled with big three-story homes and old, old trees. All lush, because Houston gets so much rain. Just green and gorgeous," says Houston native and journalist Bill Bentley. "And then, when people started moving out of that area, the rents were low, so that's why the bohemians moved in. And they started dividing up houses. The bohemians quickly evolved somewhat through the use of LSD into the hippie movement. So I would say the first hippies were right around '64, '65, when I started hanging around Montrose. And you'd see people with long hair. The University of St. Thomas had this ultra-liberal order of the Catholic priests and had the first film school. The de Menil family donated a lot of money for their art department. I remember in '65 they brought Andy Warhol in to give a talk at the Young Cinematographers Club. We high school kids went there every Saturday morning to watch movies and talk about them."

In 1964, twenty-two-year-old Guy Clark was trying to figure out where he belonged and what he wanted to do. Bob Dylan released his third studio album that year, *The Times They Are a-Changin'*, and the title track could have been Guy's theme song. Guy saw Dylan as a descendent of the beat poets he loved. Lawrence Ferlinghetti's *A Coney Island of the Mind* was one of Guy's favorite books, and Dylan was putting that kind of poetry to music.

Now that Guy was not in college, he had to contend with the Selective Service Act. Things in Vietnam were hot, and Guy received his draft letter.

"I got a piece of paper that said be in San Antonio at 8 o'clock on such and such a day," Guy says.

My father just wouldn't hear of it that I would not run right down there and be first in line, because he'd been in the service. I got there and took a written test and had the cursory physical. The written test was first, and after that we're all standing there with no clothes on. This drill sergeant who's in charge of the whole place comes up to me. "Clark. You're pretty smart, aren't you? You scored a hundred on this test. You're the only one who's ever done that in I can't remember when. We want you." I thought, *Oh, God, no.* I'm in line, and finally there's a point when you get to sit with the doctor by yourself. I started with, "Man, my father's a diabetic, and I'm pretty sure I'm gonna be a diabetic, and I'm pretty sure that should keep me out of this. And I have flat feet." This guy was just taking it in. The next thing, he said, "Give me the name of your doctor. We're going to run a glucose tolerance test on you back in Rockport.

You're going home." So I go back to Rockport and had a glucose tolerance test, which in those days was excruciating. They had to reinject
your vein on a sliding scale—like the first one's five minutes, the next
one's ten minutes, fifteen minutes—not just put a line in there to draw
blood but a new injection. And both of my arms were just pulsing like
a cartoon. I waited around for a couple of weeks, and pretty soon a letter came from the Selective Service bureau. Says, "Sorry, but you're not
capable of being inducted into the service for health reasons." That's
all it said. That's all I ever knew. When my father died, I was going
through all the paperwork and sorting everything. I found a letter from
that doctor who did the glucose tolerance test. It said, "I see no reason
why he shouldn't be inducted into the service, no diabetes." He sent
that letter back to the military doctor, and that doctor threw it in the
trash. He rarely ran across somebody in one of those rooms of inductees
who was as smart as I was and just straight-up [said], "I don't think
he ought to be doing this." That's how I got out of the service. I know
that's what that guy did. He just picked it up off his desk and threw it
away and wrote his own letter.

"Guy was giving away all his possessions because he was sure he was going
to die," Jan Clark says. "He gave me his Martin guitar. Surely he knew I
couldn't carry a tune and was tone deaf, but I was very honored and thought
it was very important. I took very good care of it—until the next day, when
they sent him back. He said [to me], 'I want my guitar back.' We were all
grateful he didn't get drafted, for whatever reason."

Guy returned to Houston a free man. No more college, no military service. All he wanted to do was play his guitar and sing. The first real job he
had as a folksinger required him to put on a coat and tie and travel to high
schools all over Texas and across the South to play and sing traditional songs
at assemblies. Ellis Clark helped his son buy a car so he could drive around
from gig to gig.

In 1964, Dick Clark and *American Bandstand* moved from Philadelphia to the
ABC Television Center in Los Angeles. Season seven included performances
by the Beach Boys, Jan and Dean, Fabian, Little Richard, Johnny Rivers, Dusty
Springfield, Sam Cooke, Marvin Gaye, and tributes to the Beatles and Elvis

Presley. But it was the short-lived ABC variety show *Hootenanny*, hosted by Jack Linkletter and featuring performances by the Journeymen, the Limeliters, the Chad Mitchell Trio, Judy Collins, and Johnny Cash that reflected and influenced what was happening in Guy Clark's Houston circle.

Traditionally, the Houston Folklore Society, lead by folk historian John Avery Lomax Jr., hosted open hootenannies once a month. By the mid sixties there was a push to do more. They added a "hoot" to one of the bimonthly Tuesday meetings at Linkwood Park Community House in addition to regular hoots on Sundays, which were often held in partnership with the Jewish Community Center. Along with the skinny young white kids, bluesmen Mance Lipscomb and Lightnin' Sam Hopkins often played the Sunday hoots. The Houston Folklore Society proudly declared that the word "hootenanny" was coined by Texas Jim Lewis, a 1930s entertainer, and claimed that Woody Guthrie and Pete Seeger had learned the term from Lewis.

In the mid-1960s, Guy traveled around the South and played traditional folk songs at high school assemblies. This is his PR photo from the "Folk Songs of Our Land" tour. Courtesy Guy Clark

John Lomax Jr. was a real estate developer by trade, but the Houston Folklore Society was an important avocation. He and his brother, Alan, had learned about music history from their father, folklorist and collector John Avery Lomax.

"John Lomax was always at Hermann Park, and we'd sit around in the summertime, just twenty or thirty people in circles singing songs," Guy says. "He didn't play any instrument. He would just stand up there and sing a cappella. Or he had one little act where he would do a prison work song and bring a fucking log with him and an axe and sing while he was chopping wood. It was really far-out, because all I knew about blues was Josh White and traditional black folk songs. He turned me on to Lead Belly and Lightnin' Hopkins: extremely primitive, extremely subtle stuff. And it certainly made a difference in my life to have it presented to me that way. That's one of the most fortunate things you can imagine, that formative part of learning about whether Josh White really played the blues or if Lightnin' Hopkins really played the blues. Lightnin' really was a good guitar player when he had just enough whiskey in him. He was pretty righteous."

Lomax introduced Guy to Mance Lipscomb, too. "Mance was a totally different guy than Lightnin'," Guy says.

Lightnin' was a city guy. Man, he was hip to everything. Wearing shades everywhere, a star, and had come from a very poor background. Lightnin' was a gambler and a drinker and a womanizer and a guitar player. Mance, on the other hand, had sharecropped all of his life. He was a poor black dirt farmer until he was sixty-five or something, when Mack McCormick discovered him living there in Texas. The thing about it is, what made those guys so cool to me was the fact that they were writing songs. They were singing the blues. They were the blues. It was just like, wow. Write songs for a living and play in honky-tonks. What a cool thing to do.

John Lomax was one of the few white guys that Lightnin' Hopkins and Mance Lipscomb trusted. That was an entrée to have Lightnin' come and play for us, you know, play for the white kids. Or go to joints, once you got to know the right people through John, and you were able to go to black joints in Houston in the early sixties and see Lightnin' play in his own element. And Mance—I actually got to go to Mance's house in Navasota. A bunch of white kids from the Jewish Community Center making a pilgrimage to see Mance Lipscomb. We all sat in his living room, and he played for us. It was far-out. Women couldn't come in the front room. They could come in if they had a plate of fried chicken, but men were all in the front room of this little frame house, and in the kitchen, through the door, there were like four or five kitchen chairs around the door, with all the women sitting there . . . but they didn't come out. I mean really patriarchal, sharecroppers and such. I'm not a blues player, and I really don't want to be. I love it and I appreciate it, but what Lightnin' brought to it for me was [that] there are no rules. He didn't play straight time, and nobody could play with him, you know, except people who really knew what he was going to do. But he put extra bars and he would stop and vamp on one for however long he felt like, and he'd take a drink of whiskey and he'd play. There were no rules, and it was the most captivating, fascinating approach to music. It was just pure music.

"Houston was very segregated at that time," journalist Bill Bentley says. "The blacks had a side of town, the whites had a side of town. And the music was the thing that bridged the races. I've always maintained that was probably the biggest catalyst for the civil rights movement, white people listening to black music and enjoying it so much they realize these people are equal to us in every way. It opened a lot of doors. And in Houston all of us young white kids are going over to the black clubs. And then the old taboos of keeping us separate, it was just like, what the hell? There's nothing different. So that really tore down a bunch of walls in Houston."

The folk singers who played Mac Webster's Jester Lounge on the corner of Westheimer Road and Mid Lane called Webster's joint a "mecca for misfits." The place was packed every weekend. It served beer on tap and allowed patrons to bring in mixers.

Performers smoked dope out in the parking lot between sets. Guy hadn't yet discovered the appeal of booze and drugs and would quietly excuse himself from a table of arguing drunks. He was there to play music, hear music, and mingle with the other performers.

"Houston was sort of out of the way for show people, but they liked to come down there to get their acts together at the Jester," songwriter Gary White recalls. "When I first arrived at the Jester, the Stoneman family, Pop and Ron Stoneman and their family, were there about six months working on their reunion. I remember Pop Stoneman playing the autoharp and Scott who was the guitar player and later played with Clarence White. Then John Denver showed up and played about three months at the Jester. He had just left the Chad Mitchell Trio, and he worked up his solo act there."

"We were seat fillers and openers for John Denver," Carl Snyder says. "Judy Collins played there too. And that's where we first saw Mance Lipscomb and Lightnin' Hopkins."

"One of my most vivid visual memories is Guy at the Jester onstage," regular Don Sanders remembers. "I remember him doing 'Cotton Mill Girls:' 'Hard times for cotton mill girls / working in a cotton mill all my life / all I've got to show is a Barlow knife.'"

Guy had recorded "Cotton Mill Girls" on a 1963 Jester Records compilation release titled *Look, It's Us!* The album was recorded at Gold Star Studios at 5626 Brock Street in Houston. It was Guy's first experience in a recording studio. Lightnin' Hopkins sang "Trouble in Mind," Kay Oslin sang "Brave Young Soldier," Frank Davis recorded "East Virginia," and Frank and Kay dueted on "My Girl." There is a group picture of the artists on an insert with the note:

> The one big happy family of Jester Strolling Players (Kay, put down that mandolin!) are: (you should pardon the expression) Left to Right (oops!)
> Back Row: Alex Martin, Arthur Hodges, Kay Oslin, Guy Clark, Mack Webster
> Middle Row: Vivian Holtzman, Frank Davis, Kenn Roberts, Sarah Wiggins, Scott Holtzman
> Seated Front: Judy Stewart, Jenny Bell Dean
> Missing in action at picture time: Lightnin' Hopkins and Jim Gunn

Musician Frank Davis, a savant who, among other things, built what he called the "daddy banjo" with a snare drum for a banjo head and a Fender guitar neck. He was an engineer at Andrus Sound, a recording studio co-owned by Walt Andrus and Leland Rogers, brother of Kenny.

"Frank Davis was crazy and innovative," Gary White says. "He played Lead Belly songs on the daddy banjo. Frank and Kay Oslin, who later had success as K.T. Oslin, were probably the big-time locals of note back then."

"Frank Davis is a genius," Guy says. "I'm probably as influenced by Frank's music as anybody's. He could do Lead Belly more primitive than Lead Belly. He's a natural guitar player and singer. It's really rough and charming as hell."

Before she teamed up with Davis, Oslin played some shows as a trio with Guy and David Jones. "My friend and I had gone to Prince's drive-in, a hamburger place, and were parked next to David and Guy," she says. I knew David from high school. They were singing at the Jester and invited me to sing with them. We worked up a few songs as a threesome and played for a month or two. It was fun."

Guy's repertoire included ragtime blues songs, Bob Dylan covers, and whatever he could learn from traditional Folkways records. He listened to Joan Baez, Ramblin' Jack Elliott, and Judy Collins, and if a song struck him, he'd work it up to play at the Jester. John Lomax III saw Guy play "San Francisco Bay Blues" at the Jester. "That is not an easy song to pick, and Guy did a bang-up job with it," Lomax says. "He was a really good guitar player."

The green room at the Jester was crowded with beer kegs and instruments and performers ready to go on stage, so everyone lingered in the Jester parking lot before and after gigs. This is where Gary White first bumped into Guy. Gary says, "I had learned how to finger-pick the guitar when I was over in Korea from a tape that friends had sent me of *The Freewheelin' Bob Dylan*. I was finger-picking 'Don't Think Twice, It's All Right,' and Guy goes, 'God, that's great. How are you doing that?'"

Guy's roommate Carl Snyder had just gotten married, and Guy needed a new place to live. White had a job at NASA working on the new Apollo space program, so he and Guy pooled their money for an upstairs duplex on Greeley Street between Westheimer Road and Alabama Street. Rent was $120 for two bedrooms and a spacious living room and kitchen. Guy used the sun porch as a workshop to repair guitars.

Minor Wilson, son of famous Austin photographer Burton Wilson, had met Guy on a beach in Rockport when they were teenagers. They kept up with each other and sealed their friendship when Wilson moved from Austin to Houston. Together, Guy and Wilson taught themselves to repair and build guitars.

"Minor Wilson and I just started doing little repair work for people," Guy says. "Fixing cracks or re-gluing bridges or whatever needed to be done. Then I really got into it. I was taking classical guitar lessons from this guy Charlie Gestantes, who was an old retired symphony fiddle player. He had taken up guitar in his old age and was grossly overweight and had two of the rarest guitars I've ever seen in my life. One which he let me have and copy and take old measurements off of it."

"Guy had a ten-dollar Mexican guitar soaking in the bathtub full of water in his apartment in Houston," Wilson says. "He wanted to figure out how to take it apart. It didn't take long to find out that this was not the right way to get a guitar apart, but it was the first shot at 'I wonder how you get inside one of these?' That's when I decided to move from Austin to Houston, because Guy and I wanted to learn to build and repair guitars together."

The guitar repair business expanded quickly. The pair loved working on guitars together and decided they needed more space. Guy and Gary White moved to a two-story house at 3703 Fannin Street, where they lived upstairs while Guy and Wilson used the first floor for their shop. "The place was a dump," White says. "It had no heat and old gaslights. We put in a cheap wood-burning stove. There was electricity, but it's a wonder we didn't burn ourselves with those gaslights."

"People would bring us Gibson L5's and stuff, when it wasn't appropriate for us to even touch one let alone take it apart, but we did it anyhow," Wilson says. "Guy and I built a twelve-string which still hangs on my wall. That's the first guitar that he and I ever built. Guy had some poplar, which was really easy to work with. We copied the bridge from a Washburn-type bridge, and it worked. We built that guitar, then we built a classical guitar, and then we built a steel-string guitar."

The year 1965 was a pivotal one. President Johnson ratified the Voting Rights Act and expanded the troops in Vietnam. Guy spent more and more time honing his skills at the Jester and Houston Folklore Society. Peter Gardner, who had preformed in the New York folk duo the Gardners with his ex-wife Isabelle, remarried, moved back to Texas, and hosted a folk radio show on KHOU, the University of Houston's radio station. Once a week, Gardner recorded the show at the home he shared with his new wife, Mary Helen. It became an important open mic opportunity for the Jester folksingers. Guy remembers meeting Townes Van Zandt for the first time at the Gardners' house. The friendship was immediate. Guy heard Van Zandt sing a couple of songs and knew that this was someone he wanted to be around.

Van Zandt was born into a prominent Fort Worth family. His great-great-great-grandfather, Isaac Van Zandt, was leader of the Republic of Texas; his great-great-grandfather, Khleber Van Zandt, was a Confederate Army major and a founder of Fort Worth. Van Zandt County, Texas, is named for his family. During his college years at the University of Colorado at Boulder, Townes showed signs of manic-depressive disorder and drank to excess. His parents sent him to a psychiatric hospital in Galveston, where he received shock therapy for several months.

By the time Van Zandt met Guy, he had been married to his college sweetheart, Fran Petters, for several months. He knew that he was going to get a draft letter and decided to join up instead. "I went by the National Guard to see if I could get in," Van Zandt told Louise O'Connor in 1991.

They laughed at me. They had been filled up for months. So I went to the post office and proceeded to join the air force in Houston. I went through this battery of tests for three days and scored [in the] 96th–98th percentile. After three days, the very last question on the sheet was "Have you ever been treated for mental illness?" I told them it was nothing—it was a college breakdown, that I was in the hospital for nine months. [They] told me I couldn't be in the air force. Then comes the draft. I had gotten greetings and I go in for the induction physical. My parents and my wife put me on a bus to Fort Hood. They said to have the letter from my doctor in my pocket. [After I arrived we heard] "All you creeps got letters from your doctors, stand up. Strip and stand at attention." We're all looking at each other. We were from farms, crack houses, from all around Houston and here we go to Vietnam. Doctor walks all the way down the line. I went to military school and never feinted, had a secret underground group called the Syndicate, I founded and headed it, sold bootleg to freshmen, rolling crap games. . . . I was in the Secret Underground in Shattuck. So, I'm in line and everyone is getting inducted, and then he calls out "Van Zandt!" He never turned around. He just said "You are permanently disbarred from any branch of the armed services. You can't even be a fucking fireman. Van Zandt, you get out of here." I was swarmed by this bunch of guys wanting to know what was in that letter. I just sort of slipped into someone else and had tears coming down my cheeks. I'm the only full-grown member of my family who never served. We were in the Revolutionary War and the Civil War. Tears are coming down my cheeks, and I scream: "I'll be the only one!" Those guys are backing away from me. I got my clothes, went outside and split. I never knew what was in that letter—but I was 4F. I was defective.

"Townes was complicated," his first wife, Fran Lohr, says. "When he was sober, you never met a kinder, more affectionate, more loving person. He wore his heart in his songs. He wrote 'I'll Be Here in the Morning' right after we found out Townes couldn't join the service because of his psychiatric treatments. Townes always needed something to hold on to. I always felt like his relationship with Guy was so strong because Guy was stronger than him. He had the ability to handle things Townes couldn't. Townes ran away from everything like that. His shock treatments weren't just insulin shock as some people think. It was electric shock, too. Three months of it. He had no picture memories of anything. He didn't even know his mother when she came in to see him. He recognized me, and he clung to me, because I was something that he remembered."

"Townes was bound and determined to have the blues," Guy says.

One of the first songs he wrote was "Waitin' Around to Die." I heard that and "Don't You Take It Too Bad" and it was one of the main reasons I started writing . . . hearing those songs. It was so literate, you know, and yet music. Wow, what a concept! Of course, I can't be Townes, and I can't be a white blues player, but I can write using the same approach, the same care and respect Townes and Lightnin' took with writing. I'll tell you my favorite piece of Townes poetry, two verses of a song called "Two Girls" I'll always remember:

*The clouds didn't look like cotton*
*They didn't even look like clouds*
*I was underneath the weather*
*My friends looked like a crowd*
*Said swimming hole was full of rum*
*I tried to find out why*
*All I learned was this, my friend*
*You've got to swim before you fly.*

*It's cold down on the bayou*
*They say it's in your mind*
*But the moccasins are treading ice*
*And leaving strange designs*
*Cajuns say the last time*
*That this happened they weren't here*
*All Beaumont's full of penguins*
*And I'm playing it by ear.*

"That's my yardstick right there, those two verses," Guy says. "That's what I try to write to every day. Is it that serious and that funny? You never get over the fact that you can't beat Townes, but you can aspire to the same quality of work in your own humbled and whispered way."

For inspiration, Guy and Townes often listened to the poet Dylan Thomas reading his own work. "Dylan Thomas used the English language better than anybody," Guy says. "We'd listen to him reading *Under Milk Wood* or *A Child's Christmas in Wales*. Amazing. I grew up reading poetry, and the roll and the rhyme is pleasing to the ear. That style evolved with singing my songs. They are a piece of poetry, and that's the way I like to perform them."

While Guy thought more about writing songs, he continued to play at the Jester and the new Sand Mountain Coffeehouse, opened by a Mrs. Carrick and her son John. It was at Sand Mountain that Guy first heard Doc Watson sing "Columbus Stockade Blues," a line he would use later in his song "Dublin Blues." Guy still visited high schools to sing traditional folk songs during assemblies. One of those schools was Bellaire High School in the Houston suburb of the same name. Senior Susan Spaw was learning to play guitar when

Guy, Frank Davis, and Carolyn Terry from the Folklore Society performed at Bellaire.

"I thought, *That's what I want to do*," Susan says. "I didn't meet Guy that day but it put the idea in my head that I could be a folksinger."

Susan graduated in the spring of 1965 at the age of seventeen. She was ready to play the Jester, but she couldn't drive and wasn't old enough to get in the club. That entire summer Susan's father took her to the Jester and nursed a beer all night while Susan waited to play her two songs.

"That's when I met Guy and a whole bunch of other people," Susan says. "Jerry Jeff [Walker] was in and out. I met Janis Joplin and John Denver at the Jester. Mac Webster, that old fart, made me play a really stupid song I'd written. It was crazy. And John Denver was the sweetest thing. He was the only person left, and he listened to the whole thing. And then he got up and played the song he wrote for his wife, Annie."

When Susan turned eighteen, she no longer needed her father to chaperone her at the Jester. She became one of the regulars and saw more of Guy. It was no secret that Guy loved beautiful women, and he had already hooked up with several of them from the Jester gang. In addition to his old friend Juliette Tawil, who had returned from New York the previous year, Guy also had dated Linda (now his friend Carl's wife), and Amy Goodenough, daughter of blind piano player Forest Goodenough. Now Susan and Guy started seeing each other regularly, and in the spring of 1966, they discovered Susan was pregnant.

"He never asked me to consider an abortion, although two wives of his friends came to the house to urge me to do so," Susan says. "A friend took me to an abortionist she knew about. He examined me on his four-poster bed and gave me some pills. If they didn't work, I was to go back. I couldn't do it. Guy understood and we agreed to marry. Our parents would have been mortified if we hadn't."

Guy Clark married Susan Spaw on June 2, 1966, at the Bellaire Methodist Church. Guy's parents drove up from Rockport for the ceremony. John Lomax Jr. gave the young couple a signed copy of his father's book *Cowboy Songs and Other Frontier Ballads*. Susan moved into the Fannin Street house with Guy and Gary White, and the Houston Folklore Society newsletter announced the marriage: "Guy Clark and Susan Spaw were married on June 2. Susan is

Guy Clark and Susan Spaw marry on June 2, 1966, at Bellaire Methodist Church near Houston. Courtesy Clark family archives

teaching guitar at the new Houston School of the Creative Arts. Guy builds guitars at 3703 Fannin."

After a short honeymoon in Nuevo Laredo, Guy and Susan returned to gigging at the Jester and Sand Mountain. Guy taught folk guitar lessons at the Jewish Community Center and continued taking classical guitar lessons from Charlie Gestantes, who owned a guitar shop nearby. Between meager income from gigging and guitar repair, the young couple just got by. Guy tried to make a comfortable home for his new wife on Fannin Street.

"The old duplex was great," Susan says. "We had a monster living room and dining room, a nasty little kitchen—it was horrible really, and an adequate bathroom. Gary had a bedroom, and our bedroom had a sunroom off of it, which was going to be a nursery. This place was really old and classy. I just loved it. It had gaslights on the wall, and they'd light those things, but they didn't have any covers on them. So these tremendous lamps would shoot up [and we had] to be careful to get them just right so we didn't burn ourselves down."

"Guy was sweet," Susan says. "I was throwing up every day, for six months straight. It was awful. He'd hold my head when I was throwing up, bring white bread, Cheese Whiz, and grapefruit to my bedside, which was all I could keep down. He even put in a window air conditioner so I could hide out in the bedroom for the Texas summer. It was a really cool place, and I know Guy didn't want to give it up, but one morning he was out back and found a large rat drowned in a bucket. He found us another place, and we moved before I delivered."

Guy and Susan moved to a three-bedroom upper duplex with a fireplace and sunroom in a brick building at 1548 Castle Court. Carl and Linda Snyder lived downstairs, and Townes and Fran Van Zandt lived a mile away. Meanwhile Jerry Jeff Walker, Pete Troutner, and Bob Bruno moved in with Gary White on Fannin Street.

"Jerry Jeff and his new rock band, Nucleus Heat, moved in with me upstairs," White says. "They had this trio, and they played acoustic guitars and sang three-part harmony, mostly songs that Jerry Jeff and Bob Bruno had written. About that time I was spending more time playing at the coffeehouse and at the Jester, and I had also joined a local Beatle copy group called the Baroque Brothers. I got sick of Fannin Street. It was getting crowded with Jerry Jeff and his boys, and I wasn't going to pay the rent for them. I moved into a one-bedroom apartment downstairs from Minor and Mary Ann Wilson. After I moved, Jerry Jeff would still end up over at my place sleeping on the couch. Lots of people dropped by. Townes Van Zandt would come in a lot. We'd go play at the Sand Mountain Coffeehouse, and they'd come over afterward, and we'd stay up until late in the morning. Johnny Winter used to come over and sit around and just play guitars with us and have a good time."

"At that time, the Beatles were happening and the Stones were happening, and original material was being put together by bands," Jerry Jeff Walker says. "We were out all night looking at what other bands were doing and trying to find gigs or playing upstairs and making tapes and trying to figure out our own shit. We thought we could put a band together because we had songs and could sing harmonies."

They asked Gary White to play electric bass in the band and took the name Lost Sea Dreamers. The new group inherited a Mercury station wagon from a friend of Bob Bruno and took off for New York.

"We got to New York, and we played at the Night Owl Cafe for quite a while, eight months or something," White says. "Then we got a job working at this place called the Electric Circus, and we became the house band. And Vanguard Records signed us. But they said they didn't want us to be the Lost Sea Dreamers, since the initials spelled LSD, so we changed the name to Circus Maximus and did a couple albums there for them."

By the mid 1960s the 13th Floor Elevators had become one of the hottest rock 'n' roll bands in Texas. Guy and Minor Wilson went down to Houston's Texas Opry House to see the pioneering psychedelic band for themselves. "It was the first time I smoked a joint," Guy says. "I sat in front of the speakers and just went into another world. Roky Erickson was the best blues guitar player I ever heard. He was a crazy motherfucker."

Although performing and going out to hear live music remained a big part of his life, Guy had a new wife and a child on the way. So he missed out the time his friends went to find the Merry Pranksters: Ken Kesey and Neal Cassady (the model for Jack Kerouac's Dean Moriarty character in his seminal beat book On the Road) and Kesey's psychedelic magic bus when the Pranksters visited Kesey's friend Larry McMurtry in Houston.

Guy and Susan rented their Castle Court apartment from Paul Montague, a sculptor and carpenter who had built himself a garage apartment and rented out the duplex. Susan furnished the apartment with items from the new Pier One Imports store, while Montague allowed Guy to set up a guitar repair shop in the garage. Now that he was going to be a father, Guy needed a full-time job. He found one drafting structural steel for Pyramid Derrick, a construction company that built oil rigs. "I hated that job," Guy says. "I burned myself out because whenever the boss wanted to build a new rig or something crashed, I had to work all night to get the drawings ready so the shop could fabricate the steel and get it to the job. I learned on the job, and I was good at it and thought I was underpaid for what I was doing."

The original Star Trek series debuted on NBC that fall. Guy's friends Dick and Suzy Mitchell brought their kids over to watch it every Thursday night. The couples cooked dinner and watched the Clarks' small television. On October 30, Guy and Susan went to the Jewish Community Center Folk

Song Series to see seventy-year-old Mance Lipscomb perform. Susan sat on the floor in front of Lipscomb, and when he couldn't find his thumb pick, Susan gave him hers.

Townes and Fran Van Zandt also spent a lot of time at Guy and Susan's. Carl and Linda Snyder came upstairs, or friends would float between the two floors. Folksingers from the Jester and Sand Mountain hung around constantly, and everyone pooled their money to buy cheap gallons of Gallo wine. "After one of those notorious parties, Townes's wife came downstairs looking for Townes," Carl Snyder says. "No one could find him for hours. He was in a closet, writing a song."

Sandra Carrick, whose mother owned Sand Mountain, often stayed up late with Guy at Castle Court. "Guy was both waifish and rakish," she says. "Somehow I could never think of Townes as a sexual sort, but Guy was a different story, a randy devil he was . . . and he did everything well—played well, sang well. There was an unbelievable number of people coming and going at Castle Court. [On] one of the most memorable evenings for me, after we'd indulged in various consciousness-raising substances, Mickey Newbury got up, walked over to Susan's old green piano, sat down and played something rather complicated. I said 'Shit, Mickey, I didn't know you could play the piano.' He lifted his shoulders, gave me a Mickey look, and said 'Neither did I.'"

Guy's ex Amy Goodenough and her new husband, Paul Johnson, were frequent visitors to Castle Court and happened to be staying with Guy and Susan when Susan went into labor on December 18, 1966. The Johnsons jumped into their VW Bug and led the Clarks in their old used car, lights flashing, to the hospital. Guy and Susan's son, Travis Carroll Clark, was born that morning.

Guy and Susan's landlord, Paul Montague, worked as the art director for the Houston Chronicle's KTRK-TV, Channel 13. After Travis was born, Montague hired Guy in the art department. Guy quit his drafting job and moved over to Channel 13's headquarters at the Herman Lloyd Design Dome on Bissonette Street. Guy put his graphic design skills to work on advertisements and logos and was part of the team responsible for creating the look and feel of the on-air graphics. He had access to a darkroom and blossomed as a photographer.

Guy Clark with his first wife, Susan Spaw, and their son, Travis Carroll Clark, circa 1967. Courtesy Clark family archives

Guy put his artistic sensibility and creativity to work at home, too. Suzy Mitchell borrowed screen-printing equipment from the high school where she taught art and set it up on the Clark's dining-room table, and Guy designed his first concert poster while Susan held the baby and watched. He repaired earrings he had bought for Susan on their honeymoon by cutting two tiny mother-of-pearl discs, inlaying them in the silver settings, and soldering them. When Guy needed new pants for work, he used Susan's treadle machine to sew a pair of slacks using bright navy corduroy with green thread. After Travis climbed over the rail of his crib one morning and fell, Guy removed the crib, set up a double box spring and mattress in the corner, cut a playpen to fit around it, attached it to the woodwork, and built a gate.

. . . . . .

Guy settled into the routine of marriage, fatherhood, and a full-time job in Houston. Meanwhile, more than 400 miles north in Oklahoma City,

Susanna Talley Wallis left her husband. Susanna, known as Susie to her family and friends, was a debutante and an extended member of the Kirkpatrick oil dynasty family. Susanna's mother, Virginia, was a first cousin to family matriarch Eleanor Kirkpatrick.

"Cousin Eleanor was the official international greeter of Oklahoma City," Susanna told Louise O'Connor in 1991. "When I was in my teens I had to have dates with short guys from India. I had to go over and pour punch for German choirs. I had to escort visitors from Africa, always with a smile on my face. I had to wear white gloves when all I really wanted to do was run in a hayfield somewhere."

Susanna was born in the East Texas town of Atlanta on March 11, 1939, the sixth of nine children born to John and Virginia Talley. "My mother was really beautiful," Susanna said. "My dad saw her walking down the street and said to his friend, 'Leroy, see that girl? I'm gonna marry her.'"

John Talley was an entrepreneur who worked as a mover and owned a trucking company. At one point he worked as a salesman for the wholesale

Guy's sisters became mothers right about the time he became a father. *Left to right*: Caroline Clark holding her son Jonathan, Susan Clark holding Travis, Jan Clark holding her son Ben, Rockport, Texas 1967. Courtesy Clark family archives

John and Virginia Talley and their nine children. *Left to right*: John Talley holding Dee,
Sally, Billie (*in the corner*), Joan, Bunny, Dan, Susanna (*looking over Dan's shoulder*), Jack
(*standing in back*) and Jim sitting in mother Virginia's lap. Circa 1948. Courtesy Sherri
Talley

grocery company Collins Dietz Morris. The Talleys were a close-knit family.
"I was loved, in my younger years, very well by my mother and especially my
father," Susanna wrote in a diary entry dated March 31, 1997. "We all called
our father John," Susanna recalled later. "We never called him Daddy. People would ask him why he let his children call him John and he said 'That's
my name.'"

Susanna's mother had been an edgy young flapper in the 1920s, complete
with rouged knees and long plaid socks. By the time she married John Talley and had children, though, Virginia had found religious salvation. "Every
time we got in a scrape she quoted the Bible to us," Susanna said. Virginia's doctrine allowed no compromise or negotiation: for her, the Bible was
the inspired and infallible word of God. She believed in the scriptures and
in eternal hell for sinners who did not repent.

While a student at Oklahoma State in 1958, Susanna landed a part-time
job at the Oklahoma division of the Federal Bureau of Investigation. Susanna

quit school, transferred to Washington, DC, and worked in the FBI department that held files on Lucille Ball and Ray Bradbury. Delusional demagogue
Joseph McCarthy had been dead for a year, yet the FBI still kept files on Americans deemed communists by McCarthy's investigations. After a few months,
Susanna was homesick for her family and returned to Oklahoma City.

With their encouragement, Susanna married John Wallis in 1961. She
was twenty-two. It may have been the high society wedding of the year in
Oklahoma City. Susanna Talley's elite social stature required her to marry
an equally privileged husband.

"I married the right person," Susanna told Louise O'Connor in 1990. "I
married a person who wore a suit and tie. He was the one my parents would
want me to marry. He wanted a lovely wife to be hostess for all the right parties for the right things. He didn't want me to paint. I had a lot of painter
friends, and he called us the 'Sambo Set.' He couldn't stand it, wanted me to
stay home, be a hostess, cook meals. We had lots of money and I didn't need
to work. John was a wonderful person and we remained good friends, but
we both realized I was hell-bent on heading in one direction, and I couldn't
be for him what he needed."

Susanna explored her feelings with a leading therapist who practiced
the new existential-humanistic psychotherapy. "I was on the couch three
times a week for three years," Susanna told O'Connor. "This guy knew how
to reach the child in me. I was down to raw meat, to new skin, ready to start
anew, and then my therapist died and I didn't know what to do."

Susanna's mother-in-law, Jewel Wallis, wrote to Susanna as the marriage
was breaking up:

Dear Susie,
We returned from Casper this past Wednesday evening and I have been
very busy getting the laundry done and all chores attended to, or I would
have written to you sooner. Johnny wrote to us saying that you and
Johnny had decided to separate. I haven't heard otherwise so presume
that you two are still apart.

I am very sorry that this happened, but if you are not happy living together I think it is best that you live apart and make a new life. I am glad
that there isn't a child involved, which would cause more heartache than

there is. I will say that I'm not surprised because we have felt it coming this past year. You have said things that let me know that you weren't really satisfied with your marriage. Clelland and I have discussed this and we are not going to take anyone's side. This trouble is between you and Johnny and you will have to make your own decisions.

We love you like a daughter and enjoyed having you in the family and we hoped that you love us. We hope that we have not caused any unhappiness between the two of you—if we did it was not intended. We want to thank you for writing to us and letting us know what you are doing. We really enjoyed and appreciated your letters.

Our main concern is happiness for both of you whether you live together or apart. If this separation continues and you would like to write to us we would love to hear from you. We are not mad at you and would still like to be friends. Love, Jewel

After Susanna moved out of the posh apartment she shared with John at 6001 North Brookline, Eleanor Kirkpatrick gave Susanna a job teaching oil painting at the family-founded Oklahoma Science and Arts Center. Susanna's sister Johna Talley, known as Bunny, was hired as the museum's publicist shortly after earning her journalism degree from the University of Oklahoma. The Talley sisters rented an apartment together in number 162 at Casa Cortez Apartments, 1602 NW 31st Street, in Oklahoma City.

Through the arts center, Susanna met landscape painter Jack Vallee. A protégé of Andrew Wyeth, Vallee lived on a goat farm outside the city and had a studio in his barn. He asked Susanna to sit for a portrait, and she agreed to be his model in exchange for painting lessons. Susanna paid seven dollars a month for a small studio near Jack, in a space formerly used to sell goat's milk ice cream. She spent a year there while Jack painted her portrait and she learned techniques from him. At the end of the year, Susanna's paintings were selected for a seven-state art show, and the recognition gave her the validation she needed. Susanna was an artist.

· · · · · ·

In August and September 1967, the 13th Floor Elevators recorded an album at Andrus Studios in Houston. *Easter Everywhere* was engineered by Frank Davis

Susanna Talley, an Oklahoma City debutante, circa 1957. Courtesy Guy Clark

and released by the International Artists label in November. Guy Clark took
photos for the packaging. "Roky and Townes would come over, and we'd
hang out and sit around and get stoned on LSD and play music," Guy says.
International Artists also hired Guy to design the cover art for the forthcoming Lightnin' Hopkins record *Free Form Patterns*. "Lightnin' wanted the
cover to be psychedelic because that was the thing," Guy says. "That cover
is just horrible. Not my proudest work."

Guy still worked as an assistant in the art department at Channel 13, and Guy and Susan continued to perform at the Jester and Sand Mountain and at Houston Folklore Society events. Guy taught Susan his arrangement of Dylan's "One Too Many Mornings." At their Castle Court home, Guy wrote his first song, "Step Inside My House":

> That picture hangin' on the wall / Was painted by a friend
> He gave it to me all down and out / When he owed me ten
> It doesn't look like much, I guess / But it's all that's left of him
> It sure is nice from right over here / When the light's a little dim
> Step inside my house, girl / I'll sing for you a song
> I'll tell you 'bout just where I've been / It shouldn't take too long.

The song goes on, with many more verses that describe items from Guy's house: a book of poetry, a prism, a guitar, a pair of boots and yellow vest, a leather jacket and bag, a hat. "Step Inside My House" is the first song Guy put on paper, and it is an artful peek into his identity and personality. The composition is reminiscent of Don Blanding's 1923 poem "Vagabond's House," a favorite around the Clark family table back in Rockport.

"Believe me, they did step inside my house," Susan says. "It got really crowded in there sometimes. We were rarely alone."

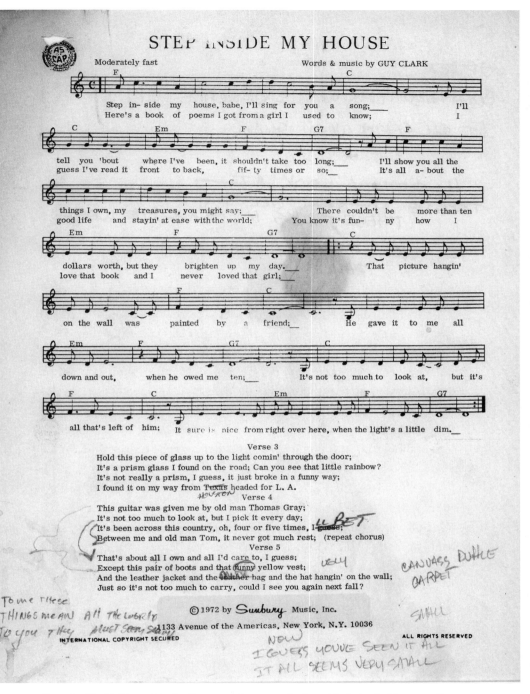

# STEP INSIDE MY HOUSE

Moderately fast

Words & music by GUY CLARK

Step in- side my house, babe, I'll sing for you a song;___ I'll
Here's a book of poems I got from a girl I used to know;___ I

tell you 'bout where I've been, it shouldn't take too long;___ I'll show you all the
guess I've read it front to back, fif- ty times or so;___ It's all a- bout the

things I own, my treasures, you might say;___ There couldn't be more than ten
good life and stayin' at ease with the world; You know it's fun- ny how I

dollars worth, but they brighten up my day.___ That picture hangin'
love that book and I never loved that girl;

on the wall was painted by a friend;___ He gave it to me all

down and out, when he owed me ten;___ It's not too much to look at, but it's

all that's left of him; It sure is nice from right over here, when the light's a little dim.___

Verse 3
Hold this piece of glass up to the light comin' through the door;
It's a prism glass I found on the road; Can you see that little rainbow?
It's not really a prism, I guess, it just broke in a funny way;
I found it on my way from ~~Texas~~ headed for L. A.
*HOUSTON*

Verse 4
This guitar was given me by old man Thomas Gray;
It's not too much to look at, but I pick it every day;
It's been across this country, oh, four or five times, ~~I guess~~; *I BET*
Between me and old man Tom, it never got much rest; (repeat chorus)

Verse 5
That's about all I own and all I'd care to, I guess;
Except this pair of boots and that ~~funny~~ yellow vest; *UGLY*
And the leather jacket and the ~~leather~~ bag and the hat hangin' on the wall;
Just so it's not too much to carry, could I see you again next fall?

*CANVASS DUFFLE CARPET*

*SMALL*

*To me these THINGS meAN All The world*
*To you They Must Seem SmAll*

*NOW*
*I GUESS YOUVE SEEN IT ALL*
*IT ALL SEEMS VERY SMALL*

"Step Inside My House" is the first song Guy wrote in the mid-sixties in Houston. He never recorded it, but Lyle Lovett would record it in 1998. Courtesy Guy Clark

## CHAPTER FIVE

# Bunny, Susanna, San Francisco, and Los Angeles

January 1968 never got warmer than zero degrees Fahrenheit in Oklahoma City, its chill an omen of the year to come. Violence monopolized the spring. Small-time criminal and racist James Earl Ray murdered civil rights leader Dr. Martin Luther King Jr. on April 4 at the Lorraine Motel in Memphis, Tennessee. Two months later, Jordanian immigrant Sirhan Sirhan drew a gun in the kitchen of the Ambassador Hotel in Los Angeles and killed presidential candidate Robert F. Kennedy after Kennedy's stirring campaign speech. The war raged on in Vietnam, Laos, and Cambodia as tens of thousands of young American soldiers were returned to the United States in body bags.

Bunny and Susanna Talley donned pencil skirts and flattop straw hats to volunteer for the presidential campaign of Eugene McCarthy, the senator from Minnesota who was running on an antiwar platform. The sisters could not fathom that so many of their contemporaries had been killed in a war few believed in.

In Houston, Guy and Susan Clark broke up. Susan had no appetite, wasn't sleeping, and weighed only eighty pounds. She was miserable in her marriage to Guy, whom she says remained emotionless and aloof no matter how hard she tried to get him to talk to her. Susan took baby Travis and moved to a dingy eight-by-twenty-foot garage apartment owned by Travis's babysitter. "Guy never asked me to stay or to consider the hazards to Travis's well-being by our trying to live on our own," Susan says. She carried on as a

Susanna Talley Wallis (*center*) celebrates with others campaigning for Eugene McCarthy for president in 1968. Courtesy Guy Clark

single parent, taking classes at the University of Houston two days a week, working for an architect three days, and gigging at night to make the rent, forty dollars a month.

Guy struggled between the love and sense of responsibility he felt for Travis and the freedom he needed to pursue his music. It was a crazy world, and Guy could not figure out where he belonged. "All this heavy shit was happening," he says. "It was changing my view of what America was about and how I wanted to live in this world. Music became even more important to me."

Guy inherited his maternal grandmother Hazel's 1957 red Chevy sedan and gave it to Susan. He brought antibiotics from an all-night drug store when Travis had croup. He still turned up to fix things at Susan's apartment. He didn't say much but appeared when Susan needed something.

Guy quit his job at Channel 13, and he and Townes roamed around Texas and the South playing folk joints together. Guy wrote songs, practiced guitar, drank, smoked, and slept with women. Many weekends, Guy and Townes played the Sword and the Stone Coffee House at Seventh and North Hudson Avenue in Oklahoma City.

Bunny Talley had moved up from publicist to executive director of the Oklahoma Science and Arts Center and was making herself known in artistic circles around Oklahoma City. She first met Guy and Townes at the Sword and the Stone. A cute, petite brunette, she resembled Guy's wife Susan in build and coloring. It's no wonder Guy fell for her. Bunny and Guy started seeing each other on the weekends when Guy and Townes came up to play the coffeehouse. She dragged the guys to parties and introduced them to the art crowd.

One day Bunny brought Guy and Townes back to her apartment. Bunny's sister Susanna walked in and found two long-haired, disheveled folksingers slouched on her sofa. Guy and Townes looked so unhealthy that Susanna offered them vitamins. The two men said little as they waited for Bunny, who was in her bedroom changing clothes. Susanna walked over to the painting she had set up in the corner and picked up her brush.

"I was painting a prairie," Susanna says. "I [had] read an article about Andrew Wyeth and wanted to use his technique to capture the movement of wheat blowing in a breeze. I got stuck and said half out loud: 'I can't make the foreground come forward in this painting.' Guy got up and walked over to me and said, 'You know what to do. You can do this and that and you can mix this color with that.' And I thought, *Geez, I like him. First of all, he's interested in painting. Second of all, he called me on my bullshit.* I hadn't run across a male who cared about the fact that I painted, much less knew something about it, much less called any bluff I was throwing out there. I liked him."

So did Bunny. She and Guy carried on a long-distance relationship as events in Guy's orbit continued to shift. Townes and Fran reunited after a long separation and were expecting a child. Jerry Jeff Walker and Gary White stayed in New York with Circus Maximus. Minor and Mary Ann Wilson had followed their friend Janis Joplin to San Francisco a few years earlier, and some of the other Jester folks had also moved west to California.

By 1969, Guy had enough of Houston. Minor and Mary Ann Wilson broke up, and Guy took off for San Francisco to hang out with his old friend Minor. The summer of love was over, and Haight-Asbury rose from the ashes as citizens banded together to rehabilitate the neighborhood. The music scene thrived at the Avalon Ballroom, Bill Graham's Fillmore, free concerts in Golden Gate Park, and the coffeehouse circuit. *Rolling Stone* magazine had

Susanna Talley with an early painting. Courtesy Guy Clark

been born in San Francisco two years prior, and the Grateful Dead, Jefferson Airplane, and Big Brother and the Holding Company personified the new San Francisco sound. Crosby, Stills, Nash, and Young recorded their first album together, *Déjà Vu*, at Wally Heider's San Francisco studio. Graham Nash renovated a house in Buena Vista Park West, near the Haight. David Crosby crashed in a hippie house in Novato in Marin County, and Neil Young owned a ranch in Woodside. Janis Joplin, Santana, Boz Skaggs, and Steve Miller all lived in the area.

Guy moved into Minor Wilson's loft at 8 Brady Street, just a few blocks down the road from the Fillmore West nightclub on Market Street and Van Ness Avenue. The two friends picked up where they left off in their guitar repair business, working on two workbenches in the storefront side of the loft and sleeping in the back.

Guy helped Wilson build an electric mandolin for their old Houston pal, blues guitarist Johnny Winter. "We got a fretboard for a mandola, a little bit longer action than a mandolin, and made a copy of a Gibson F-Hole classic mandolin, the best mandolin in the world," Wilson says. "We used two

Susanna's self-portrait, circa 1959. Courtesy Guy Clark

Fender jazz bass pickups, which have four holes on each of them, perfect for going under eight double strings, four courses, and it worked perfect. We copied that curlicue cutaway style and scaled it up and made a curved, arch-top, solid-body mandolin. We made it in black lacquer with white binding. Johnny took it in the studio and on this blistering-fast electric guitar solo goes right up to the end of the range of electric guitar, stops recording, picks up the electric mandolin, and starts on that note in a range that's likes three times as high as a guitar will go. Blew everyone's mind."

Bobby Weir from the Grateful Dead ordered a single-cutaway, hollow-body, classic, arch-top, F-hole guitar that Guy built to Weir's specifications using Gibson pickups and the best tuners available. Minor and Guy worked on all of the guitars for Big Brother and the Holding Company, and they repaired guitars for a bluegrass band. Their cover of Willie Nelson's "One Day at a Time" was Guy's first introduction to his fellow Texan. "That song really jumped out at me. It's such a great song," Guys says. "Now I know about this guy named Willie Nelson. Man, he's really far-out."

A printing operation, Rip Off Press, occupied the loft next to Guy and Minor's. Founded by fellow Texans Fred Todd and Dave Moriarty, with cartoonists Gilbert Shelton and Jack Johnson, the press printed posters and tickets for rock bands as well as underground comic books, known as comix. Rip Off printed tickets for the Fillmore and were generous with free passes for Guy and Minor. Since the Fillmore was an easy stumble down the block, the guys also went there often for a Tuesday night series featuring local bands, which Graham had dubbed Audition Night. In the summer of '69, Guy caught live shows by Johnny Winter, Lonnie Mack, Chuck Berry, Santana, Creedence Clearwater Revival, the Dead, Jefferson Airplane, Janis Joplin, and the Everly Brothers.

"The Everly Brothers played with just two acoustic guitars, a drummer, and a bass player," Guy says. "It was fuckin' amazing, their harmonies, and working just one microphone. It was just, wow. Lonnie Mack would just walk up there with a Telecaster and a little bitty amplifier on a folding chair and just blow me away. It was really good."

Although Guy frequented many shows at the Fillmore, it wasn't a venue he played. For his folk music fix, he hung out at the beatnik folk club Coffee and Confusion at 1339 Grant Avenue in North Beach, not far from Ferlinghetti's City Lights bookstore. There he played traditional folk songs along with some of the tunes he was writing.

"He was building his foundation to become what he is today," Wilson says. "Guy was writing simple songs, simple melodies, but even in the time we were together in San Francisco I could see his songs getting more and more sophisticated. He was breaking away from covering other people's stuff. He'd play them for me, and it was easy to see that he was going to be a great songwriter."

The Johnny Cash Show debuted on ABC on June 7, 1969. Cash's first guests included singer songwriters Bob Dylan and Joni Mitchell. Gordon Lightfoot appeared the following week. Guy missed seeing Linda Ronstadt on the June 21 episode of Cash's show. That day he dropped acid and went to the Old Time Fiddler's Convention in Provo Park in Berkeley. The park was just blocks away from the Freight and Salvage Coffeehouse, a new joint opened by Nancy Owens. Owens kept the name of its former occupant, a used furniture store at 1827 San Pablo Avenue. She kept the sign and telephone number and converted the room into a folk club. In later years, the Freight and

Salvage would be a regular stop on Guy's tours, but in 1969, Guy was high in Provo Park and grooving to a pretty fiddle player named Dawn.

Before long Wilson heard Guy sing "A Nickel for the Fiddler," inspired by the afternoon in Provo Park. "I was stoned on acid and just music wafting through San Francisco in the sixties," Guys says. "It just captured my imagination."

> Well, it's a nickel for the fiddler, it's a nickel for his tune
> It's a nickel for the tambourine and kind of afternoon
> And it's a high holiday on the twenty-first of June
> And it's country music in the park and everybody's ruined.

The summer of 1969 was momentous and tumultuous. On July 20, Apollo 11 landed the first humans, Americans Neil Armstrong and Buzz Aldrin, on the moon. In August the Woodstock Music & Art Fair, a three-day festival of "peace and music" showcased thirty-two artists in front of several hundred thousand people in upstate New York. *Rolling Stone* listed the festival as one of the "50 Moments That Changed the History of Rock and Roll." San Francisco–based artists Johnny Winter; the Grateful Dead; Jefferson Airplane; Santana; Crosby, Stills, Nash and Young; and Janis Joplin and the Kozmic Blues Band all played Woodstock.

As the summer of 1969 heated up, it was clear that Guy's days in San Francisco were numbered. Although he loved working on guitars during the day and hearing and playing music all night, he had responsibilities back in Houston and missed his son.

In Guy's song lyric notebook from the time this line appears: "The pain of you is so bad I don't even want my grilled cheese sandwich, but I eat it anyway."

"I was missing Travis and home," Guy says. "And that's just a really bad line that came out as I was writing."

Guy wrote song lyrics about Travis:

> Hey little boy child, I ain't seen you in a while
> Ain't heard you laugh, ain't seen you smile
> I bet you've grown a foot or more

*Only seems like yesterday*
*You were crawlin' on the floor.*

*Hey little boy child, I won't be long*
*I'm on my way back down the road to you with this song*
*I'll tell you about the things I've seen*
*You can slip back down the road with me on make-believe dreams.*

*Hey little boy child, sometimes I've cried*
*Sometimes I've felt like layin' down to die*
*Hey little boy child, son of mine*
*I ain't seen you in a long lonesome time*

*Hey little boy child, will you understand*
*When you see me coming that it's your old man*
*Will you hold me hard, look me in the eye*
*I love you and I ain't ashamed for you to see your daddy cry.*

It sealed the deal when Susan called Guy to ask him to come back. "I had gotten a hernia waiting tables and lifting Travis and everything," Susan says. "I called Guy to tell him I needed an operation to fix this hernia. I asked him to please come back and get a job and get some insurance."

Still, Guy had taken to heart the counterculture ethos of free love, and Guy and Minor Wilson shared many women while living together at the loft. Bunny Talley had also visited Guy in San Francisco a few times, and they still cared about each other. Guy wrote to her regularly and sent her small gifts. "He'd put the most beautiful notes in the boxes," Susanna says. "I thought: *This guy is a poet.*"

"I think Bunny was head over heels in love with Guy, but I mean, there were a lot of relationships at that time," Wilson says. "I had a lot of girl-friends, and we weren't possessive of each other. I was already established in San Francisco, and when Guy got there he would sleep with a lot of my girlfriends that came over. It was like 'I'm going out, you guys have fun!' We were exploring jealousy-free relationships."

In August, 1969, Guy bought Bunny a plane ticket to fly west and join

LEAVING HOUSTON FOR CALIF.

So now the time has come to leave
I dry my eyes upon my sleave
& turn upon my heel & walk away
& you revel in the sadness & think
it's so romantic, the stayin behind
you say someday we'll meet again
& maybe be more than friends
you love storybook reality
the kind with no finality

APRIL 12 - SAN FRANCISCO

The pain of you is so bad
The pain of you is so bad
The pain of you is so bad
I don't even want my grilled cheese sandwich
but I'll eat it anyway

I love you Travis my son I love you

Please somebody take away the pain
goddamn it!

                         MAN
for this boy-child son of mine
whose first breath I will always share

This small boy - wonderer
This small boy - wonderer
with a eye full of wonder why
with a handful of touch it now
with heart full of love · me · back

Guy's journal note about missing his son, Travis, San Francisco, 1969. Courtesy
Guy Clark

him for his long drive back to Texas. They rented a car to take them from San Francisco to the Greyhound bus station in Amarillo, and the road trip was sometimes tense. Bunny wanted to talk about the relationship, and Guy wanted to focus on driving and save the heavy stuff for later. "Bunny bitched the whole time because I wouldn't get into a deep conversation with her while I was driving," Guy says. "It was a typical young female and male thing: 'You won't talk to me.' 'Well, goddamn it, I'm driving.' I've always been like that, I can't carry on a conversation when I'm driving."

There were lighter moments when the couple stopped to do some sightseeing along the way. In Arizona, they went into a souvenir shop that sold turquoise jewelry. Guy spotted a ring he wanted. "Jack Prigg always wore a ring, and I always wanted my own ring like Jack's," Guy says. "This one just struck me. It was twelve dollars, which was a lot of fucking money to me at that time, but I had to have the ring." Bunny and Guy bought the ring together. Guy put it on his right ring finger, where it remains to this day.

Guy and Bunny kissed goodbye at the Greyhound station in Amarillo. Then Bunny boarded a bus to Oklahoma City and Guy hopped a bus to Houston. During the trip, Guy wrote in his song notebook:

Sometimes you can't see the sky
You get too close, you get too high
Sometimes you can't feel the pain
It hurts so bad you go insane
So stand back Mama, take a good hard look
I'm a brand new cover on the same old book

Somewhere between Flagstaff & the New Mexico border
Alone but up front like a Santa Fe freight cutting through
    the Arizona desert
Bunny & I in a drive away car from S.F. to Amarillo, Tex.
    with Travis on my mind.
Sure can get to feeling greasy driving a car cross country.
Now the west-hand side off Flagstaff
Is outrageously beautiful with Ponderosa Pine
I've just come from Northern California.

Over the next few months, Guy and Bunny kept up a long distance relationship as Bunny remained in her position as executive director of the Oklahoma Arts and Science Foundation. Guy knocked around Houston working freelance jobs to support Travis and playing in local clubs. He headed up to Oklahoma City often to play the Sword and the Stone and spend time with Bunny.

Yet, it was not a monogamous relationship from Guy's side. He was seeing other women and began to spend more and more time with his Houston girlfriend Gretchen Mueller. By January of 1970, Guy and Gretchen were pretty much living together. On January 30, 1970, Guy wrote in his journal:

> This is the weirdest Sunday afternoon, rain inside and out, outside and in. Gretchen and I going through so many changes. Travis running around with Roscoe (dog) yelling and screaming and suddenly Travis gets very quiet and I can't see him so I say Travis come here. No, he says, Daddy come here because I'm busy watching the rain. Sometimes I think I did the best I could. Sometimes I think I didn't try at all.

The following day Guy wrote a song for Bunny in his journal:

> *Oh it's north to Oklahoma*
> *That I'd like to go*
> *Get away from south Texas*
> *And see me some snow*
> *And a woman who's hair*
> *Falls black cross her face*
> *And stands ten time straighter*
> *Than the whole human race*
> *Red clay woman are you calling my name*
> *Bunny, is your face in the window*
> *With your breast against the pane*
> *Livin' and lovin' with others when we had to*
> *Livin' and lovin' together when we could*
> *Will you hold me and love me like a lost lonesome child*

*Will you hold me and love just the best that you can*
*Will you hold me and love me like I was your man*

Late at night on Saturday, May 2, Bunny went home to her old bedroom at her mother and father's house instead of returning to the apartment she shared with Susanna. Bunny was alone in the house. God only knows what she was thinking when she wrote a simple note: "At this point, this is the honorable thing I can do." The beautiful twenty-six-year-old picked up an unregistered .38 caliber revolver and shot herself in the temple.

On Sunday, May 3, 1970, Virginia Talley found her daughter's lifeless body, her hand holding a gun with four live rounds, and two spent casings. Nitrate tests on Bunny's hand proved positive. There was no doubt she had killed herself.

Guy found out about Bunny's suicide when he missed his flight to Oklahoma City that same day. He called Bunny's apartment to tell her that he wasn't going to make it, and Susanna answered the phone. It was left to Susanna to break the news.

"I didn't see it coming," Guy says. "It was just out of the clear blue sky."

"Nobody in the family knew about Bunny's relationship with Guy, but I did," Susanna says. "I asked Guy to come to Oklahoma City for the funeral. Both of us were fucking sick and vulnerable. She was my sister, and I loved Bunny more than anything in the world. She had such conflict. They wanted her to be something she wasn't, working as the director of the science and arts foundation. She really wanted to be a sculptress, but she thought she was stuck in the family business. Unless you're well-rounded, you can't do it, and my sister was not well-rounded. She couldn't take conflict because we're from a gene pool that's sensitive as shit. By the time it gets filtered down to us, we're a quivering mess."

"When Guy was at my apartment after Bunny died, someone called to talk about a casket. I picked up a sculpture and threw it across the room," Susanna says. "I said 'My sister is dead, I don't want to talk about fucking caskets!' I started breaking shit. Guy gathered me up in his arms and said 'I love you, Susanna, I love you.' We were down to love. I didn't know him; he didn't know me. All I knew was that he was my sister's friend. We were just wracked. I was hanging on to something and he was hanging on to something. I was desperately trying to hold on to my sister, and Guy was the closest thing. Both of us were quite devastated. In that torn-down state of sadness that we were both in, we fell in love."

"I remember talk amongst my parents that she was troubled," Bunny and Susanna's niece Sherri Talley says. "From what I understood about Bunny, just from knowing her as a child and from my parents talking, is that she was brilliant and real artistic, straight As, and gorgeous. She had everything in the world going for her. I remember when we got the phone call. I was in grade school. I was standing in the kitchen, and I remember how devastated Dad was, just completely floored."

Guy began writing song lyrics about Susanna immediately.

*My strength is the strength of ten*
*My love for you sees no end*
*Begun before, begin again*

*I'll never be the same again*
*I've seen your face*
*I've touched your skin*
*Walked beside you in the wind*
*Think I might have found a friend*

*I'll never be the same no more*
*Indecision found a door*
*Picked itself up off the floor*
*Tried to make it just one more*

*I'll never be the same somehow*
*Sweet Susie's on the lookout now*
*The emotional snob has made a vow*
*To heal his hurt and you're the how.*

On May 20, two weeks after Bunny's suicide, Jack Prigg died from natural causes in Monahans. Guy had driven to Monahans a few days before to see Jack. The man who had watched over Guy for more than two decades,

1420 ROSELAND
#2

I'VE SUNG A SONG FOR TEXAS & ONE FOR NEW ORLEANS
BUT I'D JUST AS SOON BE SINGIN SONGS FOR ONLY YOU
YOU & OKLAHOMA & YOU
I'VE SUNG FOR CALIFORNIA'S SHORE & THERE'S SURE TO
BE A WHOLE LOT MORE
SOMEDAY I MIGHT EVEN SING for YOU
I JUST FOUND SOME FLOWERS IN A BOTTLE ON THE TABLE
& I DON'T EVEN KNOW WHO LEFT THEM THERE
I ONLY WISH IT COULD HAVE BEEN YOU

SOMEDAYS HAS FOUND ME DOWN & OUT
SOMEDAYS HAS FOUND ME BLUE
SOME DAYS HAS FOUND ME SINGIN SONG FOR YOU

EVERY TIME I SEE YOU I STOP & WONDER WHY
I DON'T QUIT THIS LIFE I LIVE FOR YOU

I KNOW THAT YOU GOT TROUBLES I GOT TROUBLE
OF MY OWN
BUT WE COULD WORK IT OUT JUST ME & YOU

DON'T HAVE MONEY FOR HONKY TONKS
JUST SIT HERE BY MYSELF & GET DRUNK & THINK
ABOUT THE LAST TIME I SAW YOU

43          5
X

BUNNY TALLEY SHOT HERSELF IN THE HEAD
LAST SUNDAY - MAY 3, 1970

Song lyrics for Bunny and Susanna Talley, "You and Oklahoma and You," written about the time of Bunny's suicide in May 1970. Courtesy Guy Clark

taught him to play dominos and pool at the Green Frog Café, gave him the keys to the old Packard when Jack was too drunk to drive, slipped him fivers for the girls, and been like a grandfather to Guy for twenty-eight years was gone. Jack's death sent Guy into a deeper state of despair.

For the next month, Guy and Susanna burned up the phone lines between Oklahoma City and Houston. They talked long into the night, bonded by grief. During one of these calls, Susanna dropped a bombshell and admitted to Guy that Bunny had been pregnant and had an abortion a few months prior. Neither Guy nor Susanna knew if the baby was Guy's, but it didn't matter. Bunny's conscience and Virginia Talley's harping about sin and hell would have been enough to drive Bunny to the brink. In a letter to Susanna, Virginia Talley wrote: "I don't want to go to hell . . . that probably gives you a good laugh, but hell is no joke to me—it's part of the Book."

In Houston, Guy found a job in the art department at Corinthian Broadcasting's CBS affiliated KHOU-TV Channel 11 on Allen Parkway near downtown. He shared the rent for a house on Stratford Avenue with musician Pete Gorisch and his wife, Franci. And he continued to write love songs for Susanna and Bunny in his lyric journals and scrapbooks:

> I've sung a song for Texas and one for New Orleans
> I've sung for California's shore and there's sure to be a
>         whole lot more
> But I'd just as soon be singing a song for you
> But I'd just as soon be singing a song for you
> You & Oklahoma & You
> You & Oklahoma & You.

> Red clay country woman are you callin' my name
> Is your face in the window
> Does your breast feel the pain
> Will you hold me like a lonesome child
> That ain't been home in a long, long while
> Will you hold me just the best you can
> Hold me like I was your man
> Everytime I see you I stop and wonder why
> I don't quit this life I lead for you

You & Oklahoma & You
*Some days have found me down and out*
*Some days have found me blue*
*Some days have found me singing songs for you*
You & Oklahoma & You

By July, Guy had been promoted to art director. Susanna wanted to get out of Oklahoma City and away from all the reminders of Bunny, especially in the apartment they had shared together. On July 4, Guy and Susanna loaded all of Susanna's possessions into Guy's Volkswagen bus and her car and drove from Oklahoma City to Houston. "I did not know this man, and he did not know me," Susanna told Louise O'Connor in 1991. "But I packed up and left. There were too many reminders of my sister in Oklahoma City. I just wanted to start over."

Susanna kept Bunny's final subscription issues of *Vogue* and *Seventeen* magazines, dated June 1970, along with a dry cleaning receipt with Bunny's signature and a poem about Bunny written by their mutual friend Gaylon Stacy.

It took Susanna a while to adjust to her new life. She came from a high society, white bread family. Now she was sharing a house with people she didn't know, including the boyfriend of her dead sister, and spending all her time with hippies, druggies, and musicians.

"Our house was the central gathering place for people to drop in and get high. I was thrown by this," Susanna told O'Connor. "I mean, there were real dopers there, people walking around on Quaaludes. I didn't know one soul. Everybody wondered who in the hell this new girl was, and all his old girlfriends were disappointed because Guy was living with me. They didn't know me, and I pretty much ignored everything. I was painting and Guy was going to work at the TV station every day. It was a terribly lonesome time for me because Guy was the only person I knew, and he is a rather distant person. He was no bosom buddy. But he had been close to Bunny, and that was our bond."

Guy Clark was never one to wear his heart on his sleeve. He was taught from a young age to be stoic; to observe the West Texas credo, "stand up and be a man." He'd learned one should put up a strong façade no matter what he is feeling inside. Instead of talking to Susanna, Guy channeled his grief into his work and music and self-medicated with alcohol, pills, and marijuana. Yet he wrote intimately and honestly in his lyric notebooks:

Susanna's up there sleepin'
With her hair down in her eyes
I sit here playin' songs for her
She can't hear them but that's okay
I like to play them anyway

Susanna's up there layin'
With one arm across her breast
My mind is up there with her
She's sleepin' like a worn out kid
From all the love that we just did

Susanna's up there peaceful
Like I've never seen before
That peace slides down the stairway
Covers the first floor of a house
That never knew peace before.

Guy's best friend Townes Van Zandt had battled his own demons for years and was still grieving the sudden death of his father four years earlier. Townes was more openly sensitive and vulnerable than Guy. When Susanna arrived in Houston, Townes wrapped her in a bear hug and said: "If Guy loves you, so do I." Townes and Susanna spoke a private language from the beginning. They recognized the sadness in each other and it was a strong bond between them. Townes's and Susanna's I.Q. test scores classified them as gifted individuals with superior intelligence. They believed in the afterlife, visits from ghosts, and the supernatural, which Guy thought was nonsense. Townes and Susanna were accomplished artists. In time, both of them turned to pills and the bottle. Many thought they were just plain crazy. Once Townes and Susanna bonded, there was no tearing them apart. "They were best friends and soul mates," Guy says. "They both drove me fucking nuts."

Guy easily slipped back into his Houston lifestyle, playing the folk clubs nights and weekends. He still played the Jester and Sand Mountain along with two new places: George Banks's hippie restaurant the Family Hand and the Old Quarter, opened the previous year by Rex Bell and Dale Soffar. When the Armadillo World Headquarters opened in Austin, Guy drove over to check it out.

Sick of the corporate life, Guy quit his job at Channel 11 although he continued to freelance for the station. While Susanna painted, Guy wrote songs and practiced playing guitar. In early November 1970, Susanna threw a surprise party for Guy's twenty-ninth birthday. Townes showed up early and ruined the surprise, and Susanna hit him with her purse, a story Townes and Susanna would tell for the rest of their lives.

Susanna was in therapy to deal with her grief and to try to figure out what to do with her life. She sat Guy down at the kitchen table one afternoon and asked him what he wanted to do with his. "Guy said 'I want to do music,'" Susanna told Louise O'Connor. "I said, 'Well, by God, no producer is going to come knocking on your door in Houston, Texas. You've got to do something about it.' He couldn't sing at the Old Quarter the rest of his life and bitch about nothing happening. I was sad in Houston. I was in mourning over my sister. I just wanted Guy to be happy, and I wanted to be happy. I believed totally in Guy Clark, and I loved him very much. I knew that he was good. I was his biggest cheerleader."

Susanna's friend Mason Williams from Oklahoma City lived in Los Angeles. Williams had won three Grammys in 1968 for his instrumental hit "Classical Gas." Now he was writing for the Smothers Brothers Comedy Hour. Mason's success was a beacon to Susanna, a promise of what could be. Susanna sold her car and a painting to make money for the trip. Guy packed up his Volkswagen bus with everything they owned. The couple made a brief stop in Rockport to say goodbye to Guy's family, then headed west for California.

At the time, Bob Dylan, Simon & Garfunkel, James Taylor, and Carole King kept folk music afloat in the mainstream, although British rock bands Led Zeppelin, the Kinks, the Who, Jethro Tull, Black Sabbath, Deep Purple, Traffic, and Eric Clapton were on fire with top-selling albums and adventurous tours. David Geffen established Asylum Records in Los Angeles and signed Jackson Browne as his first artist.

On October 4, shortly before Guy and Susanna arrived in California, Janis Joplin was found dead of a heroin overdose at LA's Landmark Motor Hotel.

Guy and Susanna found a place to crash at the home of Susanna's friend, Japanese artist Masami Teraoka. They stayed in a spare room and slept in sleeping bags on the floor.

"I could have gotten a job in LA, but I wanted to paint and Guy wanted me to paint. He could have made a respectable living some other way, but he wanted to sing and I wanted him to sing," Susanna told O'Connor. "We lived for the sake of the art. We lost weight because we didn't have enough to eat, but it didn't bother us because we saw no other alternatives. It never even dawned on us that we could do something other than art."

However, they did want some privacy and a place of their own. Guy took his art portfolio and went out to find work. He met John Dopyera at his guitar shop in Escondido. Dopyera didn't have work for Guy but suggested Guy call his brother Ed at the Dobro factory in Long Beach. John, Ed, and Rudy Dopyera had founded the Dobro Guitar Company in 1929. The name Dobro was taken from the name Dopyera Brothers. "Dobré" also meant "good" in Czechoslovakian and sounded enough like Dopyera to make it cool. They moved their factory from Chicago to Los Angeles in 1937, but a metal shortage stopped all production in 1939 and they didn't begin manufacturing Dobros again until 1961.

"Rudy Dopyera was the crazy-wizard-looking guy [who] spent the day in his private loft pounding out brass bell mandolins and handmade stuff," Guy says. "There was one guy who worked there who had escaped from Cuba on a boat. He didn't speak any English. There was another guy who was a weird religious fanatic who fretted all the banjos, some field hippie smokin' dope, and me. It was a far-out experience. One guy would build necks, and one guy would fret the instruments, and they would bring all the parts to me. I spent all day assembling Dobros or National steel guitar bodies. I could make six in a day and made about five hundred when I was there."

Guy and Susanna found a small guesthouse for rent at 2244 Daisy in Long Beach, the property shaded by a majestic grapefruit tree. Susanna set her easel up in a corner and painted a picture of Guy's old blue shirt and a haunting portrait of Bunny.

The Dopyeras allowed Guy time off to meet with publishers and record labels. He would drive to Los Angeles with his guitar and play songs for any music executive willing to listen. On nights and weekends, Guy played writers' nights at the folkie joints up and down the coast from Long Beach. He met an upright bass player named Skinny Dennis Sanchez, and they formed a string band with a fiddle player. One night the band played the Hermitage Coffeehouse in Mission Beach. It was more than an hour back to Long Beach on Interstate 5. Guy slept in the backseat while Susanna drove. At one point he woke up, around 3:00 a.m., and said, "If I could just get off of this LA freeway without getting killed or caught." The line struck him and he grabbed Susanna's eyebrow pencil and wrote it on a crushed burger sack.

In the summer of 1971, Townes came to Los Angeles to record his fifth album, *High, Low and In Between*. Being with Townes again made Susanna happy. While Guy was at work and Townes had breaks from the studio, he'd take Susanna to the beach, where they discussed the meaning of life. Susanna confided in Townes that she had otherworldly visits from Bunny, and Townes believed her.

While Townes was in town, Susanna and Guy cowrote their first song together. Susanna says she was writing "Black Haired Boy" about Guy, but Guy thought they were writing the song about Townes:

> He's a black haired boy of some confusion
> He makes no excuse for the things that he's usin'
> And he's gentle and wild, a child of the mountain
> His words are for singing and his days are for countin'
> He's looking for a home, he's scared to find
> Some lady beside him and he's drunk on white wine.

"Susanna asked me for help with that song, and I was sure it was about Townes," Guy says. "We finished the song, and she told me it was about me. I still think it's about Townes." Perhaps the song is fitting because it describes both of Susanna's black-haired boys.

Before he came to Los Angeles to record, Townes had met a girl named Leslie Jo Richards at the Old Quarter in Houston, and now he invited Leslie Jo to come out to California. She hitchhiked from Houston and stayed with

Townes in the condo his manager, Kevin Eggers, had rented. She spent her days in the studio with Townes. Many evenings, they'd get together with Guy and Susanna. One afternoon, Townes needed something from the condo, and Leslie Jo offered to go back to get it. She stuck out her thumb for a ride. A psychotic drifter picked her up, brutally stabbed her, and dropped her body in a ditch, leaving her for dead. Leslie Jo managed to crawl to a house for help but died on the suburban front lawn before the ambulance arrived.

The murder devastated Townes. He called Guy and Susanna, and they drove up to Los Angeles. Townes and Susanna stayed up all night holding each other and weeping. Guy returned to Long Beach the next day for work while Susanna stayed with Townes. It had been a little more than a year since Bunny's suicide. Leslie Jo's death vanquished any peace Susanna may have found since leaving Houston.

In the fall of 1971, Guy landed a meeting with Gerry Teifer, the head of Sunbury Dunbar, the publishing division of RCA Records. Guy played four songs for Teifer. At the end of the audition, Teifer offered Guy a publishing contract with a $500 advance and asked him if he wanted to stay in Los Angeles or move to New York or Nashville. Guy hated LA and didn't figure he'd like New York much better. His Houston friend Mickey Newbury was enjoying success in Nashville, and there was this new guy Kris Kristofferson whom Guy admired as a songwriter.

As Guy and Susanna packed up for a road trip to Nashville, they got a call from Guy's old roommate Gary White. Gary and his wife Annie had moved to Los Angeles a month earlier after Linda Ronstadt recorded Gary's song "Long, Long Time" on her Silk Purse album. The song was a hit and about to be nominated for a Grammy. The Whites drove down to Long Beach to spend one last night with Guy and Susanna before they moved to Nashville. "They had already packed everything up, and we sat around on crates reliving the past and catching up," White says.

Gary White was the latest in a string of Guy's friends enjoying success in the music business. Now Guy and Susanna were heading for Nashville, where Guy had a paying gig as a songwriter. Maybe it would finally be his turn to make it.

# PART TWO

## Nashville, 1972–1997

## CHAPTER SIX

# Outlaws and Poets

Only a few blocks separated Sunbury Dunbar's Music Row offices from the storied Columbia Studios down the street, where Bob Dylan had recorded his *Blonde on Blonde* and *Nashville Skyline* albums. Now Guy Clark was here, working as a professional songwriter at 1204 Sixteenth Avenue South. He was paid an advance of $75 a week to write songs that Sunbury Dunbar would pitch to singers to record. It was not much of a living, but it was a start.

The counterculture generation continued to change popular culture, and country and folk music were no exception. The Nitty Gritty Dirt Band, who'd had a huge hit with Jerry Jeff Walker's "Mr. Bojangles," bridged the generation gap with *Will the Circle Be Unbroken*, a lively three-disc album recorded with several paragons of country music. The Byrds' celebrated *Sweetheart of the Rodeo* album showcased an expressive blend of folk and country. Gram Parsons joined the Flying Burrito Brothers for two cosmic folk records before stepping out solo. Carole King and James Taylor each rolled out luscious folk-pop albums, *Tapestry* and *Sweet Baby James*. Townes Van Zandt had released four albums of his own exotic compositions written since he and Guy had met in Houston. Although a name for the genre didn't exist yet, what would come to be known as Americana music simmered on the back burner, waiting for the countrypolitan sounds of Tammy Wynette, Ray Price, Charley Pride, and Lynn Anderson to fizzle out.

Van Zandt blew into Nashville the second week of January in 1972. He had been in New York until Guy called to announce that he and Susanna were tying the knot and wanted Townes to be the best man. On January 14, thirty-year-old Guy Clark and thirty-three-year-old Susanna Talley Wallis returned to Mickey Newbury's houseboat with Townes in tow. Susan Newbury baked a cake, Guy carried the weed, Townes brought vodka. Mickey piloted the boat out of Old Hickory Lake eastward up the Cumberland River to Sumner County. The five friends left the boat and caught a taxi to the county courthouse, where Judge J. C. McMahan married Guy and Susanna.

When the short ceremony ended, they backtracked down the river. "Townes and I drank a bottle of vodka and got as shitfaced as we could until we got back to the dock," Guy says.

After the party, Guy, Susanna, and Townes retreated to the cheap little rental house at 1307 Chapel Avenue in East Nashville. Together they had found an old mattress dumped behind a nearby grocery store and dragged it home. Townes tossed his sleeping bag on top of the mattress next to Susanna's easel in the second bedroom. An omen of what was to come, the trio spent the wedding night together, and Townes lived with Guy and Susanna for eight months. If Susanna had misgivings about Townes's intrusion on the honeymoon, she kept it to herself.

It didn't take long for the threesome to feel like family—perhaps a non-traditional family, but kindred spirits in every way that mattered to them. Guy, Susanna, and Townes leaned on each other and believed in each other. Guy wrote songs. Townes wrote songs. Susanna painted and composed poetry. Guy painted. Townes played a sloppy fiddle. Guy whittled on guitars. Townes brought women home from bars. It took some of the pressure off Guy to have Townes around. Now Guy didn't have to be the charming new husband all the time; Townes took up some of the slack.

"Townes was very bright, the highest-IQ person I've been around, except for maybe Susanna. That's one of the reasons they were so close, just off-the-chart-IQs," Guy says. "Susanna was closer to Townes than anybody. Townes and I were close, and he had a side he showed me, but he and Susanna would dish the dirt and talk about poetry or philosophy. My conversations with Townes were more like 'Yup. Yup. Okay, man. Yup. Okay. Don't call me drunk again. Okay.'"

The trio shared what little money they scraped together. Many nights Susanna fixed "bean surprise" for dinner, the surprise being whether there were onions or hot dogs in the beans. They showed up at music business parties, ate and drank as much as they could, filled their pockets with appetizers, and swiped bottles of booze for later. The executives at Sunbury Dunbar contributed canned goods and frozen pizzas to the household. When the good stash ran low, friends chipped in marijuana, vodka, and whiskey. Each morning they sat companionably at the kitchen table and drank coffee and smoked Guy's hand-rolled cigarettes while Townes's parakeets Loop and Lil swooped up and down. Townes woke up one morning, picked up a guitar, and played a new song called "If I Needed You." He swore to Guy and Susanna that he had dreamed the entire song.

When Townes and Guy caught the flu, Susanna looked after them. She made chicken soup and doled out cough syrup. While they slept, she conceived a new painting called The Bouncing Apple, a statement of her happiness at having a little time and space for herself.

Halfway through her work on The Bouncing Apple, Susanna ran out of white paint. No extra money existed for such luxuries, and the painting sat unfinished until one day when the threesome was flipping their last quarter to decide whether to spend it on a Coke or a Popsicle. Mickey Newbury called to tell Townes that Buffy Sainte-Marie had cut one of their songs and that a $500 check awaited him at the publisher.

"Jesus Christ! Five hundred dollars!" Susanna says. "We were so broke we were down to drinking apple Malt Duck or grape Malt Duck. Every time we got a little money Townes would give it to a veteran on the street corner."

After they picked up the check, Guy, Susanna and Townes climbed back in Guy's new Volkswagen double-cab truck to go to the liquor store. Townes insisted they stop at the art store first to buy Susanna white paint.

"Townes said: 'The first thing we are going to do with this $500 is get a tube of white paint for Susanna.' I couldn't believe it," Susanna says. "We went up there and slapped that money down. 'We want a tube of white paint.' And by god we got it. It was the most important I've ever felt in my life. That's what the household needed, was me getting some white paint."

At the liquor store, they bought good vodka, and Townes looked around for a pretty girl to pick up. There was no one. They went home without a girl for Townes, so he called the Old Quarter in Houston.

"A girl came to the phone, and Townes said, 'Do you want to come on up

to Nashville? A plane ticket is waiting for you,'" Susanna says. "He blew the rest of the $500 on a plane ticket. Mickey Newbury was just horrified when he found out what Townes had done with the money. Mickey thought he was going to save all of us, that we'd buy chicken and rice and make it last for a long time."

Living together in close quarters wasn't always a party. One night Townes threatened to kill himself. He took an X-Acto knife and cut a sideways slice through his chest.

"I yelled 'Townes!' and I jumped over the table," Susanna says. "I wrestled with him with all the strength I had, and I was sitting on him in the kitchen. I had his hand and was pounding it on the garbage can to make him let go of the X-Acto knife because I knew he wanted to do more with it. I kept saying 'Let go of it, let go of it.' He finally relaxed and said, 'Susanna, why would I do that?' I said 'Drop the knife.' Townes said later: 'I just want you to pay attention to me.' The next day or so, Townes wouldn't take care of this thing. I went out and bought all this ointment and pads and stuff. I

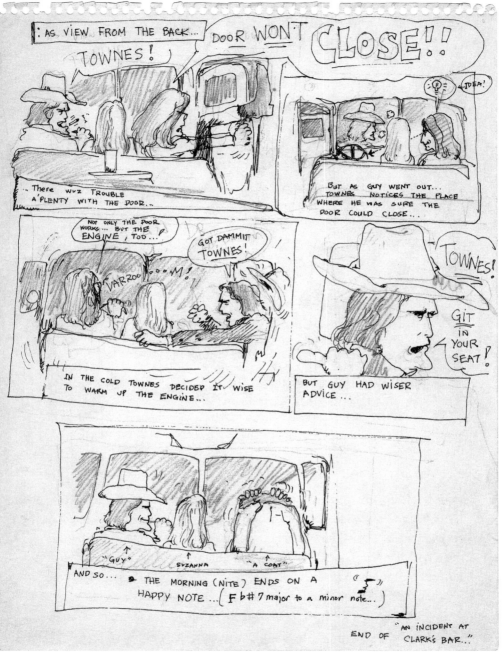

Artist Mel Chin captures the craziness of a night with Guy, Townes, and Susanna.
Courtesy Guy Clark collection

Susanna Clark and Townes Van Zandt, Susanna always Lefty to Townes's Pancho.
Courtesy Guy Clark

said 'Look, Townes, we've got to take care of this thing. It's going to fester.' I fixed him up. He said, 'You know I was going to make an X but you
stopped me. Susanna, how am I going to explain this thing on my chest to
the girls I'm going to fuck? I'm going to tell them I was bobsledding down a
hill and ran under a barbed wire fence. What do you think?' I said 'Townes,
tell them you were attacked by a psychopath. That's true, you were.'"

   But Susanna loved Townes and began writing poems about him in her
journal:

   It was just after we said I do
   That I ever knew there was anyone but you

It was one of them parties they give us newlyweds
That I started to crave another man's bed
He told me he'd rather give his own life
Than take the love of his best friend's wife
Now we've lived this way for a thousand years
Measured with tears for my husband and his wife
Now he comes to visit and we all play cards
And study the pear tree in the back yard
Then 12 o'clock comes and he must depart
One is my soul, the other my heart

Guy and Susanna were married. Guy and Townes were best friends. Susanna and Townes were soulmates. Many times, Susanna and Townes spoke their own language and it annoyed Guy.

One day, Guy was so pissed off at Susanna and Townes that he nailed himself into the bedroom. "Townes and I can do a deal that's above Guy's level,

Townes Van Zandt, Susanna Clark, Guy Clark, and Daniel Antopolsky on the porch at Guy and Susanna's house in East Nashville, 1972. Courtesy Guy Clark

and Guy does not know what to do with it," Susanna told Louise O'Connor. "At the same time, Guy's going to do something. It's going to be dramatic, because he learned drama from his mama. He just fucking had enough. Townes and I were sitting there, and we were talking, and we were on the same level. We were just eyeball-to-eyeball, and all of the sudden, we hear this *boom, boom*. He knew we would come after him, so he nailed himself in the room and nailed the window shut too."

"It all involved alcohol, I'm sure," Guy says. "Something pissed me off about the way Townes and Susanna were denigrating my intelligence, and I was offended. I had enough of those two idiots, so 'fuck you.' I took a bottle of whiskey and some ten-penny nails and pounded those nails into the oak frames with this small hammer."

"Naturally, being a woman, I was concerned about his food," Susanna says. "So we decided to make a tuna fish sandwich and flatten it so we could slide it up under the door. We tried and tried but it was one of those little bitty doors and we couldn't get it under there. I said 'Guy, listen, there's a tuna fish sandwich here if you really want it.' No response. By then, he's not even talking. Townes and I sat there all day long figuring the whole thing out. 'What do we have to do?' 'I don't know. What do you think?' We'd pound on the door. Nothing. Zero. We decided to write a note and send it under the door. 'I love you, Guy. Tomorrow will be okay.' No chance. Nothing. Not even a howdy-do. We'd write everything clever we could think of. Finally, about four o'clock in the afternoon, we heard nails being pulled out of the door. Townes looked up and went 'Oh, wow!' We thought he might come and speak to us. Oh, no. He went straight to the bathroom. Then back to the bedroom and slammed the door. By now we were just terrified, so we left him alone."

While nailed in the bedroom, Guy wrote the now classic "Let Him Roll," a song about an old merchant marine named Sinbad, who had hung around the Old Quarter in Houston and worked as an elevator man in an old hotel. "I was trying to write that talking thing, which I got from Ramblin' Jack," Guy says. "Trying to re-create Jack's approach to doing that kind of stuff, like '912 Greens,' the best talking blues." Guy also scribbled a ditty titled "I Can't Make This Flat Pick Work," which was never recorded.

Susanna studied Guy and Townes as they composed songs and believed she could do it too. She first tried her hand at it with Townes when they

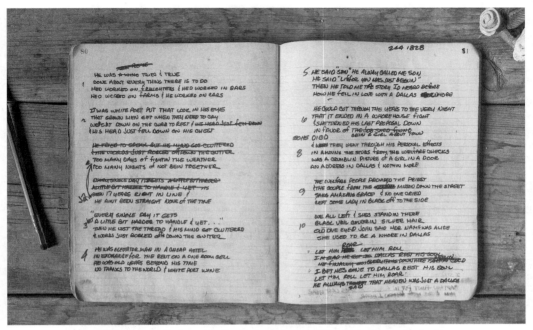

Guy wrote "Let Him Roll" in 1972 after he nailed himself in the bedroom in the East Nashville house to escape Susanna and Townes, who Guy said were "denigrating his intelligence." Courtesy Guy Clark

cowrote "Heavenly Houseboat Blues." In the liner notes for a reissue of *The Late Great Townes Van Zandt*, journalist Colin Escott called it "a trippy rewrite of the mystic hillbilly spiritual 'Great Speckled Bird.'"

"Townes and I and Guy were driving back in that same Volkswagen bus one night, real late. And Townes and I started singing 'I'm building a houseboat in heaven.' And then he'd say, 'To sail in deep in the sea'—and we wrote that song together, switching lines out," Susanna told Van Zandt biographer Robert Hardy in 2000. "And by the time we got home, we had written it. And the next day he put it on his album."

Townes added the song to his seminal 1972 album, recorded in Nashville with producer and colorful character Cowboy Jack Clement. He also cut Guy's new tune "Don't Let the Sunshine Fool Ya." Townes was only the second person to record a Guy Clark song. Harold Lee had recorded Guy's "The Old Mother's Locket Trick" as a single for Cartwheel Records shortly before Townes went into the studio.

Harold Lee's single, "The Old Mother's Locket Trick," Guy Clark's first song to be recorded by another artist. Author collection

Part of Guy's publishing deal required him to record demos of his songs so Sunbury Dunbar could pitch them to singers; the goal was for someone to record a song and make it a hit. But when Guy tried to record his new song "Pack Up All Your Dishes," Harry Jenkins at RCA told him he could not sing the line "That sumbitch has always bored me."

"Harry said, 'Look, you need to think up something beside 'son of a bitch'; we can't demo this song this way,'" Susanna says. "We're talking about the difference between the song getting cut and [making] thousands of dollars or ever getting on the radio. We're talking serious shit here. We're living on $75 a week and sending $100 a month back to Guy's first wife for child support. Harry said, 'You've got to say something else; how about *son of a gun?*,' and Guy says, 'How about *motherfucker?*' That was the first time that Nashville learned that Guy was not going to be compromised."

The struggle with RCA became moot that spring when Jerry Jeff Walker breezed through town and stopped to visit Guy, Susanna, and Townes.

"We all sat around talking and drinking some beers . . . and then Guy said: 'I've had a breakthrough. I've written something,'" Walker says. "The first song he played me was 'Old Time Feeling.' I thought: *That's really good. That's put together.*" Walker asked Guy if he had more songs, and Guy played a new one called "Pack Up All Your Dishes." One line of the song came from a canvas of Susanna's on which she had painted the words "Love's a Gift That's Handmade." Guy was writing the song when Susanna painted it.

Walker needed a couple of songs to round out his first record for Decca. He had moved back to Texas and was recording tracks near his home in Austin and at a studio in New York. He flew to New York with two new Guy Clark songs in his pocket. As he laid down "That Old Time Feeling," he talked about his old friend Guy. To teach the band "Pack Up All Your Dishes," Walker sang the chorus a few times:

*If I could just get off of this L.A. Freeway*
*Without getting killed or caught*
*I'll be down the road in a cloud of smoke*
*To some land I ain't bought, bought, bought*

As they recorded, everyone in the studio, including Walker, kept referring to the song as "L.A. Freeway."

"I called Guy and said, 'Can we quit calling it 'Pack Up All Your Dishes'?' Everybody keeps saying, 'Hey, that 'L.A. Freeway' song is good,'" Walker says.

Decca released the song as the first single on the album *Jerry Jeff Walker*. The record label was based in Los Angeles, and the promotion team broke the song in the LA market.

Susanna wrote to Guy's grandmother Rossie: "Guy's song 'L.A. Freeway' is still going up in the charts, especially in California and Texas. The music business is so slow and unpredictable we have no idea what the next

PACK UP ALL YOUR DISHES
MAKE A NOTE OF ALL GOOD WISHES
SAY GOODBY TO THE LANDLORD FOR ME
THAT SOM-BITCH HAS ALWAYS BORED ME
SAY ~~ADIOS~~ TO ALL THAT CONCRETE
GONNA FIND ~~US~~ SOME ~~DIRT ROAD~~ ~~DUSTY~~ BACKSTREET

THROW OUT ALL THOSE L.A. PAPERS
& THAT MOLDY BOX OF VANILLA WAFERS

~~HERES~~ TO YOU OLD SKINNY DENNIS
THE ONLY ONE I THINK I WILL MISS
PLEASE GIVE MY ~~BEST~~ REGARDS
TO THAT ~~FUCKIN~~ DOG IN THE LANDLORDS YARD

DONT ~~FORGET~~ TO CHECK THE CLEANERS
THROW OUT THOSE MOLDY WEINERS

I CAN HEAR YOUR BASSMAN SINGIN
SWEET & LOW LIKE A GIFT YOUR BRINGIN

PLAY IT FOR ME ONE MORE TIME NOW
~~GOODBY TO HOLLY GROUND NOW~~
WE GOT TO GIVE IT ALL WE CAN NOW
~~I~~
~~AINT~~ BELIEVE ~~EVERY WORD~~ YOUR SAYIN
JUST KEEP ON KEEP ON PLAYIN

Guy's first draft of "L.A. Freeway." Courtesy Guy Clark collection

EH SUSANNA DONT YOU CRY BABE
LOVES A GIFT THATS SURELY HAND MADE
YOU GAVE ME SOMETHING TO BELIEVE IN
DONT YOU THINK IT TIME WE WERE LEAVIN

PUT THE PINK CARD IN THE MAIL BOX
LEAVE THE KEY IN THE FRONT DOOR LOCK
THEY'LL FIND IT LIKELY AS NOT
~~SEEMS LIKE THERES SOMETHIN I FORGOT~~
I'M SURE THERES SOMETHIN I HAVE FORGOT

turn will be. It's bound to be good; we've spent enough time waiting."

In Texas, the Hill Country town of Kerrville launched its first folk festival, conceived by visionary Rod Kennedy, owner of Austin's Chequered Flag, a club Guy had played many times. Meanwhile, KOKE-FM in Austin flipped its format to "progressive country" and "redneck rock," spinning records by Waylon Jennings, Willie Nelson, Bob Dylan, and the Rolling Stones. The cosmic cowboy scene sparked in Austin, a town that embraced left-of-center artists. Doug Sahm, Steve Fromholz, Michael Martin Murphey, Willis Alan Ramsey, Rusty Wier, B. W. Stevenson, Willie Nelson, and others were shaking up the status quo at clubs including the Armadillo World Headquarters, the Soap Creek Saloon, Castle Creek, and Threadgill's. Though Austin attracted many songwriters, Houston native Rodney Crowell headed instead to Nashville, arriving in September of 1972.

"I was living in my car and hanging around Centennial Park with some out-of-work trapeze artist and his wife," Crowell says. "They posed as Russians, but they were from upstate New York. I got into a conversation with this fella, and he said, 'Look, who you want to get in touch with is Guy Clark.' I filed away the name."

As the weather got colder, Crowell decided he needed a roof over his head. He found a job busing tables at the TGI Friday's restaurant on Elliston Place and moved to an old house with a wraparound porch on Acklen Avenue in Hillsboro Village, an artistic and bohemian neighborhood on the south side of Vanderbilt University. His roommates were fellow Texan Richard Dobson and "Skinny" Dennis Sanchez, the six-foot-seven, 125-pound upright bass player who had played with Guy in a string band in Los Angeles and followed Guy to Nashville. Sanchez's height was a symptom of Marfan syndrome, a genetic disorder of the connective tissue that sometimes includes heart valve and aorta defects. Crowell worked the evening shift until 2:00 a.m. Word got around that the house on Acklen was an all-night hang. After the bars closed, the porch became the stage and the Crowell-Dobson-Sanchez house was the place to be for late-night picking parties.

Crowell came home from work one early morning and found Guy Clark passed out in his bed. "Skinny Dennis and I shared a bedroom with two little twin beds. I walked in and saw these long legs and pair of cowboy boots hanging off the end of my bed and I went, 'Okay. That's cool,'" Crowell says. "Then I went and met Susanna. My first conversation was with her. She was flirting with me, in the way Susanna used to flirt. She's teasing me, the fresh-faced kid. She was funny. We became instant friends. We talked about painting. I don't know if I was at all interested in painting, but I lied and said I was. I was ten years from getting interested in painting, but, 'Of course, yeah, I love painting. Van Gogh?' I knew that name. I think I [had] heard [of] Rembrandt."

Crowell's roommate Richard Dobson tended bar at Bishop's Pub, a place where songwriters were welcome to pass the hat and play for tips, burgers, and beer. Dobson had moved to Nashville after reading a story about Kristofferson in the *New York Times* magazine. Mutual friends suggested he look up Guy Clark.

"I called up Guy. He's very courtly on the phone and said, 'Who do you know?' I mentioned three or four people," Dobson says. "Then I mentioned a fellow named Frank Davis, who is an engineer, artist, all-around beloved Houston character. When I said 'Frank Davis', Guy said, 'Oh, why don't you come on over?' So I did, and he said, 'Let me see what you got.' I played this

Guy Clark (*end of table*) and (*clockwise*) Charlie Bundy, Susanna Clark, Danny Rowland, (unknown in hat), Chris Laird, unknown, and Rodney Crowell in the backstage green room at the Palomino, Los Angeles, circa 1975. Courtesy Guy Clark

song called 'Baby, Ride Easy.' He said, 'Oh, I like that.' He arranged a Nashville demo session, and he demoed the song for me. He also pointed out a place where I could probably find a rooming house on West End, and that worked out for me. He just took me in. Guy and Susanna are a pretty striking couple, and they were just really good to me."

Owned by Tim Bishop, Bishop's stood at West End and Thirty-Second avenues. At the time, West End, Hillsboro Village, Centennial Park, and Elliston Place neighborhoods operated as the nerve center for artists, songwriters, hippies, and performers.

Two characters who called themselves Girl George and Arizona Star came up as part of the street scene around the West End. George and Star had moved to Nashville from San Francisco on the advice of Kris Kristofferson, who told them they would be a perfect fit in the creative landscape of Music City. George wore high boots, a sword, and a Prince Valiant costume. Star floated through the park in billowing hippie tunics. Together they sang, danced, and entertained all around Centennial Park, West End, and Elliston Place.

Elliston Place, known as the rock block, held several hangouts: TGI Friday's, where Crowell worked alongside another aspiring songwriter, Marshall Chapman; the Gold Rush, a dive where musicians could find cheap eats and score some dope; and the Exit/In. Young songwriters worked their way up from playing Bishop's Pub to headlining at the Exit/In. Although he had only been in town for a year, Guy had a big enough following to play the Exit/In. He was the heart of the bohemian scene.

Crowell describes the hierarchal order of their community:

Mickey Newbury had a place on the lake, a houseboat on the lake. You rarely saw Newbury, but when you did, it was like a visit from the king. And then there was Townes, who was this satellite, who revolved around Guy and Susanna. Townes was a version of the Wandering Troubadour or the Ramblin' Jack character. When Townes came into town he would generally be kicking heroin. Word would get around that Townes is coming into town and then we'd all gather around at Amy Martin's carriage house in Hillsboro Village. The first day or so, we'd all wait downstairs while Townes was upstairs at Amy's place. We'd all be out sitting around a picnic table with guitars in hand waiting for Townes to come down—waiting for him to get over the jones and junk. That was just a movable feast, to quote Hemingway.

These characters orbited Guy. Guy was the sun, and there were a lot of planets spinning around him. Maybe Susanna was the sun sometimes and Guy was the moon, and then Guy was the sun and Susanna was the moon, and rest of these artists, in some form of development, would orbit around Guy. He was the curator of the street characters, the great artists like Newbury and Townes. People just followed Guy around. He invited me to hang and pay attention and sometimes would tell me "Just shut up and learn."

Guy didn't think of himself as a mentor, but he was a barometer for excellence, and the other songwriters looked up to him. Crowell, Sanchez, Dobson, Bobby David, Steve Young, Steve Runkle, and Harlan White were just a few of the writers who gathered around Guy.

"He sat me down and played Dylan Thomas reading poetry," Crowell says. "He said, 'Hey, man, listen to this. Our songs have to be able to speak with the eloquence of Dylan Thomas.' Now, that's setting the bar at the right place. Guy has the jeweler's eye. At four a.m. when the smoke clears and the chemistry is just right, he can identify what is true, real, and what is potentially museum-quality art. Most everybody I knew wanted to be around that. I certainly did because I wanted to learn. People have said that Guy is my mentor, and Guy bristles at that. He wasn't a mentor to me. He didn't have that self-important thing that 'I'm going to mentor you and teach you something, young man,' but it was more like, 'Hey, man, we're hanging. You know some good songs; let me hear 'em.'"

By the time John Lomax III, son of the Houston Folklore Society's John Lomax Jr., came to Nashville in the summer of 1973, Guy and Susanna had left East Nashville for good. They now lived next to Mickey Newbury at 159 Sunset Drive in a log cabin with an incredible view on the north side of Old Hickory Lake.

"I moved into an apartment out in Goodlettsville, primarily because it was reasonably close to where Guy and Susanna were out on the lake," Lomax says. "I got to hang with them some and meet a bunch of people that way. Townes, Rodney Crowell, and Steve Young were hanging out. Skinny Dennis.

Guy Clark plays guitar in his Nashville home, circa 1973. Courtesy Guy Clark

They were the ones who were having the salon at the time. They would pool the money and buy a bottle of whiskey of some kind. They'd get it and break the seal and just throw the cap away. Pass the bottle until it was gone. They didn't need the cap because they weren't going to keep it."

Sunbury Dunbar continued to pitch Guy's songs around Nashville. The Everly Brothers had a string of number one country hits on the *Billboard* chart in the late 1950s with "Bye Bye Love," "Wake Up Little Susie," and "All I Have to Do Is Dream." The brothers had impressed Guy with their harmonies back in '69 at the Fillmore West in San Francisco, right about the time he was inspired to write "A Nickel for the Fiddler." Now the Everly Brothers were in the studio to record that song for their 1973 album *Pass the Chicken and Listen*.

Guy was in good company on the Everly Brothers album, which included songs by Mickey Newbury, Kris Kristofferson, John Prine, and Willie and Waylon's "Good Hearted Woman," although Chet Atkins's production of the album is about as countrypolitan square as one can get. The brothers weren't happy with the result and were fighting among themselves, and it would be ten years before Don and Phil cut another record together.

Back in Texas, Willie Nelson rolled out his first Fourth of July picnic in the Hill Country hamlet of Dripping Springs. Kristofferson, Waylon Jennings, John Prine, and Charlie Rich were all on the ticket. Jerry Jeff Walker invited Guy to open for him at Castle Creek in Austin the same week. Drunk and eager for Walker's brand of redneck rock, the rowdy throng booed and cat-called. Guy gave up midway through his set and left the stage.

Despite that fiasco, Walker played an important role in Guy's life during this period. No slouch in the songwriting department himself, especially after the success of "Mr. Bojangles," Walker had options—either to write his own songs or let his artist and repertoire (A&R) people find songs for him. While it's true that Walker and Guy were old friends, Jerry Jeff backed Guy because of the superiority of his songs, and many fans discovered Guy thanks to Walker's recordings.

In his song "Pissin' in the Wind," Walker references the ways in which he extracts songs from Guy:

About the time I called Guy it was four in the morning
Teach me the words to the song I was humming
He just laughed and said that ol' gray cat is sneaking down the hall
But all he wants to know is who in the hell is paying for the call.

"Sometimes he'd teach me the words on the phone when I was in a session," Walker says. "Sometimes I'd call him, sometimes we'd be on the road and cross paths, and sometimes we'd be drinking together. I know Guy doesn't write bad songs, and he'd always have something of interest."

Susanna and Guy planned to go back to Texas in August to hang out with

Walker while he recorded a show at Luckenbach; the session became Walker's famous *¡Viva Terlingua!* album. Luckenbach ("more a state of mind than a town") was named for Albert Luckenbach, the first postmaster of an 1849 Comanche trading post. Ranchers Hondo Crouch (who Guy had met as a kid in Rockport) and Cathy Morgan bought the entire town in 1970. The outpost quickly became a place to relax and get away from it all. To this day chickens scratch the ground in front of singers strumming acoustic guitars under a shade tree while the audience lounges on picnic tables sipping longnecks and eating barbecue.

"I found a mobile sixteen-track truck that was willing to go to Luckenbach," Walker says. "I just decided to record with the birds and the trees. I wanted to get away from the world and just make music and play. That's what people do in Texas. On the weekend you put your shit in the car and you drive off into the Hill Country and visit some old windmill towns and stuff. You wind around and you have a couple destination spots. Some people go to Gruene Hall. There's a river where you can river raft. Or you wind

Jerry Jeff Walker records *¡Viva Terlingua!* at Luckenbach in August 1973, and the Clarks are there for the festivities. *Left to right:* "Slappy" David Gilstrap, Jerry Jeff Walker, Steve Keith, Donnie Dolan, Bob Livingston, Gary P. Nunn, Susanna Clark, Hondo Crouch. Courtesy Guy Clark

around and go to Luckenbach. You get out, somebody drinks a longneck beer, and they pitch washers, and the kids get their feet dirty."

The night before they left for Texas, Guy and Susanna partied at Chips Moman's Music Row studio. Moman had made his name producing Elvis Presley's 1969 album *From Elvis in Memphis*, which included "Suspicious Minds," "Kentucky Rain," and "In the Ghetto." Guy was more impressed with Moman's writing chops on Aretha Franklin's "Do Right Woman, Do Right Man," and a song called "The Dark End of the Street," recorded by soul singer James Carr. As they sat around and drank, Guy amused Moman with stories about Luckenbach.

"Guy and Susanna were at the studio all night, and Guy told me great stories about Hondo Crouch and Luckenbach," Moman says. "It sounded like an interesting place: one store, a post office and a dance hall. The next morning Bobby Emmons showed up to write, and I said: 'Hey Bobby, let's go to Luckenbach, Texas.' I had my guitar, he played piano, and we just wrote the song."

Jerry Jeff Walker and the Lost Gonzo Band loaded into the dance hall at Luckenbach on August 18, 1973. The band included Kelly Dunn on organ, Craig Hillis on guitar, Bob Livingston on bass and vocals, Michael McGeary on drums, Gary P. Nunn on piano and vocals, Herb Steiner on steel guitar, Mickey Raphael from Willie Nelson's band on harmonica, Mary Egan on fiddle, and Jo Ann Vent on background vocals.

Guy was there to witness Walker and the band record "Desperados Waiting for a Train," the third Guy Clark song Jerry Jeff recorded. No one could know then that Chips Moman and Bobby Emmons were in the middle of writing a classic song, one that would put Waylon Jennings (with guest vocalist Willie Nelson) on top of the *Billboard* country chart in 1977. Unless you're a regular at Luckenbach, few people know that it was Guy Clark who sparked the idea.

*Let's go to Luckenbach, Texas*
*With Waylon and Willie and the boys*
*This successful life we're livin'*
*Got us feuding like the Hatfields and McCoys*
*Between Hank Williams pain songs and*

*Newbury's train songs and "Blue Eyes Cryin' in the Rain"*
*Out in Luckenbach, Texas, ain't nobody feelin' no pain.*

When Walker and his girlfriend Susan married, Guy and Susanna joined them on their honeymoon in Barbados.

"We had a good time," Walker says. "In fact, while we were there, I learned 'Coat from the Cold.' Guy had just written it. I ended up putting it on the next album. We were sitting there at dinner one night. My wife's real salty, and we were having an argument over something, and I said something like, 'Oh, it's just like you to say that.' My wife picked up a piece of fish and threw it. Hit me right between the eyes. I think I bolted myself into the bedroom and passed out. Guy got a picture of my bare ass on the bed when I had to get up and unbolt the door to go to the bathroom.

"Susanna painted a picture on the front porch. There was one of those glass balls they use to mark where you can park your boat and anchor it. She painted it. Just as she was finishing it, a bird flew over it and shit on the side of the painting. She had to smudge it off. We still have that painting. We had it framed. It hangs in our house in Belize, and we always think of her when we're there. We smile and think of that porch. That was one of our great trips."

Another visual chronicler, photographer Jim McGuire, built a studio in an old mom-and-pop grocery store at the corner of Forty-Fifth Street and Wyoming Avenue in the Nashville neighborhood of Sylvan Park. He dug what was happening in the music scene and soon made his living photographing the coolest of the cool up-and-comers in his storefront studio. McGuire's business exploded, and he called his friend Bob Miller to join him in Nashville. Miller drove down from New Jersey. Known as the Grease Brothers, McGuire and Miller worked on cars when they weren't photographing the new class of songwriters and singers. Word spread around town that McGuire's studio was a haven for picking parties and goofing off.

Guy and Susanna moved back into Nashville when the owner of the rented log cabin on the lake reclaimed his house. The Clarks settled in an apartment on Thirty-First Street and Wellington Avenue near Vanderbilt University and stumbling distance from Bishop's Pub. Townes still crashed at their place when he was in town, which was often. "We lived in an upstairs apartment that was full of mice," Guy says. "Townes and I got drunk one afternoon, and I had a grocery paper sack. Townes got the broom. I would hold the sack. Mice would come around this wall—bap! right in that sack. We caught six or seven mice. Had them all in the sack and decided it was time to go to Bishop's Pub. Walked in and dumped that sack on the pool table. Oh shit."

Although the place was much smaller, and the bigger parties took place at McGuire's, the Clarks still opened their home to pickers and partiers.

"I was in there one night and I distinctly remember David Allan Coe being there, and Townes played 'If I Needed You,'" John Lomax III says. "David said: 'That's a great song, man. Mind if I do something with it?' Townes said, 'No, but give me credit as a writer.' So David Allan Coe came up with 'Would You Lay with Me in a Field of Stone' and claimed sole writer. Several years later, some attorney tried to sue Townes for stealing David's song until somebody pointed out that it had been on a record three years before David claimed to have written it. I would always bug Townes about that. I'd say, 'Man, why don't you get on that guy and sue him for stealing your song?' He looked at me and said, 'John, I'm out there on the road by myself. David Allan travels with a biker gang.' 'Yeah, I see your point.'"

When Walker got the test pressing for ¡Viva Terlingua!, he brought it to McGuire's studio. "I always brought my test pressings to McGuire's," Walker says. "We'd all meet over there and of course his camera was all set up, and we would mug and jump around and have a cocktail or two or eight." McGuire photographed Jerry Jeff, Susan, Guy, and Susanna together and displayed the pictures next to the ones he'd shot of Guy, Townes, and Susanna together.

Another night, McGuire, Susanna, Guy, and Townes went to the Tennessee State Fair. Townes won two oversized stuffed dogs by tossing washers into milk bottles. Guy and Townes were accomplished at washer pitching, a talent they learned in Texas where pitching washers is a poor man's horseshoes. At Luckenbach, Guy won a lot of money before his opponents realized he was unbeatable in washers. "Washer pitching is an art," Guy says. "The game was invented by oil-field workers in West Texas. It's the first game I learned as a kid. They use big old washers on the oil rigs, about

After a winning day at the Tennessee State Fair, Guy, Susanna and Townes at McGuire's studio, circa 1975. Courtesy Jim McGuire

the size of silver dollars. You bury tin cans in the ground about twenty feet apart and pitch them into the cans." After the fair, the foursome returned to McGuire's studio where he photographed Guy and Townes brandishing the stuffed dogs like bayonets.

Songwriter Keith Sykes often popped in and out of Nashville. On one trip, he stayed with Guy and Susanna in the spring of 1974. He had met the Clarks through Jerry Jeff a couple of years earlier. "I stayed with them for a week," Sykes says. "Every day Guy and I would walk to the liquor store, and there was a big fiberglass horse out in front for Palomino Whiskey, so that's the kind of whiskey we bought. We bought a fifth of that stuff every day and would have to replenish it the next day. It was such a great camaraderie. We would just sit around and play and sing. There might be six or seven of us. It would get to be my turn and Guy would always say 'Country Morning Music!' So I played that song more than any other for people because Guy just loved it and it was the one he wanted to hear."

In November of 1974 another Texas boy, nineteen-year-old Steve Earle, hitchhiked to Nashville. Earle was tired, hungry, thirsty, and down to his last six dollars when his ride left him near I-40 and West End. As luck would have it, Robert Altman was in town filming his opus *Nashville*.

"They needed the crowd scene in Centennial Park and were advertising dime hot dogs and nickel Cokes," Earle says.

> I thought, *There's lunch and dinner*. I bought all the dime hot dogs and nickel Cokes I could drink and eat. I asked somebody, 'Where can I go pass the hat and play?' They pointed me to Bishop's Pub. I walked in Bishop's and Richard Dobson was behind the bar. I knew Richard from Texas because Richard and David Olney had played the University of Houston coffeehouse. Richard was the first familiar face I saw in Nashville. I hung out, and later Guy and Susanna came in. There was a poolroom in the back of Bishop's. Somebody took me back there and introduced me to Guy. I knew who Guy was for a long time before I met him. I used to play Sand Mountain Coffeehouse when it was on its last legs. There was a mural in the back room; it was Guy, Townes, Don Sanders, Jerry Jeff Walker, and Mickey Newbury. The place was usually empty when I played, so you could see the mural really, really fucking good. It was like Mount Rushmore. It was a really, really big deal. I had an automatic verbal letter of introduction from Townes Van Zandt. I met Townes at Jerry Jeff's thirty-second birthday party that I crashed.

As with Guy and Rodney Crowell before him, the promise of Nashville seduced Steve Earle. Bob Dylan's recordings and Kristofferson's songwriting success represented a changing of the guard.

"Kris Kristofferson was the first person I saw that made me think that maybe I didn't have to go to New York, I could go to Nashville," Earle says. "The business knew what to do with "Help Me Make It through the Night," and they let Kristofferson write "The Silver Tongued Devil and I.""

As Nashville's reputation as a hub for the hippie creative class grew, scores of artists streamed there and spread all over town. "McGuire's studio was ground zero as a songwriter hangout when I got to town," Earle says.

The outlaw scene unfolded at "Hillbilly Central," a studio owned by brothers Chuck, Jim, and Tompall Glaser. Cowboy Jack Clement, who wrote Johnny Cash's hits "Ballad of a Teenage Queen," "Guess Things Happen That Way," and "The One on the Right Is on the Left" and had introduced Kristofferson to Cash, was making records with Townes and Waylon Jennings over at his cosmic empire JMI, where John Lomax III ran the publicity department. Musician, music publisher, and producer Pete Drake laid the groundwork for playing steel guitar on rock recordings, his licks heard on albums by the Everly Brothers, Carl Perkins, Bob Dylan, and George Harrison. Drake also produced Ringo Starr's country album *Beaucoups of Blues*. Open-minded songwriters, those who aspired to writing songs as great literature, collected around Guy Clark.

"I had a real, live, old-fashioned apprenticeship with Guy," Earle says.

Guy and Townes are two completely different types of songwriters on the surface. Townes is a weird one. The only thing that Townes taught me directly was to always put the cap back on the bottle because somebody would kick it over. I kicked the bottle over at one point, and I got taught that lesson really hard. Trying to analyze the whole existence of Townes's approach to songwriting . . . Dylan's all about French poets and the Beats, whereas Townes's literary influences are more conventional in a lot of ways, like Shakespeare and Robert Frost and really serious hardcore academic poets. Townes would give me a copy of *Bury My Heart at Wounded Knee* and tell me to go read it.

I figured out I'd learn faster by paying attention to what Guy was doing. He would show me how he'd go about writing songs. It doesn't necessarily mean that it'd work for me, but at least it was a place to start. There's a methodology. Laying things out on paper. Staying organized helped to keep from losing shit. He showed me a rhyme dictionary and a thesaurus. Guy was really, really generous. He paid attention to us, but he also made sure other people paid attention to us. He championed younger writers in a way that nobody else did. I had my first publishing deal because he bugged the shit out of [head of Sunbury Dunbar] Pat Carter.

Many writers and friends point to those times at Guy and Susanna's as the

Guy Clark, expert cigarette roller. Courtesy Guy Clark

Susanna Clark relaxing in bed with a book and newspaper. Courtesy Guy Clark

last real salon in Nashville. Artistic circles mingled freely. One could be a painter and a songwriter and read poetry. One could build guitars and play guitars. And although it was Guy the young bucks came to write with, it was Susanna who made them feel at home.

"Susanna was a muse for Guy, me, Steve, Jerry Jeff, Willie Nelson—Willie came under Susanna's influence," Crowell says.

"I made the very first tape that I took around to people at Guy and Susanna's," Earle says.

He had a quarter-track tape recorder at his house. We'd been smoking some pot and we made the tape. I'd play a song, and he'd say, 'All right, play another one.' I played four or five songs like that, and Susanna was cooking bacon. That first tape I took around had Susanna frying bacon on it. No stops. It was going good, and Guy's like, 'Play another one.' 'The Mercenary Song' was probably on that. I owe as much of who I turned out to be to Susanna as Guy. There's no doubt about that. It wasn't like she wasn't holding her own in a roomful of men every night. And it wasn't like she wasn't okay with that because she was. She was so strong, a real streak of feminism there. Being as young as I was . . . I did realize that I'd stumbled into this environment, this real nest of bohemia. Everybody was learning something from everybody.

Johnny Cash's daughter Rosanne also hung around the Clarks after meeting them through her beau, Rodney Crowell.

"I was in awe of Guy and Susanna," Rosanne Cash says. "I was a neophyte songwriter and they were the pinnacle. They owned this town as songwriters, and everyone looked up to them. They had a café society at their house. People would go out there and sit around the table and carve their names into the table, and talk about songs, and play each other new songs. Guy was always kind to me but Susanna was tough. She scared me. I really wanted to be friends with her. She was quite a bit older than me, and she drank real alcohol, not just wine, and she was dismissive of women who just had a glass of white wine. I remember Susanna saying about women, 'All we get is an "s". Meaning: if you got married you became a 'Mrs.' We were friends, but there was always a bit of a wall there between us. Emmylou was probably the closest to Susanna, but Susanna did not cultivate women friendships. She didn't really like women that much. She thought women in general were silly and shallow and vapid. She would much rather hang out with men. You have to admit there were a lot of silly and shallow women in the south in the seventies."

"Susanna drank a lot. She drank heavy," Crowell says. "She was two-fisted and would say, 'I'll show you. I'm hanging with Guy and Townes and can drink as much as they do. I can do as much blow as they do, and I can be more lucid than they are.' Susanna was playful. She was extremely smart and clever. She could lay a trap for you. You'd walk into it, and then she would hand you your silly boy button. She would say, 'I baited you on that one, and you walked right into it.' I had a girlfriend and thought we were going to have something going, then she would take pleasure and say, 'You know, while you were in the studio, Townes was upstairs with your girlfriend having sex with her. I'm not even sure that that was unkind. I think it was like a come-on. 'I'll show you what you don't know.' She had a magic wand, in a way. 'Tap you on the shoulders a couple of times with my magic wand and you, too, will have the magic, you, too, will be an artist, you, too, will understand that art is in the process and not the end result.'"

## CHAPTER SEVEN

# The RCA Years

In his first RCA Records press biography, Guy Clark is described as "a songwriter's songwriter in the country-flavored Austin-Nashville bag." The convoluted phrase proves that even back in the mid seventies, the Nashville music business did not know what to do with Guy.

Fifty-one-year-old guitar slinger Chet Atkins ran the RCA Records outpost in Nashville. Atkins was one of the creators of the Nashville sound, which replaced the twang of steel guitars and fiddles with lush pop instrumentation. In 1975, country radio charts reflected the old line as C. W. McCall's "Convoy" and Glen Campbell's "Rhinestone Cowboy" proved to be the biggest hits. As the business strived to sell country music to city people, the easy listening melodies of Ray Price, Charley Pride, Lynn Anderson, and Tammy Wynette ruled the day.

There was hope for change at RCA, however. Grammy winner and hit maker Bobby Bare showed that folk story songs could live on country and western radio with his recordings of the traditional "500 Miles Away from Home," Ian Tyson's classic folk song "Four Strong Winds," and "Ride Me Down Easy," a song written by Texan Billy Joe Shaver.

Two more outcast Texans, Willie Nelson and Waylon Jennings, were shaking things up on staid Music Row as well. Nelson's new *Red Headed Stranger*, coming after the success of Jennings's 1973 album *Honky Tonk Heroes* and on top of Jennings's wife Jessi Colter's breakout hit "I'm Not Lisa," had Nashville executives scratching their heads. The "outlaw" movement brewed under the radar, and of those who knew about it, no one was quite sure what to call it or whether it would last.

Elsewhere, progressive country artists attracted attention from the media and a younger generation of listeners. Gram Parsons's country-folk *Grievous Angel*, issued the year after Parsons died of morphine and alcohol overdose, later drew this assessment from *Rolling Stone*: "The record brought a pure country style and a wrecked country sensibility to rock, setting a standard that no other country-rock effort has begun to challenge." Parsons's collaborator Emmylou Harris (a friend of Guy's) released two heartfelt left-of-center country albums in 1975. *Pieces of the Sky* included the Rodney Crowell–penned "Bluebird Wine," while *Elite Hotel* showcased Crowell's "Till I Gain Control Again."

Sunbury Dunbar's Nashville chief Pat Carter thought Guy embodied the new attitude and that his songs fit this shift in country music. Jerry Jeff was running all over the world playing Guy's songs to the same rednecks and hippies Willie had first brought together in Austin. Rita Coolidge, then married to Kris Kristofferson, recorded Guy's "Desperados Waiting for a Train." Johnny Cash had just recorded Guy's "Texas 1947" on his album *Look at Them Beans*. There was something here, and Carter convinced the brass at RCA to sign Guy to a record deal.

Jerry Jeff's manager, Michael Brovsky, owned an Austin and New York–based company called Free Flow Productions. Because Brovsky was a Nashville outsider and worked with Walker, Guy hired Brovsky to manage his career. Someone had to be the go-between with RCA and take care of the business end. Free Flow had a good relationship with the label and negotiated an advance and production budget for Guy.

RCA's A&R producer Mike Lipskin signed Guy to the label with the condition that Lipskin would produce his first album, using Memphis musicians instead of the more traditional Nashville country approach. According to Lipskin, Guy agreed to the terms. "Chips Moman had a lot of hits in the sixties with the Boxtops. His rhythm section and his studio did a lot of the Neil Diamond hits and B. J. Thomas and some other people," Lipskin says. "I liked that sound, and I thought it was much more commercial than the more acoustic country. Since Jerry Jeff Walker had a hit with Guy's 'L.A. Freeway,' I wanted to do something that was more commercial that would give Guy a better chance at being successful. As a songwriter, Guy is such a treasure. Sometimes he's his own worst enemy commercially. In any case, I signed him and told him, 'We have a deal. We're not going to do country-western. We're not going to do acoustic with violin. We're going to do the Memphis sound because that way, I think, you'll have a better chance of being commercial and having a hit single.' I didn't want to do an album where you had one great single and the rest is crap. I wanted every track to be good."

In August 1974, Lipskin took Guy into RCA's famous Studio A to record his first album. For the tracking sessions, Lipskin hired the Memphis Boys, a group of studio musicians put together by producer Chips Moman at his American Studios in Memphis. The band included Bobby Emmons on organ, Bobby Wood on piano, Mike Leech on bass, and Reggie Young on guitar. Collectively, the musicians had been part of the inner circle on multiple albums: Elvis Presley, Dusty Springfield's *Dusty in Memphis*, Dionne Warwick's self-titled album, and other influential works out of Memphis. For drums, Lipskin brought in Jerry Carrigan, part of the famed Muscle Shoals rhythm section.

**GUY CLARK**                            A Free Flow Production
                                              RCA
                                          on   Records

Guy Clark's first publicity shot for Free Flow Productions and RCA Records. Courtesy Guy Clark

To sweeten "Desperados Waiting for a Train" and "The Ballad of Laverne and Captain Flint," Lipskin hired the Muscle Shoals Horns: Harrison Calloway on trumpet, Harvey Lee Thompson on saxophone, and Charles Rose on trombone. He also added cello and violin on "Desperados," "Let Him Roll," "Anyhow I Love You," "L.A. Freeway," "Like a Coat from the Cold," and "Virginia's Real."

"I'm very proud of that record," Lipskin says. "Chet Atkins thought it should be issued too, but Guy and his wife did not like the results." In fact, guitarist Atkins, who'd been in charge of RCA's Nashville division in the seventies, wrote a memo to Lipskin that reads: "This sounds good to me. Too bad it wasn't used."

"I never did anything I didn't want to do," Guy says. "After I did it, I found out it wasn't me. I never did write songs for country radio. I wasn't a country singer and am still not a country singer. I just write songs and play them. I'm Guy Clark. My songs are not really geared to sell a lot of records and have hits. I just do what I do. The producer pissed me off. I walked into the studio one day and found he'd flown in an entire horn section to play on my record. The charts had been written and the session planned out without asking me anything. It would have been an absolute disaster had I put that record out."

It might not have been a disaster, and perhaps the more popular Memphis sound would have pushed Guy into the mainstream, but Guy had been writing and playing for a decade. He knew who he was as an artist. Guy was a folksinger. He favored stripped-down, acoustic instrumentation with the vocals up front and lyrics playing a starring role on the recordings. After spending almost the entire budget and not getting what he wanted, Guy fired the RCA producer and scrapped the record.

With the budget blown and nothing to show for it, Guy was in a pickle. He turned to his friend, audio engineer Neil Wilburn. Wilburn had been a staff audio engineer at Columbia's famed Quonset Hut studio in Nashville, where he controlled the sound on important albums including Leonard Cohen's *Songs from a Room* and *Songs of Love and Hate*, Dylan's *Nashville Skyline*, Johnny Cash's *At San Quentin*, and the Byrds' *Dr. Byrds and Mr. Hyde*, among others.

"Neil had been engineering demos I had done for the publishing company, and I just liked what he was doing," Guy says. "He knew how to get the right sound, and he liked my songs, which is a pretty good start for a working relationship. No matter how sophisticated the equipment, all we're here to do is record music. We don't lose sight of that. If a thing isn't worth doing well, then it ain't worth doing at all, and to hell with it."

Neil and Guy snuck into RCA Studio B with scavenged tracks from Guy's demos, called in favors (the supporting cast included Emmylou Harris, Rodney Crowell, and Gary White), and cobbled together the record that would become Old No. 1, a collection of gritty and dazzling story songs rooted in the culture of the West Texas desert. Sparked by real people and events, Guy's vibrant narratives introduced colorful characters from his life and immediately separated him from the fluffy pop songwriters of the day.

Several songs from the Lipskin-produced sessions would not show up until Guy's later records. "Anyhow I Love You," "Don't Let the Sunshine Fool You," "The Ballad of Laverne and Captain Flint," and "Virginia's Real" didn't make it onto Old No. 1, which was released in the fall of 1975 with a list price of $6.98. The jacket cover features a photo of Guy wearing a straw cowboy hat, with a cigarette hanging from his mouth, standing next to Susanna's painting The Old Blue Shirt. The back of the jacket has a photo of Guy and Susanna, both clad in jeans and denim shirts, smiling broadly. Inked around the photo in all caps is a rambling note by Jerry Jeff Walker:

July 4th, 1975
To my friend while emotionally deranged

We've been down this road
Once
Or twice before
Guy Clark's first
Hmmm
I think of young ones makin' it
Too soon
While Tom Waits
Guy writes
Of old men
And old trains

And old memories
Like black & white movies
Etched
No, carved like crow's feet
In the corners of his past
Now he'll close his eyes
And all those faces
And places
Pass
Again
To the natural music
Of a flat-top guitar
A fiddle
A Rockport jukebox
Spilling
Stories
Texas music
Good hard workin' people
Light & dark
Like the Texas skies
Always changin'
But constantly
Texas

This is not Guy's first
Nor last
Anything
He's a Sleepy-John
Who waits
Till he knows
What he knows
Then
He'll tell ya straight
Or slightly bent
If it fits

*(Some things are slightly round)*
*(Skid ways if memory serves me)*
*Well;—*
*Anyway*
*This album's been a long time comin'*
*I, for one, have waited*
*Till Ol' Sleepy-John, Guy said*
*"All right,*
*Would you write my liner notes?"*
*And I said*
*(Just like I knew what we were doin')*
*"Sure"*
May your music set you free—
Jerry Jeff Walker

*Old No. 1* kicks off with the up-tempo "Rita Ballou," an impressionistic song of cowgirls and cowboys dancing in the open air, inspired by Guy's teenage trips to Garner State Park. The album also includes several songs that had been released by other artists: "L.A. Freeway," "That Old Time Feeling," and "Like a Coat from the Cold" from Walker's albums; "A Nickel for the Fiddler," recorded by the Everly Brothers; and "Texas 1947," recorded by Johnny Cash the same year.

"Texas 1947" is Guy's memory of the first streamlined train coming through Monahans when he was six years old. "I knew I had to write that song because it is so etched in my memory," Guy said. "I'd play down at the train station all the time because my friend Jerry Cantrell's dad, Jack, was the stationmaster. One day it was just a flurry of excitement, and everyone in town goes down to the station to wait for this train to come through. This streamline train comes barreling through, it doesn't stop, and everyone is just watching it fly by."

"That Old Time Feeling" was not the first song Guy ever wrote, but it is the first song he kept. It makes an appearance on the album along with Guy's favorite song he's ever written, "She Ain't Goin' Nowhere."

"It's a three-minute song about ten seconds in a woman's life. It's a seamless piece of writing, came out in a straight line with no editing," Guy says. "I wanted to lend dignity to the scene. She's not sitting down crying on her suitcase. It's not a self-pitying song. It's an affirmation. I grew up around strong women: my mother, my grandmothers, my sisters, and then I married Susanna. I dig strong women."

The intimate "Instant Coffee Blues," a song Guy describes as "the romance of being a songwriter on the road," is the second-to-last track. "Let Him Roll," the talking blues piece Guy wrote when he hid from Susanna and Townes in the nailed-tight bedroom on Chapel Avenue, rounds out the collection.

Maybe the most vivid and important song on *Old No. 1* is "Desperados Waiting for a Train," a remembrance of his grandmother's boyfriend Jack Prigg, the wildcatter who had shown young Guy a world of pool halls and taverns and oil wells that gushed black gold.

"We used to go to the Gulf Days picnic in Odessa in Jack's '38 Packard, and he'd drink beer all day," Guy says. "I drove the car home. I was just a kid, before I had a driver's license, driving back to Monahans at thirty miles per hour. Jack was family. He had a room at the hotel, he didn't pay rent, but he paid the water bill and fixed things when they broke. He was there before I was born. 'Red River Valley' was his favorite song. He was bald but would pass his hand over his head and that's where [the song's line] 'run his fingers through seventy years of living' came."

In "Desperados," the flesh and bone of Jack Prigg is laid bare, as is the admiration and love of his protégé:

> He's a drifter, a driller of oil wells
> He's an old school man of the world
> He taught me how to drive his car when he was too drunk to
> And he'd wink and give me money for the girls
> And our lives was like, some old Western movie
> Like desperados waitin' for a train
> Like desperados waitin' for a train.

"'Desperadoes Waiting for a Train' was written when Guy was in his late twenties or early thirties about stuff that happened when he was eight," Steve Earle says. "Guy's incredibly detailed, like details within details. I related to 'Desperados' because I had a great-uncle named Gene Wall, and he worked for the railroad. He was a section boss, in charge of maintenance for a section of the railroad. For a while, by complete serendipity, he got the section

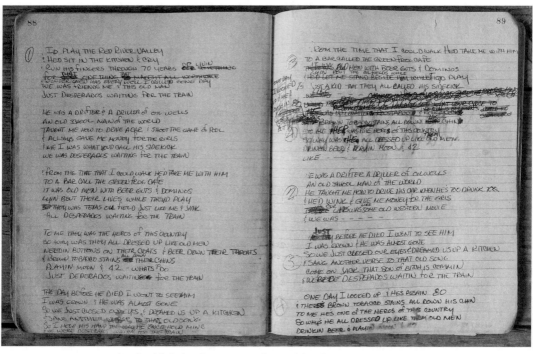

Guy's notebook with lyrics for "Desperados Waiting for a Train." Courtesy Paul Whitfield

that went from Seguin, Texas, headed to Houston by Highway 90. He was in the area and would stay with us in Schertz. The first time he came, he's like, 'I'll take the boy and buy him a soda water.' Naturally, a block away, he's like, 'Where's the nearest beer joint?' He'd buy me a Big Red and sit there and drink for three solid fucking hours until my dad got home."

Not everybody in Guy's jury was impressed with "Desperados."

"When Guy sang 'Desperados Waiting for a Train' for Townes, [Townes] said, 'Gone commercial, huh?'" Susanna says. "I remember that because Guy repeated a chorus and Townes was like 'For God's sake, you don't repeat a chorus over and over again.' Guy could go in and sing a song in front of an audience and he wouldn't give a flying fuck, but if he sang it in front of Townes, he would be crazy until Townes gave the lordly okay. I've seen Guy sweating in front of Townes. Townes was the yardstick."

The unpolished production and exquisite use of language on Old No. 1 captured the attention of fans hungry for authenticity and made music critics around the world take notice. Glowing reviews, rife with comparisons to Kris Kristofferson, rolled in to the RCA publicity department. The British weekly music newspaper *Melody Maker* declared: "There occasionally appears, without warning or advance publicity, an album so original and excellent that it pins you to the floor with surprise and delight. Guy Clark's *Old No. 1* is, without a doubt, such an album. . . . The quality of the compositions included in this collection mark Clark as the most important country artist to have emerged since the death of Gram Parsons . . . and he is currently regarded as the most valuable new songwriting discovery since Kris Kristofferson breezed into Nashville."

Critic Ed Miller claimed he had heard Kristofferson sing "Desperados Waiting for a Train" on stage in Dallas before the song made it to Jerry Jeff's album. He wrote in the *Fort Worth Star Telegram*: "If Kristofferson ever wants to stop being Kristofferson and they start lookin' around for somebody else to write Kristofferson words and live that rough road life of the travelin' picker, probably they could get Guy Clark to do it. Clark's stuff is literally at a level approaching that of Kris, so far as vivid descriptions of emotional events goes."

The *Austin Sun*'s Joe Nick Patoski said: "Right now, Guy Clark may very well turn out as the hottest pen Nashville has heard [from] since Kris Kristofferson." *Playboy* called him "Larry McMurtry set to music," while a review in *Playgirl* stated: "Like Kristofferson in his early 'Silver Tongued Devil' days, Guy Clark is a singer of country songs that speak to a mature, intelligent music audience that wants more than down-home soap operas in its popular music." Frye Gaillard in the *Charlotte Observer* also focused on the writing: "Clark is one of the best of Nashville's new-country songwriters, and the material on this album easily ranks with the best of Kris Kristofferson, John Prine or Mickey Newbury."

In the *Soho Weekly News*, Lita Eliscu addressed Guy's delivery, saying, "Clark's deep voice sounds much the way Kristofferson's might if he could stay in tune." Kristofferson was the one to whom he was most frequently compared. Greg Linder of *Twin Cities Reader* wrote: "Clark's a member of the Kris Kristofferson school of contemporary country songwriters. Losers, winos, trains and busted love affairs populate his melancholy ballads. He writes as well as anyone in the idiom, far better than Kristofferson. As an observer of sad love situations, his eloquence parallels Mickey Newbury's."

Townes opened for Guy at a record release show at the Exit/In. Critic Don Cusic reviewed the show for *Record World* and stated: "It is only a matter of time before Guy is crowned the Poet Laureate of the Honky Tonks."

Because Guy was a staff writer for RCA on Music Row in Nashville, it went without saying that *Old No. 1* was commercially categorized as country music. At the time, Joe Galante, who would later become president of RCA's country division, worked as a liaison between Nashville's satellite office and the label's main office in New York. "I was a big fan of Guy Clark and that record, but I didn't know any better, that he wasn't a country act in the sense of what we had at that point, the Charley Prides and Ronnie Milsaps," Galante says. "We had not yet had our first major hit on Waylon. We were still struggling with the sound. Guy wasn't an outlaw in the sense that Willie and Waylon were, but he was certainly left-of-center for what the format was. Artistically I thought they were tremendous songs, and Guy was engaging as he could be, but he also wasn't there to play a radio game. He did what he had to do but maintained his artistry."

Although RCA was probably the most successful record label at the time, the Nashville office was staffed with just a few radio promotion people and a couple of bodies to coordinate efforts with the New York headquarters. They had no marketing department on Music Row. In the days before technology existed to track airplay and sales, record labels had to rely on radio stations' published playlists, compiled by each individual station, to tell them what songs were played. Record stores made up their own lists of which albums sold and how many. Although radio circulated playlists and record stores published sales information, it was all a guessing game.

It could be argued that radio stations and retail accounts were still managed by old-school businessmen, and those executives were not about to give the business away to a bunch of draft-dodging, long-haired, pot smokers. Whatever the line of thinking, before Nielsen launched its sales-tracking system (Soundscan) and airplay-monitoring technology (Broadcast Data Systems) in the 1990s, there was widespread misrepresentation on playlists and sales information, and much of the time country music came up short. According to Galante, RCA didn't even get Dolly Parton on a national late-night television talk show until 1980. The common belief was that country music didn't sell, and this would hold for more than another decade, until September 1991, when country star Garth Brooks's third album, *Ropin' the*

Wind, debuted at number one on the *Billboard* 200 sales chart, knocking off heavy metal rockers Metallica, who had been in that spot for five weeks. It was the first time in history for a country music album to top the overall sales charts. Three hundred thousand records sold in the first week, and mouths dropped throughout the music industry at the news. It was not until that moment that Music Row understood the power it wielded.

In 1975, Guy's *Old No. 1* collected great reviews but didn't sell that well. It was a harbinger, though, of things to come. In January 1976, RCA released *Wanted! The Outlaws*, a compilation album of recordings by Willie Nelson, Waylon Jennings, Jessi Colter, and Tompall Glaser. Waylon and Willie's "Good Hearted Woman" stayed on the country charts for seventeen weeks, reaching number one and winning CMA Single of the Year. *Wanted!* was the first country album to sell a million copies.

*Rolling Stone* associate editor Chet Flippo wrote the liner notes:

When the smoke cleared and the fallout returned to earth, there was a major shift in country music. "Progressive Country" (for want of a better term) was on the map, was here for good. And these are the people responsible for that. Call them outlaws, call them innovators, call them revolutionaries, call them what you will, they're just some damned fine people who are also some of the most gifted songwriters and singers anywhere. . . . They're the cutting edge of a brand of American music that I find the most satisfying development in popular music in the past decade. It's not country and it's not country-rock, but there's no real need to worry about labeling it. It's just damned good music that's true and honest and you can't ask for more than that.

With favorable reviews of *Old No. 1* and the triumph of *Wanted! The Outlaws*, Guy knew "we had something that was worth doing." He says "We were getting such a great response and really great reviews. I just wasn't cut out to do the Nashville country star thing."

Yet Guy didn't exactly fit the outlaw moniker, either, as he said in an interview with the British magazine *Omaha Rainbow*:

I'm no outlaw or outcast. I don't appeal to pop or country in particular but I don't feel alienated by either and I'm influenced by both. The so-called "outlaws" is a term invented by people who had to have something to call them. What they are not is straight-ahead, old-line Nashville, what people call the "Nashville trip," referring to the way some of the musicians deal with the music business using ninety percent hindsight: "What's on the charts? Let's make a record that sounds exactly like that." If they had coined the term "outlaw" 15 years ago, then George Jones would be an outlaw. I'm sure that in ten years or so, Willie, Waylon, Townes and me will be middle of the road and some young kids will be doing acid-country or whatever.

At the same time RCA worked in vain to get Guy's single, "Texas 1947," played on radio, the promotion team scored with a song Susanna wrote. Although the men never took her seriously, Susanna had continued to experiment with songwriting. "I'll Be Your San Antone Rose," was recorded by Seguin, Texas, native and RCA artist Dottsy Brodt, who went by the stage name Dottsy. On November 22, 1975, the single peaked at number twelve on the *Billboard* Hot Country Songs radio chart. "Texas 1947" stalled at number thirty-five.

"I was so tired of hearing country songs about women who get hurt and go around feeling sorry for themselves," Susanna says. "If somebody hurts her heart, a girl can go out and boogie her heartache away same as a man can. That's what I wanted to say . . . when I wrote the song."

"When the record was going up the charts and Guy and I were sitting there . . . I mean, Guy and I got drunk for three days when 'The Wreck of the Edmund Fitzgerald' was a hit," Steve Earle says. "We thought there was some hope for us. We wrote all these long story songs and now we thought maybe we could make some money after all. But when 'San Antone Rose' was going up the charts, Susanna said, 'Guy writes the classics; I write the hits.' She also said, 'There's nothing to this silly little business.' That became her mantra. Which pissed us off."

The guys may have feigned outrage at Susanna's success, but in truth they were all proud, if a bit jealous. "Yeah, she beat us all to the punch, didn't she?" Guy says. "I'm not surprised."

Right around this time, an acquaintance of Skinny Dennis and Jim McGuire came to town. He was thinking about making a film about outlaw songwriters. "James Szalapski came to town to hang out before he started shooting stuff, just to get a feel for what he was going to shoot," McGuire says. "He found out about these picking parties that we have. He wanted one, so we just invited everybody over. One night John Hiatt, Steve Young, and Rodney Crowell sang. It was great. When he decided to shoot he wanted us to re-create that scene."

Meanwhile, John Lomax III met director Szalapski and producer Graham Leader at Jack's Tracks studio during a Townes Van Zandt recording session. Szalapski and Leader hired Lomax to help them as a talent advisor. Lomax introduced the producers to southern rocker Charlie Daniels, country rapper Gamble Rogers, and redneck bad boy David Allan Coe.

The result, *Heartworn Highways*, would grow to be a cult classic. In one part of the laid-back documentary, Guy works on a guitar while drinking wine. "I was so fucked up I strung the guitar upside down, with the bass strings on the treble side," Guy says.

Many scenes ended up on the cutting room floor. The crew filmed Guy performing at the Exit/In as the opener for Tracy Nelson. Earle says the crew was so intrusive that, as a way to get back at them, Guy suggested the team head to Austin to find Townes Van Zandt. "Townes was living in a trailer down in the Clarksville neighborhood with a dog and chickens and this mean girl," Earle says. "We knew as soon as the cameras were rolling he'd be a handful and crazy. The joke was on us. Townes was the only one who played directly to the camera, and he stole that entire film."

The final scene from the film takes place at Guy and Susanna's lake house on Christmas Eve 1975. With his advance from RCA and Susanna's money for "I'll Be Your San Antone Rose," the couple bought a 1,300-square-foot cabin at 80 West Lakeview Drive in the Crosswinds neighborhood of Mt. Juliet, Tennessee, on Old Hickory Lake. In the film, a table, softly lit with two oil lamps, is littered with half-empty wine jugs and whiskey bottles, dirty plates, broken glasses, Pabst Blue Ribbon cans, cigarette packs, and overflowing ashtrays. Susanna's paintings *The Bouncing Apple* and *The Old Blue Shirt* hang on the green-paneled walls. Guy, Rodney Crowell, Steve Earle, Steve Young, Jim McGuire, and Richard Dobson sit around the table, smoking and drinking and picking.

Guy is obviously wasted. He leads the group in a drunken round of "Country Morning Music," one of his favorite songs, written by friend Keith Sykes.

*Left to right*: Rodney Crowell (*with guitar*), Susanna Clark, Guy Clark holding son Travis, and Jim McGuire with friends at the Clark house in Mt. Juliet, Tennessee, during the filming of *Heartworn Highways*, a documentary about pickers and poets. Courtesy Guy Clark

McGuire accompanies on Dobro while the others strum acoustic guitars. Susanna, the only woman in the room, stands against the wall and looks downright bored.

"Here's a smart woman who's an artist who probably has something more grounded to offer up than any of us testosterone-crazed, competitive young fools," Crowell says. "Susanna looked at us and rolled her eyes. She just knew that we had these egos craving attention and a centered woman doesn't crave it like an off-kilter young man does. We were all competitive, trying to get in the limelight. She thought we were ridiculous. She loved us, she loved the colorful brotherhood but knew full well that we were just ridiculous with our neediness."

From the perspective of forty years later, the footage of the group at Guy and Susanna's house does look silly—a bunch of sorry winos trying too hard to be cool for the cameras. But if one looks past the cheap backdrop, the music at the heart of it is astounding. Earle, only twenty at the time, debuts profound work in "Mercenary Song" and, after Guy requests it, "Elijah's Church." Richard Dobson sings "Forever, for Always, for Certain," a song Guy would record in 1999. Earle and Crowell duet on the Bob Wills classic "Stay a Little Longer," and Steve Young sings a plaintive cover of Hank Williams's "I'm So Lonesome I Could Cry."

As the night winds down, someone off-camera begins to sing "Silent Night." The camera is squarely focused on Guy as he lights a cigarette. He looks unhappy about where this is headed—a holy song blowing the festive mood. But he goes along with the sentimental choir, which wraps up the film.

By the end of 1975, Crowell had moved to Los Angeles as a member of Emmylou Harris's Hot Band. His last apartment in Nashville, on Capers Avenue, had been condemned. Before departing, Crowell bought a bag of markers and invited everyone over for a party. They drank and sang songs and wrote messages to each other on the walls. When Crowell moved to LA, Skinny Dennis went with him, moved to Long Beach, played in a trio with folksinger John Penn, and one night fell over on stage and died. Complications from Marfan syndrome affected his heart, and it just gave out.

· · · · · ·

To succeed as a recording artist, one must travel around the country and perform in front of an audience. Radio hits drive the train but touring keeps it on the tracks. Guy was in an odd position with RCA Nashville. They knew what to do to promote and sell country records or the Elvis Presley–style Memphis sound, but acoustic folk music was not an area in which they had expertise. Because Guy's simple melodies and straightforward lyrics told stories of everyday people and the label was based in Nashville, it made sense to RCA executives to sell him to a country market. They promoted Guy to country radio stations, and they wanted him to tour with a country band. For no other reason than that it seemed to be the thing to do as a major-label artist, Guy did his due diligence and hired a band to back him on the road. Steve Earle played bass in Guy's first road band, which also included Champ Hood and Chris Laird.

In January 1976, Guy, Susanna, and the band drove to Texas in a blinding snowstorm. Guy had a gig in Houston on Westheimer, near his old neighborhood. After Houston, the band was scheduled for a five-night run at Castle Creek, next to the Texas Chili Parlor Bar in Austin.

"Guy wouldn't let anyone else drive. So he drove every fucking inch from Nashville," Earle says. "I sort of drove Guy crazy because I talk so much, especially with us riding in a van for a thousand miles. I'd been smoking a joint or something, and Susanna one time goes, 'Man, you need to get your one-liners down.' We played Houston, and then Guy takes off and goes to Rockport, which put me in charge of getting the band and Susanna to Austin for the Castle Creek run. We drove to Austin, and Townes had recommended a motel. Townes recommending accommodations was kind of a sport. It was the old Austin Motel, which is a kind of ritzy place now, but it was a total shoot-up-and-die place then. I dropped Susanna off, and she was in the motel for maybe thirty seconds [before screaming], 'Townes, goddamn son of a bitch.' She decided she wasn't staying there. That's how desperate it was: I was the youngest person in the whole equation, and I was more or less in charge for twenty-four hours. There was screaming and a lot of chaos. My twenty-first birthday was during that run. I pissed Guy off because we had a uniform—T-shirts or Wrangler denim shirts and blue jeans and cowboy boots. My grandmother was the type who would buy you a new suit of clothes every few years, whether you needed one or not. She bought me this weird western leisure suit. I showed up at the gig that night wearing it, and he was just disgusted."

During the shows, Guy insisted that Earle take the spotlight to play "Mercenary Song." They swapped places, and Guy played bass while Earle strummed the guitar and sang his song. According to Guy, one of the best perks of public attention is the chance to turn people on to good songs. Crowell, Earle, and Keith Sykes were early heirs of Guy's relentless crusade. He would come to champion many songwriters throughout the years.

Guy's second album, *Texas Cookin'*, was released in the fall of 1976. The saturated blue album cover shows a sweaty close-up of Guy squinting at the sun while holding a straw hat over his head. The back features Guy and Susanna photographed through the back window of a truck cab, Susanna looking at the camera and Guy looking at her.

Underneath the photo, a note reads:

Once upon a good time we got together & made a record of ourselves having a good time making a record—this is it. Everyone's name you see hereon & herein is hereby specially thanked for adding their own brand of craziness & care including Susanna Clark, Michael Brovsky, Steve Frank, Jim McGuire, Mel Ilberman.

Recorded at Chips Moman's American Sound Studio in Nashville and again produced by Neil Wilburn, the record is lively and joyful but suffers from an identity crisis. Guy's son Travis, then ten years old, was one of the background clappers on "Texas Cookin'" and recalls, "We were in the control room doing listen-back or whatever . . . and they started passing an album around, and Waylon Jennings passed me an album with cocaine on it. I just kind of backed up," Travis says. "On *Texas Cookin'*, I clapped on the up beat where everybody else was clapping off. I remember the piano player had really, really, really long hair, this girl."

The overzealous production is bloated by the sheer number of musicians and singers. Brian Ahern, Rodney Crowell, Waylon Jennings, Jerry Jeff Walker, Chips Moman, Chip Young, and Danny "Ruester" Rowland all play guitar on the recording, in addition to Guy. The album also includes Johnny Gimble, Tommy Williams, and Steve Keith on fiddle; Pete Grant on Dobro and steel guitar; David Briggs, Lea Jane Berinati, and Chuck Cochran on piano; Byron Bach on cello; Chris Laird and Jerry Kroon on drums; and Mickey Raphael on harmonica. Briggs even throws in some clavinet. Emmylou Harris, Tracy Nelson, and Nicolette Larson join Jennings and Berinati on harmony and background vocals, plus everyone joins in on the final choruses of "Texas Cookin'."

"In retrospect, I don't like the production on the record," Guy says. "I was trying to give RCA what they needed, a country-sounding record that they could sell to radio. It didn't work, and neither of us were happy with the results."

Yet, even with the busy production, the songs stand out.

The title track is a playful love song to the food of the Lone Star State. "I was trying to learn Mance Lipscomb songs in that country-blues style, and that goofy song came out," Guy says. "'Stop your belly and backbone bumping' is an expression I heard all my life."

The song Guy and Susanna had written in Long Beach, "Black Haired Boy," made it on this record, along with an upbeat fiddle tune, "Virginia's Real"; the barroom ballad "Broken Hearted People"; and an ode to a Rockport shrimper, "The Ballad of Laverne and Captain Flint."

*Old Flint's boat is fine and she's called the Miss-Inclined*
*And there's no home port painted on her stern*
*And they say she's like a ghost up and down that Texas coast*
*But you saw him didn't you Laverne*

*Daddy says Flint is a weird old bird*
*And what's more I have heard*
*That his nets are charmed by a woman who knew*
*How to work that Louisiana voo-doo*
*Laverne get away from that boat you hear*
*Your mama don't want you hangin' round here.*

The song was loosely based on a crusty fisherman named Fred Werhan, a character Guy knew from his years at Rob Roy Rice's shipyard. "He had the worst-smelling boat in the world," Guy says. "Once a year, we'd haul it out and have to clean it out and repaint it. I used Fred as the character and put him in another song that I really love, the Irish ballad 'Pride of Petrovar,' written by Percy French. He was a music hall songwriter in the 1920s. His song is about McGraw the old horse trader that ran off with the most beautiful girl in this little Irish village. This guy was just totally brokenhearted, couldn't figure out why she would go with a guy like McGraw. In my song, Fred Werhan is McGraw."

Around the same time Guy recorded "The Last Gunfighter Ballad," Johnny Cash also recorded it for his next album. "I always thought that was one of my best pieces of writing, the mechanics of it and the way it went down," Guy says. "It was just really tidy. I'd been reading a lot of history about that era, what they called the 'gunfighter era.' When I was a kid, there was a guy who lived at my grandmother's hotel, an old, old guy who taught me how to play dominoes and checkers, mostly dominoes. Earl something. But as a young man, he had been in the United States Cavalry, the real John Wayne cavalry through Tucumcari, New Mexico. He hung out in Belle Star's saloon; she was a famous bandit. He just had all these great stories. Earl is a teenager in 1885 and then he lives to be eighty. Imagine all the changes he saw."

Another one of Guy's favorites from *Texas Cookin'* is "Anyhow I Love You," which includes the line "I wouldn't trade a tree for how I feel about you in the morning, anyhow, I love you." "It's still one of my favorite songs," Guy says. "I've always tried to get somebody to record that song, but I think it's the line about the tree. That's just too big a leap for people. It's like, what's cooler than a tree, except you? It just seemed obvious to me. Nobody's ever called me on it, but I always have the feeling that it's a little too hip for country music. It never really bothered me that it never got cut, but I'd think that someone would have by now." The song would not be covered until 2011 when Lyle Lovett would sing it on *This One's For Him: A Tribute to Guy Clark*.

The favorable reviews on *Old No. 1* fired up the RCA promotion department for *Texas Cookin'*. They needed a hit and decided that the title track fit. The label created a national retail campaign and gave away barbecue grills. A few Texas radio stations got on board with the song, but RCA wanted a national hit on country radio, and it was not happening.

"We needed a hit single," Brovsky says. "That was constant pressure on us, much more so than we certainly would ever let Guy feel, because Guy wasn't that kind of artist. He wasn't a country single guy. We tried to protect that and maintain that for Guy, but yes, we had a great deal of pressure in getting a hit. Especially after the critical acclaim of the first record, they said, 'Okay, now let's get a hit, now let's get a hit, now let's get a hit.'"

While the label tried to sell *Texas Cookin'* to radio stations and record stores, Guy did his part on the road. To please RCA, Townes, Jerry Jeff, and Waylon joined Guy and his band to play for the Country Music Association convention in Nashville. Guy also opened shows for Waylon and Emmylou and hit the usual places in Texas. In a review of a show at Whiskey River in Dallas, Pete Oppel at *Dallas Morning News* likened Guy's songwriting and performance delivery to Kristofferson's. After Guy's opening set for Emmylou and the Hot Band at the Paramount Theater in Austin, critic Patrick Taggart wrote in the *Austin American Statesman*: "His voice is a little like Kristofferson's and a little like Joe Cocker's."

Guy and the band headed out to California for a date at the Great American Music Hall in San Francisco and stopped by Bay Area radio station KFAT for an in-studio performance and interview. In L.A., they played the famed Troubadour. Fiddle player and former Flying Burrito Brother Byron Berline showcased his new band, Sundance, in the opening spot. In a happy coincidence, Berline's newest band member was a singer and mandolin player named Vince Gill. "It was one of the great nights of my life," Gill says. "There in the flesh were all these people I was completely nuts about: Guy, Emmy, Rodney—it was great. I already felt like I knew Guy because the band I was in during high school covered several of his songs."

Harris and Crowell were at the Troubadour to cheer Guy on. Crowell was surprised to hear this new kid Vince Gill sing Crowell's "Till I Gain Control Again." Gill's performance dazzled Guy and his friends. Crowell burst into Gill's dressing room and asked "What are you doing singing my song better than I can?"

· · · · · ·

It was expensive to take a band on the road. Although RCA gave Guy a small stipend to support the tour, playing live shows cost more money than Guy made.

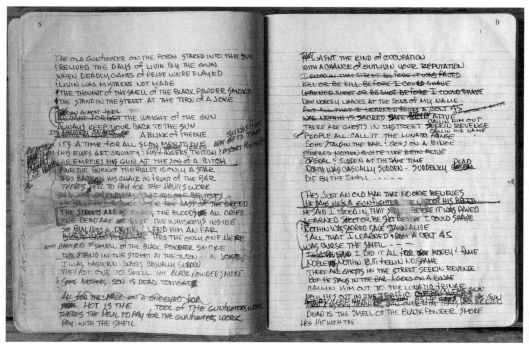

Guy's notebook with lyrics for "Last Gunfighter Ballad." Courtesy Paul Whitfield

Guy with an early incarnation of his band. *Left to right*: Charlie Bundy, Danny Rowland, Kurt Allen, Chris Laird, Mickey Raphael, and Guy. Courtesy Guy Clark

In an interesting turn of events, a Japanese promoter got in touch with Guy's manager Michael Brovsky to invite Guy and his band to perform a run of concerts in Japan, and the money was good. In the spring of 1977, Guy and Susanna, along with Guy's road band—Danny "Ruester" Rowland on electric guitar, bassist Charlie Bundy, drummer Chris Laird, and pedal steel player Pete Grant—boarded a flight to Tokyo. The band played nine shows between April 4 and April 16, beginning and ending in Tokyo, with stops up and down the country in Sapporo, Nagoya, Fukuoka, Osaka, and Okayama. Guy kept a slip of paper in his pocket that read "Hi = Konnichiwa and Hello on the phone is Moshi Moshi."

Emmylou Harris's new album, *Luxury Liner*, included Susanna's song "I'll Be Your San Antone Rose." It was the B-side to the single "Making Believe." By the time Guy and Susanna returned from Japan, *Luxury Liner* was the num-

Susanna and Guy Clark look over a Japanese magazine containing a story about Guy, Tokyo, 1977. Courtesy Guy Clark

ber one album on the *Billboard* country chart and Waylon Jennings had just released *Ol' Waylon* with "Luckenbach, Texas (Back to the Basics of Love)" as the first single. The song reached number one on the *Billboard* country chart and stayed there for a month, then crossed over to the pop charts. It would go on to be one of the biggest hits of 1977. Guy and Susanna's influence continued to snowball in music circles, yet Guy's *Texas Cookin'* album was a bust.

In May 1977, Guy scheduled recording sessions for his next RCA album. He hired Crowell and Albert Lee from Emmylou's Hot Band, Mickey Raphael and Bee Spears from Willie Nelson's band, and his friend David Briggs to play the piano. The band played together in one room and recorded live in the studio. They laid down four tracks with no overdubs. Guy loved it. RCA did not.

"We did the four tracks and then stopped," Guy says "I understand RCA was looking for hit records. Fine with me. I don't blame them—that's their job, but it's just not me. They couldn't understand why I didn't want to go into the studio with the usual bunch of session musicians and just do a nice comfortable country album. I wanted to work with my own people, people who understood me musically."

Just like that, after only two albums, Guy's career with RCA Records ended.

## CHAPTER EIGHT

# The Warner Years

B y the fall of 1977, Guy had inked a recording contract with Andy
Wickham at Warner Brothers Records. Emmylou Harris had racked
up three acclaimed records with the label and Wickham had just
signed Rodney Crowell.

"I wouldn't presume that Emmylou or I had anything to do with Guy getting signed to Warner Brothers," Crowell says. "But I would say that Andy
Wickham became aware of Guy through us because we were always talking about him. Andy had signed Gram Parsons, so he was in the business
of understanding passion. I think he and Guy probably made that happen
over some pretty good whiskey."

In November, the PBS music series *Austin City Limits* invited Guy to perform. In its second season and recorded in the communications building
on the University of Texas at Austin campus, the show was partly inspired
by Jan Reid's book *The Improbable Rise of Redneck Rock*. KLRN program director Bill Arhos, producer Paul Brosner, and director Bruce Scafe pitched an
idea to PBS to showcase Austin's progressive country, folk, and blues scene.
Guy and his band played for the live audience and television cameras on
November 10, 1977. Crowell played acoustic guitar and sang harmony for
the occasion. "We went down to Austin, and the night before the shoot—
which if somebody was thinking about stardom and image projection, we'd
have all gone to bed, got some rest, got up, and got on with the business
of becoming a star—Jerry Jeff came to the hotel [with] a couple of other
yahoos, and we stayed up all night swapping songs and talking while Jerry

held court," Crowell says. "Guy's priority was staying up all night and getting down there deep, drinking heavy. Getting down into that five-o'clock-in-the-morning moment when one of those great songs peeps through or a conversation triggers a notion or an idea for where a song might happen. Guy was more interested in that. He was passionate about that."

Crowell continues:

The next day we go around to the camera blocking for *Austin City Limits*, a big opportunity to start a career off, and we were so hung over that the director finally came around and said, "Are you guys ever going to turn around and face the audience, or do you perform looking at the drummer?" Guy turns around and halfway makes it through 'L.A. Freeway' and [says], "We'll be back in a while."

I was a little more image conscious than Guy was at the time, and I was thinking, *We need to really get this right. It'll be all right. Let's go eat some Mexican food and come back and do it.* The thing about Guy, and how he would have a lasting influence, is that he stayed there in the trenches with Joe Ely singing "Indian Cowboy." You stay up all night in search of those great songs, great ideas. That is where Guy's creativity was at its best and finest. He had a jeweler's eye in that moment and was a profound influence on me. "This is where it is and this is actually the most important thing, and whatever happens after this will just have to take care of itself." Guy wasn't in the business of farming stardom, harvesting stardom. He was in the business of harvesting art, poetry, and really insightful, incisive, true songs.

Around this time, Guy wrote a remembrance of Hondo Crouch, who had died in 1976, for Luckenbach's *Monthly Moon* newsletter:

I first met Hondo in 1958. We were down at Rockport at his sister's house. George Hill, Lola Bonner and Hondo were singing Mexican songs. It was the first time I was ever at a passing around the guitar. Now it's almost a ceremony at Luckenbach. If you're lucky enough to have a guitar and it isn't out for repairs or in the hock shop until your agent comes through with the money from your last gig, you play your bit and pass the guitar to the next girl or guy who may not have one. And then the next guy does his or her thing and it goes all around. It's real friendly like and now it's a custom under the trees at Luckenbach, but it was brand new to me then. It was just the first of many great times I had with Hondo. I lived them all again when Jerry Jeff and I were taping the special, picking in the saloon with the iron stove warming the place. Wherever pickers get together and pass the guitar, Hondo lives on.

The year 1978 was prolific for Guy's wife and friends. In January, Emmylou Harris released *Quarter Moon in a Ten Cent Town*, her fourth album for Warner Brothers. The album title came from a line in "Easy from Now On," the first track on the record, written by Susanna Clark and Carlene Carter.

"Susanna has a wonderful feminine take on the poetry of the heart," Harris says. "It's lovely and romantic but not cloying. There's a real spirit in her lyrics."

"Easy from Now On" rose to number twelve on the *Billboard* Hot Country Singles chart, and the album reached number three on the *Billboard* Country Albums Sales chart. Harris had asked Susanna to paint an image for the cover, and Susanna dreamed up a dark purple sky over a road pointing toward a light in the distance. Hanging in the sky is a sliver of a yellow moon.

"I thought *Quarter Moon* needed to be a landscape," Harris says. "I didn't want another pretty picture of myself. I felt there was a theme in that album, like there is in all records. They're like children; they each have idiosyncrasies and personalities. At first I thought the painting would be more of a town, but it's even better because it's a town from a distance."

In April, Willie Nelson followed Harris's lead and requested a painting for *Stardust*, his lovely album of pop standards. Susanna's serene painting of a star-studded sky graces the cover.

Around this time, Jerry Jeff Walker cut Susanna's "We Were Kinda Crazy Then" for his album *Contrary to Ordinary*, and "I'll Be Your San Antone Rose" appeared on his *Too Old to Change*. Meanwhile, Tomato Records issued Townes Van Zandt's eighth record, *Flyin' Shoes*, produced by Moman. The album included the song "Pueblo Waltz," with lyrics about moving to Tennessee to see Susanna and Guy.

Although Guy had left RCA because he didn't want to record a main-stream country album, here he was, just down the street on Music Row at the country division of another major record label. Warner's Andy Wickham was based in LA, but the Nashville staff was in charge of getting Guy played on country radio.

Guy didn't have enough songs for a full album yet, but his new record label wanted music. Guy and Neil Wilburn went into the studio to record *Guy Clark*, his third album and his debut for Warner Brothers. They brought in Albert Lee from Emmylou Harris's Hot Band to play lead guitar and Bee Spears and Mickey Raphael from Willie Nelson's band to play bass and harmonica respectively. David Briggs on piano, Jerry Kroon on drums, Buddy Emmons on steel guitar, and Crowell playing acoustic guitar along with Guy rounded out the band. Guy called his Houston friend Kay Oslin, who was working as an actress in New York, and asked her to come in to sing harmony on the record.

*Guy Clark* includes six originals and four covers. The album opens with "Fool on the Roof" and ends with "Fool on the Roof Blues." Guy says of the latter, "It's a strange little blues guitar piece that I love, a cross between Mance Lipscomb and Lightnin' Hopkins, somewhere in the traditional blues style but it's not straight timing. Blues players have that freedom to put in an extra bar for emphasis, and I just took that form and repeated it."

Guy also wrote "Comfort and Crazy," a song Walker had recorded for his recent *Jerry Jeff* record. "That song had some really good lines in it, and then some of it isn't. 'Using stumbling blocks for stepping stones.' Eh," Guy says. "I don't think I ever even tried to perform it. Something about it didn't come to fruition."

He wrote "Fools for Each Other" about Susanna, and "Houston Kid" is loosely based on his days living on Fannin Street with Gary White.

Guy recorded the traditional "In the Jailhouse Now," a song usually credited to Jimmie Rodgers, which was part of Guy's live repertoire for many years; Van Zandt's "Don't You Take It Too Bad"; Crowell's "Voila, an American Dream"; and "One Paper Kid" by Walter Martin Cowart, a song Emmylou Harris had sung on her last album.

For the first time, Guy and Neil paid special attention to Guy's vocals. "When we were making this record, Neil and I kept noticing that bits of

September 7, 1978


Susanna Clark
Route #4, Crosswinds
Mt. Juliet, TN 37122

Ms. Virginia Team
Art Director
C B S RECORDS
34 Music Square, East
Nashville, TN    37203

Dear Virginia:

There is no charge for the Willie Nelson STARDUST album cover.

Sincerely,

*Susanna Clark*

Susanna Clark

SC:bbs

cc:  Willie Nelson
     Rick Blackburn
     Michael Brovsky

Susanna Clark gives permission for her painting to be used for Willie Nelson's *Stardust* album. Courtesy Guy Clark

my singing were rich and full and then other parts seemed to bend off. I'd never considered myself a singer and never had any training. I had to learn how to push a sound from down low to make a fuller, stronger sound with my voice."

Warner released *Guy Clark* in October 1978 to little fanfare. The simple cover shows a newly bearded Guy wearing blue jeans, a tan shirt, and brown vest, smoking a cigarette and leaning against something out of frame. His name, written in large gold cursive letters, takes up half of the cover.

"Fools for Each Other" peaked at number ninety-six on the *Billboard* Hot Country Singles chart. There wouldn't be another single, and for all intents and purposes, the album was over before it started. Warner followed it with *On the Road Live*, a promotional album recorded at Washington DC's Cellar Door club in 1979.

While Guy contemplated his recording career and wrote songs, the personal lives of his friends changed and evolved. Rodney Crowell and Rosanne Cash married that spring; Guy and Susanna attended the reception at Johnny and June Carter Cash's home on the other side of Old Hickory Lake. In September, Emmylou Harris, who had married Brian Ahern, sent a card to Guy and Susanna announcing the birth of their daughter Meghann.

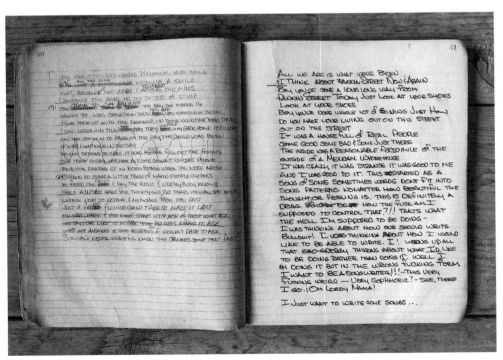

Guy writes about his time on Fannin Street in Houston. Courtesy Paul Whitfield

The same month, Guy played a show in London with a new band lineup: Bee Spears from Willie Nelson's band on bass, Willie's nephew Freddy Joe Fletcher on drums, Rodney Crowell's cousin Larry Willoughby on rhythm guitar, Lea Jane Berinati on keyboards, Dave Perkins on guitar, and Vassar Clements on fiddle. Guy shared the bill with Townes on a few dates and played around Nashville, but mostly he stuck close to home and worked on songs for the next album.

The *Urban Cowboy* era was in full swing. Thanks to the 1980 romantic hit film, based around a nightclub in Houston, the soundtrack *Urban Cowboy* was a smash. It included sugary number one country songs "Lookin' for Love" (Johnny Lee), "Stand by Me" (Mickey Gilley), "Could I Have This Dance" (Anne Murray), and "Love the World Away" (Kenny Rogers). Nightclubs all over the United States brought in mechanical bulls and country bands, while their customers dressed in western garb and learned how to two-step. The Nashville music industry responded by putting out more pop-flavored songs.

If things had gone as originally planned, Guy's 1981 album *The South Coast of Texas* would have been titled *Burnin' Daylight* and produced by Craig Leon. Leon had produced eponymous records for Blondie and the Ramones in 1976 and most recently Rodney Crowell's 1980 album *But What Will the Neighbors Think?* Crowell's song "Ashes by Now" had made the pop charts, and the brass at Warner Brothers believed Leon's approach might drive the same commercial success with Guy.

"We had been in London when the post-punk, rock, new-wave thing hit and heard Elvis Costello's 'Pump It Up' and thought we needed some edge," Crowell says. "There was an artist named Moon Martin whose record I liked, that Craig Leon had produced, so I sought out Craig. *But What Will the Neighbors Think?* turns out to be one of my least favorite records I made. I wouldn't hold that against Craig. I was chasing a style rather than being myself."

Guy and Leon didn't hit it off. Guy wanted to give the label what they needed, but his songs and his poetry were getting lost in the mix. Not only did he have to contend with a new producer, Guy's manager seemed to have his own agenda too.

After finding colossal success with artist Christopher Cross, whose self-titled debut album, with hits "Sailing" and "Ride Like the Wind," had just swept the Grammys, Michael Brovsky and his Free Flow Productions built the new Pecan Street Studios in Austin helmed by engineer Chet Himes. Brovsky cut a deal with Warner Brothers and insisted that Leon record *Burnin' Daylight* at Pecan Street. Brovsky also worked with Carole King and brought in her studio band, supplemented by Johnny Gimble on fiddle and Lloyd Maines on steel guitar.

"This is where part of the problems started," Leon says.

I had just had a very interesting crossover—Rodney's record was very, very bold. It was a relatively successful record with Rod, and was something unique, and I wanted to do the same thing with Guy. I wanted to use folkier players or more sensitive players, shall I say, similar to Rodney's band, who ended up doing *The South Coast of Texas* anyway, but I didn't want all of Rodney's band, but a couple of the guys I did want. Guy didn't want that because he didn't want [his] to be seen as a clone of Rodney's record. Michael Brovsky didn't really care what it was as long as it was done in his studio and he contracted all the players. There were only a few players that I knew, because he was contracting all the players. It was like "okay, we've got a violin player showing up at three o'clock and he's got to be out of here by six."

I didn't like the studio, quite honestly, but I was stuck there and it wasn't anything to do with Guy, who I really revere as a songwriter to this day. He made two really promising records for RCA and did some beautiful, beautiful songs. They were a bit overproduced, but it didn't matter because the songs were so good. What I wanted to do was get back to an even more stripped-down feel, which is very similar to what I did with Rodney. Rodney's album was all done pretty much live, just playing in a room like they did in Nashville a long time ago. It wasn't the right studio to do it in and they weren't the right players. I didn't want to make a Texas outlaw country record. They're good players, but they weren't sophisticated enough to do what I'm talking about in a certain way or folkie enough. They were technically sophisticated but not folkie. They didn't have this folkie kind of sophisticated thing like Tim Hardin had and Tim Buckley. They're more the people I would've lumped Guy with—Townes Van Zandt and Guy were guys that belong with all those singer-songwriters.

The musician credits on *Burnin' Daylight* are quite different than on any other Guy Clark record. Guy is credited with playing electric guitar, with Dave Perkins on lead electric guitar, 12-string guitar, acoustic guitar, and harmony vocals, Steve Meador on drums, Roscoe Beck on bass, Johnny Gimble on fiddle and mandolin, Lloyd Maines on pedal steel guitar and Dobro, and James Fenner on percussion. Reese Wynans played piano and organ on "Broken Hearted People," John Staehely played lead guitar on "She's Crazy for Leavin,'" and Craig Leon played electric piano on "Crystelle." Bonnie Bramlett, Mark Hallman, and Cassell Webb came in to sing harmony.

"I think Guy understood what I was trying to do, but he was very, very self-conscious in those days and not very secure," Leon says. "He was always second-guessing himself. The record was turned in and was approved by Guy and me. It got mastered, it has a catalog number, and a sleeve was done for it and everything else. Then he backtracked and said he wanted to change it, which is possibly because 'Heartbroke' wasn't a huge single. Rodney had had a hit single, and maybe Guy thought he had to have a hit single or whatever. I don't know."

"I believe the single version of 'Heartbroke' was from that session," Brovsky says. "Some of the tracks were smokin' hot but ultimately a bridge too far for Guy."

"I could tell Craig Leon didn't really have a clue how to treat Guy's songs," Lloyd Maines says. "I think the final straw was when Craig insisted on adding a female vocal to one of the songs and Guy said no. It pretty much collapsed then."

The best thing to come out of the *Burnin' Daylight* sessions was the marriage of Craig Leon and Cassell Webb, who got to know each other while making the album. The track listing on *Burnin' Daylight* includes three songs that did not end up on *The South Coast of Texas*: Joe Ely's "Indian Cowboy," "Broken Hearted People," and "Madonna w/Child ca. 1969."

A forty-five single for "Heartbroke" had already been issued to radio stations. With little budget left and a deadline looming, Guy was once again in a pickle.

"They had already printed twenty-five thousand record jackets on *Burnin' Daylight* when I stopped it," Guy says. "I knew it wasn't right and wanted

The single "Heartbroke," from the Warner Brothers album *Burnin' Daylight*, which was never released. Author collection

reinforcement, so I called Rodney. He was enamored with Brian Ahern and his mobile truck, so we went to Los Angeles to record there."

Guy and Susanna moved in to Rodney and Rosanne's house in Calabasas. "I had just written 'Seven Year Ache' and we were sitting at the table in our house, and I started playing it," Rosanne says. "I really wanted Guy to hear it, but I was too afraid to actually turn to Guy and say 'Do you want to hear my new song?' I just couldn't do it. So I started playing it, and Guy whipped his head around and said 'What's that?' I said, 'It's a new song I wrote called 'Seven Year Ache.' Guy gave me his approval, and it was the first time I got real approval from Guy for a song I wrote. I was just a puddle of joy. It meant so much to me."

Every morning Guy and Rodney drove to Brian Ahern's Enactron Truck, a forty-two-foot tractor-trailer decked out with recording equipment and modeled after network video trucks. He parked it outside the rented home in Laurel Canyon, which he shared with his wife Emmylou.

"I had been making records with Rosanne in that truck, and Brian and Emmy had been making her records there," Crowell says. "It had a Neve console and a couple of twenty-four-track machines—some pretty good gear. I said, 'Well, come on, Guy. I got these guys that I work with all the time: Emory Gordy, Hank DeVito, Larrie London, Tony Brown, and Richard Bennett. Let's go in the studio. We can do this really fast.'" Crowell continues:

> That record wasn't produced, it was midwifed. We were racing against the clock. We stayed up for four days and made it. Donovan Cowart was engineering, and he was working on a record with Emmylou in the same studio at the same time. Donovan didn't sleep. That's when Guy started calling him Negatory Raccoon because he just had these black circles around his eyes. Sweet Vince Gill came in and did all the harmony vocal. He and I did the background vocals, so it was a good moment. I really liked that record, and, with Vince coming on it, I think Guy felt relieved. It was a real relaxed atmosphere. Everybody was friendly. I thought it was a fine record. I'm not sure they knew how to market a poet of Guy's caliber, but I was pleased with that record, and at that time I think Guy was too.

While together in Los Angeles, Guy and Susanna turned out for the Grammys with Rodney, Rosanne, Brian, and Emmy. Harris won Best Country Vocal Performance, Female, for "Blue Kentucky Girl."

"We got suited up to go, and I had a tuxedo shirt that at the time would fit Guy, but it didn't have any buttons, [it needed} those kind of stud buttons you have to put in," Crowell says. "So we went out into the garage and found these wing nuts, a screw with wing nuts on them. We put these wing nuts all the way up his tuxedo shirt." Crowell recalls:

> While we were making that record, Emmy was recording *Rose of Cimarron*. One night we had dinner, and we were going back to Brian

and Emmy's house to play our cuts. Guy and I got there first, and we walked around the house to go in the back door because we knew the back door was unlocked. We walked past a guitar case sitting on the sidewalk around the back of the house, a guitar case just sitting there. And Guy goes, 'Wow, what's that guitar case doing just sitting out here?' We just picked it up and walked in the house, and Brian and Emmy came home and they had just been robbed. Whoever was robbing the house had set the guitar right there. We walked right past them, picked up the guitar case and took it in the house. But they had already robbed Brian and Emmy.

Guy renamed the album *The South Coast of Texas*. His hometown of Rockport appeared in living color on the cover, and Guy, then forty, sported a graying goatee. Clad in blue jeans and a tan windbreaker, he sits on a post in front of a shrimp boat in Rockport Harbor. The back of the jacket shows a fleet of boats in front of Jackson's Seafood Company, the business owned by the family of his first girlfriend, Mary Lucille.

All ten songs are written or cowritten by Guy. The title track is a rich illustration of Guy's life as a teenager in Rockport, from memories of his first car to flashbacks of working in Rob Roy Rice's shipyard:

*The south coast of Texas is a thin slice of life*
*It's salty and hard; it is stern as a knife*
*Where the wind is for blowin' up hurricanes for showin'*
*The snakes how to swim and the trees how to lean*

*The shrimpers and their ladies are out in the beer joints*
*Drinkin' 'em down for they sail with the dawn*
*They're bound for the Mexican Bay of Campeche*
*And the deck hands are singin' Adios Jole Blon*

*In the cars of my youth, how I tore through those sand dunes*
*Cut up my tires on them oyster shell roads*
*But nothin' is forever say the old men in the shipyards*
*Turnin' trees into shrimp boats, Hell I guess they ought to know.*

"Every time there was a hurricane or high water, it'd wash up all the snakes from St. Joseph's barrier island right across from Rockport," Guy says. "The water was thick with rattlesnakes. I had a gray '49 Packard, and I did tear through the sand dunes and cut up my tires on oyster shell roads. 'Living on the edge of the waters of the world' is the line that captures that feeling of having access to the entire world two blocks from your house. Fishermen are an international breed, and all languages are spoken in those bars in Rockport. The Mexican bay of Campeche was south of Rockport, and the big shrimp boats would go there for two or three weeks to shrimp and fish in that bay."

"Lone Star Hotel," "Crystelle," and "Rita Ballou" (the latter also recorded earlier, on *Old No. 1*) are songs about interesting women. "It's just those West Texas characters," Guy says. "It's the kid enamored with the older, more experienced woman, like in *The Last Picture Show*."

Guy wrote "She's Crazy for Leaving" and "The Partner Nobody Chose," with Crowell. "'The Partner Nobody Chose' was our attempt at a Carter Family song," Guy says. "It's a really charming song. I think I had 'She's Crazy for Leaving' almost finished, and something about it didn't suit me. I asked Rodney to help me fix that song. We were both coming from the same head about that scene in East Texas."

"New Cut Road" is the true story of Guy's maternal grandmother's family, the Bonners from Kentucky, who had traveled around Texas for five years in a covered wagon before settling in Oklahoma. In an interesting twist, "New Cut Road," "Rita Ballou," and a later song, "Sis Draper," would all be used as names for thoroughbred horses.

"I was in Texas at a race track, and there was a horse called New Cut Road," Jim McGuire says. "I bet it, and he won. I went down to talk to the people after and asked where they got that name. They said, 'From a Guy Clark song.' I have a photo-finish picture of it winning the race. A few months ago, there was one called Sis Draper. I started doing the research. It was a veterinarian in Maryland who owned the horse, but I could never track him down."

Guy's single, "The Partner Nobody Chose," rose to number thirty-eight on the *Billboard* Hot Country Singles chart. It was the first time in four albums that one of his songs cracked the top forty. Nothing else from *The South Coast of Texas* gained recognition, at least not for Guy. Bobby Bare delivered "New

Guy Clark goes home to Rockport for photo shoot for his *South Coast of Texas* album.
Courtesy Jim McGuire

Cut Road" as a single in late 1981, with "Let Him Roll" as the B-side. Bare's version of "New Cut Road" peaked at number eighteen.

"The reason we didn't release it as a single on my album is because of me," Guy says. "The promotion guy at Warner Brothers wanted to release it as a single, and me and Rodney and Andy Wickham and my manager Brovsky all said 'This isn't a single, it's too long, it doesn't have a chorus, there are too many words.' Bobby Bare pushed and pushed his record label to put it out as a single, and I wound up fighting to not put it out as a single for me, even though I knew it was one of the best songs on that record. All it proves to me is that I don't know a thing about the record business."

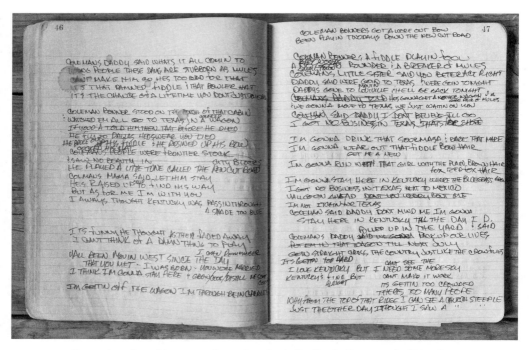

Guy writes about his maternal grandmother's family, the Bonners, in "New Cut Road." Courtesy Paul Whitfield

If that didn't hurt enough, Guy's early single of "Heartbroke" did nothing. But a rising star named Ricky Skaggs, from Emmylou's Hot Band, had sung backup on the session and had fallen in love with the song. Skaggs changed the lyric "pride is a bitch" to "cryin' when you're rich" because he didn't want his parents to hear him cuss on the radio. He put it on his debut Epic Records album *Highways & Heartaches*. After seventeen weeks, Skaggs's recording of "Heartbroke" reached number one on the *Billboard* Hot Country chart.

· · · · ·

Guy's father, Ellis Clark, died on September 1, 1981, after a long illness. "He had a bad heart, and he smoked and drank all his life," Guy says.

> He just got weaker and weaker and deteriorated. We knew he was dying. I was driving from Nashville to Rockport, and I got to Port Lavaca; it's

on the road going down the coast. I was worried and stopped to call my mother. She put my father on the phone and he was very lucid. He said "I'm getting ready to go here. You're going to have to take care of the family. It's your job." We had a conversation that healed any hard feelings that may have been between us. My father was a good man. He had worked in the oil fields when he was in high school but he was not a rough-and-tumble kind of guy. We were never punished or spanked in any way. He was not violent. He was funny. He thought it was real funny to get a big pitcher of water and pour it on you while you were in the shower. That was his best joke. He was as honest as the day is long too.

Ellis was cremated, and the family held a memorial on a fishing boat in Copano Bay. "My mother orchestrated that," Guy says. "We all piled on a sixty- or seventy-foot wooden boat with a big canvas cover on the back to get people out of the sun. My mother organized a ceremony and poured his ashes off the stern."

Ellis Leon Clark in his office, Rockport, Texas. Courtesy Clark family archives

Back at the house after the memorial service, Guy's mother asked if he wanted anything that had belonged to Ellis. As a gift to Ellis, she had taken the Randall knife, which Guy and Victor Torres had broken long ago, to a repair shop in Cuero. There someone had ground the tip down to the correct shape and sharpened and polished the knife, and Guy wanted it. When he returned to Nashville after the funeral, Guy sat down at his workbench to write a poem about Ellis. Guy says:

> I wanted to write something about my father after he died, and the first line I thought was, "My father had a Randall knife." The rest of it was just stream-of-consciousness writing. He did almost cut his thumb off. When he came home from World War II he was shaving off an oak door jamb in a house he was building for us. He put his thumb on the back of the blade and pushed, [and] his thumb slipped and he almost cut his thumb off. I was standing there watching, six years old, blood going everywhere. It was a cathartic thing to write it. I didn't even pick up a guitar. It was a poem. I never thought it would be a song. Never intended for it to be a song. We were getting ready to make a new record, and I had read it to Rodney, and he said, "Why don't you try to make a song of that?" I tried several different melodies and rhythms, but it didn't sound right. I couldn't twist it into a song. One day, I just hit on that thing that I'd used for "Let Him Roll," and it just fell together. It still amazes me that people get it, but they seem to really relate to it. It's a connection with your father that every man has to resolve. It might be more powerful for me since I was his only son. The knife is a metaphor: It's a combat knife, made to kill people. The irony is that it became a symbol of love between us because he wasn't pissed off when I brought it home broken. That was a gift.

*My father had a Randall knife*
*My mother gave it to him*
*When he went off to World War II*
*To save us all from ruin*
*If you've ever held a Randall knife*
*Then you know my father well*

If a better blade was ever made
It was probably forged in hell

My father was a good man
A lawyer by his trade
And only once did I ever see
Him misuse the blade
It almost cut his thumb off
When he took it for a tool
The knife was made for darker things
And you could not bend the rules

He let me take it camping once
On a Boy Scout jamboree
And I broke a half an inch off
Trying to stick it in a tree
I hid it from him for a while
But the knife and he were one
He put it in his bottom drawer
Without a hard word one

There it slept and there it stayed
For twenty some odd years
Sort of like Excalibur
Except waiting for a tear

My father died when I was forty
And I couldn't find a way to cry
Not because I didn't love him
Not because he didn't try
I'd cried for every lesser thing
Whiskey, pain and beauty
But he deserved a better tear
And I was not quite ready

*So we took his ashes out to sea*
*And poured 'em off the stern*
*And threw the roses in the wake*
*Of everything we'd learned*
*When we got back to the house*
*They asked me what I wanted*
*Not the law books, not the watch*
*I need the things he's haunted*

*My hand burned for the Randall knife*
*There in the bottom drawer*
*And I found a tear for my father's life*
*And all that it stood for.*

Guy reunited with Crowell as producer for his third Warner Brothers outing, Better Days. They recorded at Nashville's Bullet Recording Studio A, with additional mixing at Woodland Sound Studios. Vince Gill took the lead on electric and acoustic guitar, with Emory Gordy adding bass and acoustic guitar, Hank DeVito on steel and electric, and Gary Nicholson on acoustic and electric rhythm guitar. Johnny Gimble, now a regular on Guy's records, came in to play fiddle and mandolin. Tony Brown played keyboard, and Larrie Londin was the drummer.

"We recorded 'The Randall Knife' and I was arguing with Rodney to the last that it didn't need a fucking drummer on that song," Guy says. "That was one of the few arguments Rod and I ever got into about music. I told him the song didn't need a drummer, but he wanted it to sound like the rest of the record. I don't care how good Larrie London is. I don't care what the rest of the record sounds like."

"That was not my finest hour as a producer," Crowell says.

I didn't help Guy do what I should've. I love the songs, but I'd love to do it again and record it all around Guy's guitar playing. Because, that record, we moved away from Guy's guitar playing, and I think that was a mistake. The band became the focus, as opposed to Guy's guitar playing, the way he writes the songs and plays them. I think it may have been a

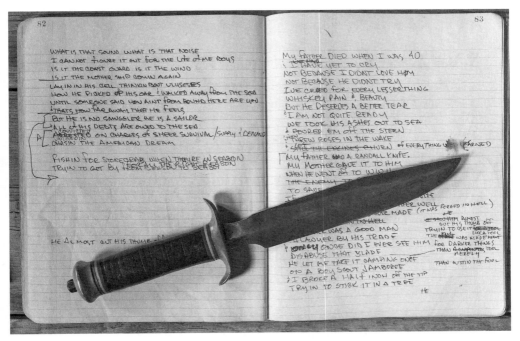

Guy's notebook pages with "The Randall Knife" lyrics and the original knife. Courtesy Paul Whitfield

Guy and the band during *Better Days* recording sessions. *Left to right*: Vince Gill, Rodney Crowell, Emory Gordy, Guy Clark, Gary Nicholson. Courtesy Jim McGuire

turning point for Guy in the methodology of making records—recording tracks with musicians and then having the lead artist come back and dub in vocals. That's not how you want to record Guy Clark, because he's an actor, narrator, and performer. He performs these songs. He's not somebody you want to produce.

Even if Guy wasn't sure about Rodney's production of "The Randall Knife," everyone had a great time recording the *Better Days* album.

"We just giggled the entire time," Crowell says.

One of my favorite stories about *Better Days* is that in the old Woodland studio there was a little side room off the control room, so we went in there to smoke a joint, the three or four of us, and this guy named Glen Snobby, who was a really sweet guy, but straight, by the book. So he happens to walk in when we're in there smoking a big fat joint. There was this spare set of drums in there, really shitty drums, and we're caught red-handed smoking dope in the side room, and so Guy says, 'Glen, I'm paying for this studio. I want to use these drums.' The next day when we come in, they're set up in the middle of the studio. We just fell over laughing. Guy was just trying to divert the attention away from the fact that we were in there getting high.

Thanks to an inside joke during the sessions, the band called themselves the Mud Flaps and even posed with a Lufkin truck mud flap for an inside sleeve photo.

Crowell says, "Guy would play guitar and Larrie London would interpret the way Guy played guitar, the feel of the music, and I said, 'That feels kind of like mud flaps you see on the back of those trucks when you go down the interstate. It's the rhythm of how they're flapping.' So we named the band Guy Clark and the Mud Flaps."

McGuire spent hours photographing the sessions, collecting priceless mementos of Guy, Crowell, and Vince Gill, who was also working on his first record for RCA at the time. On the cover of *Better Days*, Guy is clean-shaven, his hair curling above his collar. He's wearing a white button-up tuxedo shirt and black sport coat and looks more dignified than in any of his previous album cover photos. The only thing out of place is the fake bird perched on his shoulder.

"It was just a joke, a prop to go with the photo," Crowell says. "I mean, getting your picture taken by McGuire is no big deal, but still, you're getting your picture taken, and if you can get a bluebird on your shoulder, that helps. You see that smirk on Guy's face. We thought it was funny. Mr. Bluebird on my shoulder."

Guy wrote all of the songs on *Better Days*, with the exception of the Townes song "No Deal," and a cowrite with Crowell on "Uncertain Texas."

The title track is a song about a strong woman in the mood of "She Ain't Goin' Nowhere." "There's one line in that song that I hated," Guy says.

I worked on it, worked on it, worked on it, and couldn't get it to come out. I went ahead and recorded it anyhow. When that album came out and I was playing the album on the road, it was the first song I dropped because I couldn't bring myself to say, "On a ray of sunshine / She goes dancing out the door." It was just like, "Goddamn, Guy, surely you can come up with something not that goofy." Years later I was playing Australia, and after one show we were hanging out somewhere, and this woman came out and said, "I work at a shelter for battered women, and we use that song for kind of a theme song. We all sing it when we get together and have a meeting." I told her, "You know, I quit doing that song because that one line is just so cheesy that I can't bring myself to sing it anymore." Then I stood right there and fixed it: "She has no fear of flying / And now she's out the door." That was the perfect line. I changed it standing right there in front of her. It finally came to me.

"Supply and Demand" is a true story. "A friend of mine in Florida was a stone crab fisherman, just a stand-up, straight-ahead guy. Really cool," Guy says. "He was living in Steinhatchee, Florida, right in the armpit of Florida. It's traditionally been a smuggling town since the Spanish were there. He wasn't a dope smuggler, but he had an old barn by the water, and these guys he knew talked him into storing these bales of marijuana in the barn. And they got busted. He went to jail instead of turning these guys in. He went to jail for about a year because that's where he was from, that's where his wife's family was from. Had he turned those guys in, he would've been a social outcast for sure. To maintain the life he wanted to live, he did the time for it, and everybody knew it."

The label picked "Homegrown Tomatoes," which Guy always calls "a love song," as the single to market to country radio. They made up packages of "Guy Clark's Homegrown Tomato Seeds" and shipped them off to radio stations and the press. "Homegrown Tomatoes" reached number forty-two on the *Billboard* country chart on July 2, 1983, and then it dropped off.

During the release of *Better Days*, Warner Brothers and Elektra Records were in the middle of a secret merger. In the spring of 1983, Elektra's boss, Jimmy Bowen, was announced as the new head of the Warner/Elektra Nashville division. He kept his Elektra team, fired most of the old Warner staff, and dropped more than half of the artists. Bowen forced his head of A&R, Martha Sharp, to do the dirty work with Guy. They had never met and never worked together, but Sharp was the one to tell Guy he was no longer a Warner Brothers artist.

Guy was okay with the decision. He had recorded five albums with two major labels over the course of eight years and hadn't been satisfied with any of the records since *Old No. 1*. "Some of the songs were badly done, and the records didn't sound like I wanted them to sound," Guy says. "All of those records were done with someone else producing, not me having the ultimate say. They were trying to get me on country radio. It's pretty funny to think about it, but that's what they were shooting for. I see myself as a folksinger and my songs as poetry. When there is too much instrumentation the songs get lost."

It irked Guy to take a band on the road, too. He had never met a drummer until he moved to Nashville, and the full band sound was never his thing.

"I was really tired of trying to keep a band on the road, four or five pieces, and then paying them," Guy says. "I mean, it was just a nightmare to me because it's not what I do. I was doing it because I thought I should. It just wasn't the right thing for me."

At forty-two years old, Guy Clark was finished chasing hits, finished playing with a band, and finished with Brovsky and Free Flow Productions. He had no idea what was next but knew it was time to do things his way.

Susanna Talley circa 1962. Courtesy Guy Clark

Guy created the album artwork for Lightnin' Hopkins's 1968 album *Free Form Patterns*. Courtesy Guy Clark

ABOVE RIGHT: Guy and Susanna Clark with the 1963 double-cab Volkswagen at their house on Chapel Avenue in East Nashville, 1972. Guy bought the truck to replace the Volkswagen bus he drove across the country from L.A. to Nashville. Courtesy Guy Clark

RIGHT: Guy Clark's painting of Skinny Dennis Sanchez, his friend mentioned in the song "L.A. Freeway." Courtesy Guy Clark

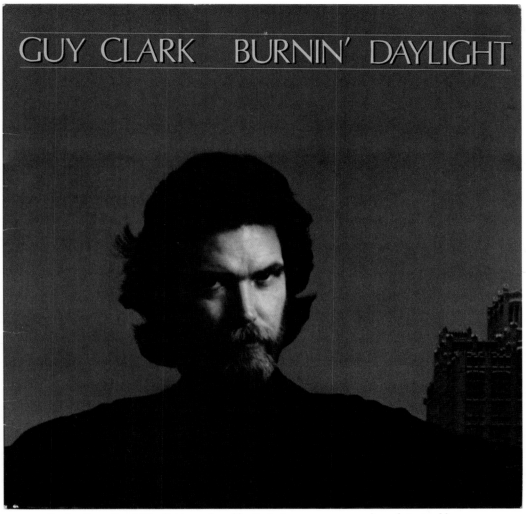

Guy's album *Burnin' Daylight*, produced by Craig Leon, was never released. Instead he recorded *The South Coast of Texas* with Rodney Crowell as producer.

ABOVE LEFT: Guy and Susanna Clark with Susan and Jerry Jeff Walker. Courtesy Guy Clark

LEFT: Guy and Susanna Clark in Nashville in the seventies. Courtesy Guy Clark

Guy Clark at home in Mt. Juliet, Tennessee, circa. 1982. Courtesy Jim McGuire

Susanna Clark. Courtesy Guy Clark

# MONAHANS

Briskly

Words & music by GUY CLARK

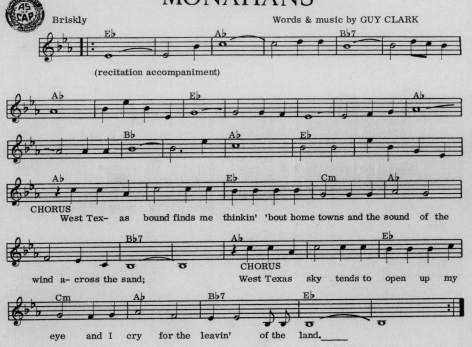

(recitation accompaniment)

**CHORUS**

West Tex- as bound finds me thinkin' 'bout home towns and the sound of the wind a- cross the sand; West Texas sky tends to open up my eye and I cry for the leavin' of the land.____

**CHORUS**

### RECITATION 1
Highway 80 'cross the Texas sand makes a little stop called Monahans;
An old Texas and Pacific Railroad depot, and 'bout twice a year, they have a rodeo;
My grandmother ran a cheap hotel; It was eight bucks a week and you know damn well
That it was nothin' but roughneck and truck drivin' fools;
And no women in your room was the only rule. (chorus)

### RECITATION 2
Old Jack Prigg, he was a friend of mine, he had me swampin' on a drillin' rig when I was nine;
Forty years of cabletoolin' Texas sand, and he never got his butt out of Monahans;
My great aunt Susan used to tell me lies 'bout the color of the grass and the country sky;
Kentucky, she said it with a someday grin; West Texas never let her go again; (chorus)

### RECITATION
It ain't much of a place to say you're from; I don't really know 'cause I left it young;
I used to get back there now and again, but now it's just a case bein' next of kin;
Highway 80 'cross the Texas sand makes a little stop called Monahans;
.An old Texas and Pacific Railroad depot, and 'bout twice a year, they have a rodeo; ;

Sheet music to the song "Monahans," by Guy Clark. Guy has never recorded the song; he says it's terrible. Courtesy Guy Clark

## CHAPTER NINE

# Fresh Voices and Old Friends

On September 17, 1985, a story in the *New York Times* announced the death of country music. "The audience for the Nashville Sound—lovesick laments, tales of marital strife and other plain-spoken lyrics, sung with a rural twang, and often accompanied by arrangements more redolent of Las Vegas than of Southern cotton fields—is dwindling, growing old along with its favorite stars."

Country music *was* changing. Artists with large crossover appeal ruled mainstream country radio. Kenny Rogers, Alabama, Exile, and Hank Williams Jr. led the pack. The countrypolitan era was over, along with the *Urban Cowboy* craze. Even Nashville's favorite outlaw, Waylon Jennings, was selling half as many records.

A new wave of Nashville country-punk blossomed on Music Row thanks to a trio of recent transplants. Jack Emerson formed Praxis International with the motto "Out of the cradle endlessly rocking" (words lifted from Walt Whitman) while majoring in English at Vanderbilt University. Soon after, childhood friend Andy McLenon and Belmont College student Kay Clary joined Emerson at the artist development and management company. Praxis accelerated the careers of Jason and the Nashville Scorchers, John Hiatt, Webb Wilder, Steve Forbert, Sonny Landreth, and the Georgia Satellites. The latter took their southern rock anthem "Keep Your Hands to Yourself" to number two on the *Billboard* Hot 100 in 1986.

"New traditionalists"—Texan George Strait and Kentucky boys Ricky Skaggs and Dwight Yoakam—also won the attention of a younger demographic of listeners. Kids that had grown up on rock 'n' roll invented new rules now that they had jobs as disc jockeys, music journalists, and entertainment executives. These young executives championed artists more similar to the bands of their youth and strived for authenticity in music. Live music became more important than canned studio creations. The *New York Times* was right. The old guard was dying, and it was anyone's guess how things would shake out on Music Row.

Guy Clark quit the country music business and practiced singing his songs in front of a mirror in his basement. He wanted to get back to the basics of putting the lyrics out front. He wanted his poetry to come first, worked to improve his fingerpicking, and designed his own combination flat pick and thumb pick.

"He's missing part of his thumb. He cut it off with a band saw, either in the shipyard or something. This corner of his right thumb is gone," Verlon Thompson says.

He puts on these artificial nails and made this special thumb pick. For a dollar, you can go buy a thumb pick, but they're rigid and he likes a more flexible pick. He'll buy a rigid thumb pick and keep the part that goes over his thumb, but he cuts off the pick part, and then he takes a flat pick, puts a rivet through it and attaches this pick to what's left of the thumb pick. That gives him the clicking, percussive sound. He started off playing nylon string guitars, Spanish stuff, which is pretty much finger-style picking. It just enhances his sound to have those nails; otherwise you're constantly breaking them or snagging them. You have to baby them.

Booking agent Keith Case, a fan since Jerry Jeff Walker recorded "L.A. Freeway," pursued Guy as a client. "I was knocked out by Guy as a songwriter. His images are so strong, like short films that paint a vivid picture of Texas back in the time when he lived there. I wanted to work with him, and he's one of only two artists I chased down to sign." Case booked Townes Van Zandt, too, and sent Guy and Townes on the road together, just the way they did it back in Houston.

The troubadours flipped a coin each night to decide who would take the stage first. Sometimes they'd join each other on songs. Whatever they

Guy Clark and Townes Van Zandt. Courtesy of Guy Clark

felt like doing on the spur of the moment, they did. Case also booked Guy on solo acoustic tours. He went out and played shows by himself, singing his songs and playing guitar with no back up, as he did it in the old days in Houston. Guy traveled to Texas for a run that included Dixie's Bar & Bus Stop in Austin and Poor David's Pub in Dallas. He played across the river from Washington, DC, at the Birchmere, where a critic likened Guy's songs to the film *The Last Picture Show.*

While his records were largely absent from music stores and radio, Guy made a name for himself with his songs. CBS Songs acquired Sunbury Dunbar, and Guy still had his publishing deal. He was obligated to turn in a set number of songs each quarter, but it wasn't the quota that made him stick around. All Guy wanted to do was write songs and be around other songwriters.

The Highwaymen, the supergroup of Johnny Cash, Willie Nelson, Kris Kristofferson, and Waylon Jennings, took "Desperados Waiting for a Train" to number fifteen on the *Billboard* Hot Country chart in late 1985. Ed Bruce and Lynn Anderson recorded Guy's "Fools for Each Other." John Conlee scored a big hit with "The Carpenter," and Johnny Cash covered "Let Him

Roll." Vince Gill's "Oklahoma Borderline," cowritten with Guy and Rodney Crowell, reached number nine on the chart.

Gill was just getting his feet wet as a songwriter, and Guy was a tremendous influence. "To me, he is a painter," Gill says. "His lyrics are familiar to me because I came from that part of the country, too. I can see oyster shell roads . . . all of those things are so real. Every word matters, and you don't waste words. 'They're bound for the Mexican bay of Campeche, and the deckhands are singing *adios Jole Blon.*' That is poetic. God, it just rolls off of you so well. There are no words that are uncomfortable. One of the greatest lessons to try to learn from Guy is how to find a common sense yet elegant way to say it. The visual side of those songs [is] what completely annihilate[s] me."

Another Okie, from the small town of Binger, landed in Nashville as a staff writer for CBS Songs. Verlon Thompson met Guy at the office. They became cowriters and friends after Thompson brought Guy a song he had started called "Indianhead Penny."

"That's when we started having fun, or I did," Thompson says. "I had mentioned that idea to several people, and nobody thought it was worth messing with. Guy immediately grabbed his paper, just like that. What impresses me is the way he uses fewer words to give you more images. With two or three words, you get a complete visual idea in your head about the character and the setting and what's going on. That's what I love about his writing. It's the economy of words. One of the songs that I think illustrates that is 'The Last Gunfighter Ballad.' Man, if you listen to that, it is a three-minute movie. Everything is there."

Rodney Crowell and Rosanne Cash had moved back to Nashville, and Emmylou Harris followed them after her divorce from Brian Ahern. Harris continued to release critically acclaimed albums on the Warner/Reprise label, and Guy and Susanna attended Harris's album release party for *The Ballad of Sally Rose*. For the first time, Harris cowrote (with Paul Kennerley) all of the songs on the album. All along, Guy had encouraged Harris to write her own songs.

"At one point, I had a song that I never ended up finishing," Harris says.

It was a song about a woman—kind of like "Your Good Girl's Gonna Go Bad." The idea was that she was going to get even with this guy, but it was obvious that he was the villain of the song. We were working on it, and at one point Guy said, "I don't like to write songs where everybody's not equal." He's very democratic. He doesn't want to pin the blame on anybody. He sees the whole story leading up to it and beyond. We're all human, and we all have our faults. You can't say, "You win and you lose." That really impressed me. I went back and thought about all of Guy's songs and characters he writes about, like "Let Him Roll" and the prostitute that the old guy was in love with. It's just a sad tragedy of two people who maybe could've found happiness. There's no judgment in Guy's songs. He writes with a great deal of care about everyone, but he doesn't give anybody a free pass either.

Guy had attended or played the Kerrville Folk Festival in Texas every year since 1975. Rod Kennedy, who had owned the Chequered Flag (later Castle Creek) folk club and had founded the Zilker Park music festival in Austin, started Kerrville in a 1,200-seat auditorium in the small Hill Country town. Within a couple of years, the festival group purchased sixty acres of land outside of town and named it Quiet Valley Ranch. By the 1980s, more than twenty thousand people descended on the ranch each May and June to take part in the eighteen-day festival. Kerrville attracts roots musicians, songwriters, and fans from all over the world. Songwriters are revered, and many of today's most respected writers played at Kerrville before everyone knew their names.

At Kerrville in 1986, Guy ran into Lubbock native and multifaceted artist Terry Allen, who became a close friend. "I recall meeting Guy, and then memory fades fast after we met, but it was at Kerrville at the folk festival at the YO Ranch Hotel," Allen says.

He was in the lobby, and we were both taking the shuttle to the stage. Guy had played, I think, the day before and was hanging around for his check. I was playing the next day. We hit it off in the van, just talking to each other, and ended up hanging out. Peter, Paul and Mary were playing, and we were a little too close to the stage and a little too rowdy because the guy that ran the thing got really, really pissed off at us. We were drinking a lot and carrying on a lot. It was all his fault, pretty much. There was a full moon that night. It's like thousands of hippies out there, stoned, just listening to "Puff, the Magic Dragon." There was a moon, and one cloud came out of nowhere, and, just like a claw, it just covered the moon. For some reason, Guy and I got so tickled seeing that, and we fell apart on the side of the stage. Peter and Paul were very upset with it, but Mary, she laughed at us. I was basically banned from then on. We just had a real good time that night and then sort of crossing tracks over the years. Every time we saw each other we got friendlier.

The Ballad Tree is a beloved tradition at Kerrville. Each weekend during the festival, a songwriter hosts a song swap under a sweeping live oak tree on a beautiful piece of the ranch called Chapel Hill. The same year he met Terry Allen, Guy hosted the Ballad Tree and spotted a young writer named Buddy Mondlock.

"I had seen Guy play at a place called Holstein's in Chicago, and I was just blown away," Mondlock says. "Like you've heard a million times, the first time someone hears Guy Clark do a set or hears one of his records, it's like, 'Oh my god, this is the best songwriter I've ever heard.' I was particularly struck by that line in 'Old Time Feeling' about an old gray cat in winter staying close to the wall. With a few words, he just nailed the complete spectrum of feeling."

Mondlock signed up to sing at the Ballad Tree so he could meet Guy and maybe shake his hand. "A bunch of people played and I was toward the end and I played a song called 'No Choice.' Afterward, I was just kind of standing around talking to a friend, and I saw Guy Clark walking in my direction," he says.

I was looking over my shoulder to see where he might be going, and he stopped in front of me and said, "Hey, I really liked that song you just played. Do you have a tape of that?" I said, "Well, yeah. I do. That's my tent right over there. Don't move, I'm going to go over and get you a tape." I came back with a cassette I had done earlier that year on a friend's little four-track. It had that one and a couple other songs on it. I thought: *That's the coolest thing that's ever going to happen to me. Guy Clark is going to listen to a song of mine, and he liked what I sang.* I went on with the rest of the festival and had a great time. Kerrville just blew my mind too. It was just, it was a great place to be and it was a perfect fit for me. I went home, and a week later I was coming into my apartment in Chicago with a basket full of laundry. I could see this little light blinking on my answering machine. I hit the play button: "Hey, Buddy. It's Guy Clark in Nashville. I really liked your song, and I liked the other ones too. Give me a call sometime." Holy shit! After I got done doing backflips in the kitchen I called him, and we talked for a minute. He said, "Well, what do you want to do?" I said, "I just want to keep making music and writing songs and trying to figure out how to make a living and a life out of that." He said, "Okay, well, let's see if we can get you in the music business."

"I heard him at the Ballad Tree, and he was so good I just kept my eye on him," Guy says. He wrote some great songs. 'The Cats of the Colosseum' is about the Colosseum in Rome that is in disrepair and full of cats. Buddy writes about the kids playing music at the Colosseum in the middle of the night. And I thought that was so good."

As Mondlock sent him more songs, Guy made mixtapes of Mondlock's work and began to pass them around Nashville. He handed out tapes to music publishers, folks at the performing rights organization ASCAP, friends, and anyone he thought should hear good songs. In turn, Nashville music executives began to call Mondlock, starting with producer Jim Rooney.

"He was one of the first people that called me, and he said, 'Hey, Guy Clark gave me this tape, and I thought it was really interesting. What are you up to?' I told him I was just starting to tour and playing clubs in Chicago," Mondlock says.

Jim said, "Well, I'm coming up to Chicago. I want to go to a Cubs game. You want to go with me?" So Rooney and I had a great afternoon going to see the Cubs play in Chicago. A little while later, Bob Doyle from ASCAP called me. Bob said Guy had given him a tape, and on that particular tape was a song I wrote called "The Kid," and that one really struck Bob. We talked a few times, and finally he said, "Well, do you ever think you might come down here to Nashville?" I said, "Well, yeah, I've been thinking about it now. I never used to think about it before." My picture of Nashville was just this stereotypical Dolly Parton and rhinestones and all that stuff. I didn't really feel any affinity toward that commercial Nashville glitz. That was my impression of Nashville, so I thought there was nothing for me there. But Bob said, "Well, you should come and check it out. It's a really cool place, and songwriting is really what it's all about here more than anything else."

Doyle offered Mondlock his spare bedroom. On Mondlock's first trip to Nashville, he signed with ASCAP, visited Guy over at CBS Songs, and was introduced to Emmylou Harris at a reception at the Country Music Hall of Fame.

"It was just so cool. I was like a kid with my eyes wide open," Mondlock says. "I met all the people at CBS Songs. It's just this little house with a few offices and writing rooms in it, really homey and comfortable, and Guy was there, and everybody's being nice. I thought it was really cool. I remember watching Guy do a demo session in the little basement studio next door. It was not at all what I was picturing Nashville to be."

By the time Mondlock signed his publishing deal, SBK Entertainment had purchased CBS Songs, but it didn't matter. Thanks to Guy Clark, Buddy Mondlock was now a professional songwriter. Within a few years, his songs would be recorded by Joan Baez, Nanci Griffith, Peter, Paul and Mary, and country superstar Garth Brooks.

Maybe the most well-known beneficiary of Guy's generosity is fellow Texan Lyle Lovett, who performed at Kerrville early in his career. Lovett says,

I was a fan of Guy's. He was one of my songwriting heroes. In 1980, I made the cut to be in the New Folk contest at the Kerrville Folk Festival. They picked tapes out of all the ones Rod Kennedy would get. They'd pick forty contestants to pick two songs. It was very democratic. They wouldn't pick a winner, they'd pick six finalists. From the six finalists, they'd pick two people to come back to play the main stage. I made that forty, and I was excited because one of the judges was Guy Clark. I thought: *As much as I like Guy, this must be a good sign.* I was still in school [at Texas A&M] and living in College Station and trying to play as much as I could. I didn't make the six finalists or the two uber-finalists.

Lovett didn't meet Guy in 1980, but by the middle of the decade Guy would become his biggest champion. Lovett says,

In 1984, I went to Nashville for the first time. My dad and mom always worked for Exxon. My dad's boss's son had gone to school at MTSU [Middle Tennessee State University] in Murfreesboro and studied in the music program. He made some calls for me and set up meetings all over town in Nashville. I had copyrighted some of my songs, and he set me up a meeting at CBS Songs with a college buddy of his named Sam Ramage. I said, "I know Guy Clark is a writer here, and if there's any way you could give him a tape, I'd be really honored." He said, "I'll see if I can give it to Guy." After that trip, I'd go to Nashville every four or six weeks to just make the rounds and talk to people and see if I could stir up any interest in my songs. I'd meet somebody, and they'd say: "Oh yeah, Guy Clark told me about you." I'd think: *That can't be. Something's wrong.* Then I'd meet someone else and they'd say: "Guy Clark gave me your tape." I'd think: *This is impossible.* Turns out Sam did give Guy my tape. I hadn't met Guy and didn't meet him those years before in Kerrville. He was just my strongest advocate.

"I listened to that tape every day for weeks. It was the best thing I'd heard in years," Guy says. "I thought everyone should hear it. That's the same way I felt about Buddy Mondlock's songs."

MCA Records A&R vice president Tony Brown had toured with Elvis, Rosanne Cash, and Emmylou Harris. He had played keyboards on Guy's *Better Days* album and was a sought-after session musician before RCA hired him for their A&R department. He signed the band Alabama and Vince Gill, among others, to RCA. When Jimmy Bowen took over MCA Records in 1984, he hired Brown to manage A&R. Perhaps in part from all the music Emmylou Harris had turned him on to during late-night bus runs while he was in her Hot Band, Brown had more eclectic tastes than many A&R people in Music City. In some circles, he was thought to be a little too radical for country music. Guy ran into Brown at lunch one day and slipped him a cassette tape of Lyle Lovett's songs. Almost immediately, Brown signed Lovett to MCA and produced Lovett's eponymous 1986 album.

"I know if it hadn't been for Guy Clark putting in a word for me with the people I eventually met and worked with, they wouldn't have had as much confidence in the decision to work with me," Lovett says. "I really feel like it was because of Guy Clark that I have a career. It's because of Guy that I was able to get signed to a label."

Brown also recruited Steve Earle for MCA and produced Earle's essential *Guitar Town* record the same year. He signed traditional singer Patty Loveless and Texan Nanci Griffith, who had been on Rounder making folkier-sounding records. Griffith issued *Lone Star State of Mind*, produced by Brown in 1987. Over at Warner Brothers, Dwight Yoakam made waves in the progressive landscape with *Guitars, Cadillacs, Etc., Etc.*, and newcomer Randy Travis's *Storms of Life* was about to make him a huge star. Left-of-center Nashville music circles still refer to this period as "the Great Credibility Scare."

Rob Bleetstein was the music director for progressive country radio station KHIP-FM near Santa Cruz, California, when he met Guy Clark in 1986. Bleetstein had gotten his start at the now defunct KFAT-FM in nearby Gilroy. "It was these renegade people smoking dope and playing George Jones and Bob Wills and Eric Clapton and the Grateful Dead all at the same time," Bleetstein says.

It wasn't just a radio station, it was a lifestyle. It was popular with artists, and they knew about it. Rodney and Rosanne would go there. Emmylou would go there when Tony Brown was in her band. They'd be on their knees pulling out records and DJ-ing. It was a real thing. When I was in college doing radio at San Jose State, KFAT was my thing, and when I moved to Santa Cruz, living the KFAT lifestyle and right when I finished college, they go off the air. Then at the beginning of 1985 these DJs reemerged at KHIP in Hollister, which is the next town over from Gilroy. If you can't be FAT you can be HIP. I drove down there the first day and said I am FAT and I'm not leaving here until I have a job. I started doing overnights and working in the office, which was basically rolling people's joints. Within a month of that I saw Dwight Yoakam open for Los Lobos in Santa Cruz, and I walk up to him after his set and say: "You are fuckin' it, man. We've got this radio station down the road and you've got to come by." He wasn't even signed to Warner yet, but we had a hand in breaking him. I became a music director within weeks and helped educate all these KFAT DJs on what was new and hip out there. Guy was a huge part of that. He and Townes played together at O. T. Price's Music Hall in Santa Cruz, and Guy came over to the station.

Guy invited Bleetstein to visit him in Nashville sometime. Bleetstein took him up on the offer and showed up for songwriter Harlan Howard's annual birthday bash and concert in the BMI parking lot.

"All my heroes were there," Bleetstein says.

But that was extremely misleading because that didn't happen every day or every week or every month, especially in 1986. Guy and Susanna took me out to dinner, and he just laid it on the line for me: this is what this place is about, this is what you can and can't do. The thing you are involved in, this whole part of the music business you're in is small, and you care about it, and we care about it, but everyone for miles around does not care. I'm young and leftist, and I'm thinking we're going to change the world, you know. Tony Brown is running MCA with Lyle Lovett, Steve Earle, Nanci Griffith. Rosanne was queen and Rodney was about to become king. I'm like, "Yeah, we're going to take over and reclaim country music."

During the Great Credibility Scare, the only recording studio Guy spent any time in was the tiny publishing company workshop where he laid down demos so other artists could hear his songs. Miles Wilkinson, who had worked as an engineer with Brian Ahern in his mobile recording studio, built the demo studio with help from Guy and Verlon Thompson.

"Guy called me about the studio, so I met him over at CBS Songs and we walked across the alley and into a dark, damp, dingy basement and found odds and ends of some old, unused recording equipment," Wilkinson says. "Most of it was crap and run down, but the prize was some amazing vintage Neumann U67 tubes and a few other great mics. After this inspection, Guy asked me if he thought I could put together a demo studio with this equipment. In a few weeks, CBS Songs had a very simple and basic eight-track demo studio in that same basement. After we got it running, several of the other CBS Songs writers started using the studio, with me engineering."

When he wasn't working (and even sometimes when he was), Guy cut loose and drank large quantities of alcohol, smoked a ton of weed, and spent significant money on cocaine. Coke was the hot drug of the 1980s, and Guy loved it. "I remember this drag racer asking us if we wanted to do some cocaine at the old Exit/In," Crowell says. "We go out to the back of his car. He opens up the back of his Cadillac, and he's got five pounds. We were in trouble there for a couple days. Or I was. I didn't have Guy's stamina. I could go for a little while, and then I'd have to bow out. He'd keep going."

While drunk and stoned, Guy and Susanna argued, and it made for a difficult home life.

Guy watches Susanna work on a painting. Mt. Juliet, Tennessee, circa 1980.

More than a decade later, Susanna still grieved for Bunny and when things got tough at home, she contemplated suicide. Around this time she wrote in her journal:

It'll all be over soon. I won't have to worry about a cheating man and a lying tongue or where my next meal is coming from. I won't have to worry about right or wrong. Soon it will all be over, won't take too long. Won't have to worry about a dying father or a mother grown cold. Won't have to worry about making a rhyme. I will be free and my spirit all mine.

Guy and Susanna each tried rehab—Guy at the Betty Ford Clinic in Rancho Mirage, California. It didn't stick for either of them. "The Betty Ford era," Rodney Crowell says. "Johnny Cash started it. Cash went to Betty Ford first. The next thing you know Rosanne is in treatment somewhere outside Georgia, and then Guy's off to Betty Ford. It was like a Shirley MacLaine book at the time—everybody went to see some psychic. I can't be the judge of it. I just know it was fashionable to go to rehab."

Crowell and Rosanne Cash also had marital problems, in no small part because of Crowell's drug use and the time he spent with Guy and Susanna. "I was having multiple children then," Crowell says. "I had a house full of little girls. Those years from '83 to '86 were kind of crunched for me. I was pretty miserable. I needed to get present because I was a father, and I had active kids and a marriage that was eventually going to fall apart and had probably already started. I just remember dinners in restaurants in Nashville. Drinking a lot of wine. Ordering cocaine from a dealer over on Music Row. At some point, that stopped being fun. It had a really negative effect on me. I had to pull away from it because it just put me in anything but a creative space. I don't recall having any creativity with that. All of the debris that collects around it is not conducive to doing good work. That's what became really obvious to me. I'm not doing any good work."

Rodney got clean and landed a new deal with Columbia Records for his 1986 album *Street Language*, followed by 1988's *Diamonds and Dirt*, and 1989's *Keys to the Highway*, which includes "I Guess We've Been Together

Too Long," written with Guy. From *Diamonds and Dirt*, Crowell scored five number one hit songs: "It's Such a Small World," his duet with Rosanne; "I Couldn't Leave You If I Tried"; "After All"; the Harlan Howard–penned "Above and Beyond"; and "She's Crazy for Leaving," written with Guy.

"The eighties were strange. It was really pretentious," Crowell says. "Guy was never into that pretense. If he felt like he needed to be part of a trend, you couldn't see it. And if he did feel it, my guess is that he knew himself well enough:

> "That ain't me. I'm not going there. You guys can do it if you want, but you look silly to me," Guy said. And I concur. In hindsight, I concur. Guy and I kind of got estranged for a while when I stopped doing drugs altogether. I just stopped on the dime. Part of that program, they tell you to change your friends. It's one regret I've had about that twelve-step program. I followed those directions, and I distanced myself from Guy and Susanna. Also, during that period I had the *Diamonds and Dirt* record, and I was gone all the time. Got full of myself. Was just an asshole. I was really the guy who stepped out. I have regret, because Guy didn't change—I did. Guy stayed the same. I know it hurt him. I've regretted that. I was a really shitty friend for five, six years there.

In 1988, country singer Steve Wariner had a number two hit with "Baby I'm Yours," cowritten with Guy. Texas swing band Asleep at the Wheel recorded Guy's "Blowin' Like a Bandit." Tony Brown wooed Vince Gill over to MCA, and Gill recorded *When I Call Your Name*, an album that included Guy's "Rita Ballou" and "Sight For Sore Eyes," a song Gill wrote with Guy.

More and more, Guy grew comfortable with cowriting. He was open-minded and willing to explore new partnerships. He wrote with others at CBS Songs and writers from different publishing companies. "I really enjoy the nuts and bolts of writing. Probably my weakest link as I've gotten older is dialing up the ideas," Guy says. "It's not that my ideas aren't good; it's just that I don't see them like I see other people's. It's a strange thing. I'll get so far into someone else's three-line idea, when I have probably a hundred times better stuff here and can't focus like that on it."

Guy was proud of the songs in his catalog, enjoyed his high profile as a writer, and was thrilled that artists sought out songs. He got to thinking it might be time to record again. Instead of going out to find a label deal, Guy decided to lay down some tracks in the demo studio he had built with Miles Wilkinson.

For the first time, Guy was in control in the studio. He changed his recording style to complement the verses, parsing sparse musical arrangements to give the words more weight and put the vocals out front.

"Guy always had definite ideas of what he wanted on his recordings," Wilkinson says.

The first thing he said to me was, "I've got two rules: no reverb and no fades." No reverb meant we would not be adding reverb or echo or delays to either his voice or any other instrument. Very dry. And no fades. Each song had to end with the musicians coming to a conclusion on their own, instead of having them play on and the engineer slowly pulling the master mix fader down to fade the song out. Along with this, he insisted that the lead vocal be very up-front and predominate in the mix. Possibly because of bad past experiences, Guy wanted the vocals way up front. On the first CD we made together, he had me mix his voice so loud that when you listened in a car the road noise would wipe out all the accompanying music. You heard nothing but the voice. Once I demonstrated this to Guy and showed him that there was a way to keep his vocal front and center and still hear the music he relented and never complained about his vocal levels again. I learned from Guy how to produce in a way that supported not only the singer but, most importantly, the story. It was through Guy Clark that I developed an organic approach to music production.

With Wilkinson at the controls, Guy came in each day and played a set of songs without stopping to fix anything. He played his songs one after the other, over and over, and ran through them for several days until he got them recorded in a way that pleased him. It was only then that Guy called in other musicians and overdubbed their parts—guitar, mandolin, bass, and a little percussion but no big rock 'n' roll drums.

Guy invited Verlon Thompson to play on the record. "One day he said, 'Man, come down here and play something on this thing.' It was real spur-of-the-moment," Thompson says. "One thing led to another, and that's where it all took off. At the time, I didn't know if he was just doing a demo or if it was really going to be a record. We were doing stuff like, instead of a kick drum, we'd take the microphone and put a towel over it and hit it. We got on this experimental thing, making a record in a different way. We had fun doing it."

With the understated production, for the first time since *Old No. 1*, the songs took a starring role. "It was the first time I finally got to make the record I've always wanted to make, with an acoustic approach and no drums," Guy says. "I quit trying to please everyone else in the room and only worried about pleasing myself."

"Guy always entered the studio like a larger-than-life Texas gentleman. Gently upbeat, confident and positive, with a smile on his face but in a supremely dignified way," Wilkinson says.

He had a Clark Gable [in] *Gone with the Wind* style of dignity. He knew his songs were good, but there was no conceit to it. And he just made everyone glad to be there. Working with Guy was often like he was holding court, because Guy was always bigger than life. He would walk into the studio, and the room was filled with dignity. He'd be polite, charming, sweet, and was there to take care of business. And another of Guy Clark's hard recording rules: no couch in the control room. Guy said that a studio was for working, not lounging or sleeping. So we never had a couch. Usually about three-quarters of the way through the session, after he had done his part, things would loosen up. Perhaps some whiskey would be brought out. This was a frequent pattern, take care of business, work hard and [be] diligent, and then celebrate.

Guy titled the album *Old Friends*, the same as the title of a song he wrote with Susanna and Richard Dobson. "Susanna and I had been writing songs, and there were a couple that Guy seemed interested in," Dobson says. "Of course, we weren't going to turn down his help. Susanna and I had started on 'Old Friends,' and we had the chorus, pretty much. I went home that night and then talked to them on the phone later that evening. Guy had already gone in and started writing the verses. Susanna and I were really just responsible for the chorus, and Guy wrote the rest."

Other cowrites on *Old Friends* include "Heavy Metal," a song about a D10 Caterpillar tractor, written with Jim McBride; "Hands," a three-way collaboration with Verlon Thompson and Joe Henry; and "Immigrant Eyes," with Roger Murrah. Guy wrote "Watermelon Dream" and "Doctor Good Doctor" by himself. He'd always loved Van Zandt's "To Live Is to Fly," and he recorded it here with the lyrics rearranged. "Steve Earle gets so pissed at me for changing Townes's lyrics," Guy says. "But 'Days up and down they come, like rain on a conga drum' should be the first line to that song, and that's the way I sing it."

Guy had been talking about recording Joe Ely's "Indian Cowboy" since the first time he'd heard Ely play it in the 1970s. Ely was a Lubbock native, friend of Terry Allen's, and part of a Texas roots band called the Flatlanders with fellow writers Jimmie Dale Gilmore and Butch Hancock. "I'd been away from Lubbock a while and came back just as Ringling Brothers was setting up the circus over at Texas Tech, putting up a tent for their elephants," Ely says.

I got hired on the spot; somebody just gave me a sledgehammer and said "Go help those guys." I stayed with them for a couple of months, on every stop in Texas, New Mexico, and Oklahoma. It was hard work and low wages and too much romance, and everything was over the top. The song is about a big rainstorm coming up through the tent. A lot of the horses and elephants broke away, and a couple of them got loose. It was an actual event, but I painted it a little differently. I never wrote it down. It was not written in any notebook. I wrote it in my head while I was shoveling hay. A couple of months after I left the circus, I ran into Guy at someone's house. I remember how awestruck I was with Guy's songs. You can listen to a song on the record player or the radio, but when you listen to it firsthand sitting in a room, that song is magnified about a million times. We started playing songs back and forth, and it just went all night long. About sunrise, I just about had it. I said, "I got one more song," and I played "Indian Cowboy." That was the first time I had played it for anyone. Guy said something like, "Would you play that again?" He grabbed a little old cassette recorder. I played it again, and then I didn't even think about that song.

Ely had no idea that Guy remembered the song. He was driving around
Austin listening to public radio when Guy's recording of "Indian Cowboy"
came on. "It took me a minute to even realize it was my song," Ely says. "I
was touched and flattered. Then I headed straight to Waterloo Records to
get a copy of the album."

*If you ever go out to the circus*
*Where the Wallendas walk on the wire*
*I'll tell you a tale to remember*
*When the white horses leap rings of fire*

*It was a cold night in Oklahoma*
*The show was about to begin*
*The animals they were all restless*
*When the star pony broke from her pen*

*Now she was a mare of high spirit*
*Like a whore on a Saturday night*
*Kickin' and buckin' past the men who were brushin'*
*The elephants lyin' on their sides*

*Close to the tents set some lanterns*
*Dangerously next to the hay*
*That mare headed straight for those lanterns*
*Some fool had put there by mistake*

*Up stepped some Indian Cowboy*
*His lasso he whirled through the air*
*In the full dead middle of danger*
*He roped that runaway mare*

*The elephants raised up their trumpets*
*Two of them broke from their chains*
*Stampeded that Indian cowboy*
*Who had saved the Big Top from flames*

*So if you ever go out to the circus*
*Where the Wallendas walk on the wire*
*Remember that Indian Cowboy*
*When the white horses leap rings of fire*

Through the CBS Songs merger, Guy and Susanna met Richard Leigh. Leigh had won a Grammy in 1978 for writing "Don't It Make My Brown Eyes Blue," a song about a dog, according to Leigh, and a huge hit for country singer Crystal Gayle. "I came in the front door at CBS Songs one day and to my left was this beautiful lady," Leigh says.

It was Susanna on the couch next to the fireplace. She glanced up at me, and I glanced down at her, and as I walked to the receptionist I heard her say something like, "Who's that?" And somebody said, "That's Richard Leigh." And she just said something sweet. I can't remember what it was. So I walked back in there and introduced myself. I had been visiting with Guy from time to time down at his little office, and I had been completely charmed by him. His honest approach to songwriting blew my mind and changed my mind about my own songs too. I became friends with Susanna, and she was so, so witty. She's one of the brightest people anyone would ever meet. She was so fun, and we just hit it off. We'd go to lunch all the time. And we'd write, but mostly we just loved to talk and philosophize and just be friends. I was transformed by those meetings with Susanna and Guy. The influence of hanging around such an ordained writer as Guy made me think that a lot of my songs were very superficial and kind of unimportant by comparison. I started thinking about putting more of me in my own songs. It was a philosophy that I adopted. I just thought: if you write a song and you put a lot of detail and honesty into it, the money will follow. We do it for a living, but do it to make a difference, not a dollar. Guy never said those words, but that was always the feeling I got. I admired him for that.

Leigh and Guy wrote "All Through Throwing Good Love after Bad," which Guy recorded for *Old Friends*. "He saved that song," Leigh says. "I had it like a Ray Charles song. Real slow and bluesy. And we wrote it that way. I really liked the lyric. He went home and made it like [a] bluegrass thing, Texas deal. And I said, 'Oh, man. It's so much better.'"

"It's always been one of my favorite songs," Guy says. "We wrote it as a 6/8 Ray Charles waltz, and I just couldn't do it. I can't sing like that. There's something musically about songs in 6/8 that translate immediately to 4/4. It's just easy to do. I changed it to that bluegrass feel. Tammy Wynette recorded it in 6/8 time."

Leigh and Susanna wrote "Come from the Heart," a song that would change both of their lives. The chorus goes:

> You've got to sing like you don't need the money
> Love like you'll never get hurt
> You've got to dance like nobody's watching
> It's gotta come from the heart if you want it to work.

"That song couldn't have been written with anybody but Susanna Clark," Leigh says. "I mean, she's the only woman that would pull something like that out of both of us. It's just her. Just magic."

"I honestly believe there are only two emotions—fear and love," Susanna told Louise O'Connor in 1991. "I think fear takes many forms. It can take the form of anger. It can take the form of rage. It can take the form of a lot of self-hurt. The opposite of fear is love, and we all have this love inside us. And if we're not scared, we show it. That's how we got the line 'Love like you'll never get hurt.' The greatest protection in the world is love. That's the greatest armor you can wear is love—it's not really armor, it's total vulnerability. When the fear is relinquished, the only thing we've got is love."

"Come from the Heart" was recorded first by Don Williams on his 1987 album Traces. About the time Guy tracked it for Old Friends, country artist Kathy Mattea also recorded the song for her 1989 album Willow in the Wind. Mattea's single of the song climbed to number one on Billboard's Hot Country chart. But she almost didn't pick up the song because of Don Williams's album.

"It's a funny story, actually," Mattea says.

I was in Allen Reynolds's listening room at the studio. We were listening through songs and talking about the next album, and the receptionist buzzed in to say it was my manager, Bob Titley, on the phone. Bob said, "I have a song you need to hear, but you can't have it. I'm coming over right now." He played the song, and I looked at him and threw out a few cuss words, jokingly, but only partly. I can still remember the feeling that came over me at the end of the first chorus. I'm always looking for a song that makes me react like that. I think it was the universal theme—something in me resonated with the truth of the song. And also, the sheer joy of it struck me too. I instantly fell in love with the song, but it was on hold for Don Williams, and that meant I couldn't touch it. How could you let me know this song exists and tell me I can't have it? That's just mean. So I waited. I watched. I made my album without the song. Eventually Don Williams's album came out. I pored over every review I could find. No one mentioned the song. It didn't seem like they were thinking of releasing it as a single. I held my breath. When it came time to start thinking about my next album, I started with that song. After a song has been recorded once, there [are] no more licensing hoops to jump through—it's fair game for anyone. So I jumped on it. When it was time to learn the song for the album, we called Guy and had him come over to the studio and play it for us. We knew he'd been doing it in his shows and we wanted a different perspective on it. It was a sweet way to spend the afternoon.

"I had a giant fight with my publishing company when they gave the song to Don Williams first," Susanna says. "Kathy was new, but I wanted her to have the song. I knew she was good. Richard and I agreed we wanted to give it to Kathy, but the publisher had the last legal word on it. So they give it to Don. Well, Don is mad at his label. He was making a shit record on purpose. I was so furious. Well, Kathy's album went platinum. It was a huge song for her. The rest is history."

Once Guy finished the bare bones production of *Old Friends*, it was time to decide how to get it out to the people. He discussed it with Keith Case, and they both thought of Sugar Hill Records, a small independent roots music label based in Durham, North Carolina, owned by entrepreneur Barry Poss. It was a gutsy move at a time when Rodney Crowell was having mega-success at country radio with slickly produced albums. Major label country-pop artists including Reba McEntire, the Judds, Eddie Rabbitt, Restless Heart, Alabama, Steve Wariner, and Garth Brooks rode the wave of the Urban Cowboy era into the next decade; Guy moved in the opposite direction. Case called Poss at Sugar Hill to see if he might be interested.

"I'd been listening to Guy since the early RCA albums and I had seen him perform over the years at festivals and clubs," Poss says.

> I didn't know the man yet, but from the start you can't miss that Guy is a striking figure in so many ways. Physically he casts this powerful presence. He's tall. He's ruggedly handsome. He's got a strong bearing. He's one of these guys that doesn't need to work at making his presence felt; it just is. And then those songs. The gorgeous poetry. He understands that you can convey emotional power through a few perfectly crafted lines. That is what struck me about him in the beginning. He creates these little intimate, personal narratives that speak to a larger landscape. He may be writing about a knife or a boat or a dance or a road or a hooker or even a tomato, but they're also about the human condition and all its complexities and flaws. They're just beautiful, powerful poems of life. I don't think I can convey his importance as elegantly and articulately as the man deserves, so simply put: His work matters. To me, to his audiences, to music, to understanding life, all of that.

As a label, Sugar Hill enjoyed a distinct identity, and Poss was well known for his impeccable taste in music. Sugar Hill had a prestigious roster of artists. "Guy not only fit the aesthetic at Sugar Hill, he defined it for us," Poss says.

> That first record was a one-off. Normally it wasn't my practice to do one-offs, but the opportunity to have a Guy album was just too hard to resist. And I loved the idea for the album. It would be stripped down. It would be focused. It would be direct. The songs were the key. They would be front and center and have supportive arrangements. Not the other way around, which I think was the problem with some of the early records.

In November 1988, Sugar Hill Records released *Old Friends*. Guy felt so strongly about this album that the cover is a self-portrait painting. He had spent hours

Guy set up his camera to take this self-portrait, created a painting of it, and used the painting as cover art for his *Old Friends* album. Courtesy Guy Clark

setting up a camera with a timer in his home workshop. Once the camera was set, Guy moved to the other side of the table and posed casually for the shot. He insisted on taking photographs of Rodney Crowell using the same setup. Then he created paintings of both photos. He titled them *Hands* and *Knees*, and the paintings hang next to each other in his house to this day.

Guy used the painting of himself on the cover of *Old Friends*, and it made a statement. The Sugar Hill press release put it into words: "Listening to *Old Friends* is like a wonderfully intimate visit with old picking friends on a Sunday evening in Guy Clark's living room. His guests include singers Emmylou Harris, Rodney Crowell & Rosanne Cash, fiddle/mandolin wizard Sam Bush, and guitarist Vince Gill, but the evening belongs to Guy, the singer and his songs. Guy Clark is a master of condensing the very deepest and most powerful feelings into a few simple words."

As Sugar Hill released *Old Friends*, Guy's lawyer Ken Levitan traveled to Europe with his management client Nanci Griffith. Guy had handed Levitan a cassette of *Old Friends* before the trip. At a dinner in Dublin, Bono, the lead

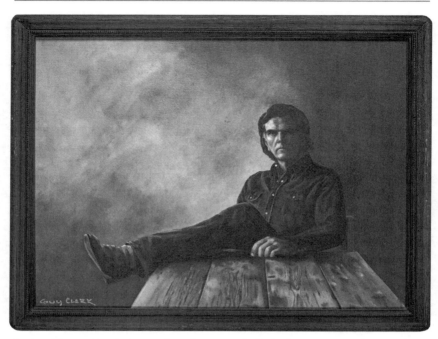

Guy's self-portrait painting used on the cover of *Old Friends*. Courtesy Paul Whitfield

singer of rock band U2, asked Ken if he knew any good music in Nashville. "I ran up to my room and got Guy's cassette to give to him," Levitan says. "The next day I got a call from a guy named Dave Pennyfather who worked for MCA but also ran U2's label, Mother Records. He said Bono just loved the record and wanted to put it out. I came back to the states and told Guy, 'U2's label in Europe wants to put out your record.' Guy says: 'Who's U2?' Of course, at the time they were one of the biggest bands in the world, and Mother Records was a formidable little label in Ireland."

Now that Guy had a record out, he stepped up his tour dates. He played with Townes at McCabe's Guitar Shop in Santa Monica and the Great American Music Hall and Sacred Grounds Coffee House in San Francisco. They played the Birchmere in Alexandria, Virginia, with Robert Earl Keen as the opener.

In early 1989 Guy toured Australia, New Zealand, England, Scotland, and Ireland and returned to the states in time for Jerry Jeff Walker's forty-seventh birthday bash in Austin on March 18, followed by dates at the Cactus Cafe,

Leon Springs Café in San Antonio, and Poor David's Pub in Dallas. In May, Guy and Townes played the Bottom Line in New York City before Guy flew to Frutigen, Switzerland, for two performances at the Marlboro-sponsored International Singer/Songwriter Festival. He returned to Texas for two nights at the Chisholm Trail Roundup Days in Fort Worth, then headed to Canada for a run that included the Edmonton Folk Festival.

In the fall of 1989, Guy partnered with Joe Ely, Lyle Lovett, and John Hiatt for a songwriting workshop, sponsored by Marlboro, back at the Bottom Line. It was the beginning of what would become a many-years-long partnership with Lovett, Ely, and Hiatt as they took their acoustic song swap show on the road.

As Guy toured the world playing songs from *Old Friends*, Kathy Mattea's version of "Come from the Heart" grew to be a smash record. "It was a big record and it was really meaningful," Richard Leigh says.

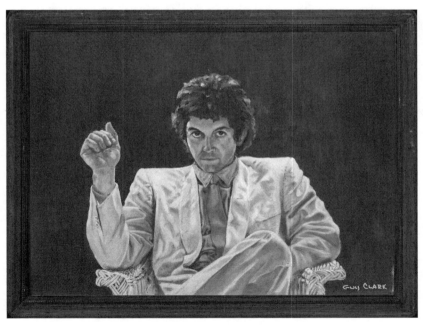

Guy created this painting of Rodney Crowell to go with his self-portrait. Hanging next to each other in Guy's home, he has titled them *Hands* and *Knees*. Courtesy Paul Whitfield

Guy Clark, Joe Ely, John Hiatt, and Lyle Lovett toured together often in the 1990s and 2000s on the acoustic songwriter tour, swapping songs and stories. Courtesy Jim McGuire

People jumped all over it wanting to record it. That was a pivotal time. And here's where it gets good. Reebok calls, wants the license to "Come from the Heart" to sell their tennis shoes. Now, I'm so altered by then that I tell my publisher that I don't want to license it for a quarter of a million dollars. I don't care. I said, "I'm going to call Susanna and tell her that I think it'll bruise the copyright." This is a magical song. We don't want it selling sneakers. And that's how Guy and Susanna had changed me, and they didn't mean to change me. I started thinking songs were little sermons. They were written in homiletic form. They were meant to help people, not sell tennis shoes, so I was a changed man. But thank the lord, the publishers had control over both our contracts so we not only got the money, we got to feel good about our decision. It was the best of both worlds.

On November 10, 1989, Guy played *Austin City Limits* with fiddle player Stuart Duncan and upright bass player Edgar Meyer. When he sang "Better Days," Guy showed off the lyric he had fixed with the woman from the battered women's shelter in Australia:

> *Now see the wings unfolding*
> *that weren't there just before*
> *She has no fear of flying,*
> *and now she's out the door*
>
> *Out into the morning light*
> *where the sky is all ablaze*
> *This looks like the first of better days.*

Susanna had grown her own wings. With the money and confidence she earned from "Come from the Heart," she rented an apartment just south of Nashville in the small town of Franklin, Tennessee. She didn't complain or explain—she just moved out. And, of course, she wrote a song:

> *I gave you my heart*
> *I gave you my soul*
> *Let you have my life*
> *You took control*
> *Can't go on like this*
> *When I see the cost*
>
> *I'm at the edge of a cliff*
> *And you pushed me off*
> *Surprise, Baby, I can fly*
>
> *I take back the way I walk*
> *The pride in my stride*
> *My honest talk*
> *I take back the sparkle in my eye*
> *I take back my kind of grace*

Susanna Clark and Rodney Crowell at Rodney's wedding to Rosanne
Cash, Hotel Bel-Air, Los Angeles. Courtesy Guy Clark

*My smile when the sunshine warms my face*
*I almost let you steal my style*
*Surprise, Baby, I can fly*

*You can keep the tears*
*You can have the fear*
*Of losing you when the wind hits my hair*
*I don't care about the blues*

*I'm taking back all of my stuff*
*I'm over it now and that's enough*
*Can you hear the fat lady sing goodbye?*

*Surprise, Baby, I can fly*
*It's over.*

## CHAPTER TEN

# Hangin' Your Life on the Wall

The new decade ushered in country music's storied class of 1989, a group of artists that dominated the country music charts and record sales. Hat acts Clint Black, Alan Jackson, and Garth Brooks led the pack, which also included country rocker Travis Tritt. Black sailed to number one right out of the gate with his first four singles and racked up nine Top 10 hits by the end of 1991. Alan Jackson scored six Top 10 hits, and by the end of 1991 he'd had three consecutive number one hits. Garth Brooks, the heavyweight, had ten Top 10 hits and seven of them soared to number one.

The progressive side of country dovetailed with mainstream music at major labels. Record companies made more and more money thanks in part to the popularity of new artists, the proliferation of country radio, and the rise of nightclubs that catered to the line-dancing crowd. In the 1990s, labels could well afford to keep a couple of literate songwriters for the cool factor alone. Many executives had eclectic tastes. In business they were obliged to please country radio, but their personal record collections did not always reflect what happened in the mainstream. Some were determined to break acoustic artists and songwriters such as the O'Kanes, Mary Chapin Carpenter, Kevin Welch, Alison Krauss, and Tish Hinojosa, all of whom had signed record deals with major labels. They attained limited chart success, yet attracted a passionate fan base.

The thirty-second annual Grammy Awards, held February 21, 1990, at the Shrine Auditorium in Los Angeles, honored the leaders of the progressive faction. The country category included nominees Lyle Lovett, Emmylou Harris, Rodney Crowell, and Rosanne Cash. Lovett and Crowell walked away with statues for Best Country Vocal Performance Male (Lovett) and Best Country Song (Crowell) for "After All This Time." Guy Clark's *Old Friends* album was nominated for Best Contemporary Folk Album. It was his sixth album and first crack at an award. He lost to the Indigo Girls, who took home the honors for their self-titled record.

Grammy or not, Guy continued to rake in rave reviews for *Old Friends*. The *Village Voice* wrote: "In Clark's best songs he climbs right into a moment, sits down, looks around and describes it without the heavy hand of judgment." The *Washington Post* wrote: "His grave, gently ironic stage presence gives him the air of a 19th century southern senator." Perhaps the biggest compliment came from Bob Allen in *Country Music* magazine: "[Clark] is, in many ways, what Picasso was to modern art, or what Raymond Carver was to the American short story: a master of expression and conciseness who has often set the benchmark standards for artistry, originality and integrity in his chosen field."

In early 1990, Guy shared the bill on *Austin City Limits* with Lucinda Williams. He taped the Nashville Network's music series *American Music Shop* with Nanci Griffith and James McMurtry and played dates in England, Scotland, and Ireland with Robert Earl Keen. In 1991, Sugar Hill Records reissued Guy's out-of-print RCA albums *Old No. 1* and *Texas Cookin'*.

Meanwhile, Carlene Carter, daughter of June Carter Cash and Rosanne's stepsister, released *I Fell in Love* on Reprise Records. The album included her version of the song she cowrote with Susanna Clark, "Easy from Now On":

> *There he goes gone again*
> *Same old story's gotta come to an end*
> *Lovin' him was a one-way street*
> *But I'm getting off where the crossroads meet.*

The lyrics illustrate what Susanna felt during those days. She lived alone in her Franklin apartment and even bought a parcel of land in the country not far from there. She savored the time alone and relished her success as a songwriter and an artist. For the first time in a long time, Susanna took care of herself. She went on a Sugar Busters diet and avoided refined sugars and white flour. She walked daily and cut back on drinking. There was no doubt Susanna and Guy still loved each other, and they saw each other often, but Susanna had some issues to work out, and she couldn't do it living in the same house with Guy.

"She'd had enough of my bullshit, and she just went and rented herself an apartment in Franklin," Guy says. "That was it. It wasn't like we're breaking up, we're getting a divorce. It was just like, 'I'm going to live in Franklin for a little while. I like this town.' I wouldn't have thought that she had her shit together enough to do that. I think she was proving a point—that she didn't have to depend on me for everything."

"I gave Guy a comfortable place to be so he could be an artist," Susanna told Louise O'Connor in 1991. "I poured love into him. I knew that he was hurting, and I poured attentiveness into him. He's not your Lone Star loner standing there. I attended to what he needed, and I did that until I realized that it wasn't being returned. He just goes out, gets drunk, gets coked up, and yells. No fun. I had spoiled him. I spoiled him to the point where he thought he could get away with anything. Then I got back into therapy myself and moved out, and we broke ground on being able to get along, still love each other, still have a wonderful relationship, but not live in the same place. We're better friends and have more fun now."

Susanna later wrote in her journal:

I was a peace-seeking missile. I had just left my house and husband without his blessing and was looking forward to a long overdue shot at self-reclamation. I went as far south of Nashville as our house is north. Safe and in Franklin, a beautiful, quiet setting noted as the best small town in Tennessee. I also found a very good person of a therapist who held a very large bottle of Elmer's glue and helped me glue myself back together again after I carefully found and picked up the pieces of myself. Slowly this treasure hunt for myself was surprisingly powerful, sometimes scary and amazing, and I didn't even know it existed. I had slowly dropped parts of myself along the way so miniscule, but so determinedly deliberate, that sometimes I realized that there was nothing left. With museum-like repairing, I set about to call my new apartment "my church and hard hat area." All under construction. Little did I know the help and activity silently guarded and helped with a power so great and surprising that I feel compelled to tell you now.

Rodney Crowell and Rosanne Cash also separated, and Cash moved to New York. Townes Van Zandt and his wife Jeanene had marital problems too. Eventually, Townes moved into Nashville's Close Quarters, also known as the Rock and Roll Hotel.

Susanna and Townes spent a lot of time together at the Franklin apartment. They sang songs, played music, and stayed up late engrossed in deep philosophical discussions. When Susanna was sick, Townes cooked for her, taking a serving tray filled with food and flowers to her bed. "It was a beautiful time. He was a beautiful, beautiful man," Susanna says.

Living on her own without Guy, Susanna was free to explore her mystical side. "I'm having a lot of spiritual visits," Susanna told O'Connor at the time. "I'm seeing things with my third eye. I can see everything more clearly." Susanna visited a psychic in Atlanta and practiced what she called "automatic writing" — words thought to be presented by the subconscious soul. During this time, she visited Townes in a rehab hospital.

"Townes told me that they had put him on these very powerful barbiturates that were making him crazy, because they said he was having hallucinations," Susanna told Van Zandt biographer Robert Hardy.

He said: "I looked out my window, and very quietly, there was an Indian woman and her husband, an Indian man, and a little baby Indian. And the little baby Indian was sitting in the tree. And they were all around there. And a plane flew over, and the little baby Indian pointed up at the plane and said, 'Mommy, what's that, what's that?' And the mommy Indian said, 'Oh, that's just some humans who think they can fly.'" I said, "Townes, those aren't hallucinations. You are seeing spirits. That's real." He said, "Really? Oh, that gives me hope." And I said, "You're connected to another part of the world." He said, "Oh, that makes me feel so much better. That gives me a reason to stay sober, because knowing that I'm connected to a spiritual world, now I have something to look forward to when I get out of here. It really makes me want to not drink anymore, so I can see what's going on out there." He was convinced that he wasn't crazy after all. They had tried to convince him that he was crazy, and [were] giving him these horrible drugs.

Susanna believed that she and Townes shared a strong spiritual connection and that they possibly had known each other in a different life. "We could read each other's thoughts," Susanna told O'Connor. "I could walk in a room to find something, and he would tell me where it was without even asking what I was looking for. He knew what I was thinking all the time and answered my questions before I even asked them."

"You see the beauty in Townes if you feel beautiful," Susanna says. "But if you're hiding your own depression, Townes will bring you down. It's your own fucking shit. But if you're already up, you get it. Way down deep, there's Townes Van Zandt love. He's full of it. He doesn't bring you down. Townes comes from the most beautiful, uplifting places in the world. Think about his songs. 'Brother Flower.' 'Maybe she just has to sing for the sake of the song.' I mean, that's a beautiful, loving, kind, gorgeous place to come from. The most power you can have in the world is love, and that's what Townes has in abundance."

·  ·  ·  ·  ·

On March 17, 1990, Guy played at Jerry Jeff Walker's forty-eighth birthday bash at the Paramount Theater in Austin. The theme was "A Salute to the Cowboy Way of Life." Ramblin' Jack Elliott was on the bill, along with world champion rodeo cowboy Larry Mahan. Ramblin' Jack had left his hometown of Brooklyn, New York, at sixteen and joined a traveling rodeo. After he made his way back to the budding Greenwich Village folk scene in the early 1950s, he had hung out with Woody Guthrie, then followed him to California. Guy loved Ramblin' Jack, musically and as a good friend.

The Driskill Hotel was always the playground during Walker's annual birthday shows, and this year was no different. Guy and Richard Leigh later wrote a song about it:

Stayin' up all night
In the Driskill Hotel
Ramblin' Jack and Mahan
Was cowboyed all to hell
The room smelled like bulls
The words sound like songs

# JERRY JEFF WALKER

### BIRTHDAY CONCERT
### "A Salute to the Cowboy Way of Life"

Paramount Theatre
Austin, Texas
Saturday, March 17, 1990
8:00 p.m.

JERRY JEFF WALKER
LARRY MAHAN
RAMBLIN' JACK ELLIOTT
U. UTAH PHILLIPS
GUY CLARK
TOM BEALE (Trick Roper)

### INTERMISSION

PATSY MONTANA
IAN TYSON
CHRIS WALL
JERRY JEFF WALKER

## LARRY MAHAN

His heroes, he says, have always been cowboys. That's no small irony, given that Larry Mahan has attained something of a heroic stature among cowboys himself. During the course of a 14-year rodeo career, Mahan amassed no fewer than six World Champion All-Around Cowboy titles. That feat put Mahan in the Guinness book of records, and it remains unmatched to this day.

It's not unfair to say that Mahan revolutionized modern rodeo, and took it to the masses. A cowboy gypsy who chased the old cattle trails in his private jet, he became a megagenic star in both the board room and the bucking chute. The Oscar-winning documentary, *The Great American Cowboy*, even made Mahan a star in the Soviet Union. Today, Mahan's competitive instincts are funnelled into business ventures as varied as horse and cattle ranches, a best-selling catalog of Western wear, and a new food line that includes chili and salsa. It's a long way from a-dollar-a-day-and-found, but then the range that Larry Mahan rides is a long way from Charles Goodnight's.

*About 1975, my friend Bud Shrake was doing a story for* Sports Illustrated *on All-Around Cowboy Larry Mahan. He called me from the road and said, "You've got to come see this guy; he's the best athlete I've ever seen. During one ten-day rodeo, he rode three different animals a day (thirty in all), flirted with all the girls, and then flew off in his own plane." So I went to the National Finals that year and Larry did all of the above, won the All-Around, and sat up and sang songs with us all night. Over the next couple of years, we followed Larry by booking concerts in towns where he was "up." I wouldn't trade any of those memories, but I might share a few during the Birthday Weekend. I'm proud to call Larry Mahan my friend.—JJW*

## RAMBLIN' JACK ELLIOTT

Ramblin' Jack Elliott, "The Last of the Brooklyn Cowboys" has been celebrated variously a a world-class rambler, a folk music pioneer, and a mentor to Bob Dylan and an entire generation of storytelling songwriters.

In the spirit of a picaresque tradition that stretches from Huck Finn to Elvis Presley, Elliott (born Elliott Charles Adnopoz) virtually invented himself. Leaving his Brooklyn birthplace at 16, he first joined a traveling rodeo, and eventually wound up in the midst of the budding Greenwich Village folk scene in the early 1950s. It was there that he became an intimate of Depression balladeer Woody Guthrie. When Guthrie moved to California, Elliott went too. It was the first of decades of hegiras to Los Angeles, Europe and New York. Along the way, he proved a profound influence on the careers of both Dylan and Woody's son Arlo.

Dylan sought to repay the debt when he made Elliott a featured performer in his celebrated 1975 road show, the Rolling Thunder Revue. But validation has never been all that high on Jack Elliott's list of priorities—he's more partial to an open road and a new song.

*What can I say about my "Dad?" Jack Elliott has let his music take him around the world. He is always in character, and that character can tell the stories and play the songs he's picked up in his travels. If part of the cowboy legacy is story tellin', Jack is living proof that that legacy is alive and well. He just keeps ramblin' on.—JJW*

The inspiration for "Ramblin' Jack and Mahan," from Jerry Jeff Walker's birthday party in 1990. Courtesy Christopher Joyce

*Now there's a pair to draw to, boys*
*I would not steer you wrong.*

After Walker's birthday celebration, Guy went back on the road with Townes. Sharing a booking agent worked to their advantage. Splitting the bill brought in more money for Townes and Guy, and they played many shows together.

"Sometimes we'd just walk on together, have a coin toss, call it in the air for who goes first. 'Okay, heads. You go first.' That's the way we'd start the show," Guy says.

Then we'd sit there and trade songs if we felt like we wanted to, or if one of us had to go pee, the other guy would do two songs. We'd just do that for two or three hours. Townes thought he was better than [comedian] Chevy Chase at pratfalls. It got to the point where it was part of his show. If he had two sets, he'd do it twice. He'd act like he lost his balance or he was too drunk to stand up and fall with his guitar strap and rolled and come back on his feet. He usually wound up flat on his back with his guitar up in the air. "I didn't break the guitar. I think my hip's shattered, but the guitar's okay." He hurt himself a couple of times. One time he did, and we were in Madison, Wisconsin. Townes played first and he was so drunk. He was sitting in a chair. Playing, crying, singing, and telling stories, and right at the very end he just fell over backwards in the chair and just hit the floor. He couldn't walk, but he had the guitar up. "I saved the guitar, man!" A doctor came in. "How many fingers can you see?" All this shit, you know. Townes is laying there in a daze, and I just walked up and sang: "If I had no place to fall, and I needed to, could I count on you?" I mean, that was our sense of humor. It was, "Okay man, you're that fucked up, ought to laugh a bit."

Townes was my best friend. That's how I would characterize him, and he was hard to be best friends with. Our friendship revolved around getting drunk and just being big jerks. I finally got to the point where I couldn't do it with him. I had Susanna, and I had responsibilities, like a commitment with the publishing company. Townes, if he had a publishing deal—and he had two or three substantial deals—he would just not turn in any songs. He just didn't do his job. That was just the way he was, and there was nothing you could do about it. You had to learn to tolerate Townes.

"Townes always spoke with tremendous respect for Guy," says Van Zandt's eldest son, J. T.

I'm sure they got tired of one another, probably pretty upset at different times just from caring about one another. I know that Townes's behavior and decisions upset Guy a lot, but Townes was always very respectful, almost to a code, about Guy. I think they both benefited greatly from having each other in their lives. They respected what each other wrote

Guy and Townes, intimate friends. Courtesy Guy Clark.

more than they could believe it in themselves. If Townes saw that he genuinely blew Guy away with something, that meant more to Townes than I think Guy realized. What Townes's songs and what Guy's songs mean to people is extraordinary. They are equals in that Guy feels the same about Townes's songs as Townes felt about Guy's songs. At least I know—Townes would talk to me about how perfect Guy would insist that a song be, and how long and hard he would work on those songs. Townes didn't really have the capability of going at it like that. If Townes had inspiration, it would just spill out of him, and then he was back on his horse, whereas Guy went through a process that's so difficult. His discipline is extraordinary. Is there anyone from Texas or anywhere else that can match up to either one of them? Unfortunately, for everyone out there, I think the answer is no. It is pure Texas music—from a modern standpoint, from a folk standpoint, from an uncorrupted standpoint—both of them writing with the simple goal of making their songs the best that they possibly could be. It didn't include the idea of getting rich or traveling and playing songs. I don't think that either one of them could've made the impact that they did on music without the other one, as best friends, in the time that they did it. It was delivered from heaven. The fact that they both exist and existed together is not a coincidence. It was meant to be that way.

Texas singer-songwriter Ray Wylie Hubbard had an occasion to witness Guy and Townes in action during a gig at the Three Teardrops Tavern in Dallas. "They were doing a song swap and I'm standing at the back wall by the soundboard," Hubbard says. "About fifty minutes into the show I see Guy lean over and whisper something to Townes, and Townes nods his head. All of the sudden, Guy gets up to the microphone and says, 'Ladies and gentleman, we have a very special guest in the audience tonight, Ray Wylie Hubbard.' There's a smattering of applause, and Guy goes, 'Ray. Why don't you come up and do a song?' I walk up there and Townes hands me his J200 guitar. They walk off. I'm up there playing, and I see the front door open. I see Guy and Townes get in a cab. I finished the song and everybody just looks around. I said, 'There'll be a short break.' They came back about thirty minutes later."

Keith Case booked Robert Earl Keen as an opener for Guy and Townes on a run of Texas songwriter dates in 1990 and 1991. In the spring of 1990, they played at the Old Town School of Folk Music in Chicago and the Ark in Ann Arbor, Michigan. That summer, the threesome headed west to Salt Lake City, Aspen, and Boulder. They closed out the year with dates at the Birchmere in Virginia and the Bottom Line in New York. In 1991, the trio jumped around from San Francisco to Minneapolis, then to Dallas, Austin, and Houston, and then to Colorado and New Mexico.

"I was totally raring to go. Both those guys were heroes of mine." Keen says.

I'd do twenty minutes, Townes would do forty-five minutes, and Guy would do like two hours. It was amazing. People would sit there completely quiet as they could be through the entire thing. It was great to be able to see them and ride around with them and sit after the show and wind down and have a drink or have a laugh. Guy and Townes had a dynamic. Well, other than brothers, I can't imagine people being so connected. There was definitely a complementary aspect to their relationship. Guy had the work ethic. Get there on time, make sure everything's going right. Townes had the "I don't give a shit" attitude, which made Guy loosen up. I also saw Guy really keep Townes together. On his own, Townes could disappear from the gig, flat out disappear. You go to a sound check, and there'd be no Townes.

Particular shows that I remember [include one in] Tampa, Florida, for the public radio station WMNF. They used it as one of their fundraisers. They had a little wooden hall there that we played in. I remember that very well because I would sell merchandise, and Guy and Townes wouldn't sell merchandise, and I said, "Hey, you guys oughta think about it." Guy said, "So how much money did you get doing that?" I said, "I don't know, seven hundred to eight hundred bucks." He said, "Really? Is that what you're getting?" Half of the fans were saying, "Where's the Guy and Townes stuff?" "They don't have any." "Fine, just give me whatever." So they would buy my stuff by default. People want a souvenir from a show. I remember Guy just being shocked that I was walking out of there with a pocketful of cash. He wasn't really hip to it. Also, I think it was that old hippie world of not capitalizing on everything all the time.

Keen didn't use cocaine, and Guy's open attitude about it made him nervous:

Some of his tactics were too exposed. He'd stop bellboys in hotels and say, "Hey, got any drugs?" He started giving me a hard time about being nervous about it. One time we were staying in this little crappy place, and we had a room as big as a closet, and we were sitting there, and I'm holding my guitar and fixing to go on, and he goes, "Hey, Robert," and I turned around, and he had a big old spoon of coke, and he dumps it in my guitar and he says, "Try to get that through security." He's just laughing and laughing. We had a lot of laughs. We weren't like the three amigos or anything. Most of the time it was those two guys driving together and me by myself, but we had a lot of fun.

During that tour, the owner of a club in Massachusetts tried to stiff the three songwriters when he didn't make enough money on the show. "It was like being in school," Keen says. "He called Guy in, then Guy goes to Townes, 'Your turn.' Townes comes out and goes, 'Good luck,' to me. I raised hell. I walked away without the money, but I threatened his life. I called the union. I don't think people should do that to you, you know. Anyway, Guy and Townes were very cool about stuff like that."

Keen says he saw some of the best Townes shows because Townes drank only beer during the tour and claimed that beer didn't make him drunk.

I saw the really great stuff. Somewhere in there, we were booked at the Granada Theater in Dallas. In Dallas, I had a lot of cachet because I had played there for years. I had built up an audience and made a record there in '88, and the guy who was the promoter, David Card, comes to me before the show and says, "I can't have you on first and Townes on after you. They'll just go crazy. I want to put Townes on first and then you and then Guy." I said, "You're the promoter, whatever you want to do." In general, I was happy with just the way it was. Man, when Guy heard this, he was livid. He doesn't get mad often. He was furious. He said, "That is not going to happen. Townes is going to go up with me. We're gonna share the stage. Robert's gonna go on, and then we're gonna go on, and that's how it's gonna be." I said, "Fine." I think I played longer, maybe an hour. From then on, it was that way. They had this mildly amusing banter or would throw in these really, really dry jokes. They'd just trade off songs. They just got up there and split the show.

One of Keen's favorite stories about Guy is the time the threesome played in Seattle and met a local fisherman.

At a show in Seattle there was this kid who was a salmon fisherman, and he wanted to talk about salmon, and Guy was looking for some drugs, and it was one of those crazy Halloween sort of nights where everybody's in costume. Everybody was nuts. . . . About a month later, I was packing to go to Nashville, and this big box comes, and it's full of salmon. One of them is separated, and it says, "Please give to Guy Clark." So, I think, *I'm going to Nashville anyway. I'll just get some more ice.* I put it on ice, and I drive all the way to Nashville, and I call Guy. I'm playing at the Station Inn, and I said, "You've gotta come down here because I've got this gift for you." He comes down, and Susanna's totally full tilt. She's smoking, she's drinking, she's going, "That goddamn Guy Clark, he's telling me I've gotta go see a fucking songwriter. Why do I want to see a songwriter? I am a fucking songwriter. He's a songwriter, and you want us to come down and see your sorry ass." I said, "Look. I didn't ask you to come to the show. I asked you to come here because I have this gift."

So we go backstage and we unwrap this salmon, which had thawed out by this time. It's a salmon, this big. Guy goes, "What am I gonna do with a fucking salmon, Robert?" "I don't know, man. The dude sent it to me and asked me to give it to you, so I'm giving it to you." He says, "All right. I'm gonna auction it off." So he goes out there, and he holds up this salmon, and he starts this auction thing. "Can I have a dollar?" I think somebody gave ten dollars and walked off with it, and that was the end of it. Then they left. The crazy couple.

In June 1991, Guy appeared at the Kennedy Center in D.C. on a Texas-themed weekend that also included Keen, Van Zandt, Butch Hancock, Jimmie Dale Gilmore, Willie Nelson, and Nanci Griffith. Guy and Townes played Austin's Cactus Cafe that month, and Guy closed out June with another songwriter date with Lovett, Ely, and Hiatt. In August, he performed a run of dates with Townes, Peter Rowan, and John Stewart in the UK and Ireland. In the fall, Guy split dates with Townes and the Lovett/Ely/Hiatt roundup.

"Besides just being fun to do, for me they were a way to see how each person approached writing songs," Ely says.

It opens you up to all kinds of new images, new ways of telling a story. Sitting next to Guy every night is liberating and terrifying at the same time. There'd be times at the end of a song I couldn't even open my mouth. How do you follow a tearjerker about a Dallas whore in church? That ends so majestically and then the chorus comes in. It would take me a while to recover, just like seeing a great movie and then the end scene rips you up. That's the way a lot of Guy's songs are. To follow that, I'd have to play something funny or fast or something to break the mood, because it's so heavy in the air, plus you're crying and stuff.

Ely says Guy takes command of a stage like no other artist. It might also be said that Guy pays little attention to rules or the decorum of any given venue. Along with whatever he is drinking, Guy has been known to light up a cigarette or joint onstage. Most venue owners and promoters are happy to have Guy on their stages and turn a blind eye to it.

I remember one time we were playing in Houston in a hall that [they were] just finished building. They had been working on it the same day getting ready for the show, putting covers on the seats," Ely says.

Here's a brand-new, fancy, two-thousand-seat listening room, and some of these workers had worked around the clock. They hadn't even slept in order to finish it for our concert. So the organizer of the place allowed the workers to have some of the seats right in the very front. There was a group of about twenty old construction workers sitting there and watching the concert. There were "no smoking" signs everywhere. Most stages have exceptions to that rule. You can smoke a cigarette onstage if it's a prop, and Guy always invoked the prop clause. He sat down and started playing, and after the first song he reached down and lit up a cigarette, and the crowd kind of gasped, and I think Lyle said something about it, and Guy kind of sarcastically said, "Yeah, it's a prop." And then we looked down [at] the front row, and here these construction workers all got out their cigarettes and were lighting their cigarettes . . . it was the five-hundred-dollar seats down there, and they were just horrified. So the whole front row's filled up with smoke, and Guy just snickered, just barely, but you could tell he was really glad that he had liberated those guys.

"Guy's role in those guitar pulls is whatever Guy wants it to be," Lyle Lovett says, adding:

I think that's Guy's role in life. I think that's what's great about Guy. He's always himself. Guy is one of the most honest people you'll ever meet. He tells you just what he feels and what he sees, and I think that's what draws all of us to him. Guy Clark speaks the truth. I think we all want that. Whether Guy's happy or not so happy on a given night, he steps onstage, and he is how he is. There is something to gain from watching

and listening to that every single time. To get to sit on stage and watch
him play one of his songs is incredible. To see his expression, to feel
what he feels as he plays, is really an incredible experience. You get that
in the audience as well, but it's quite an honor to be on stage. When
we've done those tours in the past, Guy's sometimes ridden the bus with
us. I'll never forget getting to hang out with Guy after the shows and
having something to eat and listen to him talk. It means so much to me.

"I liked the guys, you know, John, Joe, and Lyle," Guy says. "It's fun to be on
a stage with them and listen to and see them from the best seat in the house.
It was all very cool. But it also gets boring sitting in a line of four people and
knowing that you're only going to perform once in four songs. That is not
conducive to enjoying yourself. It might be the greatest thing since sliced
bread for the audience, but I don't care. I want to have some fun."

· · · · ·

Guy's cowriter Verlon Thompson released a self-titled record on Capitol
Records in 1990. All his life, Thompson had dreamed of the big record deal
and making his living as a songwriter and artist. But the reality of being on
a major label didn't jibe with Thompson's dream. Guy invited Thompson
to join him on the road.

"That was a turning point in my whole life," Thompson says:

When I started going out with him, I was in the middle of a record deal,
and it wasn't what I thought. I said to Guy, "This is bullshit." He said,
"Come out with me." Guy introduced me to the real troubadour world.
I didn't even know this other world was out there, that you could go
and just sit down in a room, and it didn't have to be a huge stage or
auditorium. It's wherever people will gather to listen. Thank goodness
he showed me another way to do it. It literally changed the course of
my thinking and my dreams and aspirations. I realize it was what I was
after and didn't even know it was there.

Basically, the day starts when I cruise by and grab Guy, and we go to
the airport and battle all that security and everything and try to get a seat
with legroom. If it's in this region, in the Southeast, we might drive to
it. A lot of the time we fly to the nearest major place and then grab a

car and fan out from there. It's just the two of us. It's pretty laid-back, if we can make it that way. We try to keep it as simple as we can, both the performing and the travel. We got a guitar and a bag. That's all we carry. I told Guy we need to have tour T-shirts printed up that just say: "Eat. Nap. Eat. Nap. Sound check. Play. Sleep."

Although Guy was on the road for much of the early 1990s, he still had a publishing deal and was required to turn in songs. EMI Music Publishing had bought SBK and moved into the old Combine Music Publishing office, where Kris Kristofferson had written his biggest songs. Gary Overton was hired to run the EMI Nashville division. "I had been reaching out to some of the writers, and some of the writers had been calling and asking for meetings because, 'Uh-oh, it's the new boss,'" Overton says. "A few weeks into it, I was actually outside my office, and Guy Clark comes around the corner. He was almost like Texas tumbleweed himself. He's kind of half off balance, hair just flying. I'll never forget it: one of his eyes—he'd broken a blood vessel, and the eye was all red, and he's just standing there, and he just stops. We're a few feet apart and he goes, 'So you're running this place now?' 'Yes, sir.' Guy says: 'Well, do you want to just kick me out now or do you want to fuck around for a while?' I said, 'Let's fuck around for a while.' He says, 'Sounds good.' And he just turns around and floats back off. That was the start of me working with Guy Clark."

Although people call him Gary, Overton's given name is Garland, which led to Guy nicknaming him Darling. "He'd walk in and go, 'Hello, Darling,' with this kind of a Conway Twitty thing, and it was always funny," Overton says. "I was in such awe of Guy because he could've made a lot more money had he decided to go the pure Music Row songwriter route. Everybody wanted to write with him. The artists loved him. He could've done that and made a lot more money, but that's not what he was built for. He just did what he did."

Guy invited Overton to come over late one afternoon after Guy and Pat Green had been writing all day in Guy's workshop. "It was like walking into a Cheech and Chong movie," Overton says.

It's just smoke everywhere. It was just the two of them, and there's four ashtrays going, four bottles of wine almost empty, and I'm, like,

Road warriors Verlon Thompson and Guy Clark. Verlon spent more than twenty years playing guitar on the road with Guy. Courtesy Guy Clark

"Working hard today, boys, huh?" They said, "Let us play you what we have." They play the verse, chorus, whatever they had, and Guy throws a bag of pot to me and says, "Why don't you roll one up there, Darlin'?" I said, "Well, Guy, I sure don't mind rolling them for you, but I haven't smoked in many, many years." "Aww. Mother gonna get mad at you?" Or something like that. So he took the baggie back, and I'm sitting close enough to him, and he turns . . . and he puts it back over my face and says, "Well, you're gonna have to breathe it." We laughed. I said, "You know, if I look up 'peer pressure' in the dictionary, it'd have your photo, wouldn't it?" So we laughed. They were out of wine, and we were supposed to go to dinner, and Guy says, "Aww, hell, I don't want to go to dinner. Gary, you know Steve Nelson? You know *Winnie the Pooh*? He wrote the music." He picks up the phone and calls Steve. "I'm over here with Pat Green and Gary Overton, and we're gonna have a guitar pull. Why don't you come on over. And, hey, why don't you bring some of that really good wine of yours." So Steve comes in with bottles of wine. So we're drinking more wine and having a great time, and Guy said to Steve, "Hey, why don't you sing one of your songs," and Steve sang, and then it goes to Pat, and Pat sings a song, and then they hand me the guitar, and I gave it to Guy, and Guy says, "You've got to play if you're gonna stay"—or something like that. They forced me. He said, "Play me one of your favorite songs, and it can't be mine or Pat's." I played a Sonny Throckmorton song, "The Way I Am," as best I could, in a hushed voice, and the whole time I'm not believing this. This is totally ruining my evening. Guy just sat there and listened, and then he said, "That's not bad. It's a good thing you're a publisher." I told my wife when I got home it was one of those days that I could have never scripted, and it is going to be one of the highlights of my career. All the times I won publisher of the year, managed artists who became entertainers—all that stuff. None of it matters. Sitting in that room with Guy Clark and doing that, just spectating, much less being part of it, was unbelievable. Guy is like human comfort food. You feel good when you're there. You just want to be there. You walk away going, "Man, I want to do that some more."

Guy talked EMI management into fixing up an attic with a big dormer window overlooking Music Square East. It was in his new alcove above Music Row that Guy wrote "Picasso's Mandolin" with Radney Foster and Bill Lloyd. "I was stoned out of my gourd," Guy says. "I had an old cheap Korean mandolin laying up against the wall. The more I looked at it, the more it looked like a drawing by Picasso—out of shape, ill-formed. It sounded like an autoharp."

It was so oddly angular and goofy-looking that we started laughing about it," Foster says. "I said, 'It looks almost Cubist,' and Bill says, 'It looks like Picasso. Maybe it's Picasso's mandolin.' Guy said, 'That's a song title. We're going to write that.' Guy had the sense to know 'Picasso's mandolin' is a song title. We said, 'Really? Are you sure?' We were sketchy and scared. Who at radio is going to play a song called 'Picasso's Mandolin'? We were trying to write songs for the radio because we had a band and we're only twenty-eight years old. Guy's smart enough to go, "No, no, no, no, no."

"While we were there, the phone starts ringing and Guy answers it," Foster says. "He's talking, 'Yeah, I'm writing with these guys, Foster and Lloyd,' and then he said, 'No, hang on. Let me find out.' He puts his hand over the receiver, and he goes, 'Do you guys mind if Townes Van Zandt comes by?' We're trying to keep from wetting our pants at that point. Maybe Bill's capable of writing after that, but I was not," Foster says.

I'm just sitting there pretending by looking at a piece of paper, thinking, *Townes Van Zandt is going to come over. Oh, my god. I'm going to be in the same room with Guy Clark and Townes Van Zandt.* About ten minutes later, we start hearing *beep, beep, beep, beep, beep, beep, beep, beep, beep, beep* down in the street. We all go looking through the dormer window, and Guy throws open the sash, and all three of us stick our heads out. Townes Van Zandt is cutting doughnuts on a Vespa in the middle of Sixteenth Avenue. We all go running downstairs, and he has a brand-new cream-colored Vespa with a matching Italian helmet. He wanted to show us his new scooter. I even took a couple of turns around the parking lot on it. Then we all go back up to Guy's office. I really didn't smoke much weed, but needless to say there was some weed smoked, because I'm not going to let this opportunity pass me up. You could tell that their friendship was long and deep. Townes was really excited because his whole catalog was going to come out on CD. He told Bill and me to give him our addresses. Two weeks later, Townes sent a note with ten CDs, which was really unbelievable. I was just so stunned by the whole thing.

Guy is about to make a new album, and he decides to put "Picasso's Mandolin" on it. He takes the bridge we wrote out and the guitar riff out, and he writes a whole other verse, which is very typical of Guy.

When Guy told us he was putting it on the record, I damned near cried. Because that's like Mozart saying he's going to do one of your pieces. I mean, it was just so unbelievable to me. It still is to this day. A lot of people write songs, and they write them well, and they're in love with songwriting, but they're really in love with their own songwriting. Guy's in love with the art form of songwriting—everybody's songs. He's bored with petty conversation when he's in the presence of someone who could be playing a song. Every time I've ever been around Guy, he's like, "Play me a new song."

From all accounts, it is clear that songs were the sturdy rope that kept Guy's life from unraveling. When he wasn't listening to songs, writing songs, or playing songs, he was pitching songs. One day Guy called John Condon, the head of A&R at Asylum Records Nashville, because he wanted to pitch Condon songs for Asylum artist Mandy Barnett. "Guy was a serious songwriter and wanted to cast his tunes," Condon says. "He had some relevant pitches."

Mandy was not a writer, and she needed songs. He loved her singing. They were birds of a feather. I went over to his house about six o'clock one night. There was a note on the door that said "Come on in." I walked in the glass door, and Guy is walking up the stairs as I was walking in. He had the large glass with ice and orange juice and vodka, mostly vodka. He just handed it to me, and it was full. It was overflowing. It was splashing onto the carpet. That was the beginning of my listening session, my pitch session with Guy Clark. He takes me downstairs, and Susanna's upstairs in bed. We go down into the lair and past the models of planes he had suspended from the walls, and he's working on one of his guitars. After about forty-five minutes of some pretty serious pitching on his behalf, I was a little intimidated. Going to Guy Clark's house and having him pitch you songs, and you try to critique them. How far do you go? "No, you asshole, that's not going to fly on radio. We're not doing that."

Condon wisely kept his mouth shut and did not lecture Guy on what radio would and would not play. "We ended up just really partying pretty hard that night. It was an amazing night, educational and super fun. He kept pulling these cassettes of the wall and saying, "You like that, let me play you this." I kept calling my wife. I called her at seven o'clock: "I can't make it home for dinner." And ten: "Not going to be home before bedtime." Not sure how many other calls after that. I got home at five a.m. It was an eleven-hour deal and a night I do not regret. I think that Guy is just one of the most compassionate and honest, sincere people that you could meet. He's a gentleman, a true gentleman. His music reflects that, I think, and vice versa. Guy is one of the greatest American songwriters ever."

Overton concurs. "Guy is so loud without talking loudly, by what he has to say and how he says it, whether it's just talking or in songs. People are like children around him. They're mesmerized by him and what he has to say. He's truthful. He's funny as hell. He's not trying to be something else. I think at the heart of it all, one of the things that draws people to Guy Clark is he is really what every writer starts out to be. Sometimes when they get to the fork in the road, they take it. They become much more commercial. They're interested in money and rewards. They write songs for other reasons. Guy's never done that. I think that's one of the special things about him: He writes songs for the songs' sake."

## CHAPTER ELEVEN

# Americana Music Comes to Town

Guy teamed up with producer/engineer Miles Wilkinson again for 1992's *Boats to Build* after being courted by Kyle Lehning, who had been hired to manage the Nashville office for the revamped Asylum Records label. Lehning released *Boats to Build* as part of the American Explorers series in partnership with Elektra/Nonesuch.

"I remember it being kind of exciting," Guy says. "I was certainly pleased to work with Kyle because he was producing Randy Travis, and I liked the records that he made with him."

At the time, many artists played on mainstream country radio were selling hundreds of thousands of albums. Progressive artists didn't typically show those kinds of numbers, then or now. But there existed a few faithful executives who believed things could be different.

"The original reason that we started Asylum was to do a boutiquey, left-of-center country label, which lasted about a year and a half before I just about had a nervous breakdown and we had to shift gears," Lehning says. "Guy was part of that first year and a half. This was right on the heels of Alison Krauss's success; it was post-O'Kanes and Foster and Lloyd, and Alison was making noise. It almost seemed possible. Today it sounds completely ludicrous to think that we might try to take a chance, but at the time there was this woody, acoustic kind of thing floating around. There was a vibe in the air where it seemed possible we could sell a lot of records on these left-of-center artists."

For *Boats to Build*, Guy wrote two songs by himself: "Madonna w/Child ca. 1969" and "Must Be My Baby." But it is the cowritten songs that really stand out on the album. Guy reunited with Richard Leigh, with whom he wrote "Ramblin' Jack and Mahan," to write "I Don't Love You Much Do I." He's joined by Emmylou Harris on the track. He wrote "How'd You Get This Number" with Susanna, "Too Much" with Lee Roy Parnell, "Jack of All Trades" with Rodney Crowell, and the title track with Verlon Thompson. The latter song became a fixture in his live shows, along with its backstory. Of course, Guy couldn't help but be influenced by his own boatbuilding experience in Rockport, but he and Thompson wrote "Boats to Build" as an homage to their friend Richard Leigh, who loved to sail. Guy sometimes sailed with Leigh on Old Hickory Lake. Knowing how much he loved boats, Leigh's wife presented him with the gift of a boatbuilding class at a school in Maine. The story Guy tells on stage is that Richard's wife left him when he returned from boatbuilding school, but "Richard ended up with a nice boat, and Verlon and I wrote a good song."

Guy wrote "Baton Rouge" with J. C. Crowley, a member of the 1970s rock band Player, which scored a number hit with 1978's "Baby Come Back." When recording "Baton Rouge," Wilkinson envisioned a New Orleans style Dixieland jazz feel. "Guy was reluctant at first but let me try it anyway," Wilkinson said. "It would not be right to have trumpet, slide trombone, and clarinet in the song, which is what I heard in my head, so we gathered Sam Bush on mandolin, Jerry Douglas on slide Dobro, and Stuart Duncan on fiddle. I told these guys that I wanted them to think and play like a Dixieland band—Jerry was to think like a trombone player since he was playing the slide instrument, Sam was to think like a clarinet, and the fiddle player like a trumpet. Then I let them work it out by themselves. And they did it, masterfully. Guy loved it. We ended up opening the *Boats to Build* album with that cut."

To promote the record, Asylum produced an eight-and-a-half-minute video salute to Guy, with testimonials from artists including Townes, Crowell, Emmylou, Kathy Mattea, Vince Gill, Radney Foster, Lee Roy Parnell, and Hal Ketchum. Harris, Foster, Parnell and Crowell all appear on the album.

"We wanted to present him in the proper light with his peers and with people that understood what he was about," Lehning says. "You have to understand that I'd never run a record company. To say I didn't know what I was doing is the understatement of the century. We were just stumbling in the dark, trying to do the best we could. With Guy, you have to go that route. You have to do an EPK [electronic press kit] in lieu of some flashy tour, in lieu of radio, in lieu of sales, in lieu of everything else, what do you have? You have these great accolades. You have peers. What a dynamic presence Guy is. Let's get it out there."

The Asylum staff had plenty of experience promoting mainstream country artists, and they used those tools to try to get Guy's record heard by members of the music press and radio. At Country Radio Seminar, a conference for radio programmers and music directors, Guy performed in a hotel suite to introduce his album. During Fan Fair, a music festival for country fans, Guy performed on the Asylum stage and did interviews with country music press.

"I got him to do the interviews when he came off the stage by standing there with two solo cups full of beer," former Asylum publicist Wendy Pearl says.

I handed him one, and I told him he'd get the other one when he was finished with his interviews. It was like the carrot in front of a horse's nose. He rolled his eyes at me and said, "You know me!" I told him I'd make this as painless as possible, but [he'd need] to do his part of it, and so he did. He was kind of reluctant but also accepted the game that he had to play at the time and what he needed to do. And he was always kind. I always just assumed that somebody with that kind of talent, people who live on a different plane, don't often see the people who are down here on this plane. He connected with people. It could be the janitor, and he would treat the janitor the same way he would treat the talent producer, the booker. It did not matter to him. In fact, I think he preferred the janitor because those were the people that he really, really connected with. Guy was also incredibly generous. I don't think people realize how generous he really is, because he is so stoic. People don't think of stoic people as having that kind of magnanimous personality. When Guy needed to show up to work, he would show up. When he agreed to do it, he was going to be there and be committed. He was also so stubborn, and it's the quality I respect about him the most. That he was totally 100 percent aware of who he was and what he was going to do and how he was going to do it. As a publicist, I would ask him if he could just make this one exception. Things that I thought were fantastic opportunities that he would say no to, and I had no recourse whatsoever. If it was against his personal feelings or if he said no, it meant no. All the arguing, all of the positioning, all of the begging I was going to do was not going to change that.

Lehning hired veteran promotion executive Steven Sharp to garner radio interest in *Boats to Build*. Sharp had worked with mainstream artists and radio stations at the Arista label. It was his idea to take Guy out to meet radio programmers. "Guy didn't like Steven at all, but he was a great promotion guy," Lehning says. "Steven could walk in a door and make you pay attention to whatever it was he brought in there. All I can say is, he did his job. We had this little radio tour planned up the West Coast, San Francisco. I think we went from San Francisco all the way down to Santa Barbara at some places. He had this campfire thing going where he'd invite radio people out to this little camp area. It was a little lodge, everything like that. I don't know how he figured it out or what he did, but he did. Guy would sit around this campfire and play a couple tunes."

As they did with *Old No. 1* and *Old Friends*, music critics loved *Boats to Build*. Writing for the *Los Angeles Times*, Robert Hilburn said: "As much as any album since John Prine's *The Missing Years* in 1991, Clark's latest collection, the character-rich *Boats to Build* seems wholly an expression of artistic instincts rather than commercial considerations." *Tower Pulse* called him "more Beat poet than balladeer," and All Music called the album "an ambitious, soulful, and state-of-the-art batch of songs."

Travis Clark, Guy's son, then twenty-five, played bass on *Boats to Build*, and Guy thought it would be a great opportunity to take Travis out on the road to play live. "Travis is a great bass player," he says. "He reads Count Basie charts. He's a really well-schooled bass player. And I thought it would be cool. Get Travis to play; be my bass player. We could do it just with the two of us. He can sing and he can play. That's quite a big step for him as far as being able to make money playing music. We played together really good. We sang together well."

It also gave father and son a chance to get to know each other better. "I've always been proud of who he is, but I never really knew him," Travis says. "We hadn't spent a whole lot of time together, maybe a week at Christmas or maybe two weeks. When we went on the road, we spent a lot of time together. That was a good thing to get to know him."

It also gave the younger Clark a chance to witness his father in all his complexity. Producer Dub Cornett put together a run of shows in Colorado for Guy with Travis as his accompaniment. Rosie Flores and Steve Young were also on the bill. "There was this gal June McHugh and she'd been an oil and gas heiress out in Colorado. She was a fan of the music, and she wanted to put them out on tour and do this thing," Cornett says. "She has a great heart. You can just tell she watched the music business, not knowing the mechanics but wanting to throw money at it. It was misguided as all get-out. I produced the damn thing, put it all together, and somehow ended up being the den mother. It was an ill-fated tour of the state of Colorado. A snowstorm hit, and we drove from Aspen in a blizzard back over to Breckenridge. I've never seen Guy so pissed in his life. He was actually scared. I think everybody was scared. I know I was."

"We were driving after the show to this little place that somebody in June's family owned," Rosie Flores says.

It was up in the mountains, and that late-night drive was really, really, really scary. The roads were really thin, really slender, and we were way up high. We can't see where we were going. I remember Dub white-knuckling the seats. Dub was sweating. Guy was cussing. Steve was really quiet, and I kept trying to do small talk to get everybody's mind off the fact that we might drive off the cliff and die any second.

Finally, Guy just said, "Let me out of the fucking car. You've got to get me a hotel. I want a hotel now." He thought if we didn't get out, we weren't going to make it. I got that feeling from him. There was a little town, and there was a motel, and I almost got out with him. Then I thought, "Nah, I guess I'll stick it out with you guys." We dropped Guy off. I remember looking out the window, and Guy was just flipping the bird at us while we were leaving. He's the only one that got out. Travis stayed with us.

One date was scheduled at the Wheeler Opera House in Aspen, Colorado, but somehow ended up at a local high school.

"Only fifteen fans showed up. Guy proceeded to get as drunk as he could ever get," Cornett says. "He was having a little problem with altitude, and we got him an oxygen tank. Guy comes rolling out on the stage of this high school with oxygen going in his nose, a cigarette in his mouth, his guitar sitting in a shopping cart that he'd found, and a fifth of Jack or Jim Beam, whatever he was drinking at the time. He was drunk as hell and . . . pissed because nobody's there. Then he just started to own the room in the way he does and the few people there were served with a classic, incredible show."

"Everybody just had this attitude. We were just upset with the promoters because the gigs were not very good," Flores says. "In the backstage [area] of the high school were all these props. There was this . . . pink Barbie Corvette little car. I remember I sat in it with my guitar and my boots over it. Travis pushed me out on the stage in it. We were using the props. Guy put his guitar in a shopping cart, like a grocery store, and wheeled his guitar out onto the stage. We were all just a little nutty by that point."

Around the same time, Cornett produced a run of shows with Guy, Townes, Steve Earle, and Lucinda Williams. "We played Greenville, South Carolina. We did Raleigh/Durham, Chapel Hill, Knoxville, Atlanta. At the Variety Playhouse in Atlanta they had a full house, and it was really incredibly well received," Cornett says.

It was the first sellout big crowd that we had. Atlanta was the show that Lucinda refused to go on because Guy made fun of her or something. He was drunk, being Guy. He didn't bother me. I matched quarters with him and would win his money and go, "What's the matter, old man? Can't you take it?" I'd mess with him. You'd put two quarters in your hand. It'd be heads or tails. We'd start betting . . . Guy'd get real cocky about it, and Townes was happier to lose. Guy saw it as gambling. Townes was just as happy being a loser as he was a winner. Guy really cared whether you beat him or not. I'd get a couple up on Guy, and he'd be mad. He'd walk around stoked up about it, like, "Come on, let's go." He wasn't interested in coke; he wasn't interested in nothing. He wanted to win that money back. Once you get him down, then you pick on him, get under his skin. He was so Texan he had to be the winner. Travis looking at me going, "Quit, please." You could get Guy on the ropes, and he'd lose everything he had to get back on top.

Travis accompanied Guy on some radio station visits that Travis calls painful. "It wasn't really his gig. Not a good fit," Travis says. "Once somebody met us at an airport. She might've worked for Asylum. She said, 'How did such and such go?' I made some terrible smartass comment about the radio station not getting it. It was uncalled for, and my dad jumped down my throat later. 'Don't you ever say anything like that again.' He's right. Even if he's thinking it, he's much more gracious than I am."

In Seattle, Sharp set up a dinner with a big country station. "We didn't think it was ludicrous to think they might play something from the album," Lehning says. "These guys that ran these radio stations and their wives are sitting around this big table in the middle of this nice restaurant in the hotel. People were ordering wine. Guy comes down, and I say, 'I'd like to introduce you to Guy Clark.' He goes around the table and says hello to everyone. As he starts to sit down, Guy says, 'Do you mind if I smoke?' One of the women says, 'Well, as a matter of fact, yes, I do.' Guy says, 'Well, then, fuck y'all.' He just walked over to this table in the corner by himself and sat at this little two-top and lit up a cigarette. He never came back. I just said, 'Well, this is the Guy Clark experience. I hope you consider playing some of his music.'"

At the time, Cyndi Hoelzle was the country editor for radio-industry trade magazine *Gavin Report*, based in San Francisco. *Gavin*'s charts were used as a guide for radio programmers to decide what songs to play. The publication also hosted the Gavin Seminar, a convention for the radio industry.

"Kyle Lehning had an ally with us at *Gavin*. We loved Guy Clark," Hoelzle says. "I remember that radio tour. You could tell Guy was not into it. We went out to dinner at some really nice restaurant in San Francisco. I sat across from Guy. He's totally pissed during dinner, just grouchy. After dinner was over, he says, 'Let's go out. Come on. Let's go do something.' Everybody said they had to go home. He looks at me and says 'You, c'mon, what is there to do? Let's go hear some music.' I couldn't go out. My brother had just gotten into town that night. I still regret not going out with Guy."

Along with Guy's California radio friend Rob Bleetstein, Hoelzle played a major role in developing the Americana Music Chart at *Gavin*. It would be the precursor to the Americana Music Association and play a significant role in raising the profiles of Guy and other artists like him. There seemed to be hope for a new format. In Nashville, progressive country artists Kevin Welch, Kieran Kane, Mike Henderson, Tammy Rogers, and Harry Stinson had launched Dead Reckoning Records, an indie label to release their own records so they would not be at the mercy of upheavals at a major label. Around the same time, musicians Alison Brown and Garry West started the roots label Compass Records, specializing in bluegrass and newgrass. Bloodshot Records opened in Chicago, championing what they call "the good stuff nestled in the dark, nebulous cracks where punk, country, soul, pop, bluegrass, blues and rock mix and mingle and mutate." In North Carolina, Barry Poss's Sugar Hill Records continued to sign interesting folk and bluegrass artists and singer-songwriters including Townes Van Zandt, Peter Rowan, New Grass Revival, and Jesse Winchester. In Austin, partners Robert Earl Keen, Waterloo Record Store owner John Kunz, and Heinz Geissler started Watermelon Records (named after Guy Clark's song "Watermelon Dream") and had released critically acclaimed work by Alejandro Escovedo, the Austin Lounge Lizards, the Derailers, Tish Hinojosa, and others.

In the summer of 1994, Bleetstein and Hoelzle attended a party with some of the *Gavin* staff. Bleetstein had just returned to California from Austin after working for Keen for a year. Inspired by talk at the party, Bleetstein went home that night and began to outline a pitch to create a new chart for the *Gavin Report*. "I sat down at my computer and thought about what needed to happen," Bleetstein says.

I made a list of all these artists who couldn't break at Triple A [Adult Album Alternative] or on the country charts. There was no room for Junior Brown; there was no room for Emmy. Johnny Cash had been dropped. Radio wouldn't play Waylon and Willie anymore. I thought back to KFAT. It was bluegrass, it was folk, it was hardcore country, it was alternative country, and you just had to know how to make it work together. So I go in to *Gavin* with this pitch. "Here's this list of artists. They tour successfully, the press loves them, they sell records, and they have fan bases. Radio is the black sheep in this family. You have two formats, in country and Triple A, that won't give an inch. We needed to create a new format." Of course, Guy is the fucking Mount Rushmore of it all.

"There was a group of us in the country industry who loved stuff that wasn't fitting in anymore," Hoelzle says.

> When I first started at *Gavin* it was right during the Great Credibility Scare. We had Lyle Lovett, Nanci Griffith, Steve Earle, Foster and Lloyd, and the O'Kanes. There was a group of people in Nashville who loved that music, too. After the Class of 1986, and then Garth Brooks comes in, those artists aren't being played at all. There's no place for them, but there's still a lot of people who love that kind of music. On the *Gavin* country chart, we did have a lot of smaller-market stations that were still playing good music. Rob had this idea to try to stitch all those together. He came in and pitched it to me. We pitched it to Kent Zimmerman, who was the Triple A editor at the time. His chart would accept some singer-songwriters. They played Shawn Colvin, but they're not going to play Robert Earl Keen or Jim Lauderdale because they are too twangy. They played Lyle Lovett because he was hip, but if it was too country, Triple A stations just didn't want anything to do with it. There was that gap there.

The *Gavin Report* hired Bleetstein, but the new radio format did not yet have a name. Gavin put together a casual think tank with industry insiders who loved the music and understood the potential. Jon Grimson worked at Warner Brothers in the progressive music department, managing radio promotion for artists including Iris Dement, Uncle Tupelo, and Bela Fleck and the Flecktones, among others. It was his job to find radio stations to play those artists before there was a radio format for them. "You take a group like the Flecktones," Grimson says. "Every format pointed to the other format to say, 'Well, they belong over there.' The jazz stations wouldn't take them and the bluegrass guys wouldn't take them. Jazz guys said, 'Well, that sounds like bluegrass to me.' Bluegrass said 'That sounds like jazz to me.' I interfaced with all the rock regionals all around the country, but it was always this no-man's-land for these artists out of Nashville who were not mainstream country."

After talking with *Gavin* management about their plans to start a new chart, Grimson left his job at Warner to start his own radio promotion company—specifically to promote this new genre of artists to radio. Grimson came up with the name "Americana" to describe the music. "I've never been one to try and lay any kind of wild giant claims about stuff like that, and I think a lot of people didn't like it at first, the idea of a brand called Americana," Grimson says.

> I really wanted to think beyond "what do we call the chart?" to "what do we call this music?" And "what do we call this category?" "How do we create a brand identity that can function for radio, function for retail, and that the artists actually want to use?" My idea of Americana was that it was the AOR [Album-oriented Rock] format of country. Or it could have been, if Nashville would have come to terms with how this could really benefit us in much the same way that LA and New York divisions had multiple formats that fed into CHR [Contemporary Hit Radio] radio. But in LA and New York they didn't oppose that stuff. They wanted it to happen. In Nashville, kind of universally, with the exception of people like Jim Ed Norman and Tony Brown, who were signing these artists, it was: "We're in the hits business. Come back later and talk to us when you have some hits."

In the fall of 1994, the *Gavin Report* opened a Nashville office. Hoelzle moved to town to run it as Bleetstein and Grimson prepared to launch the new Americana chart in January of 1995. Grimson sent out an Americana starter package to radio of forty CDs, including music by the Bottle Rockets, Jim Lauderdale, Nick Lowe, and Lyle Lovett, and even Guy Clark's *Boats to Build*.

"I don't think anybody ever before in the music business just up and decided to start a radio chart with a new format," Grimson says.

> *Gavin* conjured it and then published a trademarked Americana chart. They decided to advocate on behalf of the record industry and the art-

ist, unlike *Radio & Records*, which advocated for the radio stations and didn't care about the record labels or artists. It was a big risk for *Gavin* to go out there and lead and get the credit or get all the heat and all the criticism. And that's exactly what happened. It was equal amounts praise and criticism in those early years. The *Gavin* attitude was "Why not do this? We're trying to make things happen," while R&R would say, "We're trying to reflect what radio does." It was a big deal that *Gavin* stepped out there.

"The chart started out with only forty-seven stations playing little nighttime shows," Hoelzle says. "But we were committed. If we do this chart, it will give Americana legitimacy, and then other stations will say 'We can do this.' The format was already there. The artists were already doing it, but we wanted to create a movement among radio with the legitimacy of a chart."

In December of 1994, the *Gavin Report* threw a party at Nashville's ASCAP office to celebrate the launch of the Americana chart. Guy was there, along with Emmylou Harris, Sam Bush, Rodney Crowell, Jim Lauderdale, Junior Brown, and many other artists now associated with the genre.

In the spring of 1995, Guy's latest album, *Dublin Blues*, shot to number one on *Gavin*'s new Americana Music Chart. At the same time, perhaps icing on the cake, the weekly alternative newspaper *Nashville Scene* in their "Best of Nashville" issue gave Guy the "Best Barfly" honor.

Guy and Susanna had gotten back together on the condition that they buy a house closer to town. They closed on a house on the dead end street of Stoneway Close in West Nashville. Susanna took over the upstairs. Guy made the bottom level his own, with a guitar-building studio that doubled as a place to write songs. The Clarks sold their Mt. Juliet house to Townes, who had divorced his wife Jeanene.

Back in those days, Susanna showed up at EMI Music Publishing late in the afternoons, dressed to the nines. She'd park her Cadillac in the lot and take a seat in the lobby waiting for songwriters to drift downstairs ready to leave for the night. Susanna would grab a group and head over to the patio at San Antonio Taco Company next to Vanderbilt, the Chicken Coop on the alley behind the Iguana, the Sunset Grill in Hillsboro Village, or whatever

bar she felt like going to that night. The antics of the songwriter club, especially Susanna, Guy, and Townes, overshadowed whatever else might have
been happening at whatever joint they took over.

Producer Dub Cornett was a regular at the Chicken Coop.

"I don't ever remember seeing Guy Clark inside the actual Iguana restaurant," Cornett says. "In the alley with a separate entrance, there was a place
that nobody knew. They called it the Chicken Coop because it was open air.
In the winter, they'd put plastic around it, but it was more like a patio bar.
The real bullshit and drinking and cigarette smoking happened there. That
is where the serious drinking went down. That's where Pat McLaughlin and
Guy and John Prine all held court. It was just an alcoholic bath."

Meanwhile, Guy had a new album to celebrate. The title track of his new
offering, "Dublin Blues," is based on the traditional Irish melody "Handsome Molly":

Well I wish I was in London
Or some other seaport town
Step my foot in a steamboat
And sail the ocean round

Sailing round the ocean
Sailing round the sea
I'd think of Handsome Molly
Wherever she may be

"That melody has just always charmed the pants off of me," Guy says. "It's
just so cool. I guess I'm still going through that period of where I want to
preserve those old songs that are just so incredibly beautiful. That happens
to be one of them. I've been called on it several times, and my answer is,
'You bet, I did steal it.' I know what I'm doing."

Despite returning to Guy, Susanna still asserted her independence. She
also inspired "Dublin Blues." "Guy and I had gone to Ireland together, but
Guy had to go to Oklahoma to play a golf tournament, and since I was already
over there, I thought I might as well go to Italy," Susanna says. I called my
friend Tom Gribbin and asked him to meet me in Ireland."

Gribbin recalls: "Susanna called me and said, 'Guy is playing at the music festival in Galway, and we're going to go for five days, and then I want to go to Italy. Why don't you come over and be our guest, and I'll take care of everything? Guy and Susanna are getting in a cab, and Susanna puts me on the phone with a travel agent."

Although Guy's favorite 'Irish' pub is a place called Hughes, Guy and Travis played at the folk club Róisín Dubh (translation Black Little Rose), named for a famous Irish political song. The place was packed when Guy and Travis took the stage and sang "Dublin Blues."

> *I wish I was in Austin*
> *In the Chili Parlor Bar*
> *Drinkin' Mad Dog Margaritas*
> *And not carin' where you are*
>
> *But here I sit in Dublin*
> *Just rollin' cigarettes*
> *Holdin' back and chokin' back*
> *The shakes with every breath.*

The Texas Chili Parlor on Lavaca Street in downtown Austin was the scene of many shenanigans perpetrated by Guy and his friends. "There was a clique of people in Austin: Bud Shrake, Gary Cartwright, Jerry Jeff, just all these crazy people," Guy says. "They decided to call this thing Mad Dog Inc. We had cards printed up. I still have my card. I was a member in good standing. Everyone was hanging out at the Chili Parlor, and they started ordering margaritas made with mescal, which is just horrible. The only reason it came about was because nobody had any money, and it was cheap. That was a Mad Dog Margarita. I had the line 'I wish I was in Austin in the Chili Parlor Bar.' I kept trying to get Rodney to write it with me, and he refused. I sat down one day and wrote it myself. It may have been the last good song I wrote by myself. It was just an existential look at how crazy that was."

"Turning Guy down wasn't one of the smartest things I ever did," Crowell says.

Guy came over to my house one day, and he said, "Hey, I got an idea for a song," and it was "Dublin Blues." I had been on this rant with Guy.

Songwriters would come over and hang with Guy, and they would get an idea and something started, and then they would split, and Guy would go back and write the song. I was harping at him about, "Hey, you're giving up half the song when you're really doing all the work." He pointed out to me that it started with a conversation, and the song is only there because the other writers sat with them. I said, "Yeah, but they didn't come back and do the revisions and turn it into the song that it is." So, to prove a point on "Dublin Blues," I said, "No. You go home and write it yourself. You're the best songwriter I know." So he did. Then I heard it, and I went, "Damn! I could have been part of this."

The song gained such popularity that people showed up at the Texas Chili Parlor to order Mad Dog Margaritas. Guy recalls, "One day after that song came out, I walked in there and the girl behind the bar said, 'You're Guy Clark, aren't you? You son of a bitch. You wrote that song about Mad Dog Margaritas. Now people come in here and order them and spit them out and want their money back.'"

Playing "Dublin Blues" provides one of the most powerful moments in Guy's shows. It's usually an encore, especially in Texas, and it seems the entire audience holds its breath when Guy starts "Well, I wish I was in Austin, hmm, hmmm."

"I can feel it from the audience," Guy says. "It's exactly what I'm trying to do. I love scaring people to death."

For *Dublin Blues*, Guy also wrote "Black Diamond Strings," which he calls "a love song to Rodney."

*J. W. Crowell was a hell of a man*
*He played two nights a week in a hillbilly band*
*He played at the Ice House on Telephone Road*
*And he played in the yard just to lighten his load*

*Black Diamond Strings*
*Oh, Black Diamond Strings*
*Drinkin' One W. Harper*
*Playin' Black Diamond Strings.*

"It is about the way Rodney grew up playing country music with his dad," Guy says. "Rodney . . . jokingly used 'One W. Harper' in a sentence [in reference to the bourbon brand I. W. Harper], and I just loved the sound of that."

"We used to laugh a lot about my dad," Crowell says. "I'd tell Guy stories. My dad's favorite whiskey was I. W. Harper. He would say, 'Last night, I got on that One W. Harper.' Guy would laugh at the One W. Harper part. Guy knew my mom and dad. They would come through now and again. By the time Guy and Susanna got to know my mom and dad, they were teetotalers and had been converted to Christianity. I was staying at Guy and Susanna's place on the lake once, and they were coming through, and I remember going around and gathering up all the whiskey bottles, cleaning up for them to come. And then my dad came and played guitar. Guy introduces it as a love song. I bawled like a baby when he played that for me."

After some prodding from Guy, Crowell joined him to write "Stuff That Works."

"I was getting a divorce, and I'd had my fifteen minutes of country music stardom, and that was all dismantling itself," Crowell says.

An old structure was falling away, and I was whining a little bit and said, "I'm quitting; I'm through with it." Guy showed up at my house one day. I opened the door, and before I said anything he said, "Shut up," as only Guy can deliver a line with that much gravity and finality. He said, "I've got an idea for a song." It was "Stuff That Works." We spent an afternoon writing that song, and I was back in the music business just like that. Just back on it. It was a happy moment, and it probably was the beginning of me coming out of a real funk that I was in—getting divorced, wasn't going to be a country star anymore, and now I didn't *want* to be one anymore. It was a good moment. Guy said "Hey, look. You're obviously talented. You want to be an artist or do you want to be a star?" He said, "You have the talent to be a star if you want to do that. Do it. There's nothing wrong with that. It's a different mind set. You want to be an artist, you dedicate yourself to that." I'm going, "I want to be an artist. I know the right answer." And then, that was a turning

Rodney Crowell and Guy Clark: many years of brotherhood, friendship, and creative partnership. Courtesy Guy Clark

point for me, actually where I started to dedicate myself . . . to realizing how to write, more than realizing how to charm. That was a sweet and friendly thing to do.

*I got an ol' blue shirt*
*And it suits me just fine*
*I like the way it feels*

So I wear it all the time
I got an old guitar
It won't ever stay in tune
I like the way it sounds
In a dark and empty room

I got an ol' pair of boots
And they fit just right
I can work all day
And I can dance all night
I got an ol' used car
And it runs just like a top
I get the feelin' it ain't
Ever gonna stop

Stuff that works, stuff that holds up
The kind of stuff you don't hang on the wall
Stuff that's real, stuff you feel
The kind of stuff you reach for when you fall

I got a pretty good friend
Who's seen me at my worst
He can't tell if I'm a blessing or a curse
But he always shows up
When the chips are down
That's the kind of stuff
I like to be around

I got a woman I love
She's crazy and paints like God
She's got a playground sense of justice
She won't take odds
I got a tattoo with her name
Right through my soul
I think everything she touches
Turns to gold.

"I had some of the verses started and it was a waltz," Guy says. "Rodney and I were writing, and I told him it was something I just couldn't get right. He changed it to 4/4, and then we wrote the rest of it. The recording I did of it was a little tedious, too long, but I eventually learned how to do it and how it should be paced. That's a standard piece of my repertoire."

Guy thinks "Hank Williams Said It Best" is too long but Susanna wouldn't let him change it. "I should've edited about half [of] that out," Guy says. "That was one of those songs that just poured out. Usually I'm meticulous about going back and editing my work, but on the work tape I made, I just decided to sing everything I'd written down, not go back and tidy it up and rearrange lines and really work on it. I played it for Susanna, and she said 'Man, don't you dare change one word of that.' That really is a line from a Hank Williams song recorded under his Luke the Drifter alter ego: 'Unless you have made no mistakes in your life be careful of the stones that you throw.' It just came out of my mouth and made me laugh so hard that I couldn't pass it up."

Susanna had the idea for "The Cape" while hanging out with Willie Nelson after a show. She told Nelson about jumping off the garage when she was a little kid. Susanna took the idea to her friend Jim Janosky, but, after failing to figure it out, they took it to Guy. "That's a really well-written song, and basically I wrote it," Guy says. "Susanna and Jim and I got together and talked about it a few times. Once again, I couldn't leave them out because I wouldn't have done it without the idea. The idea of the cape, the first time it was ever used like that was Superman in 1939. It wasn't a longtime, universal thing. Everybody knows what it means now, but fifty years ago, I don't think anyone knew. People love that song. I constantly hear: 'It changed my life.' It's even the theme song at some camp. 'Always trust your cape.' It's kind of like, 'Don't lose your inner child, nurture it.'"

Susanna was Guy's muse yet again for "Baby Took a Limo to Memphis." "She actually did exactly that," Guy says. "Susanna was going to Memphis to write with Keith Sykes. She had a plane ticket and called a limo to go to the airport. They were on their way to the airport, and this limo driver said, 'You're Susanna Clark, aren't you? You're married to Guy Clark. You know, I beat him out of about $300 the other night pitching quarters.' Susanna says, 'Take me to Memphis.' I didn't know it until she got back and told me she took a limo to Memphis. It was just so Susanna. She looked around, and there's a TV set and a bar. 'Fuck you guys, why would I want to take an airline to Memphis?'"

"Susanna always told me that Guy and Townes were staying out late gambling their money away," Keith Sykes says.

So she gets this big hit record with Richard Leigh and has plenty of money. Says she's going to come to Memphis to write with me, and she shows up and gets out of this big old limousine in our front driveway. It cost her like fifteen hundred dollars, and that was a pretty good chunk back then for regular working songwriting guys. We spent that week together writing at my house, and then we drove up to Kentucky to see Rodney play a show at Murray State University. Murray is the town where I was born, so I know the area. We got a cabin at Kentucky Lake and hung out there. We sat up and talked and had a great weekend together. I drove Susanna back to Nashville. The next time I called, I hear Guy wrote a song called "Baby Took a Limo to Memphis" and every line in that song is just dead solid on; it's just great.

Guy and Verlon Thompson wrote "Hangin' Your Life on the Wall" together, and Ramblin' Jack Elliott joined Guy on the recording. "One thing that influenced me was a song Jack did called '912 Greens,'" Guy says. "That's where 'Let Him Roll' and 'The Randall Knife' came from—that style of slow-talkin' blues. Jack had a line in there about an ex-ballet dancer, so I took it and changed it to 'I used to be an ex-bull rider.' Verlon had the first line, 'I used to be Juanita's old boyfriend,' and we threw lines back and forth until we had it."

Although Guy had recorded "The Randall Knife" on the Better Days album, he was never happy with the arrangement and tempo. Asylum president Kyle Lehning witnessed Guy perform the song at a show in Texas and asked him to record it again for Dublin Blues. "I thought I was going to have to call an ambulance to come get me after I heard him sing that song," Lehning says. "How does somebody do that emotional thing for a five-minute song? It killed me."

Like Old Friends and Boats to Build before it, Dublin Blues garnered rave reviews from critics. John T. Davis wrote in the Austin American Statesman that

Clark "pared away superfluous details and images until his tales of hard-scrabble characters, star-crossed lovers, out-of-time dreamers and des-peradoes, and vignettes of Lone Star life achieved the parched lyricism of a Georgia O'Keeffe painting or a Dorothea Lange photograph." *Modern Screen's Country Music* noted: "He's carved an indelible niche somewhere between the Willie 'n' Waylon outlaws, the poets, the folkies, the rebels and the true country legends."

Songwriters and music journalists who admire Guy often comment that his approach to writing lyrics is comparable to his skills as a luthier—that he crafts songs with the same detail and precision of an artisan wood-worker. In 1995, Rounder Records released a thirty-song, double-CD collection of Guy's three Warner Brothers albums, titled *Craftsman*, building on this master craftsman theme. Although he gave the okay to use the title for the record, it didn't sit well with Guy. He says that craftsmanship and songwriting use two different parts of his brain.

"I should have put a stop to that 'craftsman' shit a long time ago," Guy says. "It makes my skin crawl. It's nobody's fault but mine because I didn't step up and say, 'No, that's not right.' I consider what I do poetry. I don't need to prove I'm a poet in every line, and I'm not afraid to speak plainly in my songs. Not everything needs to be metaphor, and I don't need lofty words. But it is my obligation as a poet to be faithful to the verse. I write what I know. I write what I see."

"Guy at the core is a poet and an artist," Crowell agrees.

Guy has the best command of a paintbrush of anybody I think I've ever seen. I often said, "Guy, if I could paint like you, it's all I would do." He has a master's right hand. Maybe the confusion lies in the fact that he is also a very fine craftsman. He's a luthier. He builds things, and he builds things with care and with the exactitude of a master carpenter. I think it's important to separate the two. Somewhere along the line people started saying he crafts songs the way he builds guitars. That's the part that pisses him off. I think what makes him an even better poet and has elevated him above most is that self-editing, which comes from that craftsman sensibility. It doesn't negate the poetry. It actually refines it and frames it. It's understandable that if you're not really trying to understand your own creative process and how to access the poetry, you may just throw the luthier in with the poet, the songwriter, but to me it works as a whole.

"The first time I heard someone call Guy a craftsman, I knew it was a totally inadequate description," J. T. Van Zandt says. "Craft is like stringing beads onto a rope or shaping clay. It's something that can be taught and learned. I think that to write songs like Guy Clark requires living a certain way. It also requires a great deal of understanding for the human condition, and those aren't things you can learn necessarily. You can develop a skill, but you can't develop raw talent. You certainly can't write songs like Guy Clark. No one else can. To call it a craft or to call him a craftsman is—it's not even an understatement. It's just totally inaccurate."

"His songs are art," Verlon Thompson says.

You think of the great painters or sculptors; they do it every day. They tweak on this, and they throw it out, and they start over and do it again and again. That's what Guy's done. It's so much more nuanced. It's not construction. It's a layer, and you let it dry and see how that affects the layer beneath it and what's coming through and what's not. That's why going to an art museum with Guy is one of the coolest things. He's taught me stuff about art that I never knew about—what kind of paint you use and how certain paint reflects differently than another. I think Guy is as good an artist as he is a songwriter. He doesn't do it as much, but when he does . . . he just gets his stuff out and one day, there it is, a masterpiece. I think his painting is incredible. He's an artist in every sense of the word.

"Guy Clark is a poet," Lyle Lovett says. "His songs are literature. The first time I heard a Guy Clark song, I thought it made everything I'd heard up to that point something other than a song. It's his imagery, his subject matter and how he does it. It's poetry. And his sense of melody is wonderful. The musicality is as inspiring as the lyrics."

With *Boats to Build* and *Dublin Blues*, Guy made a strong statement about his commitment to his poetry. The songs were written with insight and

Townes, Susanna, and Guy at the Americana number one party for *Dublin Blues*.
Courtesy Guy Clark

authority about grown-up themes of hardship, risk, and consequences. All
of the arrangements and sounds are in service to the song. At age fifty-four,
Guy was finally living the writer-artist life he had always imagined.

·  ·  ·  ·  ·

*Gavin*'s Americana chart and Asylum Records cohosted a party at the
Iguana and Chicken Coop to celebrate *Dublin Blues*, Guy's first number one
album. Emmylou Harris presented Guy with a package of Black Diamond
strings. Guy, Susanna, and Townes got roaring drunk. Artists, agents, managers, publishers, and countless members of the Music Row elite filled the
restaurant and bar to celebrate the rise of Americana and toast its new king-
pin, Guy Clark.

## CHAPTER TWELVE

# To Live Is to Fly

In the fall of 1995 and spring of 1996, Guy and Townes toured the country together, trading songs on stages up and down the East Coast and West Coast and throughout the Midwest and South. They invited Steve Earle, Emmylou Harris, and Nashville blues singer Jonell Mosser to join them on September 3, 1995, for a show at Nashville's famed listening room, the Bluebird Cafe. The Bluebird, a club they would not typically play, holds only one hundred people and is a little uptight for the organized chaos of a Guy and Townes co-bill. The primary rule at the Bluebird is "Shhhh"—a reminder that no one is allowed to talk during the performances. It's a great policy if one wants to hang on every word a songwriter sings but difficult to follow if a performer wishes to loosen up a crowd. Guy and Townes needed the audience to pay attention to them but they also wanted the room to be relaxed and spontaneous.

Guy, Townes, Steve, and Emmylou agreed to play the Bluebird as a favor to Susanna. The show was a fundraiser for the Interfaith Dental Clinic, run by Susanna and Guy's friend Tom Underwood. "Tom needed support for the dental work he did for battered women who'd had their teeth knocked out by some jerk," Guy says. "Tom fixed their teeth so they would be presentable for job interviews."

Twenty recorded tracks from the live show, titled *Steve Earle, Townes Van Zandt, Guy Clark Together at the Bluebird Café*, was issued a few years later by American Originals Records out of New Jersey. A second disc of eighteen tracks was never released. It includes performances by Emmylou Harris and Jonell Mosser, as well as a rare duet of Townes and Jonell singing "If I Needed You." Earlier that year, Townes and Jonell had recorded "If I Needed You" for the soundtrack to Joyce Maynard's novel *Where Love Goes*. At the time, Maynard was well known for her novel *To Die For*, inspired by a true-crime story and adapted for a film starring Nicole Kidman. Maynard had also written *At Home in the World*, a memoir detailing her romantic relationship with acclaimed writer J. D. Salinger.

"All through my writing, I was listening to a lot of heartbreak music, as I always do," Maynard says. "I came up with the idea of producing a CD soundtrack to accompany my novel. My publishers thought this was a crazy idea, but I went ahead and did it anyway—which meant that I personally contacted a lot of artists, asking their permission to use cuts from their albums, chosen by me, on the CD. In the novel the main character, a woman, imagines she's Emmylou and sings a duet with her lover of 'If I Needed You.' I love that song, so I wanted it on my CD but as a duet. I couldn't get the rights to the Emmylou–Don Williams version, and I really wanted a duet, not the Townes version alone. So I tracked down Townes. He was pretty sick by this point and definitely in advance-stage alcoholism but a beautiful man. He said he'd sing the song for me as a duet if I'd get a recording studio and put together the musicians."

Producer Dub Cornett jumped in to help Maynard. They recorded at Javelina Studios in Nashville. Jonell joined Townes on vocals and Steve Earle played guitar, with Kieran Kane on octave mandolin, Tammy Rogers on fiddle, and Dave Jacques on bass.

I think maybe that was the last recorded session of Townes Van Zandt. "I don't know of anything he did after that. I remember Jonell, Guy, and especially Steve Earle really trying to backfill what Townes was not capable of doing that day. We had to work around him, if you want to know the truth. He was pretty frail. There wasn't a whole lot of Townes left at that time. I let him move at his pace, and I knew to use Jonell because Jonell really wanted this. She was pulling him along because it was something she wanted. Because of Townes everyone had a sense of finality about that session. I could smell that in the room. You could tell it. I could feel it in Guy; you could feel it in Steve. You could feel it in everybody that was around. There was something . . . it was important in that this might not happen again. I don't know whether it felt foreboding, but there was just something about it that it felt different than an average day that we were doing something. There was a reverence about it. Looking at Townes, it seemed everyone sensed that this [wasn't] going to happen again.

"Of course, Townes was in love with Joyce, so he was ready to do anything," Keith Case says. "She was spectacular looking, and Townes was just gaga about her."

Later that fall, Guy and Townes traveled the Northeast. They returned to the Bottom Line in New York City on Guy's fifty-fourth birthday and played the Iron Horse in Northampton, Massachusetts. Joyce Maynard was on the guest list at the Iron Horse. It was her birthday, and thanks to a little prompting from Susanna, Townes made up a birthday song and sang it to her backstage.

Everywhere Guy and Townes played, they filled rooms, and fans praised *Boats to Build* and *Dublin Blues*. Guy was on a roll and ready to start his next record. In his contract with Asylum Records, there was an option for a third record.

"We put out *Dublin Blues*, which I absolutely loved," says Kyle Lehning. "But, about that time, I had a nervous breakdown. It was clear that everything we were putting out was just failing miserably, and I was in the darkest possible place you can be. I had what I thought was the greatest opportunity on Music Row, and it was for shit. We put out records, and they wouldn't just fail, they would throw themselves into a big hole and cover themselves up with their own dirt. This record company thing was not working, and it was heartbreaking, and there's nothing I could do to change it."

Lehning got on a plane to New York to meet with the chairman of Elektra Records, Bob Krasnow. "He's the guy who hired me to start Asylum," Lehning says. I just told him, 'This is not going to work. We're trying. We're butting our heads against the wall, and we're losing money. I don't want to pretend to you that this concept of ours is actually going to be able to work because I just don't see it working.' Krasnow said 'Well, what will work?' I told him we can just start going mainstream and start putting records out that are similar to the ones that are already out there, and we can probably sell some records."

"Part of me was thinking, *well, that's not really what I signed up for*, but the other part of me was thinking *I have this whole company of people back in Nashville that deserve jobs*. I came back to Nashville and called a staff meeting. I said, 'The record company that I hired you to work for was the record company that we were working for when I left yesterday. The record company that you are now working for is a very different record company today. We're going to make some changes, and we're going to start signing things [acts] that are way more mainstream.' We did, and we started selling records."

When Guy called Lehning to ask about recording the next album, Lehning wasn't ready to have a conversation with him. "Guy said: 'My option is up. Are you going to do another record on me?' and I said 'Well, not right now,'" Lehning says. "Guy said, 'Well, the option's due now.' I said, 'We just put out *Dublin Blues*. We really need a little time to do this.' I think what happened is Guy just wanted the money. It was how he would get the next pile of dough. I said, 'Guy, I don't need another record from you for a year. We've got this record. I think it's brilliant. I want to work this record. I'm not ready to do another record right now.'"

> He said, "Well, so are you going to drop me?" I said, "I don't really want to drop you, but I don't want to start another record now. We couldn't put it out for a year." He says, "Well, does that mean you're going to drop me?" I really was trying to find some way to put this conversation off, but I wasn't in a headspace where I could really think clearly. I wasn't ready to do the next record. I didn't want to start spending the money. I didn't want to do it. I wanted to give it some time to work the record we had. He just couldn't hear it. I said "I don't want to do this record now." Guy says, "So you drop me?" I said, "Okay, I'm dropping you," and he said, "Well, fuck you," and he hung up.
>
> It would have been prudent for me to say, "Hey, time out. Let me talk to my people and see what's going on," but I was in the middle of this transition and it was just me, sideways record producer, running a record company, thinking that I don't want to be bullied into making a record I don't want to make right now. If the only option I've got is to either make a record or drop you, I'm going to drop you.

A few weeks later, Lehning attended a business luncheon in the back room of the Sunset Grill, a restaurant in Hillsboro Village that was a regular hangout for Guy. "There must've been two hundred people crammed into that room to talk about the state of the music business," Lehning says

> We're sitting there trying to have a conversation and all of the sudden I hear, "Hey, Kyle." The whole room looks toward the door. It's David Briggs and Guy, and they're both bombed. They're barely able to stand up at the door. I said, "Hi, Guy. How you doing?" He just gave me the finger. Just gave me the finger. I said, "It's nice to see you, too." He left, and Joe Galante looks over at me and says, "Don't feel bad. I had to drop him, too." The more I think about it, the sadder I get about the way we ended up not being able to do more together. My head went to a totally different place. I wasn't able to backpedal from that place. That's really on me, not on him. I should've been able to take a deep breath and look at this from a little different perspective. We could have done another record or two, and it would just fill the catalog and be ultimately good for him. I do have regret about that.

"That's just the business, and it's a different business than what I do," Guy says. "They are in the business of selling records, not of supporting the arts. I am an artist, a songwriter. I did the best I could, and they did the best they could with what they had to work with. It doesn't change a thing about what I do or how I do it."

Now Guy had it in his head that it was time to do a live album. He had an entire body of work from RCA and Warner Brothers that had never been recorded in the acoustic fashion he had embraced since *Old Friends*. "These are songs I played every night that are now twenty years old and I wanted to give them a different treatment on a record," Guy says.

He invited Barry Poss from Sugar Hill over to talk about returning to the indie label that had done so well with *Old Friends*. "*Old Friends* was a one-off, and I obviously didn't have any say in the matter what happened after that," Poss says.

> Honestly, after *Dublin Blues* came out, it was such a beautiful record, I never thought Guy would return to Sugar Hill. But, you know, the truth is, the business was already changing, and Guy was changing, too. At

that time, the major-label music business got more major. It got bigger. But that also left a ton of room for niche labels like us to be successful. Niches are not mainstream, but these niches can be plenty large. I went to Guy's house and talked a little bit to Susanna and then went down to the basement. Guy proceeded to work at the workbench on his guitars and we talked. Just about nothing, about life, about music, about everything. And somewhere in the course of all that, we talked about business. I clearly didn't need to tell him how great he was, and he didn't need to hear it from me. I do remember telling him what I thought we could do as a label, without any hype or bullshit.

"This was a time when I think roots music was exciting, and there was a business to support it in a very hands-on way all up and down the chain," Poss says.

There were stores to sell records, there was radio to play them, there were clubs and festivals to perform them. All this made careers possible at a bunch of different levels. You didn't have to have a massive, mega-hit to exist. That change in the business was a benefit to us. Guy and I certainly did talk about how he wanted to present himself and how he wanted his work to be presented. As a practical matter, the big-time approach of handling Guy didn't really work for him. Certainly financially I don't think it worked. And it really wasn't a very honest portrayal of his music. I think Guy thought that on his early albums the songs were in service of the arrangements and not the other way around as it should be.

Guy recorded his first live album, *Keepers*, at Douglas Corner on Eighth Avenue South in Nashville's Melrose neighborhood, over the nights of October 31 to November 2, 1996. In recording lingo, a "keeper" is a good take on a recording. In songwriter jargon, a "keeper" is a well-written line or phrase. It's a term Guy uses often and a perfect description for the type of live album he intended to record. Guy picked Douglas Corner after hearing *Out of Our Hands*, a live album Verlon Thompson and Suzi Ragsdale had recorded in the club. "It sounded live, and it sounded like a lot of fun," Guy says. "I liked playing with people I don't play with every night. The attractive thing about sitting in a circle is being able to look at each other and communicate instead of me standing onstage in front of a band."

Guy and his chosen musicians sat in a circle on comfortable chairs, with throw rugs and dimmed lamps, which added to the intimacy. Travis Clark played bass. Verlon Thompson played acoustic guitar and sang harmony vocals. Darrell Scott played acoustic guitar, mandolin, Dobro, Weissenborn, and upright dulcimer, while Suzi Ragsdale joined in on accordion and harmony vocals. Kenny Malone played percussion. "It was a loose setting, but I had three nights of music and had to choose only fifteen songs," Guy says.

"I just remember Verlon and Darrell and Travis and Suzy and Kenny Malone seemed to be ecstatic to be there and doing this recording, which was more like a living room jam amongst friends than a formal recording session," says Poss.

Guy played two new songs for the *Keepers* album, "A Little of Both," written with Verlon Thompson, and "Out in the Parking Lot," written with Darrell Scott. Along with recording songs for the album, Guy called on some of his favorite artists to come up and sing. "He called up Vince Gill, Verlon, Darrell, and then he called up this fella who was sitting beside me who I didn't know and maybe even looked a little out of place to me," Poss says. "The fella gets up and says, 'What should I sing?' I said, 'Well, sing something you wrote.' So he started into 'Wild Thing' and I was about ready to chuckle, thinking maybe this was a joke. It's Halloween after all. Then I realized nobody else is chuckling. And I said, 'Sing another,' and he starts singing 'Angel of the Morning,' you know, the massive Juice Newton hit. That was my introduction to Chip Taylor, who I didn't know before that night."

Susanna spent all three nights of the *Keepers* recordings at Douglas Corner with Guy. After ending their separation, Susanna and Guy made a commitment to stay together. They promised each other that nothing and no one would come between them again. "Guy and Susanna were a universe unto themselves," Rosanne Cash says. "You almost didn't think of their names separately. They were as close as any couple I ever knew. It was like they were a unit. They weren't besotted with each other and all over each other. They were like a power bloc looking out onto the rest of the world. Very powerful."

Yet the marriage continued to be volatile. They both continued to drink a lot, and Guy hadn't slowed his cocaine and marijuana habits. Guy's career soared. He was finally getting recognition for his albums, and Keith Case had him booked on nonstop concert dates. But, Susanna hadn't been writing songs. She started a book project with a music journalist and had planned to write about her relationship with Guy and Townes, but, according to her journals, she wasn't sure she wanted to explore those bonds too deeply. It's clear from her writing that Susanna was restless and unsure about what was next for her own career.

"Songwriting is not a competitive sport," Guy says. "But at that time it seemed that Susanna wanted to be competitive with me. I don't know why. She wasn't getting something that she needed."

The recording of *Keepers* was the highlight of 1996. Guy was happy to be back with Sugar Hill and eager for the album's release, set for spring 1997.

Guy left for Ireland on November 12 and Susanna wrote in her journal: "Guy left for Ireland. My icy heart finally melted into a river of tears. He said 'I can't take this' and left. I'm over listening to people remind me of the early painful days when guyandsusanna was all one syllable. People want to cling to the illusion of the ideal us."

Guy returned a week later, and he and Susanna spent a quiet holiday together. They likely had dinner at Emmylou Harris's house on Thanksgiving, which was an annual tradition. For Christmas they stayed home, and friends dropped in to visit in the weeks around the holiday. On New Year's Eve, Townes's ex-wife Jeanene called to let Guy and Susanna know that Townes was in emergency surgery for a broken hip.

Jeanene signed Townes out of Summit Medical Center late on January 1, 1997, and took him home against medical advice. Doctors had insisted that Townes go to rehab and alcohol detox, but Jeanene had promised Townes she'd take him home after surgery. Jeanene was on the phone with Susanna when her son Will yelled for her.

Susanna recalls: "Her son came in the room where she was talking on the phone and said, 'Mama, it looks like Daddy's dead!' Jeanene went back there and said, 'Oh my god. Susanna, let me call you back.' Click. That's the way I found out. And he was going out of the driveway in an ambulance. And Jeanene said, 'They're lingering. You know they don't linger unless they're dying.'"

Forty-four years after Hank Williams died from heart failure exacerbated by alcohol and pills, Townes Van Zandt followed suit. Shocked by the sudden death of Susanna and Guy's best friend, their closest circle swooped in to prop them up. "When Townes died, Susanna called me and said, 'Townes has died.' I said, 'Hang on; I'll be over in a minute,'" Rodney Crowell says. "I went over, and we sat at the table, and Guy had a bottle of Johnny Walker Red, a quart, and he was hurting. He was drinking whiskey. When the pain is so deep, it's that moan, it's that timeless moan, and pain. Susanna was— that conversation was, 'You know, it's over.' She was just saying, 'It's over.' Guy was just trying to deal with the pain. Susanna surrendered something that night, as far as I could tell."

Her diary entries in the weeks after Townes's death hint at her pain. Susanna wrote in her journal on January 8:

The last time I talked to Townes he thought he had a pulled muscle, said he was in so much pain but it always made him feel better to talk to me. Harold had gotten him a wheelchair so since he always called just before he left for the road he called and said as always "Going out there, Babe, gotta roll, Babe, gotta roll." He always made me feel better, too. We dearly love each other very deeply. It may look on the surface like a very superficial silly thing, but there's a depth there that can't be touched. There's this electrical arc of understanding between the two of us. Last night Guy called from the studio and sounded so down. I asked if he was all right and he said crying, "My heart hurts." I said "Is there anything I can do for you?" He said "Say it ain't so."

On January 9, Susanna wrote:

I know your voice on the phone
first thing in the morning
I know your handwriting
scribbling a drunken song
Your soul's been released now
First thing in the morning
I know its you by your ring on the phone
I know your handwriting of last night's drunken song
Your soul's been released now

And you're probably better off
But what about me now?
We rode this life together
I'm feeling kinda lost
I'm stuck with the cast
Got to roll babe
Got to roll he said
You're on a roll now aren't you
That's what it's like being dead

Guy was dealing with his own pain from the loss. "I remember the first time I was alone after Townes had died, I was driving a car back to town. And all I could say all the way to town was, 'Oh no, oh no, oh no,'" Guy says.

At the Nashville memorial service, Guy joked that he had booked this gig long ago. "I was getting ready to play a song of Townes's and said 'I hope I can get through this. I booked this gig thirty years ago and I'm not gonna miss it,'" Guy says. "Townes was my best friend ever, but he also pissed me off more than anyone else could, except maybe Susanna. When the two of them got together they were impossible in their craziness. But he was brilliant and funny and the best songwriter I ever heard. He wrote literature and was the funniest and smartest guy I ever met. We were just best friends forever."

Susanna also got up to speak about her long, close relationship with Townes.

Every single morning at 8:30 for years Townes called me . . . Guy would usually bring me a cup of coffee because he knew we'd be on the phone for at least an hour. He'd say, "Hey, Babe." Townes was the only man I let call me Babe. We talked about art and artists and history, especially Texas history and Hank Williams and Lightnin' Hopkins and Vincent Van Gogh and Indians. We talked about the Bible and European ways and the sky that day and angels and ghosts and demons and Dylan Thomas and the birds and his dog. We talked about all the different kinds of love. He described each kind in detail. We talked about the language and words and poetry and songs. More often than not he'd read me his new poem of the day. Songs always had to work as a poem on paper first. Townes's rule. We always agreed about what we thought the first day of spring really was. He'd call and say "Hey, this is it." I would know exactly what he was talking about. I'd say, "Yep, I was just thinking the same thing." We did that year after year. Sometimes he'd tell me those terrible jokes of his. Sometimes he'd cry. Sometimes I'd cry for him. When I told him he drank too much he'd say, "Hey, there are sober people in India." We talked about the *Andy Griffith Show*. He couldn't watch violence on T.V. Only Nick at Nite usually. Yet he'd say: "If anybody touches you I'll slit their throat and drink their blood like wine." He'd make me laugh till it hurt regaling me with stories about his wildness. Or he'd let me cry till it didn't hurt. All he'd have to say was "Aw, Babe" and that would work. Sometimes I was spellbound. His words were always gentle and loving but like in his songs, mighty words they were. Sure, sometimes we'd fight about nothing, like the real meaning of the word innocence. Then we'd make jokes out of that word. He let me in his soul and I let him in mine. I had the honor and privilege of having this noble, wild soul in my life. He called me his best friend and sister. I called him my best friend and brother. We always said "I love you" before we hung up. This morning 8:30 came and the phone didn't ring.

"Townes's death really destroyed Susanna," Guy says. "She was grievous at Townes's death and really never got over it."

"When my father died, Susanna was very present and was kind of the hostess of the wake, which was at their house," J. T. Van Zandt says. "I was kind of leaning toward them for strength, really, because they were the representatives, just the stately sort of presence that Guy has. It's just natural to want to fall in close to him and especially in any threatening times. I was twenty-eight [in] 1997. Susanna was just real strong and making sure everyone—Lyle, Emmylou, Guy, Steve—everyone was there at the house. She was very functional, beautiful."

Townes had made provisions for Guy to be the executor of his estate. Guy had no intention of getting in the middle of the Van Zandt family drama and recused himself.

"It's none of my business," Guy says. "Jeanene assumed this position and attitude of being Townes's widow. She was not his widow. She was divorced from him before he died, but she just promoted that. She was bound and determined to make a living off of Townes because of all the shit she put up with and [because she'd] had two kids by him. She's pushy. She got the publishing, pretty much. The house was in her name. She bought that house in Mt. Juliet that was mine and Susanna's out on Old Hickory Lake. She moved Townes into it when they separated. I mean, he's never been able to take care of himself. He never went out of the apartment to have the gas turned on or the electricity. Jeanene is very smart, very Machiavellian. She and Harold Eggers have been fighting about putting out Townes's music all these years. Harold was Townes's road guy. Townes was his project. He really did take good care of him. When Townes died, he wanted his fucking pound of flesh, and I don't blame him, for all the shit he went through."

Although publicly Susanna held it together well enough in the beginning, her journals reflect the deep grief she felt at Townes's death.

JANUARY 10:

I miss Townes's gentleness. I feel like I married two men. Guy is fake tough, though I know fragile, he never much let it show except through his songs. Townes was gentle out loud to me, though his songs were there, too. This morning Guy and I were laughing about the difference in our friendship with Townes. Townes would be crying about something and Guy'd walk into the room and he'd straighten up and say "Don't tell Guy I was crying" and say "Hey Amigo," and act tough, throw knives, throw dice and try to out throw each other. . . . Wish one thing I'd said at the funeral was how Townes was concerned about how Guy would take the fact that Walter Cronkite was off the air. . . . Guy said that Dan Rather was only a replacement and Walter would be back soon. That was the only way Guy could deal with it and Townes knew it and worried about him. All true. Very often Townes would come up to me and say "If Jeanene and Guy were in a car wreck and both died would you marry me?" I'd say "Of course, Townes." Then he'd say "I'll fix the brakes tomorrow."

Townes once said to me "Very few men have known you, very few men have known you well, and it's been a privilege to be on this earth at the same time you were. And it's been a privilege to be one of the few men who did know you well." Tears would run down, and I'd say, It's a privilege to know you, too. One time I told him he was just my other husband, in a way. He was the sensitive one. And many a time I could call him if I felt wronged by Guy and Townes would always say, Guy loves you. Guy loves you. And all he would have to say to me—I handed him—I let him have so much power that all he would have to do was say, "Oh, babe," and it would just work. And I immediately felt better.

I remember when Jim Janosky brought a girlfriend over and she was nervous to meet me because she thought I'd judge her. Jim said "Susanna, you can be a cobra." I told Townes about it and he said "Susanna, you are an orchid." After Townes died, we were sitting around the table the night before the memorial and a florist delivered one orchid in a big fish bowl, just one orchid. The card was signed by Diane Dickerson and just as I was trying to figure out why Diane sent me an orchid, she called me and said that Townes came to her in a dream and said send an orchid to Susanna and tell her to put it beside her bed. Townes told her to sign the card Townes and Diane, but Diane didn't want to do that because she was afraid she'd freak me out and that's why she called.

Susanna's niece, Sherri Talley, called Susanna to say she'd had a dream about Townes. Susanna insisted that Sherri write it all down and send it in a letter so Susanna might keep the story close to her. Sherri's letter reads:

JANUARY 10
On the night Townes died, I had a dream about him. I've never seen him, did not know he'd been hospitalized earlier and wasn't aware of anything that happened that night prior to dreaming this wonderful dream. Here it is:

He and I were in a hospital room together—both patients. He told me his name was Townes Van Zandt. He had long (past, just barely) his shoulders—brown hair. He was young—maybe in his twenties—thin and really healthy. He got up out of his bed and walked down the hall. Before he did, we talked. I don't remember what was said but I remember the feeling. I feel it every time I think about this dream. He had an overwhelming sense of kindness and gentleness. It was so powerful—like it engulfed the room and me. I feel it in my heart now—it bears down really strong. He wasn't of this world in the dream. I felt at the time that one of us was there to help the other but couldn't tell which. Now I know he was there so I'd tell you he's okay.

Susanna wrote in her journal:

JANUARY 13
Dear Townes,
How can I feel so bad? It's been 13 days since your soul was released and your spirit now flies. I hope to keep your soul here in my heart. I think you gave it to me from time to time. I selfishly want it safe from everyone. But I know that you're lightnin' fast and just visit me, let me take of your graces and watch me like you always did. I taught you of angels and you taught me of time so come to me now in my dreams. Carry me with you. Let love guide me like it did you so it seems.
Love, Susanna

JANUARY 25
God, I miss Townes! It's 8:30 and no phone call. The last couple of days have been the hardest of all. I asked Bill for copies of all the safety tapes we made of Townes and I talking about the early days. Bill emailed me back that he had *taped over* that interview. I completely came unglued. How could he be so insensitive? I had insisted we tape Townes first because we knew we were losing him. I had a long cry with Sherri, then Louise. Robin, my attorney, called and I was crying with her. I'm not taking any phone calls from Bill, can't even hear his voice. Between Tom and Robin he was convinced to send me everything. Hope it comes today. Can't fathom my despair. Before that happened, Rodney called with a command that I get outside and walk with him around Radnor Lake. Said I needed the gentleness of nature and fresh air. Rod and I talked gently and he said I would have a ball of grief come up in the next few days because the forest loves me and fresh air is related to emotions. Well, it came up all right when I heard Bill taped over the last words of Townes and me on tape. God it hurts, still. Crying now. I remember when I lived in Franklin and Townes took care of me during my

hysterectomy—cooking cowboy stew with flowers on the tray, singing for me. Talked to Rod about my agoraphobia and all the trees I was afraid to go amongst. He said "their bark's worse than their bite." I love him, taking such good care of me.

JANUARY 31
Townes says "I'm up and safe in the eyes of heaven." I came home from lunch and had a major meltdown crying so hard missing Townes's kindness, forgiveness, and voice. Wish I could get it together.

Susanna often mentioned to Guy that she believed Townes was in the room with them. With his immutable logic, Guy dismissed any otherworldly notions Susanna had about Townes's spirit lingering.

"I don't think Townes is in the room. Susanna does. Townes is dead," Guy says. "I can tell stories about him, remember him fondly or not so fondly. Mostly he just pisses me off, unresolved bullshit that I put up with."

January 14, 1997 was Guy and Susanna's twenty-fifth wedding anniversary. Because of her grief, Susanna didn't remember the occasion. Guy set up a surprise luncheon for his wife.

Susanna wrote in her journal:

What a wonderful day! It started by Ramblin' Jack Elliott calling and asking us to go to lunch. Just before we left for the Sunset Grill, Jeanene called to tell me about Townes's services in Dido, Texas. I cried all the way to the Sunset Grill. At the table was Jan Curry, Ramblin' Jack, Keith Case, Roy Rogers and his wife Gaynell, Waylon Holyfield, me and Guy. Suddenly the maitre'd brought over a bouquet of red roses and gave it to me. I said "What for?" Guy announced "Susanna has forgotten that today is our 25th wedding anniversary." I had, but I was delighted, and then Guy gave me a gift of two silver champagne glasses engraved with 1–14–97 – Guy and Susanna. The whole table got happy and people started sending wine over.

Asylum Records president Kyle Lehning was at the Sunset Grill that afternoon with two executives from the New York office. He hadn't spoken to Guy for more than a year. The last time Lehning ran into Guy was also at the Sunset Grill when Guy flipped him the bird.

I had not seen Guy since Townes passed away. I knew how close they
were and everything, but having not left under the best of circumstances,
I thought maybe silence was the best way to go. We walk in to Sunset,
and they seat us at a table two tables from Guy and his whole crew. I just
thought, *Okay, I just have to go over there right now.* I went over, and I said,
"Guy, it's really good to see you. I'm so sorry about Townes." He got up
and gave me a hug. I said hello to Susanna and everyone. We had a nice
moment. I went back to my table and I thought everything was okay.

Lehning and his party finished lunch and left the restaurant. As they walked
around the outside of the windowed atrium, Guy yelled from inside, "Hey,
Kyle!" Lehning recalls, "I turn around and look, and Guy shot me both middle fingers with the white man overbite, the whole deal. I'd had enough. So I
took my pants down and stuck my ass on the glass window and just pressed.
I didn't spread and press. I just pressed. I just smashed it. Got it up there
really good for a couple seconds, left it there. Then I pulled my pants up, but-

Guy surprised Susanna with red roses, wine glasses, and a lunch with friends for their
twenty-fifth wedding anniversary, January 14, 1997. Courtesy Guy Clark

toned up, zipped up, turned around and blew him a kiss, and walked off."

Lehning's mooning worked. Guy has deep respect for anyone who doesn't put up with his bad behavior. He never gave Kyle Lehning a hard time again. Susanna called Lehning the next day and said, "It was the best thing that could've happened. Guy loved it, and he said, 'All's forgiven.'"

A month after Townes died, RCA released The Essential Guy Clark, a twenty-track reissue of songs from Guy's first two RCA albums. RCA got the jump on Sugar Hill because the street date for Keepers wasn't until March, but the one thing RCA could not do with the old recordings is capture the intimacy of Guy's live performances. Only Keepers could bring fans a similar experience. On March 18, Guy and the band returned to Douglas Corner to celebrate the album release. On Keepers, Guy revisited many of his best-loved songs: "L.A. Freeway," "Texas 1947," "Like a Coat from the Cold," "Heartbroke," "The Last Gunfighter Ballad," "Better Days," "Homegrown Tomatoes," "She Ain't Goin' Nowhere," "South Coast of Texas," "That Old Time Feeling," "Let Him Roll," "Texas Cookin'," and "Desperados Waiting for a Train."

"Recording Keepers was some of the most fun I've had," Guy says. "I felt like I was going back and making what was wrong right again. I hated the arrangements of those songs on my early albums, and this was a way to bring them back to life."

Working with an independent label like Sugar Hill gave Guy the creative freedom to produce the kinds of records he desired. Guy knew what he wanted to record, who he wanted to record with, how he wanted it to sound, and in what order the songs should be presented. He also worked closely with the in-house art department on the aesthetics of the album packaging. Jim McGuire was the photographer for all of Guy's projects, and Guy had final say on the design.

"If it had to do with the artistic presentation of the music, he was in charge," Barry Poss says. "I also believe that Guy left room for input, which sometimes was accepted and sometimes not. Guy gave us latitude with the design but always with his final approval. Then there would be a shift. Our responsibilities kicked in, in terms of the sales, marketing, promotion of the album. I didn't have to tell him everything we were doing. I don't think he wanted to know everything we were doing, but if it had to do with the artistic presentation, that was key."

Although Guy missed Townes, his days were busy and filled with good work and good times. Guy and John Prine wrote together throughout February and March. After *Keepers* was released, Guy hit the road to support the record, starting with a showcase at La Zona Rosa in Austin during the South by Southwest conference. While he was in Austin, Guy attended an album release party for a young Texas artist named Jack Ingram. Ingram had just released *Livin' or Dyin'* on Ken Levitan's new independent Americana record label, Rising Tide. Although Ingram wrote most of the songs on *Livin' or Dyin'*, he covered a couple of his favorite songwriters, including Guy's "Rita Ballou."

"If you live in Texas and you're into music, and certainly if you're into singer-songwriters and country music and Jerry Jeff and Willie and all the crew, you just know Guy Clark like you know English," Ingram says,

> like you know Willie Nelson, like Americans know the national anthem. You just know Guy Clark songs. I don't remember ever learning about Guy Clark. I do remember uncovering the fact that Guy was so much a part of so many records that I grew up listening to, whether it was Rodney Crowell or certainly Jerry Jeff. The first experience I really had intimately with a Guy Clark song was when I cut "Rita Ballou" on *Livin' or Dyin'*. Steve Earle and Ray Kennedy produced that record. We had a listening party in Austin during South by Southwest at the Iron Works barbecue. I didn't know Guy was going to show up. I'm sitting over there on the back porch of the Iron Works, and in walks Guy Clark. The air left the room. I can't even think about anything else other than the fact that Guy Clark showed up to one of my release parties. This is the coolest thing that ever happened to a songwriter from Texas. At that same party we were talking about the fact I cut "Rita Ballou" and my take on it and the language. Just the lyrics of that song were so conversational for a Texan. Texas has never left Guy. He may not have lived here for forty years, but it doesn't matter if he lives to be 120 and never steps foot in the state again. Texas never left him in the way he talks, in the way he holds himself, in the way he methodically makes guitars, methodically writes songs. Those characteristics are certainly front and center down here of doing things the right way. There's just a thing about being from Texas where it just feels thick. That's what Guy has always felt like to

me. There's just depth and breadth and thickness. It's not heavy. It's just like trying to punch through the water. It's always going to be just thick, and your emotions become exaggerated. I don't even know how all that makes sense. I just know that it makes sense to me when I think about Guy. He reminds me of what a Texan should be.

At the end of March 1997, Guy and Verlon Thompson headed out for dates up and down the California coast. He came back to Nashville in time to attend Ramblin' Jack Elliott's show at the Bluebird.

In May, Guy and Verlon traveled east for shows at the Birchmere outside Washington, DC, the Bottom Line in New York, and back to the Iron Horse in Northampton, Massachusetts. Guy played the Summer Lights Festival in Nashville at the end of May and went to Telluride in Colorado before heading back to Texas for a run of dates. Darrell Scott opened for Guy on June 24 and 25 at the Cactus Café in Austin.

Over the Independence Day weekend, Susanna accompanied Guy to the thirty-fifth wedding anniversary gathering for their friends Terry and Jo Harvey Allen. "We all stayed at the Camino Real Hotel in El Paso," Terry Allen says.

It was walking distance from the bridge over to Juarez. We played two nights in a sleazy-ass club called Wild Hairs, Blues and Adventure. Players were Will and Charlie Sexton, Ian Moore, Tom Russell, Dave Alvin, Joe Ely, my sons Bukka and Bale, Guy and me. We charged five dollars at the door and planned to go over to Juarez and spend it on a big meal at Martino's, a notorious French-Mexican restaurant. Instead we gave it to the priest of the Juarez dump and ate at Martino's anyway. This began a tradition of when we played an anniversary, wherever it was, we gave the door money to a local charity or someone who needed it. What a bunch of do-gooders, eh? We raised plenty of hell in various towns and clubs to atone for it.

After the anniversary party, Susanna went back to Nashville and Guy headed out on tour. He was on a roll, and when work was offered, he intended to take it. He finished out the summer with dates around the South and Midwest, and returned to the East Coast in the fall. In October 1997, Steve Earle released El Corazon. The album included a song Earle wrote about Townes called "Fort Worth Blues."

Guy had tried to write a song about Townes after his death but couldn't find the right words to describe Townes, their friendship, or his grief. It was emotional territory, which is one reason Guy and Townes never wrote a song together. They tried once with a tune called "Dr. Rippy," about a hippie doctor who practiced on Church Street in Nashville. They never made it past one verse. And Guy says he isn't sure he'll ever be able to write about Townes:

I've got about twenty pages of one-liners—emotional, tear-stained, wine-stained, coffee-stained one liners. I've been writing about Townes since the day I met him. One night we had a gig at Old Quarter in Houston. The show was about to start, and Townes wasn't there yet. Everybody's sitting around drinking and asking "Where's Townes? Is Townes here yet?" This whole club was just abuzz about Townes's whereabouts. They had good reason. I always thought that was part of Townes's charm. He knew exactly what he was doing. So I took a garbage sack and tore off a piece and filled it with stream-of-consciousness cinema verité about waiting for Townes and the whole crowd and all the girls and junkies and dope dealers and the winos. Everybody's just sitting in this fucking joint waiting for Townes until he finally shows up. I kept that piece of garbage sack. Something funny he did will flash in my head, and I'll start a page of just shit that comes into my head or just how pissed off I am at him still. The son of a bitch.

I always thought I'd finish a song about him, but then Steve Earle wrote "Fort Worth Blues," and that floored me. Emmylou came over and played me that song. She said, "Have you heard Steve's new song about Townes?" It just blew me away. I was in tears. Made her put it down on a disc right then. I just learned it immediately, absorbed it. I guess I didn't have to learn it. I already knew it. It became part of my set. It is really well-written. That was exactly what I wanted to say, but I couldn't have said it. That put a dent in my Townes song. I still have pages and pages of old stuff. I've never tried to push it out. I'm just allowing it to sit and fester.

During the year after Townes died, his friends and fans staged many tribute concerts. By then, the legend of Townes Van Zandt had already grown, raising him to mythical status and engendering hero worship. On December 7, 1997, Guy and Susanna hosted a "Celebration of Townes Van Zandt" for *Austin City Limits*.

"I think the most emotional time that Guy appeared on our show was with the tribute to Townes Van Zandt," producer Terry Lickona says.

I remember . . . just a few days after Townes had died, calling Guy, telling him that we wanted to do a tribute to Townes, and we wanted him to be our ringleader and help us round up the right artists to come and pay tribute. We asked Guy to be the conductor of that show. Talk about a guitar pull. We had about a dozen people on stage for that show. Lyle was back. We had Nanci Griffith. We had Steve Earle. We had Willie. We had Emmylou. We had some amazing people, but Guy really pulled it all together. He didn't say much about Townes, but what he did say really put it in perspective and showed the deep love and respect that Guy had for Townes. That's still one of my favorite *Austin City Limits* shows, over all these years. A lot of the credit for the way it turned out is thanks to Guy.

Crowell recalls:

After that tribute to Townes, that night Susanna told me, "I have a pain in my back." From then on, there was this mythical pain in Susanna's back. As time went on, I started to argue with her about the pain in her back, and I started to not believe that there was a pain in her back. I started this thing with her, "Well, you know, a lot of people have had pain in their back. I can give you three or four people who went and got surgery and corrected the pain." Susanna wanted pain pills. Guy and I talked about this. I'd be really open about it and say, "I don't know if there's real pain in there." Guy would say, "Who are we to say? If she says she's in pain, she's in pain." As far back as the 1970s, Susanna had described herself to me as an agoraphobic. I said, "What's an agoraphobic?" and she said, "[Someone who has] fear of the marketplace." After Townes died, that back pain set in, and she went to bed and didn't get up.

# PART THREE

## Guy and Me, 1998–Present

## CHAPTER THIRTEEN

# Always Trust Your Cape

I first met Guy Clark when I was managing editor at *Country Music* magazine. *Country Music* had been acquired by New York–based Sussex Publishers, the company behind *Spy*, *Psychology Today*, and *Mother Earth News*. It was Sussex's first foray into music. Because my colleagues (editor-in-chief Deb Barnes and senior editor Michael McCall) and I had long histories working in country music, Sussex gave us freedom to create the magazine we wanted. We covered mainstream country but also made plenty of room for the left-of-center stuff. It was the early days of Americana, and we admired the work of Americana bible *No Depression* magazine and often hired the same freelance writers. The album review section was my domain, and a quick look at back issues confirms my preference for Americana artists. Within just a few issues we covered Todd Snider, Gurf Morlix, Alison Krauss, Asleep at the Wheel, Buddy and Julie Miller, Billy Joe Shaver, Kelly Hogan and the Pine Valley Cosmonauts, Slaid Cleaves, Robin and Linda Williams, Nickel Creek, Walt Wilkins Band, Marty Stuart, Lynn Miles, Kim Richey, Stacy Dean Campbell, Old 97's, Townes, Bela Fleck, Jack Ingram, Matraca Berg, Jim Lauderdale, Kim Lenz and the Jaguars, Kris Kristofferson, Jon Randall, Bruce Robison, Kelly Willis, John Prine, Jimmie Dale Gilmore, the Mavericks, and, of course, Guy Clark.

At the same time we launched the updated version of *Country Music* magazine, a group of industry insiders formed the Americana Music Association. The radio chart was a few years old; it seemed a good time to organize around it and bring together record labels, artist managers, agents, publicists, venue owners, concert promoters, festivals, and record store owners to advocate for artists writing and playing the music we now called Americana. It was a heady time.

By the end of the twentieth century, Guy was at the top of his game. His live album, *Keepers*, picked up a nomination for Best Contemporary Folk Album at the fortieth annual Grammy Awards on February 25, 1998, at Radio City Music Hall in New York. Guy attended the ceremony with Barry Poss from Sugar Hill Records. Bob Dylan bested Guy. Dylan's *Time Out of Mind* album nabbed the folk record honors and also won big for Album of the Year. Shawn Colvin clinched Record of the Year honors for "Sunny Came Home." Both wins were a shot in the arm for folk and Americana music.

"There was an openness to roots music in general that was present and palpable," Poss says. "More people were writing about it. More people were listening to it, and consequently, in the end, maybe more people bought it. I think the Americana situation changed over time. It did become more relevant in terms of how consequential it was. It was great from the start as a promotional tool, because it gave us something to put a handle on things. For Sugar Hill, we were never really a bluegrass label, we were never really a folk label—we were all of the above. That Americana tag helped us a lot. Coinciding with that was the growth of festivals. For example, Merlefest went quickly from a few thousand people to one hundred thousand people. There was a lot more happening, and people seemed hungry for it."

In the last years of the millennium, Guy lived on the road. He roamed the United States playing solo dates, cavorted on bills with Terry Allen and Ramblin' Jack Elliott, and, in 1998, ran through Ireland with Eric Taylor as an opener. His tour calendar proves that he wasn't home more than a few days at a time for most of the year.

At South by Southwest, Guy played a show at Las Manitas restaurant with Rodney Crowell and Nanci Griffith. Griffith was gearing up to release her album *Other Voices, Too (A Trip Back to Bountiful)*, an album of cover songs that included "Desperados Waiting for a Train." It thrilled Guy to be in the company of traditional and influential folk standard bearers such as Stephen Foster, Pete Seeger, Woody Guthrie, Johnny Cash, and Ian Tyson. It seemed like the beginning of a new era for Guy. For many years he had influenced a small circle of artists and songwriters. Now in his late fifties, with a profound body of work, the ripple effect of Guy's influence on the greater music world was undeniable.

In July, Guy joined Griffith and friends to perform "Desperados Waiting for a Train" on the CBS *Late Show with David Letterman*. Letterman introduced the segment:

> Here's where we're going to straighten your life out. Just listen to the song and everything will be fine. Our next guest has recruited the best names in the business for her masterful new CD, and I'm telling you something, this is just terrific here. It's called *Other Voices, Too*, and performing with her tonight: Guy Clark, Jerry Jeff Walker, Rodney Crowell, Steve Earle, Jimmie Dale Gilmore—please hold your applause until I've mentioned everyone—Eric Taylor, and, of course, my hero, Nanci Griffith.

Guy kicked off the first verse, with Griffith singing harmony and everyone joining in on the chorus. Crowell and Gilmore shared the second verse, Earle and Walker shared the third, and Taylor and Griffith took the fourth verse. Guy sang the poignant last verse. Although meant to be Nanci Griffith's star turn on Letterman, it's clear that Guy is in the spotlight, his six friends looking upon him with reverence.

The following month, Vince Gill delivered his new album *The Key*. The title track, "The Key to Life" is a tribute to Gill's dad, influenced by Guy's "The Randall Knife":

> *I will honor my father with these words I write down*
> *As long as I remember him he'll always be around*
> *And the pain of losin' him cuts like a Randall Knife*
> *I learned a few chords on the banjo as the key to life.*

"I played on Guy's original version on *Better Days*, and that song just destroyed me," Gill says. "It reminded me of my life with my father. I broke a four-iron of my dad's. I never [confessed to] my dad about it. I hid it and got it reshafted. I finally told him when I was about thirty-five, and he still kicked my ass—he let me have it. I don't know what it was about that song, but every word of it fit me. There was such an interesting parallel. Ironically, my father then died when I was forty, just like Guy's did."

After Gill's father died, Guy presented him with handwritten lyrics to "The Randall Knife." The framed words hang in a prominent place in Gill's home studio.

In September of 1998, Lyle Lovett issued *Step Inside This House*, a two-disc set of cover songs written by Lovett's favorite Texas songwriters. The title track is the first song Guy committed to paper back in Houston. Although Guy never recorded it, the song was shared in and around Houston by other folksingers, passed around from stage to stage, much like Stephen Foster's "Oh Susanna" made its way from Pittsburgh to the California Gold Rush in the nineteenth century. Originally titled "Step Inside My House," the song morphed to "Step Inside This House" as singers learned it from one another.

"I learned 'Step Inside This House' from Eric Taylor," Lovett says.

Eric and Vince Bell and Don Sanders were people I would listen to when I was eighteen. They played places like Anderson Fair in Houston. Eric was one of the young guys who hung around Guy and Townes when they lived in Houston, a twenty-year-old kid from Georgia who moved to Houston to play and write songs. I loved hanging out in the back room at Anderson Fair listening to Eric and Vince tell stories about hanging out with Townes and Guy. Eric learned "Step Inside This House" from hearing Guy do it. The version that Eric does is a little bit different than Guy's. Guy's song is called "Step Inside My House." When I asked Guy if I could record the song and he said yes, I asked if he'd send me the words. I love to look at Guy's handwriting. The lyric that I sing, that I heard from Eric, is "Step inside this house, girl." Guy's lyric was "Step inside my house, babe." I think Guy Clark can pull off singing "babe," but I can't. So I sang it the way I'd learned it from Eric.

After one of the guitar pulls at the Paramount Theatre in Vancouver, we were riding in the elevator after the show. I had ended with "Step Inside This House." Guy said, "Man, I wish you would stop doing that song. That song is too long. There's a reason I never recorded it." I laughed. I think it's a brilliant song. "Step Inside This House" always seemed to be an invitation into someone's life. The way Guy describes his life through his surroundings is elegant and beautiful. I thought that would be the perfect title song for that record because it was a collection of songs I grew up on. It was my way of saying, "Hey, come here and check this out. Check out these songs that I love so much. I think you'll love them too."

The following month, Lovett presented Guy with the ASCAP Foundation Lifetime Achievement Award. Guy had signed with the performing rights organization at the beginning of his career in Nashville. In part, Lovett said:

> The man we honor and the great songs he's written have always had a special meaning for me and for many others as well. For twenty-five years, this Texan has served as an inspiration and mentor and a friend to generations of singer-songwriters. I speak for writer artists like Rodney Crowell, Emmylou Harris, Nanci Griffith, Hal Ketchum, Jimmie Dale Gilmore, Joe Ely, Steve Earle, Radney Foster, Robert Earl Keen, and, most of all, myself. He's also influenced and inspired his contemporaries like Mickey Newbury, Jerry Jeff Walker, and the late Townes Van Zandt. . . . In addition to being one of the preeminent singer-songwriters to come out of the state of Texas, he's also an accomplished poet, painter, and guitar maker.

Rodney Crowell walked out on stage with only an acoustic guitar and sang "L.A. Freeway" and "She Ain't Goin' Nowhere." Vince Gill joined him on the choruses for the latter song. After he finished singing, an emotional Crowell said: "I've known Guy for twenty-five years or more. I love Guy. Guy is probably the most intimidating man I've ever met. He's also the most kind-hearted, gentle, and sweet man I've ever met. He had a great impact on me. For twenty-five years plus, Guy's been writing the best songs I've heard. It's always museum-quality when it comes to Guy Clark. My hat's off to ASCAP for recognizing who I think is the finest artist in Nashville, Tennessee.

As Lovett called Guy to the stage, the several thousand writers in the hall jumped to their feet to applaud. The standing ovation lasted several minutes as Guy hugged Lovett and whispered to him before stepping to the microphone. Sighing heavily as he studied the award, he said: "Thank you.

Thank you very much. This is breathtaking. Susanna, my wife Susanna, and I moved here twenty-seven years ago. I figure another ten or fifteen. I'll probably break even." The crowd laughed. "Without wonderful friends like these—Rodney and Lyle and Vince and a thousand others too numerous to mention—this wouldn't be possible. And especially without Susanna. Thank you very much."

The crowd hopped up for a second round of long applause as Guy took his seat in the audience. We never see Susanna. Guy doesn't recall if she was with him that night. Her agoraphobia kept Susanna away from many big events. It had been ten months since Townes's death, and Susanna had mostly checked out. She couldn't seem to find her way out of the pain.

She wrote often about Townes in her 1998 journals: "How do you know Townes Van Zandt and not fall in love with him? You don't. It was easy to love you until the day you died. But it's so hard loving you for the rest of mine. When we meet again will you walk beside me and sing sweetly to my soul like you always did? I have more than a friend, a love that won't end."

As Susanna lifted Townes on a pedestal that rose higher and higher, Guy's stock plummeted in her eyes. At the same time she wrote lovingly about Townes, Susanna complained about her husband: "Guy Clark has an uneasy relationship with the truth. He will never be able to tell me the truth and most surely will never be set free by the truth. He'll never be shiny to me."

"Susanna was in love with Townes. Guy knows that. He talks about it," Crowell says. "Susanna was in love with Townes, but Townes was a satellite. Guy was the sun. Townes was Mars and Guy was the sun."

Susanna wasn't the only one who missed Townes. "Guy was in Durham to play a gig at the Carolina Theater, and we were backstage just talking and having a drink after the show," Barry Poss says. "At some point I asked him how he was dealing with the loss of Townes. He looked down and looked up and sort of looked at me, and he said, in a deadpan way, 'I don't have anyone to tell me whether my songs are any good.' I thought that was the saddest thing I'd ever heard. I mean, not in a maudlin way, don't get me wrong. It was just a very powerful commentary on their deep friendship."

Guy's mother, Frances, died in November 1998. He returned to Rockport for the memorial service in early December. Guy and Susanna then flew to

Albuquerque on Christmas Day to spend a week with Terry and Jo Harvey Allen. They came home shortly after the new year began. Susanna wrote in her journal: "Just got back from Santa Fe. Had a wonderful time. Had a terrible time. How must they see us? 'Marriage is the Kevorkian of romance.' From the movie *The Story of Us*."

Yet a month later, she was in better spirits, seemingly more hopeful:

FEB 11, 1999
I have exactly one month to be in my 50s. On March 11, I'll be 60. Thank God. What to do? What to do? What a massive change. I am going to sing and have fun from now on.

Guy hosted a sixtieth birthday party for his wife. Susanna's niece Sherri came up from Louisiana for the festivities. She recalls,

I noticed at this party how important to Susanna it was that she and her friends gave gifts of significance, not extravagance, something that meant something to the friendship. The gifts that were given to her at that party had significant meaning. It just really struck me as cool. That's something that I really valued in my relationship with her. When I went through my divorce Susanna sent me a pair of socks with a note, "These are for when someone knocks yours off." You know, I think everyone knows that she was witty and talented and a force in her profession. I don't know if people know how sensitive and kindhearted Susanna was. That was my experience. She cared deeply about us as a family. The hours that we spent talking, she wanted to know every detail about how our relationships were going, how work was. She really tried to offer advice and help and paid a lot of attention to each one of us.

In the first few years after Townes's death, Susanna was up and down. She was engaged enough to paint the cover art for Nanci Griffith's *Dust Bowl Symphony*, and she worked with the Country Music Hall of Fame to pull together an exhibit called *Workshirts and Stardust: Paintings by Guy and Susanna Clark*. She had stopped cowriting songs, however, and her journals were filled with nonsensical "automatic writing." For the most part she didn't leave the house.

Guy hadn't recorded an album of new material in nearly five years. Learning from his work on *Keepers*, he assembled his friends in the EMI studio to record *Cold Dog Soup*. Guy took control as producer and shared credit with Darrell Scott, Verlon Thompson, and engineer Chris Latham. It was the beginning of his tradition to coproduce his records with whomever was in the room, in a true collaborative spirit. Scott played accordion, autoharp, acoustic guitar, bass, mandocello, and mandolin. Thompson played banjo, acoustic guitar, and harmonica. Shawn Camp played fiddle and acoustic guitar. All of them joined Guy in singing.

Although Guy is happy with the work on *Cold Dog Soup*, the title song has a checkered past, and he's still mad about it.

"I'm very careful about lifting stuff from other people's work," Guy says.

I was writing with Mark Sanders. We had played in the same place in San Diego—the Heritage Coffeehouse. Tom Waits was the doorman at the time. I was living in L.A. Mark came over, and we were just talking, getting to know each other, and we started talking about this place, Heritage. He figured out that we were there at exactly the same time, both traditional folksingers. He comes over to write and has his list of hook lines and titles that everybody has. I was looking through it and saw "Cold Dog Soup," and I said, "I like that. It says something to me." We started talking about the old folkie days and Ramblin' Jack and Rosalie Sorrels and people they knew, like Kerouac. I don't know, it was just kind of a song that seemed pretty cool at the time. After the record was out, Keith [Case] got an email, not terribly irate, but very miffed, from the guy who wrote the book and consequently the movie called *Cold Dog Soup*. He knew he didn't have any control over titles as copyright holder, but he was miffed that someone he thought was good would lift his work. I was crushed. I didn't know what to do. I couldn't get a hold of Mark. I finally found him: "Mark, what is this?" "Oh, that's the title of a book. I saw it in a bookstore and just jotted it down. You know, they can't copyright the title." "Mark, that's not the point. The point is taking somebody's work and not telling me." There was nothing I could do. I had Keith write him a letter of apology. So: lesson learned.

Guy Clark, Ramblin' Jack Elliott, and Tom Waits outside a studio near San Francisco, circa 1995. They recorded "Old Time Feeling" together, but it was never released. Courtesy of the Guy Clark Collection.

Although he cowrote more than not these days, Guy wrote "Water Under the Bridge" and "Red River" by himself. "Red River" is Guy's romantic take on a piece of geography that's always been part of his life. "My grandmother lived right at the Red River," he says. "My mother was back and forth across it. I thought it would be a cool song."

My great grandfather came to that Red River line
And camped on the north side until it was time
To cross or to stay, to be Sooner or not
He headed south to San Antone, they said he liked it hot

Red River I know you, I know you of old
You have filled up my pockets with quicksand and gold
Susanna oh Susanna when it comes my time
Bury me south of that Red River line.

Guy and Verlon Thompson cowrote three tracks for the album: "Men Will Be Boys," "Indian Head Penny," and "Bunkhouse Blues."

"'Indian head Penny' was a song Verlon and I wrote the first day that we met," Guy says. "Verlon said, 'Hey, I have an idea about a coin that you carry around and all the stuff it's seen.' I said, 'I'm in.' I always thought it was a really good song. Verlon's rewritten the music a little bit, which is fine by me, and it sounds better than it was. We used to pitch it around. We went to a coin store and bought twenty-five 1909 Indianhead pennies. We couldn't get the originals, the ones that were minted in San Francisco. They're really rare and like fifty bucks apiece. The ones that were minted in Philadelphia and Denver aren't that rare. Anyway, we'd tape them to the cassette box every time we'd pitch it. The only person who cut it was a friend of Verlon's, Billy Dean."

"Indian Head Penny" was on Billy Dean's 1994 album Men'll Be Boys. Dean also recorded "Men Will Be Boys" and Dean's single of the song reached number sixty on the Billboard country chart. "'Men Will Be Boys' was just like a joke song, a play on words," Guy says. "I always thought a girl should do it. I've got a demo of it by Gretchen Peters before she got to be famous."

Guy recorded three cover songs on Cold Dog Soup, all written by his close friends: Richard Dobson's "Forever, for Always, for Certain"; Keith Sykes and Anna McGarrigle's "Be Gone Forever"; and Steve Earle's tribute to Townes, "Fort Worth Blues." Cold Dog Soup also introduced "Sis Draper," a true story about a fiddler from Arkansas known by Guy's cowriter Shawn Camp. "We really hadn't written much and really were just feeling each other out. 'Where you from?' That kind of stuff," Guy says. "He started talking about how he learned to play the fiddle. It was just this wonderful story about Sis Draper and his [Shawn's] family, all from Arkansas, and on and on. I finally stopped him and said, 'Shawn, this is the song.' It never occurred to him to write that close to home. It just took off from there."

"We were stuck on 'Sis Draper,'" Camp says. "We were due to record his album the next morning. Guy called me at midnight and he was up rockin'. I mean, he had been rockin' and he was rockin' right then. He said, 'Man, I think I've got it.' He quotes the last verse, and it doesn't match the other verses at all. It's totally different chord structure and rhyme scheme, and I was, like, 'This is it.' It was just whacked out enough to be beautiful. At ten the next morning, we cut that song. He was writing the final verse at midnight. He jackhammered it together. I think he stayed up the whole night."

"Good cocaine, I know that," Guy says.

For *Country Music*, I assigned a review of *Cold Dog Soup* to *No Depression* magazine cofounder Grant Alden. He wrote:

Of course, Guy Clark has little left to prove. For 25 years he has been an acclaimed singer and a successful songwriter. At 58 he is asked neither to expect nor to reject the footlights of fame, for what he has will endure, and there's little enough to be gained by arguing about the rest. Only the work itself, then, matters; that, and the will to continue to do that work. If Clark writes less compulsively than Texas compadres Steve Earle and the late Townes Van Zandt, he also sands his words to a more exact fit. *Cold Dog Soup* is his first collection of new songs in five years, his accustomed pace. More than ever Clark now sings with the patience of the thick, proud old men he once witnessed waiting for that train. . . . At some point Clark inevitably runs into his own legacy. Is it a triumph if he is merely as good as before? Well, yes, as a matter of fact.

During the same period, I worked with Lee Roy Parnell on a feature story for *Country Music*. We spent several days at Parnell's ranch in Fredericksburg, Texas, and while together cooked up a scheme to write an extensive book on Texas music. The ambitious book project never came to fruition, but it was Lee Roy who brought me to Guy Clark's house for the first time on April 1, 2000.

We arrived at noon that Saturday. Guy sat at the kitchen table rolling a cigarette and drinking coffee. Guy's house is so familiar and comfortable to me now that it's hard to recall the first visit, yet I know I was apprehensive. I had been a Guy Clark fan for so many years, and I suppose I may have been worried about the possible disappointment that often comes with meeting someone you've admired from afar. After Guy finished rolling a cigarette and a joint, we moved to the basement workshop, which fifteen years later looks exactly as it did that day.

My journal entry:

I interviewed Guy Clark. Lee Roy was there and it's a good thing he was. He and Guy are friends and I don't think Guy would have opened up nearly as much without Lee Roy there. When we started, Guy said "Well, let's smoke some pot and talk!" He smoked a lot of pot. Guy, Lee Roy and Donna [Lee Roy's girlfriend] passed a joint around several times and I kept saying, "No, I'm concentrating on these questions." I haven't smoked pot in so many years and it's really not my thing, but finally I felt like I had to at least pretend. It's pretty juvenile, I know, but when you're sitting around with a couple of stoned people and they start getting paranoid because you're not joining in—well—I just knew it would make things more comfortable if I took a hit. Anyhow, it was an absolutely AMAZING experience spending a day with Guy Clark. He's an incredible storyteller and his life is filled with incredible stories. He also talked a lot about Townes Van Zandt and Guy's wife Susanna invited me to come back any time to talk more about Townes.

We spent nine hours at Guy and Susanna's that day. Early in the afternoon, Susanna was dressed and hanging out with us in Guy's workshop. By early evening, she was in her nightgown in bed. "Susanna's been trying to rehabilitate a ruptured disk," Guy said. "When it happened, she actually turned white with pain. It was the worst thing I'd ever seen a human being go through. We finally got her to a neurologist who took a syringe full of Demerol and hit her with this giant thing, and it just didn't even touch it. So she is taking her time rehabilitating her back and sometimes she just has to lay down."

Susanna invited me to sit with her to talk about Townes. I was hesitant; I had never interviewed someone at bedside before, although it became a common occurrence for Susanna and me, and suppose I was too shy for that kind of intimacy with someone I had just met. Guy encouraged me to do it. "She is receiving in full court and would probably talk to you about Townes until the day after tomorrow if you let her. Susanna is the most eloquent about Townes because they were the best together, you know."

Susanna and I spent an hour together in her bedroom. We did talk about Townes, but she also asked a lot about me. "Do you like your work? If you could do anything you wanted to do, what would that be? Do you get a lot of flak from the good old boy network in Nashville? What is it about Guy's songs that speak to you?" She also told me that I didn't have to go back downstairs and take any bullshit from "those drunk guys."

In 2002, Sugar Hill hired me to write the media materials for Guy's next album, *The Dark*. Barry Poss had sold Sugar Hill to Welk Music Group (founded by the late Lawrence Welk), and because Poss planned to retire from the label, this was Guy's last hurrah with Sugar Hill.

This time I went to Guy's house alone to interview him. I arrived at noon on the dot, he offered me a drink, and we headed down to the workshop to talk. The saga of "Sis Draper" continued on *The Dark* with "Magnolia Wind" and "Soldier's Joy, 1864," two of several songs Guy and Shawn Camp had written featuring fictional characters they created around Sis. "'Magnolia Wind' is a song about Sis," Guy says. "'Soldier's Joy' is also part of that suite of songs. . . . We fantasized how a fiddle player would get started in Sis's family. This is about her great-great-grandfather who lost his leg in the Civil War, and he couldn't dance so he became a fiddle player. In chronological order, it all starts with 'Sis Draper' because all the characters come from that song. There are several more that are works in progress or pretty close to finished. These are the two I wanted to do on this album."

Although Guy had discovered Buddy Mondlock fifteen years earlier at the Kerrville Folk Festival, they had never written together until that time. "This year we wrote two songs together, 'Mud' and 'The Dark,'" Guy says. "Both of these were Buddy's ideas. When I write with other people, it brings out different parts of what I do, and I'm always surprised. It's really fun. When we wrote 'The Dark,' Buddy was in a really dark mood, and I was up and happy. He said, 'I'm a little darker than you are today.' It's really not a dark song, it's an uplifting song that is a take on life."

"I was just laying in bed the night before, and I was writing down whatever was going through my head, and I had a couple lines like, 'In the dark you can hear your own heart beat,' and stuff like that," Mondlock says.

I had a couple of chords that I was playing along with it. I brought in that run of images to start us off, and Guy was into it. We just kept brainstorming, and Guy came up with most of it. Just that string of stuff like firefly sparks, lightning, and stars. You can't see that stuff in the day. At the end, we really didn't have any kind of melody or even like a straight structure you could put a melody to. It was just really kind of free-form. Little rhymes popping up here and there. And at the end of the day, Guy said, "Well, tell you what, I'm just going to get the tape out and we're going to just record it. We don't have a melody yet, so just play those chords and just say whatever we've got so far. Just recite it." So I did, and we listened back to it, and it was like, "You know, that's kind of cool just like that."

"Queenie's Song" was written with Terry Allen. "We were out visiting Terry around Christmas and he said, 'Man, they shot my dog.' Someone shot his dog, and it crawled up under a tree and died. I just looked at him and said, 'We gotta write that.'"

Guy also cowrote the poignant "Homeless," this one with Ray Stephenson. "Ray was downtown on Lower Broad and saw some guy with that sign: 'Friend for Life, 25 cents.' It seems to be a simple song, but it's great," Guy says. "I glanced over it in my mind for several years, and, after dissecting it, it's strong as mare's breath. It's really wild."

The Dark includes "Arizona Star," a song about a character Guy knew from his early days in Nashville hanging around Hillsboro Village and Centennial Park. "She Loves to Ride Horses" was written with Keith Sykes about Sykes's wife, and "Bag of Bones" was written with Gary Nicholson about Nicholson's father. Guy wrote two songs with his neighbor Steve Nelson, "Dancin' Days" and "Off the Map." "Steve is a great songwriter," Guy says. "He's written musical lyrics for the Winnie the Pooh stuff and for Barbra Streisand."

As was by now tradition, Guy included a Townes song on the album. "Rex's Blues" was the choice. "I've loved that song since the day Townes wrote it, and I promised myself that I am going to put a Townes song on every record I do until the day I die because he was my friend and a great songwriter," Guy says. "This one was next on the list."

Guy had a little dustup with Sugar Hill over the artwork for *The Dark*. He wanted to use a photo of the sound hole of a guitar he had built, with his signature and bloody thumbprint (the way he marks all of his guitars) showing through the bracing. The Sugar Hill art director, Tasha Thomas, had another idea.

"We had this incredible image of Guy's thumbprint in red which our designer wanted to place on a black background," Poss says.

> It was very stark, very dramatic, very fitting, I think, for an album called *The Dark*. Guy wanted something else. He and Tasha got into it a little bit about that. I interceded. Nobody asked me to, but I was caught, like I really felt schizophrenic about his. On the one hand, I had this incredible respect for Guy, and on the other hand I had incredible respect for Tasha. I also knew that Tasha loved Guy. She didn't ask me to do it. I just picked up the phone and said, "Look, Guy, this is your choice, but regardless of anything, you need to know that Tasha's the one person who would never do anything to hurt you in any way." He went along with it, and I don't know if he was ever very happy about it, to be honest. Do I think it was the right decision? Sure. Do I think it matters in the long run? No.

"In the end, I think Tasha was right," Guy says. "I did have a different idea of what I wanted, but when I look at the album cover now, it is fitting."

*The Dark* was released in September of 2002. During the Americana Music Conference in Nashville, Sugar Hill Records hosted a small dinner for Guy at the Sunset Grill. After dinner, I climbed into the passenger seat of Guy's Jeep, and we headed downtown to Twelfth and Porter to see Jim Lauderdale play. I wrote in my journal later that night: "Why is it when I'm with Guy I want to be just like him? I drank so much wine and smoked and felt invincible. He is such a bad influence on me but it's so much fun. Here's this 60-year-old man who is just the coolest cat in the world. He just likes to get loose and party, talk to people, listen to music, and watch the scene. It's difficult to explain his presence because he's bigger than life."

That night, Guy and I talked about Susanna. I'm sure the weed and wine and Bailey's Irish Cream loosened his tongue more than if we had been down in his workshop during the day. We stood at the bar waiting for our drinks while Lauderdale sang in the next room. I asked how Susanna was doing with her back.

"She won't get out of bed," Guy said. "She won't go to a doctor. She just takes pain pills and smokes and smokes. I don't know what to do." He took a big swig from his tumbler of Irish Cream and crooked his arm in my direction and said, "So, let's go hear some music!"

I've been privy to many years of discussion about Susanna's condition. Did her back hurt as much as she claimed? Did she go downhill solely because of her grief over Townes? No one can say for sure, but those closest to her believe that Susanna just gave up after Townes died. The beautiful, enigmatic artist that half the men in Nashville were in love with was gone, and left in her place was the ghost of the woman she once was.

"When Townes died, she kind of died, too," Keith Sykes says. "It was very strange; she went to bed, and just seemed like she never got up. Every time I went to the house, and this went on for years. It was like a slow spiral, and it was just like Townes's spiral."

Susanna mostly hid in her bedroom, surrounded by many bottles of pain pills and cigarette packs. Guy and Rodney Crowell say they believe Susanna decided to slowly kill herself.

"I don't think she ever got over Bunny," Guy says. "Susanna always talked about it, how she wanted to kill herself because Bunny did."

"When her sister committed suicide, Susanna said that was her conscious choice," Crowell says.

Part of what she was saying was, "I could do the same thing." Susanna hung suicide out there pretty openly when I first met her. Part of her marriage and being with Guy and the threesome was that she could set that aside as long as she want[ed] to. That's why I think when Townes died and she went to bed, the choice she made was a long, slow one. I've fought with her about being in bed. I'd say, "I don't want to sit here by your bed. Get the fuck up." She'd look at me like, "You know what I'm doing." She said, "You know you're not gonna talk me out of this." She'd decided that that's how she's going to go out. Her sister committed suicide. Susanna decided she's gonna get behind that agoraphobia. She loves to describe it as fear of the marketplace. She decided that she was going to bed, and that's where she's gonna stay. I went through so many attempts, from tough love, to "Okay, I'm sorry," to "I need to talk to you," to "I'll come sit with you," to "All right, I'm not gonna indulge this behavior anymore."

"Susanna didn't care anymore," Guy says. "She didn't like being alive. She had no desire to do anything creative, which is what she was good at. She was a great painter. She wrote hit songs. Then she just gave up. I always felt like she blamed it on me because I was actually doing something. You know, I was out there doing it. She always thought I was competing with her, and she was the most competitive person I ever met. But when Townes died, that was the clicker. She didn't care after that. She lost Townes and it was all over."

## CHAPTER FOURTEEN

# Exposé

In the first years of the twenty-first century, Guy stayed on the road non-stop. Susanna needed a full-time caregiver, which was expensive, and Guy didn't like being home much anyhow. In 2002 and 2003, Mary Gauthier opened a span of shows. They played the East Coast at the Rams Head in Maryland, the Birchmere in the D.C. area, the Regent Theatre outside Boston, the Bottom Line in New York, the Beachland Ballroom in Cleveland, and the Rosebud in Pittsburgh. A run through California included stops in Santa Cruz and San Francisco. Gauthier wrote in her road journal: "Working with Guy is like riding a magic carpet. People fill the rooms for the show every single night, the promoters love having him come in, and the general attitude wherever we go is positive. People love Guy Clark. I love being his sidekick."

Gauthier says that Guy's audience is exactly the kind of audience she wants to find for her songs: "Educated, well-read, and well-spoken people that love literate songs."

Guy also spent time touring with Lovett, Ely, and Hiatt as part of the song swap they'd been performing together for more than a decade. Between 2003 and 2005, the foursome hit the road for long stretches to play theaters and performing arts centers all over North America.

The honors and accolades piled up. The Nashville Songwriters Hall of Fame installed Guy in October of 2004. The following year, the Americana Music Association, which had moved to Nashville's historic Ryman Auditorium for its fourth annual awards program, gave Guy a lifetime achievement award for songwriting. As a board member and incoming president of the association, I produced the show.

In retrospect, those seemed to be the last days of Guy's good health. Although clearly aging, Guy stood tall and appeared robust as he performed "Dublin Blues," joined by Emmylou Harris on harmony, Verlon Thompson on guitar, and Shawn Camp on fiddle. After a long standing ovation, Guy accepted the award humbly and with few words.

Barry Poss retired from Sugar Hill after selling the label to Welk Music Group. Guy moved over to the independent Dualtone Music Group for the remainder of his recording career. In early 2006, Scott Robinson from Dualtone called to ask me if I was interested in leading the public relations campaign for Guy's new album, scheduled for release in September. I walked up the block to pick up a copy of *Workbench Songs* (although I knew without

Emmylou Harris and Guy Clark during the Americana Honors and Awards 2005 at Ryman Auditorium in Nashville, where Guy was honored with a lifetime achievement award for songwriting. Courtesy Guy Clark

hearing it that I was definitely in). After listening to the record, I called Guy to tell him how much I loved it and was looking forward to working with him. "C'mon over and visit me," he said. "I have cancer." Guy had been diagnosed with non-Hodgkin's lymphoma, a cancer of the lymph nodes and lymphatic system that affects white blood cells.

Guy persevered through chemotherapy treatment that spring. He lost his hair and took to wearing an oversized cowboy hat. His hair loss was the only outward indication that Guy was sick.

"One day he came and stood in my doorway. He's wearing a straw cowboy hat, and I don't remember ever seeing Guy with a cowboy hat on," Gary Overton says. "He walks up to the chair and takes his hat off. His hair looked more like Uncle Remus than it did Guy Clark. It was all white. I said, 'What's going on, Guy?' He said, 'Well.' He pulled a little handful out. He said, 'I'm losing my hair. I got cancer.' 'Damn, man, I'm sorry.' He goes, 'Well, it's all right. I'm going through the treatments and stuff like that.' I said 'I'm really sorry. I understand those treatments are really rough.' Guy says, 'Oh, hell. I've had hangovers worse than this.'"

The treatments did affect how Guy felt from day to day, but his stoicism never wavered, and he carried on with his life as best he could. When Terry and Jo Harvey Allen hosted their forty-fourth wedding anniversary party in Marfa, Texas, over the July 4 holiday, much to the surprise of all their friends, Guy and Susanna showed up for the festivities.

"We had about ten cars in a circle facing each other with headlights on, and we were dancing in the dirt with the boom box," Joe Ely says. "We were all shocked when Guy and Susanna came walking through the dust out of the horizon in the middle of nowhere."

"It was such a big deal for her to come all that way. That's a long trip," Sharon Ely says. "We were all so glad to see her, even though she didn't come out of her room much."

"They holed up in the hotel room, except for the nights that we played," Terry Allen says. "Guy wasn't feeling that great then either. He had just [come] off some chemo. After the party was over, they had to put humidifiers and all kinds of stuff in that hotel room for about a month to get the smoke out before they could actually rent the room again."

"Terry and Jo Harvey invited everyone," Robert Earl Keen recalls.

Artists, writers, sculptors, musicians of every stripe went to the party. Every night there was a big jam at this hole in the wall, Joe's. Ray owned the bar, and the sign above the door said "Ray's," but everyone referred to the joint as Joe's. Each night there was a party. There was music playing like Marfa had not seen since the end of World War II. Joe Ely, Butch Hancock, Ryan Bingham, and a slew of the best acts anywhere played every night for four days. David Byrne played one night. You couldn't find a place to stand. Joe's was packed to the walls, and people were out of their minds with excitement. One of the nights, Guy played. People were screaming and hollering. Guy got up. Everybody shut up. We all settled in and listened to every word Guy Clark sang. His delivery was perfect and his singing never better. The night was exquisite. He played a wonderful, albeit short set. I was standing outside afterward, smoking a cigarette and drinking a beer, when Guy walked by carrying his guitar. Guy was all by himself, walking tall, holding that white guitar case. I started to ask him if he wanted some help. He seemed to be off in his own world so I decided to leave him alone. He put the guitar in the trunk and got behind the wheel, drove out of the parking lot. I remember thinking, *Man, he's already down the road and on his way to the next gig.* Joe's erupted in an explosion of twang and holler. I went back into the bar knowing the best part of the night was halfway to the interstate.

Although Susanna did go to Marfa, by the mid 2000s she rarely left the house unless it was for a doctor appointment.

"Susanna's friend Beth and Emmylou would mount an expedition to come over here once in awhile," Guy says. "They always got together on their birthdays, and any little occasion that came up they would come over and sit around and smoke. At least Susanna wasn't drinking anymore. That was a hard one for her to get over. I had seen her go through that for forty years, but this time she just didn't drink anymore. Cigarettes were enough. She went to the doctor all the time. She had cancer in her lung and they did surgery. It just gave her more impetus to smoke."

"Emmylou and I would huddle up outside and develop a strategy," Rodney recalls. "'I'm going to be the bad cop; you're going to be the good cop. I'm going to go in there and give her shit, and you're going to love on her.

Let's flip-flop. I can't be the bad guy all the time.' Susanna would be back in the bed. She'd say, 'Rod.' I'd say, 'I'm in the kitchen.' She'd say, 'Come in and see me,' and I'd say, 'I'm in the kitchen.' I wouldn't go in and see her. I tried everything, but I was no match for what she had decided she wanted to do. She wanted to die slowly and she did. Guy paid a high price for that. I was angry with her. She quit on me, she quit on Emmy, she quit on Guy, and she quit on herself. I was really angry about it, and it brought out some of my worst traits. There would be times when I would think, 'I've got to go and sit next to her, breathe her cigarette smoke, and tell her I love her,' because I do. I wasn't getting anything back. It was a selfish move on her part, and I'm still angry about it."

Keith Case adds, "We used to be the best of buddies, and I still love her dearly. "We would talk maybe four or five times a year, but they were always kind of lengthy, chatty, full of gossip and fun chats. I always had a lovely relationship with Susanna. We always had fun, and she's so smart and clever. After she was bedridden for several years, she seemed kind of hollow. I started avoiding her because I was so uncomfortable on the phone with her and seeing her like that. Once in a while there'd be a little glimmer of the old Susanna, but mostly just this hollow face. It's really sad."

Dualtone released *Workbench Songs* in September of 2006. The album included songs Guy had written with a couple of young writers.

"I get something out of writing with these young guys. It's not a one-way thing," Guy says. "When you're younger you're on fire with it. I'm still a songwriter and want to be a songwriter, but I'm not on fire, I guess, is the only way to describe it. I haven't written all the stories from my life yet. I feel like I have, but I know I haven't."

On *Workbench Songs*, Guy wrote "Magdalene" and "Funny Bone" with Ray Stephenson. "Ray had the title 'Magdalene,' and then he left and I pretty much wrote the song," Guy says. "Ray comes up with really interesting ideas. If I can get him to focus on it, I enjoy it even if I end up writing the song. Ray's refreshing in a way, but he wants to be a Nashville songwriter and write that trashy stuff. He's still trying to sleep with every girl he sees and put that in every song. I'm like, 'Goddamnit, Ray, don't bring that shit in here.' It'll take two, three weeks to get him out of that. We'll have a good idea started, and he'll go off in another direction, and I'll finally have to tell him, 'Ray, that's trash. Don't do that. I'm not gonna write like that.'"

"I would say as a rule that Guy is very generous," Gary Overton says. "I think most writers in Guy's position, if someone brought them an idea and said here's a title and then left, they wouldn't have touched it and [would] never [have] looked at it again. Guy must've looked at it and said, 'Hmm. There's something very interesting about this.' I don't think Guy ever in his life has set out to write a hit. He just writes the best song. I'm sure as he thought about it, it just started flowing from him, and it had to be written, whether Ray was there or not. I think it is pretty unusual [for] Guy or someone in Guy's position to give away half the song. Most writers would ask their publisher to give Ray only 10 percent of the song. It was just his idea, but Guy wrote the thing. I don't think it would've crossed Guy's mind to do that."

Overton is right. Guy is happy to share credit, and the financial windfall, if there is one, no matter how much his partner contributes to the actual writing of the song. He says without the ideas they bring to the table, there would be no song.

Steve Nelson brought the idea of "Walkin' Man" to the writing session and actually stuck around to see the song through. "It's like the wandering Jew who goes through history. It's the Trail of Tears, Woody Guthrie, Chuck Berry, Gandhi, Martin Luther King," Guy says. He also notes that "Walkin' Man" is the most political song he's written, although the social commentary of "Homeless" and "El Coyote" would soon join the sphere.

For *Workbench Songs*, Guy revamped "Out in the Parking Lot," which he had recorded first on the live *Keepers* album. He wrote "Tornado Time in Texas" and "Analog Girl" with Verlon Thompson, "Exposé" with Rodney Crowell and Hank DeVito, and "Cinco de Mayo in Memphis" with Chuck Mead. Gary Nicholson and Lee Roy Parnell came over to Guy's house one day, and they dreamed up "Worry B Gone" based on a title Nicholson had in his head. They went back and forth with the line "Give me one sip of that Worry B Gone" to "Give me one puff of that Worry B Gone." When Kenny Chesney recorded the song, he sang "sip," while Willie Nelson sang "puff."

"We were thinking if we wanted to get it cut it would have to be 'sip,'" Gary Nicholson said. "But I think Guy wanted it to be 'puff' all along."

Guy rounded out *Workbench Songs* with the traditional "Diamond Joe."

As tradition now dictated, Guy recorded the album at the EMI Publishing studio with Chris Latham as engineer and coproducer, along with Guy and Verlon Thompson. Thompson played guitar, mandolin, and harmonica and sang. Shawn Camp played guitar, fiddle, and mandolin and sang. Bryn Davies played upright acoustic bass and cello. Davies and Morgane Hayes shared harmony vocals on the tracks. Wayne Killius played drums, and Kevin Grant played piano.

Calling the album *Workbench Songs* gave the media an easy opportunity to compare the way Guy writes songs to the way he builds guitars. Guy invited journalists and editors from all over the country to join him in his workshop for interviews. The tired "craftsman" tag stained most of the reviews and features written about the album.

"I can't help that," Guy says. "They'll write what they write. I don't write songs at the same workbench that I build guitars, they just happen to be in the same room. I don't use the same side of my brain to build guitars and write songs. To me they are completely opposite endeavors."

Craig Havighurst did write a particularly stunning story for the *Nashville Tennessean* about what separates Guy as a songwriter and luthier:

Guy Clark is such a good songwriter that a metaphor follows him around. The Craftsman, he is often called, suggesting an especially deliberate approach to giving songs structural integrity and the proper balance between what's there and what's left out. This is something Clark learned about in three dimensions, for even as he's pursued the cerebral art of musical storytelling, Clark has spent a good portion of his 62 years making things with his hands. The first toy he can remember getting growing up in Texas is a pocket knife, followed by the toys he made from disused fruit crates with said pocket knife. He's been a carpenter, a draughtsman and the art director at a television station in the pre-digital era, when backgrounds and logos had to be cut, painted and assembled.

But even for somebody good with his hands, to set about building guitars takes nerve. Acoustic guitars especially are bewildering in their beauty, delicate enough to resonate boldly but strong enough to hold

The workbench where Guy Clark builds guitars with antique hand tools. Courtesy Paul Whitfield

several hundred pounds of string tension. They're laced with delicate braces and other parts that require precise hand carving. The differences between a great guitar and a good guitar or even a lousy guitar are elusive and hard to see, sometimes even hard to measure with precise tools. One of Clark's recent instruments came out sounding particularly good, but he can't figure out how to duplicate what worked about it. "I built two exactly alike," he says, "and the other's a red-headed stepchild." So he sent the fine one to a master builder who pored over it and a month later sent it back to Clark with a note: "It ain't in the numbers; you just got lucky."

And just as there has been trial, there has been error. One six-string Clark made decades ago for fellow songwriting great Mickey Newbury had its top sanded too thin, and the thing just collapsed. It sits on a shelf in Clark's workshop like a wrecked glider.

Guy has built mostly traditional flamenco guitars, based on Spanish ones made in the nineteenth century, and a blueprint for this style of guitar hangs

A portrait of Townes Van Zandt overlooks Guy's workshop, where he builds guitars and writes poetry. Courtesy Paul Whitfield

in his workshop. He's built ten guitars as of this writing, including one steel-string guitar, which Guy says is the best guitar he's ever played. Each guitar is marked with his thumbprint in blood and his unique autograph inside the sound hole.

"The most mysterious part of building a guitar is choosing the wood for the top," Guy says. "There are theories about the cross-grain stiffness and the note that it sings when you tap the raw wood and about how thick the braces have to be to affect the tone. I just experiment and build two at once and do different things to each of them to see how they sound."

Although a few people have made generous offers to purchase a Guy Clark original guitar, Guy refuses to sell them. He gave one to his grandson, Dylan, and one to Rodney Crowell. But as an extraordinary gift, Guy offered to teach a couple of his young friends to build guitars.

"Guy knew that I was making a living as a woodworker and had built some boats and stuff like that, so he made the suggestion that he would teach me how to build a guitar at his shop," J. T. Van Zandt says. "I just did what I could to make that happen with a full-time job. Two separate weeks I flew up there and got a hotel room pretty close to him and went over every day. I didn't really care about building a guitar at all, but it was an opportunity. For me to not take advantage of that would have been absolutely foolish."

He said like ten words an hour maybe, but to watch him with his tools is very cool. He is good with them. His favorite tool is this little drawknife. It's a very good piece of steel. It looks like a small pruning knife: big, thick, short wooden handle, but meaty. Then there's this tiny paring blade, but he was really comfortable carving into the curvature of the neck with it. He would say, "There are numerous ways to take off this material, but I like this knife here and you're welcome to use it." Then he would show me, draw a centerline and then start carving in that spot. He wasn't heavy on the verbal description, but he would get me started on something and then sit down and sigh and roll a cigarette. He'd sigh really heavy because he was in pain, he [had] hurt his knee, and he wasn't having a good time, and Susanna would call to him on the telephone or sometimes from the top of the stairs, and he was very attentive to that, very urgent and attentive to that.

Guy Clark with his grandchildren Dylan and Elissa, circa 1999. Courtesy Guy Clark

There would be periods when I would be left to the task, and I screwed up a little bit where the neck dovetails into the body of the guitar. I took the meat of the wood down too far, leaving it fairly thin. It's supposed to taper from thinnest at the top to thicker at the bottom, but I'd taken it to the point where it was gonna have to be the same thickness all the way down, and I was a little disappointed about that.

Guy is a hard worker. Any one of the tools on the magnet board above his bench, which are all high-quality Swiss, German, Japanese steel—they're all immaculately sharp. Keeping steel from rusting, keeping everything oiled. . . . He's got hundreds of . . . little tools and edges that he's gotta maintain, and they're all super sharp. For a guy who's on the road constantly and moving slow around the house, he gets a lot done.

I think he is gifted with an innate understanding of all things quality. Tools, the understanding of wood, making guitars, all that's just peripheral stuff to keep himself busy outside of traveling and writing and playing music, but it comes so easy to him. It's extraordinary to watch him work. He was gracious enough to allow me to build a guitar with him in his workshop, and I fancy myself as a woodworker. I've done it as a career for quite some time. He could take the knife from me and show me a certain way of doing stuff. It was just so amazing to watch him work that way and to be close to him.

Noel McKay is another young artist that sits at the feet of the master luthier. "I've learned a lot from watching how he does things," McKay says. "[Of] the guitars that Guy has built, one in particular, Number Ten, that's the best-sounding guitar that I've ever played in my entire life. I'm hoping that this guitar that I'm building with Guy will even sound a fraction as good as that one. It's been a really slow process. Guy is constantly telling me to slow down. He's a good teacher. He's patient most of the time. While I am looking forward to having the guitar finished and playing it, it's really a lot more about just getting to spend time with him."

The Country Music Hall of Fame invited Guy to anchor its fourth annual Artist-in-Residence series on September 6, 13, and 27, 2006. Cowboy Jack Clement, Earl Scruggs, and Tom T. Hall initiated the prestigious series in the first three seasons. Kris Kristofferson would follow Guy for year five in 2007, and then Jerry Douglas, Vince Gill, Buddy Miller, Connie Smith, Kenny Rogers, Ricky Skaggs, Alan Jackson, and Rosanne Cash rounded out the series through 2015. The resident artist curates three shows and often invites special guests.

For the first show in 2006, Verlon Thompson joined Guy. They rolled out their typical road show, playing acoustic guitars and singing more than twenty songs, putting the lyrics on display. On September 13, Guy traded songs with Rodney Crowell and Vince Gill. Thompson and Will Kimbrough added guitars to the mix. As one of Guy's favorite songwriters, Thompson also performed a couple of his own songs, impressing the audience as usual with his astonishing guitar chops and beautiful singing voice.

Guy brought in his studio band for the final show on September 27. Shawn Camp played fiddle and mandolin, Bryn Davies played upright acoustic bass, and Jamie Hartford played guitar and mandolin. The group played *Workbench Songs* from start to finish in the first set. The second half of the show, Guy and Camp showcased their suite of songs from the "Sis Draper" series, Emmylou Harris joined the band for a few songs, Guy paid tribute to Townes, and the performance ended with a stunning solo version of "The Randall Knife."

In October, Vince Gill released his album *These Days*, which includes a duet with Guy, a spoken-word vocal within the song "Almost Home," a poignant reading about the love between a father and a son. Gill invited Guy to sing the song with him at the Grand Ole Opry.

In the video from the show, Gill is visibly sensitive and passionate during the performance. Guy, his gray hair growing in curly after chemotherapy, is calm and composed.

"It was moving to get to do that song live with Guy," Gill says. "It may be the only time I've done that song live. There's a really neat unspoken love that Guy and I have for each other that doesn't need words. It was a great night for me. I remember writing that song and knowing that Guy had to be the voice that spoke the other part. And even then he changed phrases. 'Can I not say this? Can I say this instead?' He was remaking a song he didn't write and making it even cooler."

That December, *Workbench Songs* received a Grammy nomination for Best Contemporary Folk/Americana Album. Bob Dylan was nominated for *Modern*

Guy Clark joins Vince Gill at the Grand Ole Opry to sing "Almost Home." Courtesy
Vince Gill

*Times.* Guy shrugged his shoulders when Dylan took the honors at the forty-
ninth annual Grammy Awards in February 2007. "I'm always up against Dylan,
and he always wins," Guy says.

Guy spent the first part of 2007 on the road with Lovett, Ely, and Hiatt.
In March, New West Records released one of Guy's early *Austin City Limits*
shows on DVD as part of the *Live from Austin* series. That spring, Asleep at
the Wheel included "The Cape" on their album *Reinventing the Wheel*, and
Miranda Lambert recorded Susanna's song "Easy From Now On" on *Crazy
Ex-Girlfriend*. Guy cowrote "Salt of the Earth" with Tracy Nelson and Alice
Newman Vestal and sang with the two on a recording for Nelson's *You'll
Never Be a Stranger at My Door.*

Guy still liked being on the road and tried to tour as much as possible,
although, due to his health, it was getting harder and harder. When he was
home in Nashville, he showed up often for local happenings.

On October 28, the Country Music Hall of Fame inducted Vince Gill at its
annual Medallion Ceremony. Guy sang "The Randall Knife" as part of the
celebration. Before the show, Guy and I stood out on the back porch of the
museum as he smoked a cigarette. I asked about Susanna. "I told Susanna

it was time to see a new doctor," Guy said. "A lot has changed since she last saw one. Who knows what kind of new treatments they have? All she does is pop pain pills and watch TV—not that it's a bad life—they are pretty good pills."

A few days later, on November 1, we were back at the Ryman Auditorium for the Americana Honors and Awards. Lyle Lovett was there to receive the Americana Trailblazer Award (on his fiftieth birthday) and Joe Ely was on hand to accept the Lifetime Achievement Award for Performance. Each year, the president of the Americana Music Association presents the President's Award, a posthumous honor to recognize artists who exemplified the genre prior to their deaths. In 2006, I gave the award to Mickey Newbury. This year I wanted to celebrate Townes Van Zandt. Because I hate speaking in public, I recruited Joe Ely and Rodney Crowell to help me present the award to Townes's children Will and Katie Belle. Guy sang "To Live Is to Fly." After the show, we all gathered for press photos and our traditional champagne toast. Guy declined a drink. He told me the chemotherapy had made him lose his taste for alcohol, and he was still pissed off about it.

At South by Southwest in 2008, Gary and Francine Hartman took me to the Texas Chili Parlor bar. While we were there, Guy returned my call from earlier in the day. My ringtone is the first few lines of "Dublin Blues": "I wish I was in Austin, at the Chili Parlor bar drinking Mad Dog Margaritas and not caring where you are." When the phone rang with the ringtone and Guy was on the other end, the three of us laughed and laughed. Once we got hold of ourselves, Gary said: "Would you ever consider writing a book about Guy for our John and Robin Dickson series?" I said: "I would love to write a book about Guy, but there is no way he'd go for it." I told Gary and Francine about Guy's last album, Workbench Songs, and its song "Exposé." "Do not write my exposé / I do not kiss and tell." I just never believed for a moment that Guy would agree to me mucking around in his life.

Gary encouraged me to explore the idea with Guy, but I was too chicken to ask. A few months after the initial conversation with Gary, I pitched Keith Case the idea in an email. Keith called me the same day to say that Guy was enthusiastically in to do the book with me. Because of his tour schedule and my own obligations, we didn't have our first interview until December 2008. At first I visited Guy's workshop about once a week when he was in town. Guy dove right in, telling me the story of Bunny's suicide during our first meeting.

As we began working on the book, Guy was ready to record *Somedays the Song Writes You*. Dualtone hired me again to lead the publicity charge for the record release.

More and more, Guy found himself in a patriarchal position with young songwriters, as when he worked with Patrick Davis on "All She Wants Is You" and "Wrong Side of the Tracks."

Ray Stephenson brought his friend Joe Leathers over to Guy's house. Leathers wanted to write a song named "Hemingway's Whiskey," and Stephenson knew Guy would get it done. Guy was most excited about working with Jedd Hughes and Ashley Monroe. For Guy's new album, Hughes and Guy wrote "Hollywood," and Monroe joined them for "The Coat" and "One Way Ticket Down." Sometime earlier, Monroe had written a song with Guy and Jon Randall.

"I'd always been a fan of Guy's," Monroe says.

The first time I went over there with Jon Randall, I was real nervous. Susanna's sitting in her nightgown smoking Marlboro Reds. Guy takes us downstairs back into his workshop, which was amazing. I'm looking at all these guitars. He's got his rolling papers here, more rolling papers here. He's got tobacco and another little box of smokable things, and I thought *This is going to be fun.* He handed me a joint. I took a little puff of that, set it down. Then, as he keeps talking to me, I picked up one of his cigarettes and thought it was the joint and took a big puff, and I was coughing because I held it in. I started coughing, coughing, and coughing. He got so tickled. He thought that was just the funniest thing. Then I calmed down, and he started making jokes and making light of all the tobacco products.

We were on a roll to songwriting. I came in with a lot of ideas. I'd been up for days before because I wanted him to think I was a real songwriter. I had all these ideas, and I think Jon had a few ideas too. Jon and Guy kind of bullshitted, and all was good. We threw around a couple of ideas. He didn't say no or yes; he just said "Hmmm, hmmm" a few times. I thought that was it: *I just gave him my ideas and he hates them. I'm done.* Then Guy said: "Well, tell me about yourself." I told him I moved to Nashville when I was fifteen, and my dad died when I was thirteen. I went into this whole big long story, talking really fast. Then I said: "But look at me, I came up like a rose." He said, "Well, why don't we just write that?"

"Writing with Guy is so different because he doesn't have a system like a lot of Nashville songwriters can have, me included," Monroe says. "You think, okay, *verse, chorus, verse, chorus,* but he writes on graph paper, and it's so, so neat with the pencil. It's almost like a puzzle piece because he'll say a line and he'll put it up top. Then he'll say another line and put it at the bottom. I'm trying to follow along, almost trying to copy him, like, *okay, where's he putting these lines?* Then, sure enough, about an hour, an hour and a half into the writing process, you see a song. Every time, it's so rewarding because— he's just got his own way of doing it."

The first song Monroe wrote with Guy and Jon Randall, "Like a Rose," is the title of Monroe's 2013 album, produced by Vince Gill.

> *I was only 13 when my daddy died*
> *Mama started drinking and my brother just quit trying*
> *I'm still bouncing back, heaven only knows*
> *How I came out like a rose*
>
> *Ran off with what's his name when I turned 18*
> *Got me out of North Dakota, but it did not change a thing*
> *I left it in the yard, all covered up with snow*
> *And I came out like a rose*

For *Somedays the Song Writes You,* Monroe showed up to write with Guy and Jedd Hughes. "With Jedd and Guy and me, I feel like we each throw out a line, and then we just go around and it comes fairly easy," Monroe says.

Time stands still when I'm over there. Sometimes I forget what time it is. I had the title "One Way Ticket Down." I think I just brought it up as Jedd was noodling on Guy's guitars. I said, "Hey, I have this title I thought might be a good one." Guy said, "Huh. We should call it 'Rehab'!" Yes, we should; that makes sense. It kind of is, if you listen to it: it could be about either real drugs or a relationship that's toxic, definitely that you're happier getting away from. It turned out exactly how we meant it to, I guess. It didn't say "Rehab" on the title list, but we know.

One thing Guy's taught me, . . . just in life, is to be 100 percent who you are and 100 percent unapologetic. That's one of the reasons why I think people are so intimidated by his presence because he's 100 percent him. He really doesn't give a shit what anybody thinks, at all. He's respected for that. He hasn't given in to radio or to anything. He writes from his heart. He's nice. He's kind, and he's lived his life exactly how he's wanted to. When I'm in his presence, I'm constantly reminded of that. Everyone's trying to be something. All these songwriters who come over to his house are trying to make it, trying to be big, and are easily influenced by what people think or what people want. When you go and sit with Guy you're reminded to just be you. Say what you want to say. Do what you want to do. Live the songs you sing, and you'll still love doing it in fifty years.

Guy and Verlon Thompson wrote "The Guitar" during a workshop they taught at Jorma Kaukonen's Fur Peace Ranch Guitar Camp in Ohio. All the people in the room became part of the creation of the song. Guy asked Gary Overton at EMI if they could give everyone in the room a piece of the song.

"I asked 'What was their input?' and Guy said they were pretty much spectators on how a song gets written," Overton says. "I said, 'Well, to be honest, it's not out of greed, Guy, but it would be a nightmare trying to get ten others on a song like that.' His idea was the hippie 'Just make 'em all a part of this thing.' Guy is so giving of his time and his talent. He doesn't seem like he's expecting anything back, which is very rare, especially in this business."

"The class was supposedly going to write a song with Guy and Verlon," participant Jack Secord wrote in a letter to me. Secord suggested the topic for the song should be a guitar because Fur Peace is a guitar camp. Guy and Verlon took the suggestion for the topic, but it ended there. "The reality was we gave suggestions which they graciously considered, but they wrote the song allowing us to watch their process."

Thompson and Shawn Camp wrote "Maybe I Can Paint over That" with Guy, Rodney Crowell joined him on "Eamon," and Gary Nicholson and Jon Randall wrote "Somedays You Write the Song" with Guy. Guy chose Townes's "If I Needed You" for the customary nod to his best friend.

Guy was nearly sixty-eight when *Somedays* was issued in late September 2009. By that time, I had produced three tribute albums. *Beautiful Dreamer: The Songs of Stephen Foster, The Pilgrim: A Celebration of Kris Kristofferson* for Kris's seventieth birthday in 2006, and *The Bluegrass Elvises* with Shawn Camp and Billy Burnette for the thirtieth anniversary of Elvis Presley's death in 2007. Since Guy and I had been spending time together for the book, I started thinking about producing a tribute album to Guy in time for his seventieth birthday. I pitched it to one label in Nashville, and they declined. Gary Hartman suggested I talk with Icehouse Music in Houston, and he set up a meeting to introduce me to David Gardner, the president of Icehouse. Gardner was immediately enthusiastic about the project. It didn't take long to come to terms and to determine that we would make it a fundraiser for the Center for Texas Music History.

I didn't tell Guy until we were close to a deal. Guy's friends had recorded a beautiful, private tribute for his sixtieth birthday that was never commercially released. I wanted this to be different. I wished for the world to know and love Guy Clark and his songs and wanted those closest to him, the artists that knew him best or had been notably influenced by Guy, to record them. I wanted Shawn Camp and Verlon Thompson to lead the house band, and I wanted to record half of the album in Nashville and half of the album in Austin, with both Nashville and Austin musicians. There was no doubt this project would cost money and take time, but we had two years, we had a champion in Icehouse Music, and, as time unfolded, Austin's Music Road Records came to the table with significant contributions.

One day as Guy and I sat together working on this book, I told him I wanted to produce a tribute album for him. He was familiar with my work, and I think he liked it. "Why would you want to do that, Tamara?" he asked. "Because you deserve it," I said. "Well, I guess that's true," he said. Guy gave me his blessing, and I asked how involved he wanted to be. "It's your project, do what you want," Guy said. It didn't surprise me that he said that. What did surprise me is that Guy took a much more active role than I imagined he would. He never came to the studio, but each time I brought him the rough mixes from the day, he listened to them immediately, made comments, and often called me later to mention something else.

We recorded our first sessions in Nashville on January 27 and 28, 2010, at Blackbird Studio. John McBride, owner of Blackbird and husband of country star Martina McBride, gave us a sweet deal on the studio. He knew it was a low-budget record, and he loves Guy Clark. After I left John a message, he returned my call within twenty minutes. I soon found that to be true with everyone I called about the tribute album.

Niko Bolas engineered our initial Nashville sessions, and it was a thrill to work with him. When I hired Niko, we had a long talk about how I wanted the record to sound. Niko set up the studio so the band could play all in one room with the singer. I wanted to record old-school: no headphones, no isolation booths, with acoustic instruments and following in the footsteps of Guy. We set up baffles and arranged the room to get the best natural sound. It felt like RCA Studio B in the sixties in there.

Rodney Crowell kicked it off the first morning with "That Old Time Feeling," which he did in one take. I had blocked out considerable time for Rodney because I wanted to give him the time and space to do whatever he wanted to do. In addition to Shawn Camp playing guitar, mandolin and whatever else we needed and Verlon Thompson on acoustic guitar, our house band included Mike Bubb on upright acoustic bass, Kenny Malone on drums and percussion, and my friend Jen Gunderman on keyboard, accordion, and harmonium. Rodney brought Steuart Smith from the Eagles in to play on the track as well. It was magic the way it went down.

After Rodney, the band laid down the track for "Desperados Waiting for a Train," and Shawn did a scratch vocal. Willie Nelson recorded his vocal a few weeks later.

Kristofferson came in that day to sing "Hemingway's Whiskey." All of the musicians were excited to play with Kris, and he was equally as nervous about having to sing live with a band.

Radney Foster sang "L.A. Freeway." He had an electric guitar with him, and I said, "Uh, Rad, no electric on this record." He said, "Tamara, trust me." I let it go and figured we could do more takes without the electric if necessary. Of course, he was right. It was perfect.

Another magic moment was Jack Ingram singing "Stuff That Works." When Jack sat down with the band, he was looking for headphones, and I

Vince Gill, Billy Joe Shaver, Guy Clark, and Todd Snider pay tribute to Kris
Kristofferson as he is inducted into the Country Music Hall of Fame at the annual
Medallion Ceremony in 2004. Author photo

got on the speaker and said, "What do you think this is, Jack? Some mainstream studio session? Just sing the song. No headphones." He said "All
right!" and sang that song like he was living it, in one take. He flubbed a lyric
when he sang "She's got a playground sense of humor" instead of "playground sense of justice" but caught himself, laughed, and kept going. The
track is so charming with the mistake that I was half-tempted to use it. Guy
put a stop to that.

"The line has a completely different meaning if you say 'sense of humor'
instead of 'sense of justice,'" Guy said. Good thing we had Jack do more
than one take.

Verlon sang "I'm All through Throwing Good Love after Bad," and I love
Verlon's version much more than Guy's. I don't mind putting that in writing.

We got out of the studio late on Thursday night, and I planned to drop
off the first mixes to Guy the following morning. He was scheduled to have
sinus surgery on Monday, and because his health had been precarious I
was worried about him. The next morning, we woke up to several inches of
snow and a city that had shut down. For some reason, I just had to get those

mixes to Guy. My husband Paul and I ventured out in the snow. It took us more than thirty minutes to get the few miles to Guy's. There was no way to get up the hill on Stoneway Trail. Paul pulled over and I hiked the rest of the way up the hill and then slid and skittered my way down the Stoneway Close hill to Guy's house. I left the CD in the doorway and called him from the car to tell him it was there. "Tamara, you came out in the weather just for this?" Guy said. I didn't want to tell him I was worried about him.

We were scheduled to record at Cedar Creek Studios in March, but my mother had a serious accident. I canceled the sessions and went to Phoenix for several months to be with my mom. While I was there, Shawn Camp called to tell me that Guy was in the intensive care unit at Vanderbilt hospital, and they weren't sure he would make it. Shawn told me that Susanna had called Rodney to come over, and when Rodney got there Guy was near death in his bed. Rod called 911 and it saved Guy's life. Rodney also made arrangements to put Susanna in rehab while Guy was in Vanderbilt. He was persona non grata around Guy's house for months because of what Susanna called "meddling."

On August 29, 2010, the Nashville music community gathered for the Leadership Music Dale Franklin Awards, honoring Kris Kristofferson, Willie Nelson, and Monument Records founder Fred Foster. Vince Gill hosted the event. Lyle Lovett came to sing "Me and Bobby McGee" for Kristofferson, Shawn Camp led the house band, and I was there to present the award to Kris. None of us expected to see Guy. Between my mother's accident and Guy's illness, I hadn't seen him since January. No one else had seen him in many months. We were all stunned at his appearance. Guy looked thin and sallow. His hair had markedly thinned, and he had grown a goatee and walked with a cane. It was obvious that he was in a lot of pain. Vince Gill's wife Amy didn't make it to the event, so I brought Guy to Amy's place at our table. Vince sat between Guy and me. They talked for a few minutes, and then Vince leaned over and whispered to me: "Guy looks like the coolest Confederate soldier that ever lived. Oh, and I can't believe I'm sitting at a table with Kris Kristofferson, Guy Clark, and Lyle Lovett."

I took that opportunity to ask Vince to sing "The Randall Knife" for the tribute album. He said "Man, Tamara, I don't know if I can get through it." I said, "Of course you can. No one else can do this song. If you don't do it, I won't put it on the album."

After my speech for Kris, I came back to the table. Because Vince was up on the stage hosting, I took his seat next to Guy. He grabbed my hand and said "Good job, Tamara." Then he said he was hurting too much to sit there and needed to get home to Susanna. I walked out into the hallway with Guy. For me it was the beginning of believing that each time I saw Guy might be the last. That was five years ago, and I still think it.

Much to our collective surprise, Guy agreed to play a showcase at the Station Inn during the Americana Music Conference the following month. On September 8, hundreds of people lined up around the block to try to get in to see Guy's 11:00 p.m. set. Word had gotten out that Guy was ill, and many people believed he might be dying. Me included. I waited in the parking lot at the Station Inn at the parking spot reserved for Guy. He pulled up in his Jeep. It took him forever to get out, but when he did, he looked at me and said: "I don't need any help, Tamara." Showcases at the Americana festival are typically forty-five minutes long and start on the hour at 8:00 p.m., 9:00 p.m., 10:00 p.m., 11:00 p.m., midnight, and sometimes even 1:00 a.m. No one was scheduled to play after Guy. If Guy was willing to play, by God, they were going to give him all the time he wanted. Verlon Thompson was on the road, and Shawn Camp accompanied Guy in Verlon's place.

The show was transcendent. Maybe the best Guy Clark show I'd ever seen and heard (and I've experienced more than my share). Guy took request after request and played each song with reverence. Although he looked worse for wear, his voice sounded pristine. It felt like a long, slow good-bye, and the people in the room talked about it. "Is this going to be the last time we see a Guy Clark show?" someone next to me asked. In the restroom I overheard a tipsy woman crying to her girlfriend: "This is his last show. I just know this is his last show!"

Guy played for nearly two hours. He took a short break in the middle, and I was surprised when he got back up on stage. At the end of the show, everyone mobbed him. I appealed to fans to give him some breathing room, but they weren't having it. The entire room tried to get to him at once, just to tell him he was loved, that his songs mattered. After awhile, when he couldn't stand anymore, Guy spoke up and said to those in the immediate vicinity that he was sorry, he wasn't feeling well, and that he really had to go. Because the crowd was largely drunk, it wasn't easy to get them to back off. Shawn and I finally got Guy to his car. I hugged him. Guy is not a hugger. I hugged him again.

In October 2010 and January 2011, Shawn, Verlon, Jen Gunderman, and I went to Austin to record tracks for the tribute album at Cedar Creek Studios. Fred Remmert was our engineer. Lloyd Maines came in to play Dobro, mandolin and other instruments. Glenn Fukunaga played upright acoustic bass, and John Ross Silva played cajón on some of the tracks.

In October, we recorded the Trishas ("She Ain't Goin' Nowhere"), Terry Allen ("Old Friends"), Joe Ely ("Dublin Blues"), Robert Earl Keen ("Texas 1947"), and Hayes Carll ("Worry B Gone").

Hayes told a great story about visiting Guy's house, getting stoned with Guy in his workshop, and then walking upstairs to the kitchen to get a cup of coffee. He startled Susanna, who was in her bathrobe and pulling a tray of frozen taquitos out of the oven. Susanna screamed, the taquitos flew up into the air, and Hayes almost had a marijuana-induced heart attack.

"I was totally unprepared," Hayes says.

I smoked for fifteen years and thought I could handle my marijuana. The first time I ended up at his house I realized that I was not in his league. I spent the first three hours just sitting there thinking, *Man, I'm in Guy Clark's basement, and I'm too stoned to talk, let alone come up with any solid song ideas.* He just kept staring at me, going, "What've you got, kid?" I was, like, "Nothing! I'm freaking out here!" He was very gracious and tolerated me until I came up with a good line.

I kind of just kept throwing out lines and he'd say, "What else have you got?" I would play another one, and I was getting close to running out of ideas. I had this one line, "No rings upon my fingers / No ink beneath my skin / I'll be as clean going out / As I was going in." He said, "Let's write a song about that." So we just created this scene. We wrote about two-thirds of the song ["Rivertown"], and I remember going home and trying to finish it up. I mailed him a disc that I'd recorded it on, and he called me back and said, "I think you should change this to that"—very minute changes and ideas and suggestions and things that I would've completely let slip but in retrospect made a ton of difference for the worth of the song and its ability to last. Instead of just throwing up stuff and hoping it sticks, he thought through every part of it. It was really educational for me.

During the October sessions, Guy had a gig at the Paramount Theatre in Austin. The night before the show, the band and I met Guy over at Polvo's on South First Street for dinner. We sat on the patio, and Guy regaled us with stories from the old days in Houston.

The show at the Paramount was fantastic. Guy was in good form, and the audience was completely silent during his set, hanging on every word.

Back in Nashville at the end of October, Bob Edwards from Sirius XM Satellite Radio came to Guy's house for an interview. I arrived shortly before Edwards and his crew. Susanna looked terrible. She had lung cancer and had recently had surgery to remove part of a lung. She sat at the table smoking. Guy sat next to her with a brace on his knee and a medical boot on his foot. He told me he had to go back to the doctor after the interview to get infection scraped off one of his toes. He'd been trying to schedule knee replacement surgery, but they'd had to delay yet again because they could not operate if he had an infection. Guy had a hell of a time getting downstairs. His knee buckled at one point, and he almost fell. I tried to help him, but he said, "I'm okay. I can do this!" He was frustrated and in pain. The following day, the doctors amputated his toe.

On December 7, 2010, Emmylou Harris and John Prine joined us in the studio to sing "Magnolia Wind" for the tribute album. I had invited Emmy to be part of the record, and she took it upon herself to invite Prine, which saved me a phone call and made the album extra special to have a duet with the two of them. Emmy and John had gotten together the night before to rehearse. Emmylou told me she was nervous to record a Guy Clark song she had never sung before. "I'm so used to doing the Guy songs I know well," Emmy said. "This took me out of my comfort zone, but it's a good thing. I didn't know 'Magnolia Wind' and it's such a beautiful song."

I spent several days with Guy throughout the remainder of December. He seemed eager to get as much done as possible. I usually left after three or four hours with him, and each time he said: "Tamara, you come over here and get me all wound up, and then you leave." He would get on a roll, telling me stories from his life, but after a few hours I needed a break to absorb everything and get my thoughts together for our next session. And after a few hours it was tough to bear the cloud of cigarette and marijuana smoke.

In January 2011 we returned to Austin to continue recording for the tribute album. On January 4, Kevin Welch came in to sing "Magdalene" and Terri Hendrix recorded "The Dark." The next day, Verlon's birthday, Ray Wylie Hubbard came in to sing "Homegrown Tomatoes" and Rosie Flores recorded "Baby Took a Limo to Memphis." On January 6, Patty Griffin laid down "The Cape" and then stuck around to sing harmony when Lyle Lovett recorded "Anyhow I Love You." Shawn Camp sang the Waylon Jennings harmony part on Lyle's track.

When I returned to Nashville, I heard that Guy had more toes amputated. I met Steve Earle over at Guy's house and interviewed Guy and Steve for the book. Steve talked for four hours straight. Guy jumped in a few times to comment, but for the most part, he sat and quietly smoked while Steve told me stories about the early days in Nashville. Although Guy appeared composed as always, the pain etched on his face told a different story.

At the fifty-third Grammy Awards on February 13, *Somedays the Song Writes You* was up for Best Contemporary Folk Album. This time Guy lost to Ray LaMontagne and the Pariah Dogs for *God Willin' & the Creek Don't Rise*.

"I don't think it makes a bit of difference to me artistically to win a Grammy, but it'd be nice to know that my peers appreciate it enough," Guy said. "I've been to two Grammy Awards thinking I might win and would never go to that fucking thing again. It's such a cattle call of schmoozing, and if you don't do things in the order they tell you, you're in some deep shit with the Grammys. The last time I went, I just said, "Man, I'm never doing this again even if they call me and tell me I'm winning. Every time I'm nominated, Bob Dylan wins, so what the fuck."

# My Favorite Picture of You

We went back in the Nashville studio February 15, 16, and 17, 2011, to finish tracking *This One's for Him: A Tribute to Guy Clark*. Suzy Bogguss recorded "Instant Coffee Blues" and Shawn Camp recorded "Homeless." The band laid down tracks for "Better Days" and "All She Wants Is You" so Rosanne Cash and Shawn Colvin could add vocals later.

Ron Sexsmith was a last-minute addition and an anomaly on the album. Ron lives in Toronto and wasn't that familiar with Guy, and Guy doesn't know much about Ron, either. But I am a huge fan of Ron as a songwriter and performer and knew he would be a great fit for the album. The minute I heard he was in town, I began making phone calls to track him down, get him a couple of Guy songs, and find out if he was interested in covering one. The band was puzzled that I went out of my way to find Ron. None of them knew Ron's work and didn't understand why it was important to me to get him on the album. When Ron came in on our last day of tracking to sing "Broken Hearted People," he charmed everyone in the studio. Although he had only heard the song for the first time the day before, Ron just took it and branded it as his own. He insisted on doing several takes to get it just right, danced, played a mean guitar, and told great jokes. We had a wonderful time.

Jerry Jeff Walker came in later in the afternoon. He had agreed to cover "Water under the Bridge" but called Guy at the last minute to ask if Guy had a new song for him to record. "I just wasn't feeling 'Water under the Bridge' and thought it would be fun to record something new since I've recorded several of Guy's songs before he ever did," Jerry Jeff said. "When I called Guy to ask him what he had, he said, 'Well, I just wrote this new song about Susanna called 'My Favorite Picture of You.' Do you want to hear it?' Jerry Jeff pulled out a photocopy of the picture of Susanna to show the band. "Guy faxed me this picture. The words are exactly what he sees in this picture of Susanna."

> My favorite picture of you
> Is bent and it's faded and it's pinned to my wall
> You were so angry it's hard to believe we were lovers at all
> A fire in your eyes your heart on your sleeve
> A curse on your lips but all I can see
> Is beautiful
>
> My favorite picture of you
> Is the one where your wings are showin'
> Your arms are crossed and your fists are clenched
> Not gone but goin'
> A stand up angel who won't back down
> Nobody's fool nobody's clown
> You were smarter than that
>
> My favorite picture of you
> Is the one where it hasn't rained yet
> As I recall there came a winter squall
> And we got soakin' wet
> A thousand words in the blink of an eye
> The camera loves you and so do I
> Click.

Guy had played "My Favorite Picture of You" for Susanna shortly after he and Gordy Sampson finished writing the song. "I don't think we talked much about the song. Susanna was so far gone she didn't talk about much," Guy says. "I sat on the edge of the bed and played it for her. She was still in bed in her nightgown."

On June 7, 2011, Guy and Verlon picked me up in a brand-new black Cadillac rental car for a road trip down to Baton Rouge and then over to Texas.

We weren't in the car more than thirty minutes when Guy asked me what music I had brought. I handed over a CD by a young artist named Brian Wright. Guy popped it in, listened to it carefully, and even hit the rewind button a few times to go back and hear certain lyrics a second or third time. "He's good," Guy said. "I like his songs. He kind of reminds me of Joe Ely." We listened to Guy's demo sessions from the newest songs he had written: "My Favorite Picture of You," "El Coyote," "I'll Show Me," and "The High Price of Inspiration"—songs that would make it onto his next album.

About the time it was getting dark, we checked into the Embassy Suites in Baton Rouge. Guy struggled to walk, and it was up to Verlon to grab the suitcases and guitars and get everything to Guy's room. I stayed with Guy as he walked slowly and gingerly to the front desk. I tagged along on the road trip as a journalist, to cover the trip for this book, and expected to pay my own expenses. Guy would have none of it. He asked Keith Case to make sure the venues covered my hotel rooms, and when they weren't part of the contract he insisted on paying. I tried to argue, but there is no winning with Guy Clark. When I tried to present my credit card at the desk, Guy actually got snippy with me. "Tamara, I said no. You are my guest on this trip, and that's final."

On Wednesday, June 8, Guy and Verlon had a gig at a place called the Red Dragon in Baton Rouge. "It's not a club. It's more like a warehouse," Guy said. "They charge a hundred dollars a ticket, a hundred people come, and I walk out of there with six thousand dollars. The front rows are lined with couches, and everyone brings coolers with their liquor and wine and beer. There's usually food. It's a fun gig."

"All of our regular shows are twenty dollars each, but for Guy we charged a hundred dollars," the Red Dragon's Chris Maxwell says. "There was a good reason for the price. Six years ago we started trying to book Guy. An agent at Keith Case agency kept turning us down. I am very persistent. He finally responded with these exact words. 'Let me see if I can make this perfectly clear to you: Not just *no*, but *never*.' A couple of years later we enticed Keith Case to give us a shot. A friend described us to Keith by saying we were nuts but harmless. We got Guy and that agent has long since moved on. We've met that same price for every show and are happy to do it. I only wish we could pay more."

Knowing that Guy's knees were bad, the Red Dragon installed a parking spot permanently reserved for Guy, including a sign with his name on it.

The Red Dragon show was a tough one for Guy. He was in a lot of pain with his knees and hips. During sound check, Guy was testy and rude with the sound engineer. I had never seen Guy behave that way, and it disturbed me. He was usually so sweet and gentle.

The opening band was a fun bluegrass band named Fugitive Poets. They warmed up the crowd, and everyone was excited to see Guy play. He kicked off the show with "The Cape," a favorite of Red Dragon regular Ray Cate. Then, appropriately, he played "Baton Rouge" to large applause. After "L.A. Freeway," Guy performed "My Favorite Picture of You" for the first time in front of an audience. He forgot the words to "Hemingway's Whiskey" and "Magdalene" and scrapped both songs. After that, he started play "Homegrown Tomatoes" to the tune of "Baton Rouge." Verlon tried to get him back on track, and they started over again. Guy said: "Shit, I was going to do that song so good." Verlon had to bail Guy out and help with lyrics on "Out in the Parking Lot" and "The Guitar." He confused the verses on "The Randall Knife" but got through "Tornado Time in Texas" and "Stuff That Works."

Patrons George Fourmaux and Rick Colucci had invited me to sit with them on a couch in the second row. Verlon and I locked eyes a few times during the set. I think we were both heartsick about the whole thing. I was thankful that George and Rick shared their red wine with me. Finally Guy took a break, and Verlon sang a few songs. After Verlon's short set, Guy came back and finished the show with "Dublin Blues," "Desperados," "Boats to Build," "Old Friends," "Texas 1947," "Rita Ballou," and "She Ain't Goin' Nowhere." It was a strong second half, and he redeemed himself with most of the audience, although Keith Case did get a letter from one disgruntled fan who said the show was terrible, demanded a refund, and said that it was time for Guy to retire.

After the show, we stuck around to socialize with the crowd and eat delicious jambalaya that George had made. When we left for the hotel, Guy said he was in a lot of pain. The next morning we got in the car to drive to Rockport. Guy said, "I'm going to whine all day." He rolled a joint instead. When we crossed the Texas state line, "American Pie" was on the radio and Guy sang along. He rolled down his window and breathed deeply. I asked him if he was happy to be back in Texas. "Hell yeah," Guy said. "Home."

As we crossed the bridge between Copano and Aransas Bay on Highway 35 on our way into Rockport, Guy pointed out Copano Bay and told me it was where they had taken his father's ashes out to sea. He asked Verlon to cut over to Fulton Beach Road to drive the scenic route to the Inn at Fulton Harbor.

I spent the next day with Guy's sisters Caro and Jan looking through the family archives and interviewing them for the book. Guy took me back over to the house for dinner with his sisters, nieces, and nephews. The Rockport Music Festival was Saturday. Backstage before Guy's set, Jerry Jeff Walker and Guy sat at a picnic table and talked and laughed. Jerry Jeff asked Guy if he planned to perform "My Favorite Picture of You" that night. Guy said no, and Jerry Jeff sang it in his set instead. Guy's set was good. He stumbled a bit on "Hemingway's Whiskey" but otherwise his performance was perfect.

"I hate these kind of gigs outside when the sun is still up and kids and dogs are running around," Guy said. He believes his shows are more appropriate for listening rooms rather than festivals, but it was a special thing to play in Rockport. Although Guy's parents were long gone and Lola Bonner had died two years prior, many people in the audience were people he'd known since the sixth grade.

Guy's high school pals came backstage to say hello. I met Carl Snyder and told him I'd be calling him. Carl asked Guy if he could tell me everything. Guy said, "Yes, I want you to give Tamara whatever she wants."

We left Rockport on Sunday, June 12, to drive back to Austin. A local Americana radio programmer texted me to ask if Guy needed any weed. I said "Guy, so and so from this radio station is texting me to ask if you need some weed. He says he can get it for you." Guy said, "No, I think I'm all set here." After a pause he said: "Now, *that's* Americana." Verlon and I cracked up.

The next afternoon before the show, Guy, Verlon and I went to a little Mexican place for lunch. Guy had been paying my way the entire week although I continually protested and told him it was inappropriate. Discreetly, I found the waiter and paid the $15 check for our *migas*. When Guy found out I paid the check, he was miffed. "Tamara, I can't believe you're sneaking around behind my back." I said "A girl's gotta do what a girl's gotta do." Guy laughed at that one.

Guy smoked a joint before his show at Gruene Hall, which was not a good idea. The show was okay, not the semi-disaster Baton Rouge had been, but he was uneven and forgot a lot of lyrics. Shawn Camp met us there to play with Guy, and Verlon and Shawn saved the show. By the time we got Guy out of Gruene Hall, he could barely move, he was in so much pain. The tour had been rough on him, and it was only half over.

The next day, Guy and Verlon dropped me off at the Austin airport to get a rental car. They were continuing the tour, and I stayed in Austin to mix the tribute album. I leaned over to the front seat to kiss Guy on the cheek before I got out of the car. I said "Guy, this trip has been amazing—beyond my expectations. Thank you for letting me tag along and for your help on this book." He actually blushed when I kissed his cheek. He said, "It was fun having you along, and I'm glad it worked out. Call me and let me know what you need."

Shawn and I stayed in Austin for a week to work with Fred Remmert on the album mixes. At the last minute we pulled a track that just wasn't working. All along I had wanted J. T. Van Zandt to sing something for the album, but it hadn't worked out. I called J. T. and on the spur of the moment he came in to record "Let Him Roll." While we had him, I also asked J. T. to play "No Lonesome Tune," which I had intended to use as a hidden track at the end of the album, a nod to the fact that Guy usually has a Townes Van Zandt song on his records.

The next time I saw Guy, I told him about it. He said, "Tamara, I wish you wouldn't do that." I said, "Okay, why?" Guy said, "Can't I have something of my own that has nothing to do with Townes?" Since Townes's death, his legacy had been inflated to hero worship, and I suppose Guy was just tired of hearing about the legendary Townes Van Zandt all the time.

I talked with Emmylou Harris about it. "It's hard to deny dying young. It's hard to compete with that," Emmylou said. "I see it with Gram [Parsons]. I would have much rather that Gram lived and seen what he would do. He didn't live long enough to really fuck up in the way where people decided he wasn't really that good and that important or he was a flash in the pan. You escape all those things when you die young. It is a lot harder to grow old. You don't get any credit for carrying on with the dreariness and weariness of life."

Dualtone delivered Guy's second live record, *Songs and Stories*, on August 16. It had been recorded at Nashville's Belcourt Theater during an album release show for *Somedays the Song Writes You*. Although Guy agreed to put the album out, he isn't happy with the recording and now regrets that he allowed Dualtone to release it. "I suppose I need to just get over it," Guy says. "That night at the Belcourt was a hard night for me, and everything just felt off. Not one of my best shows."

In September, I headed to Monahans for a research trip and then met Guy and Verlon in Abilene. They played the Paramount Theatre as part of the West Texas Book and Music Fest. Guy's show was great. He remembered all the songs and was in top form. We had a glass of red wine together back stage. He was using a cane for balance but walking pretty well. He said physical therapy had been helping him. It was the strongest I'd seen him look since before his lymphoma treatments in 2006.

After Abilene, I went back to Austin and picked up advance copies of the tribute album. For cover art, I had commissioned a painting by Guy's co-writer Ray Stephenson, a beautiful visual artist. Although the painting is stunning, shrunk down to CD size it was clear it was not going to work. The printer couldn't get the color or detail right. Instead of looking crisp and clear, it was a muddy mess. I could live with it for advance press copies, but there was no way it was going to work for the commercial release. We were out of time, and we were out of money. Fred Remmert from Music Road talked to his partners Jimmy LaFave and Kelcy Warren, and Music Road generously and graciously stepped in to cover the new packaging. Now we just needed to find the right cover image, and fast.

I flew up to San Francisco with Kristofferson for the Hardly Strictly Bluegrass Festival. Guy and Verlon were scheduled to play the same day on a different stage. I tracked Guy down in his backstage tent to ask if I could use a Polaroid of Susanna and him in front of his Volkswagen truck for the album cover. The photo had been snapped in front of their first house in East Nashville. Guy thought it was a great idea. At the same time, I handed Guy a printout of the liner notes so he could go over the lyrics and make sure we had them right.

Fred Remmert introduced me via email to Shauna and Sarah Dodds from Backstage Design Studio in Austin. Shauna and Sarah took on the project and designed the entire package in less than two weeks. Music Road and Backstage Design Studio saved the day and allowed us to get the record out in time for Guy's seventieth birthday celebration.

On November 2, we gathered at the Long Center in Austin for *Wish I Was in Austin: A 70th Birthday Tribute to Guy Clark.* The artists from the tribute album played as a fund-raiser for the Center for Texas Music History and the launch of *This One's for Him: A Tribute to Guy Clark.* Guy's friends Jim McGuire, Tim DuBois, Liz Thiels, and Keith Case came in from Nashville. Other friends came in from all over the country to celebrate Guy's birthday. The house band for the show was the same one we used on our studio recordings: Shawn Camp, Verlon Thompson, Jen Gunderman, Lloyd Maines, Glenn Fukunaga, and John Ross Silva.

After we ran through the songs from the tribute album, Guy came to the stage to do a set. I introduced Guy:

I was fourteen years old in 1975 when I heard Guy's first LP, *Old No. 1.* Those ten perfect songs changed everything for me. Story song after story song—from "Rita Ballou" to "Desperados Waiting for a Train" to "Texas 1947"—took me to wild and wonderful places I'd never imagined. I was a teenager in Wisconsin, but somehow related to all these colorful Texans who danced the slow Uvalde and played Moon and 42. "She Ain't Goin' Nowhere" immediately became the theme song for my teen angst. All of you here know what a glorious experience it is to be moved by Guy Clark's songs. Guy is a poet whose words invite us into his stories. His melodies awaken our emotions. We taste and touch and feel all the heartache and hope that he delivers like no one else. He teaches lessons. When I was a young girl with feelings that needed some repairing, Guy taught me that it's all right to lay it down and live it like I please. Talk about a gift. Guy has given all of us so many great gifts. His songs continually enrich our lives. I hope this tribute album and my forthcoming biography will play a small part in celebrating and preserving Guy's unparalleled musical legacy for future generations. I'm proud to be here tonight to introduce the finest songwriter from the great state of Texas—Guy Clark.

Although Guy did his best to hold it together, even he got emotional when all of his friends gathered on stage with a cake to sing "Happy Birthday" and the crowd at the sold-out event sang along. It was a beautiful night.

I spent significant time at Guy's house in December. One day, as we were finishing up, I asked about interviewing Susanna again. We had spent time together over the years, but, as my research revealed more and more, I wanted to go deeper with Susanna. Honestly, I didn't believe I'd get anything useful from her at this point, but I wanted to try. Guy said, "Let's go upstairs to talk to her." He hollered up the stairs to Susanna, who was sitting at the dining room table and smoking. "Susanna, don't go to bed yet, I want to talk to you about something." He got in his chairlift to go upstairs, and I followed. When we reached Susanna at the dining room table, Guy bent down close to her face.

"Susanna, Tamara needs to interview you for this book. I want you to do this before you die."

I was mortified. "Guy, Guy, don't say that," I said. "Don't put her on the spot." Susanna looked up and me and said, "Well, not today, but maybe tomorrow." I said I'd call her to see how she felt before I came over.

The next day I interviewed Susanna for about an hour. We talked more about Townes than Guy. She kept confusing the two of them.

In January 2012, Guy spent a week or more in the hospital after emergency surgery to clean an artery in his leg in an effort to get blood flowing to his feet. Right before his surgery, he fell outside while trying to fix his mailbox. Verlon said it looked like someone beat him up. Fortunately, the surgeons were able to save Guy's leg. Guy said he was in screaming pain. In addition, his lymphoma flared up, and Guy had to endure another round of aggressive chemotherapy. During all of this, I continued to spend considerable time at Guy's house. I gave him every opportunity to stop, but he insisted we continue. Every time I was with Guy, he thanked me profusely for the tribute album and for taking on the challenge of writing the book. He was so tender with me, and it made me think he knew something bad was going to happen to him. I left his house one day to go interview Gary Overton. Guy said "Tamara, please, please give Gary my warmest, warmest regards."

By March, Guy was back on the road. His ability to rebound from the worst of the worst is extraordinary. I met Guy in Dallas for two shows at

Poor David's Pub. The second night, I had dinner plans with a friend who lived in Dallas that I hadn't seen in many years. Guy said, "Are you going to get to Poor David's in time to see my opening act?" I said, "I will do my best." Guy said, "Well, Tamara, if you can't make it for the first part of the show, don't come at all."

Brennen Leigh and Noel McKay opened for Guy that night. He knew I would fall in love with them. Guy had met Noel through his friend Kathleen Hudson at a Jimmie Rodgers Festival in 1993.

"My brother and I had a band called the Laughing Dogs," Noel says.

I remember seeing Kathleen drag Guy Clark out to sit in the audience and watch our set. Guy and Townes Van Zandt were the headliners of the festival. I remember looking out at the audience and thinking that we were completely bombing. Then we got offstage, and here comes Guy. He was this huge towering person. He had Lee Press-On Nails on his right hand to play guitar. He shook my hand, and he said, "I really loved that. I thought that was great." He wanted me to send everything that I had recorded to him on a cassette tape, to his house in Nashville, so that's what I did. He tried to get my brother and me a record deal. I mean, really, we were unprepared for that, but I stayed in touch with Guy over the years. When we started doing the McKay Brothers thing and would drive through Nashville, we would always go to Guy's house and hang out and watch him smoke. I didn't meet Susanna until years later. She was always in the bedroom lying on the bed. I could see her legs on the bed with the TV on really loud. We'd go downstairs to the shop and hang out and trade songs. He'd play us new songs, and he'd get us to play new songs for him. Every now and then the phone would ring, and Guy would answer. I guess about 30 percent of the time when Guy would answer it would be Susanna calling him from upstairs, and saying, "Guy, will you roll me one of those joints?" He'd roll her a joint and say, "I got to go take this to Susanna."

Guy was always really supportive of whatever project I had going on, whether it was the Laughing Dogs and the McKay Brothers, or when I started performing with Brennen Leigh. He was really supportive of that. My solo stuff too. Whenever we would go to his house, he'd always say,

"I got a new song. You want to hear it?" I mean, whenever he would say that, you would know that it was something that he was really proud of, and it was something really special.

On June 7, 2012, I spent the day with Guy. We talked for several hours, and then I spent several more hours sifting through files and photos and slides. I called Shawn Camp to ask him to help me load everything into my car. It took two trips to bring all of Guy's stuff back to my office. Two weeks later, after scanning and copying and organizing all of it, I took everything back to Guy's house.

My journal entry reads:

THURSDAY, JUNE 14

It was an interesting day at Guy's house. I went over there at noon to return his archives. Guy and Susanna were there alone without Susanna's caregiver. Susanna sat at the table in her LL Bean flannel nightgown chain-smoking her Marlboro Reds. I asked Guy if I should put everything back where I found it or if he wanted it stored somewhere else. He said: "Stack those photos on the table. I thought Susanna and I might look through them and take a trip down memory lane." I sat down next to Susanna and pulled out a photo of her parents. Before I could say anything, Susanna started talking about her family. Thankfully, I had my MP3 recorder in my bag and I pulled it out. This is the most lucid I've seen Susanna since 2000. She was bright-eyed, animated and spoke clearly. She was able to answer every question I threw at her, something that seemed a struggle in our last few interviews. Susanna talked about her parents, her siblings and her first husband. Then she turned to stories about Bunny and Guy and Townes. Guy and I sat at the table with her for more than two hours while she talked. Every once in awhile Guy and I would look at each other in disbelief. It was so unlike the Susanna I have known these many years. Finally, the phone rang and when Guy went to the kitchen to talk, Susanna asked me to help her to bed. In our last few minutes together, Susanna said "Tamara, you've got a big job on your hands to write this book." I said, "Yes, I know, but it's fun." Susanna laughed, raised her eyebrows and said

"Fun!?" Then she chuckled to herself and asked me to lift her legs up on to the bed and under the covers. I tucked her in the way I tucked my daughter in when she was small. I returned to the dining room, where Guy was waiting for his friend from Rockport, Robert Shivers, who was in town for the day. Susanna got up once while Guy's friends were over. She said a quick hello and Guy took her back to bed. As he came out of the room and closed the door he called back to her, "You just sleep, Baby, I'll take care of everything here." It was an endearing moment and sweet afternoon.

Two weeks later, on June 28, 2012, Susanna Clark died in her sleep.

"I was gone somewhere, I think the studio maybe, and I came home around eight thirty and Susanna was asleep in bed," Guy says.

I got in bed and went to sleep, and at some point she had a coughing jag. She always had them, so I didn't take it as anything out of the ordinary. I just went to sleep. I was tired. About midnight I just had this feeling and woke up and looked at her, and I didn't see her breathing and I was looking real hard to see, and I reached over and put my hand on her, and she was cold. I mean cold. I knew immediately. One of the girls that worked for us was downstairs asleep, and I called her and said, "I think Susanna died." Tisha took her pulse and temperature, and she called 911, and I sat there and kept an eye on Susanna. It seems like the police and the emergency [medical personnel] came at the same time. They did what they were supposed to do. I was in shock. I didn't break down and cry because I had already been through all that with Susanna. I had been through it all. I had grieved. I had been pissed off. I had been sad. I had been through all the emotions that go along with that kind of death. I felt like I had done my part already for years. For years. I just couldn't conjure up anything. I just sat in the kitchen and smoked. I still haven't cried.

Susanna had told Guy that she did not want a funeral or memorial service of any kind, and Guy respected her wishes despite pressure from Rodney Crowell and Emmylou Harris.

"I told Emmy and Rodney when they came over, 'No, we're not doing anything. Susanna didn't want that shit. She didn't like it. She hated having to go to them, and I'm not going to do it. You can do it if you want to—I might show up—but I'm not going to do it, because she didn't want it.' They didn't get it. I could tell they didn't get where I was coming from. They wanted me to break down so they could comfort me. That ain't gonna happen. They couldn't comprehend that I wouldn't do something and I think [they] finally acquiesced in some way, but they still wanted to do it."

Although there was never an official memorial service for Susanna, both Emmy and Rodney grieved the loss of Susanna in their own ways. Rodney sang "Angel Eyes," the song he had written for Susanna, in his live shows, and Emmy did a tribute to Susanna in her shows.

"On Susanna's birthday before she died, I sat there and sang 'Angel Eyes' to her and bawled like a baby," Crowell says. "That's how I was saying goodbye to my friend who's not there anymore. Then I started doing it in some shows after she died. Susanna was always enigmatic. Always an enigma. She and I became really close because I listened to her. She would open up about how she saw it all, and I would listen because she was a poet. When she really opened up about it, it came out as poetry."

A few weeks after Susanna's death, Jim McGuire, Claire Armbruster from Keith Case's office, and I took Guy to lunch. He looked great and seemed happy. He ate a huge meal and laughed and joked throughout. Guy's knee replacement surgery was scheduled for the following week, and he assured us that nothing was going to keep him from having that surgery. He said he'd be ready to dance by September.

Guy's sister Jan came to Nashville from San Antonio to help Guy after the surgery. She stayed for a couple of months. Jan was with us at the Americana Honors and Awards show on September 12. I wrote in my journal:

WEDNESDAY SEPT 12, 2012
*This One's For Him: A Tribute to Guy Clark* took home top honors at the Americana Awards for Album of the Year! I can't believe it. All the time, love, effort and drama that went into making that record. . . . It is a beautiful record and I am so proud of it and thrilled that others liked it enough to vote for it. Guy performed "My Favorite Picture of You" with

Verlon and Shawn. When he introduced the song he said "I wrote this song for my wife Susanna who died a few weeks ago. I wish she was here to hear me sing it." He got a bit emotional and stumbled through some of the lyrics, but it was charming and he got a much-deserved standing ovation. The guys walked off stage left and Jim Lauderdale came to the podium and said "Here to announce the winner of Album of the Year are Rodney Crowell and Brandi Carlisle." At that moment, a video camera was pointed at me from the end of our row and with Rodney up on the stage, I had a feeling it was going to be us. Rod said, "Here are the nominees for Album of the Year in alphabetical order: Steve Earle, Jason Isbell, *This One's For Him: A Tribute to Guy Clark*, and Gillian Welch. Brandi Carlisle opened the envelope and looked at Rodney and said, "Do you want to read this?" Rodney looked teary-eyed and his voice wavered when he said, "The award goes to *This One's For Him*. I was sitting with Guy's sister Jan and Jen Gunderman, who played piano and accordion on the album, along with some good friends. Our group jumped up and down and screamed and Jen and I held hands and ran to the stage. It was emotional and joyful and I couldn't wait to get up there to hug Guy. Once we got to the stage, we hugged Guy, Rodney, Verlon and Shawn and anyone who happened to be standing in our path. I was so nervous, my heart was pounding and I felt like a total dork up there. I said a few words of thanks and then Shawn did the same. Guy kept his arm around me while Shawn was speaking. I could feel him shaking, although, being calm, cool and collected Guy Clark, he was quiet and dignified through it all.

Between Susanna's death and Guy's health woes, he struggled to finish recording his album *My Favorite Picture of You*. Guy was determined to turn it in to Dualtone by the end of the year.

In November, Noel McKay came to town to play guitar on "El Coyote," the song he had written with Guy. "We were on the phone one day when Guy pitched me the idea for 'El Coyote,'" Noel says.

I was thrilled that he would pitch a song idea to me. The next time I drove up to Nashville and hung out at his house he showed me some lyrics that he'd written on his graph paper. We looked at it and started knocking ideas around for it. Guy said, "Take it home and see what you can do with it," and so I did. I had a fifteen-hour drive home all by myself and worked on that song the whole way back to Austin. I just thought and thought about it and would have to pull over to write lyrics. I worked on "El Coyote" for a long time. When I brought it back to Guy, I was really nervous. I had no idea what his response was going to be. I played what I had for him. When the last chord ended, it seemed like an eternity, and Guy said, "Good work." I felt this burden lift off of me. I felt an immense amount of relief and pride. Then Guy said, "Well, I think you need to fix this, and this, and this." It took us a couple of years to edit the song. One time Guy called me on the phone, and said, "Hey, there's a half of a last verse that I want you to write, and I want you to listen to some Woody Guthrie and think about that. Write a last half and bring that to me." I spent a couple of days and went off into my own little world to try to write this half a verse. I thought and thought

*This One's for Him: A Tribute to Guy Clark* wins Album of the Year at the 2012 Americana Honors and Awards. *Left to right:* pianist Jen Gunderman, producer Tamara Saviano, Guy Clark, producer and multi-instrumentalist Shawn Camp, guitarist Verlon Thompson. Courtesy Americana Music Association

and thought about it and finally came up with something that I thought was right. When I played it for Guy, I was expecting him to like it, but he said, "Oh, no. That's too much like Woody Guthrie. If you want to play it, then that's fine, but I can't play it." The only way that I knew that he thought the song was finished was when I heard him perform it. He called me and said, "Here it is. This is what I think it should be." He played it over the phone. It was amazing to hear him sing this song that we had worked on.

Noel kept the Woody Guthrie–sounding half-verse in his own version of the song. "To me," he says, "the last verse of the song ties it up in a way. I tried not to editorialize, but the last verse talks about the way that people who immigrate to this country can be taken advantage of easily. 'Some men will rob you with a sword or a pistol, and some by the shade of your skin. Some will lie to you. Leave you for dead, and no one even knows your name in the end.' That's the verse."

Grammy nominations were announced on December 5, and This One's for Him: A Tribute to Guy Clark was nominated for Best Folk Album. The album had become such an embarrassment of riches that I started to feel like I was standing out in public in my underwear. I'm proud of the album and was excited about the Grammy nomination, as we all were, but the most important thing to me is that we had paid tribute to Guy and that he liked the album. Guy was too sick to go to Los Angeles for the awards, but a group of us headed to L.A. to represent.

I wrote in my journal:

FEB 9, 2013
It is my 52nd birthday and the day before the Grammy Awards. Icehouse Music took our team out to lunch at the Beverly Hills Hotel and it was lovely to eat in the garden and have some downtime with friends before the craziness sets in. I miss Guy. He was too sick to travel although he really wanted to come with us. He's so proud that we were nominated for a Grammy for the tribute album. He's been nominated many times and has never won. You wouldn't think winning a Grammy would mean anything to Guy but it does because it's voted on by peers. Emmylou Harris and Rodney Crowell played the Troubadour and we went over there

after the Grammy nominee reception. Shawn Camp and his girlfriend Judith Hill, Jack Ingram and his wife Amy, Paul and me, our radio promoter Jenni Finlay, Brian Atkinson who wrote the liner notes and was the journalist for the project. Jen Gunderman from the band. Our engineer Fred Remmert. As producers, Shawn and I are the official nominees but that part is meaningless to me, this was a team effort all the way.

FEB 10
We didn't win a Grammy, I never expected we would so I didn't even feel a twinge of disappointment. It wouldn't have been any fun to win without Guy here anyhow. We had so much fun that the award doesn't matter. We started recording the album three years ago and it is past time for it to take its place in history so we can all move on. We had a great after party at the Foundry on Melrose, a restaurant owned by our friends. The food was delicious, lots of our friends from LA and Nashville and Austin and New York came to the party.

The Goat Rodeo Sessions with Yo-Yo Ma, Stuart Duncan, Edgar Meyer, and Chris Thile won in our category. It's a great album, and they deserved the Grammy just as much as we did.

Guy managed to make it to Austin for the Mack, Jack & McConaughey charity event on April 12. MJ&M is a joint fund-raising event started by actor Matthew McConaughey, songwriter and musician Jack Ingram, and University of Texas football coaching legend Mack Brown. Guy could barely climb the four stairs to the stage. He sang "Desperados Waiting for a Train." It was his last performance.

In July, Dualtone released Guy's album My Favorite Picture of You.

Although he had begun a romantic relationship with his caregiver, Joy, Guy's mind was squarely focused on Susanna. On the album cover, he holds his favorite Polaroid of his wife. "It doesn't matter how it ended with Susanna, or how many more years I live," Guy says. "Susanna is, and always will be, the only woman for me. No one will ever match her in beauty, brains, and how crazy she made me. If My Favorite Picture of You is my last album, well, at least it is a dedication to the one I've loved more than anyone or anything in this life."

"I think 'My Favorite Picture of You' is probably Guy's best work out of all of the stuff that he's written," Noel McKay says. "Out of all the brilliant stuff from all the decades, I think that might be his best composition and his best work. I just remember trying to hold it together while I was listening to him perform that. It just blew my mind."

The disc includes more songs from the Sis Draper series: "Cornmeal Waltz," and "The Death of Sis Draper." "We probably have several more Sis Draper songs," Guy says. "Shawn is going to have to record the rest of them."

"I like the Sis Draper songs that Guy wrote with Shawn Camp," Brennen Leigh says. "You feel like you know the characters in them. Guy does this really unusual thing. He writes women as people. That's a unique thing, and I appreciate it. When you hear those songs it's like watching an exciting film, an emotional film."

Guy wrote "Hell Bent on a Heartache" with Morgane Hayes and Chris Stapleton, who also appear on the recording. "Heroes" was written with Ray Stephenson and Jeremy Campbell.

"We were talking about that subject [Iraq veterans] because all three of us had seen it in the paper or heard it on all the news or something. It just seemed like a subject that needed to be addressed, so we wrote it," Guy says.

Along with "My Favorite Picture of You," Gordy Sampson cowrote "Good Advice." Guy wrote "Rain in Durango" with Shawn Camp and Ray Stephenson, "The High Price of Inspiration" with Jedd Hughes, and "I'll Show Me" with Crowell.

For the first time in many years, there was not a Townes Van Zandt song on Guy's album. In its stead is Lyle Lovett's "Waltzing Fool." "That has always been my favorite Lyle song," Guy says. "I performed it that night at the ASCAP awards for Lyle, and the next morning I just went in the studio and did it. I thought, *well, I always do a Townes song, now I'll do somebody else.* It wasn't anything planned until after I'd done that song that night. We had the studio booked, and it was just so on my mind that I decided to do it right then."

*My Favorite Picture of You* is the last album ever recorded in the EMI Publishing studio. Guy had recorded eight albums in the studio, which was usually used only for demo recordings. EMI had been sold to Sony Music Publishing, and the historic building, the former home of Combine Music, where

Kris Kristofferson had written his classic songs, was bulldozed to make room for SESAC's new Nashville headquarters.

The release of *My Favorite Picture of You* is the only good thing that happened for Guy in the summer of 2013. In August, Susanna's niece Sherri Talley stopped in to visit Guy on her way through town from Chicago to Shreveport. I wrote in my journal:

SUNDAY AUGUST 25, 2013

Guy has bladder cancer and is having surgery on Tuesday. He told me he had it a few years ago and this is a recurrence. He showed me the X-rays of his bladder full of blood clots. He said he is bleeding a lot and feels weak. Until they get in there to do the surgery, they don't know what stage it is or how bad. Susanna's niece Sherri Talley is in town today to visit Guy. Sherri got to Guy's 30 minutes before me. By the time I arrived, she was sitting at the kitchen table surrounded by boxes and Susanna's paintings. Guy was ordering Joy to pull out canvases and to find Susanna's jewelry, her songwriter awards, photos, handwritten lyrics and all of Susanna's archives. He wanted Sherri to take everything back to Louisiana with her that day. Guy also asked Sherri to go through a box in the garage. He said Susanna had been moving that box around since she was in college. There were a few gems in the box, an old address book, a few personal letters and books, and Bunny's last two issues of Seventeen Magazine and Vogue from June 1970 and a dry cleaning slip for Bunny from 1966.

Guy scooped some of Susanna's cremains into a small container, gave Sherri the large urn, and said, "Please spread them somewhere nice in Atlanta, Texas."

Guy seemed adamant about unloading all of Susanna's stuff to Sherri. It made me sad. He looks weak. He looks resigned, like his life is coming to an end and he's okay with it. I'm in denial. I don't want to believe this is the end. It's bizarre to be so much up in Guy's business and life and hard to figure out where I fit. Journalist and biographer, yes. Friend? Well, yes. The lines are blurry. I love Guy. We're friends and colleagues. We've known each other for a long time and our conversations for the book have been so intimate. I want to be honest and objective but there is no denying that I love Guy.

Once again, Guy bounced back.

FRIDAY AUGUST 30
Guy looks so much better. Surgery was successful and they think they got it all. Battered knees and hips, lymphoma, bladder cancer, heart arrhythmia, diabetes, health scare after health scare, and Guy is still here. He soldiers through his pain. "I'm from Texas; that's what we do."

On September 10, the Academy of Country Music honored Guy with its Poet Award in a ceremony at the Ryman. Rodney and Emmylou performed "She Ain't Goin' Nowhere." Robert Earl Keen played "Let Him Roll." When Guy accepted the award he quoted lyrics from Townes's song "To Live Is to Fly." Then he said, "I always thought of myself as a poet, and this means a lot to me."

"Townes would have liked that one," Guy said. "I wish he was here for that."

On January 26, 2014, at the Staples Center in Los Angeles, Guy Clark finally won a Grammy, on his seventh nomination. *My Favorite Picture of You* took home the honors for best folk album. Guy Clark was not there to accept his award.

"Of course, it means more to me now than I thought it would," Guy says. "I thought I would just blow this shit off and get to work. Ironic to do this for forty years and finally win the best award you can get, and now I can't do it anymore. I'd love to do another album if I could write some more songs. I don't think I'm done, but the reality of it is, I probably am. It's hard to lose that momentum. Writing songs is what I decided I was going to do a long time ago. I don't want to be a producer. I don't want to be a publisher. I don't want to do any of that crap. All I want to do is write songs and sing them. You never write the best song you can write, and I just want to continue to try."

"I think sometimes people may not appreciate how hard Guy has to work to do this," Verlon Thompson says. "I don't mean this with one single speck of disrespect. In fact, I mean it with even more respect, because it doesn't come easy for Guy. I see guys who walk in and can play a song, can play with anybody. Guy really has to knuckle down. Even when he writes a song, he works really hard on figuring out the right way to play it and how to play it, and recently I know he's been sitting with a metronome to improve his timing. At more than seventy years old, he's still interested in improving his timing. People might think he can just conjure up these wonderful images and that they just come to him. He sits there and goes through reams and reams of paper. As he says, big erasers bite the dust. Editing never ends. He'll change one tonight, if he thinks it's better."

"It was always about the songs," Rosanne Cash says. "We were always talking about songs: playing new songs, playing other people's songs that we loved. Guy is the one who said 'You have to throw out the best line of your song if it doesn't serve the rest of the song.' So many things he said

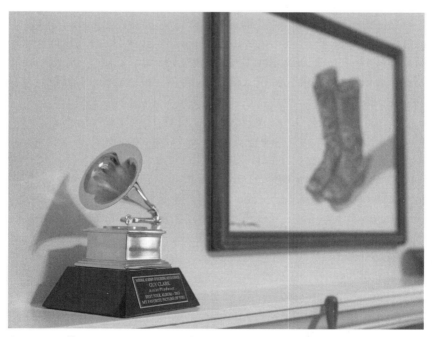

Guy's 2013 album *My Favorite Picture of You* won the Grammy for Best Folk Album, his first Grammy win after seven nominations. The award sits on his mantle next to Guy's painting of his old boots. Courtesy Paul Whitfield

in conversations about songs I have taken as my mandate as a songwriter: the discipline required, honing your poetry, and being willing to throw out the best line in the song if it doesn't serve the song. His rigor and discipline and how uncompromising [he is] about his work seems rare. It's good to know that those people exist, people that think that songwriting is a truly honorable profession."

"One of the things that makes him special is that he is not jaded about music," Brennen Leigh says.

Guy still enjoys music in its purest form. He likes to hear somebody sing and play a new song. Sometimes I would play one, and he'd say, 'That's just great.' Sometimes I'd play one, and he'd say, 'Mm-hmm.' You can tell which ones he really liked, and which ones were his style, and which ones didn't quite hit the mark for him.

It's weird to hear people call a songwriter like Guy a craftsman. Is William Butler Yeats a craftsman? Does anybody ever call Shakespeare a craftsman? No. I like to think of Guy's songs as three-minute novels. There's no denying that Guy's at the top of his field. He's the best, and I think everyone knows that. What people may not know is that Guy's a great person. I just love him. He's been very nice to me. I will never forget his kindness.

"I really can't think of anybody else in my life that's done quite so much to try to encourage me," Noel McKay says. "Every time I turn around he's saying, 'Hey, I want you to meet this person,' or 'You should listen to this.' He's always been really gentle about stuff. When I come to him with songs, he always focuses on the ones that he thinks are good. I don't know that I can really effectively convey my gratitude to Guy Clark for all of the amazing things that he's done for me . . . but I am extraordinarily grateful to have him in my life."

"When I was coming up in my twenties and thirties, people would talk about Guy—other songwriters would talk about Guy—as if he was scary or ultra-intimidating, almost mean," Jack Ingram says.

They [said], "He doesn't suffer fools." Sometimes that can be thought of as . . . not having an open heart, but that's just so not true. It's so not

Guy. Once I met him and hung out with him it was exactly what I thought it would be, which is, if you want to talk about songwriting you'd better have your shit together. You'd better care about it as much as he does. If you're going to talk about talent and talk about great songwriters and talk with Guy Clark about it, he doesn't have time to take you through elementary [school]. We're going to start on a higher level than that, and if you can't [keep up], then don't hang with me. I don't care what bad songwriters do. I don't care what lazy songwriters do. Just don't try to do it with me. Even if I'm not going to be that great I'm damned sure going to try to be.

"He's one of the joys of my life," Keith Case says. "The closest relationships I've had have been with my artists, and he's been at the top of the heap forever."

"If you can go down in that basement and hang with him and be comfortable without a whole lot of verbal exchange and hold your own and stay entertained and not feel uncomfortable, then you're batting on a pretty high level," J. T. Van Zandt says.

He's soft. He's a total sweetheart. He's a pillar of a man. When I listen to his songs, I'm fortunate enough to have that proximity and affection for him, but I want the rest of the world to know he is a great example of a true man. How gentle, kind, patient and loving he was to his wife at the end of her days, and how he could turn from that to being just so self-convicted and so strong. I never saw him shed a tear, but I'm sure that he had the desire to on numerous occasions. He gave me something to aspire to, not only as a poet, and a songwriter, and a musician, a guitar player, guitar maker, but just as a man. Now that I'm a father, I think a lot more about how Guy is than how my dad was in terms of caring for my children.

"Anybody who's ever met Guy Clark can form their own conclusion about who he is and what he is." Terry Allen says. "In my mind, other than the obvious great songwriter, storyteller, and poet, he's a character. In that sense, he's true to his roots. He may have lived in Nashville most of his life, but he is just a classic Texas character right down to his toes. When he makes up his mind to do something, you can't stop him or tell him how to do it—he will do it his way. If you meet Guy Clark for the first time and you don't know much about him, you would be well advised to let him take the lead and follow along and just enjoy the ride."

# Epilogue

May 26, 2016
Santa Fe, New Mexico

With his friend Verlon Thompson and his caregiver Joy Brogdon at his side, Guy Charles Clark died at 3:41 a.m. on Tuesday, May 17, 2016. He drew his last breath at home, in his own bed, wearing his favorite T-shirt—the pink one depicting Shawn Camp, co-producer of his last album.

Guy had suffered from a long list of health problems—lymphoma, heart disease, diabetes, and bladder cancer among them—and we were lucky to have him years longer than we'd expected. The last three months of his life were especially brutal; he spent most of them in a nursing home. By the end, Guy's only goal was to go home to die—to be in the place he loved, surrounded by his art, books, and music. With the help of friends and hospice workers, he made it.

It didn't become real to me until I saw Guy's body at the funeral home two days after his death. In the last months, he had become thin and frail. Yet, plumped up with embalming fluid, he looked like Guy Clark again. How weird is that? Because he was going to be cremated, he was laid out in a simple box just for a short time so a few of us could see him. The funny thing is, Guy is so dang tall they had to take his boots off to fit him in the box. The top of his head was pressed against one end of the box and his feet pressed against the other. Guy Clark does not fit in a box.

Guy's last wishes were clear. At some point in his waning years, his lyrical request—"Susanna, oh Susanna, when it comes my time, won't you bury me south of that Red River line"—changed to instructions to be cremated, with his cremains sent to Terry Allen to be incorporated into a sculpture. "I think that would be so fucking cool," Guy said at the time. "Sure, leave me with a job to do," Allen joked. But it's no joke now. In the days after his death, Guy's closest friends pulled together a plan to honor his wishes.

Jim McGuire hosted a wake—a typical Guy Clark picking party, one of many that took place at McGuire's studio over the years. Guy's family and

Nashville friends gathered around an altar on which we'd placed his ashes, his old boots, and our favorite picture of him, and we took turns playing Guy Clark songs. At the end of the night, Thompson led a chorus of "Old Friends" that knocked the wind out of the room.

At midnight, Thompson; Camp; McGuire; Brogdon; Rodney Crowell; Steve Earle; Guy's son, Travis; and I boarded a tour bus in Nashville that would take us—and Guy—to Santa Fe and Terry Allen. Guy's last road trip. We slept little during the 18-hour drive; we all had too many Guy stories we wanted to tell. Grief shared is grief diminished.

We arrived in Santa Fe in time for dinner on Wednesday, May 25. Allen; his wife, Jo Harvey; and their son, Bukka, hosted another wake. Emmylou Harris; Vince Gill; Lyle Lovett; his partner, April Kimble; Robert Earl and Kathleen Keen; Joe and Sharon Ely; their daughter, Marie; Jack Ingram; and painter Paul Milosevich flew in from all parts to be there. We set up another altar, gathered around, and told more Guy stories. After a feast of green chili enchiladas, tamales, guacamole, and homemade salsa, we huddled around a fire pit on the stone and adobe patio. Hanging wisteria perfumed the air as old friends toasted Guy, clinking glasses of wine against bottles of Topo Chico and cans of Robert Earl Keen beer. Under a night sky blanketed with stars, a guitar came out. This time there was a rule, and it was simple. "Play a song Guy would have made you play," Earle said. Three among this group had written songs about Guy. Camp sang "This Guy, Guy," written with Gary Nicholson. (They got to play it for Guy shortly before his death. When they'd finished, he deadpanned, "Well, isn't that cute.") Next, Thompson played his ode, "Sideman's Dream." Then Gill shared the song he wrote— "There Ain't Nothin' Like a Guy Clark Song"— one that provides a perfect benediction to the master songwriter's life. Through this song—and many more of his own—there's no doubt Guy Clark will live forever.

### There Ain't Nothin' Like a Guy Clark Song

*There ain't nothin' like a Guy Clark song*
*When you're feeling fragile, afraid you don't belong*
*If it's a lonely road you're traveling on*
*There ain't nothin' like a Guy Clark song*

Old Friends, Boats and Stuff That Works
A Randall Knife, an old blue shirt
Strong and steady like Texas dirt
A place to hide when you really hurt
Coleman Bonner and his fiddle case
Old Skinny Dennis singing bass
That workbench was a holy place
His favorite picture, Susanna's face
Homegrown tomatoes and a Dallas whore
Rita Ballou on a dancehall floor
He rolled his own and loved to roar
It's been forty years since The Troubadour
What do you do when your heroes die?
You let him roll and you let him fly
Desperados don't worry or wonder why
Son of a bitch, we're going to miss you, Guy
There ain't nothin' like a Guy Clark song
When you feel abandoned and your friends are gone
Whatever road you're traveling on
There ain't nothin' like a Guy Clark song

## NOTES ON SOURCES

As a writer for *Country Weekly* from 1996–98 and managing editor of *Country Music* from 1998–2000, I interviewed Guy several times, including a nine-hour on-the-record interview for a Texas music book that never came to fruition. Sugar Hill Records hired me to interview Guy and to write the media materials for his 2002 album, *The Dark*. I worked as Guy's publicist 2006–2009 for his albums *Workbench Songs* and *Somedays the Song Writes You*, and in December 2008 I began interviewing Guy for this book, spending many hours with him each month through the summer of 2015. In 2010 and 2011, I produced *This One's for Him: A Tribute to Guy Clark* and spent many hours listening to his recordings and discussing songs with Guy as part of the production of the tribute album.

Guy opened up his personal archives to me, which included his lyric books and journals, his wife Susanna's journals, personal correspondence, booking contracts, tour calendars, family letters, photos, posters, awards, and other historical documents.

Guy's sisters Caroline Clark Dugan and Janis Clark opened the Clark family home in Rockport, Texas, to me numerous times over the years. They shared genealogical records from the archives of their mother (Frances Greene Clark), family history documents, letters that their father Ellis Clark wrote to his wife Frances during World War II, photos, newspaper clippings, personal correspondence, and high school yearbooks. Caro and Jan also gave dozens of hours of interviews about the family and Guy in his younger years.

Several journalists and historians graciously shared historical interviews with Guy, Susanna, and others close to the story. Historian Louise O'Connor offered her 1990 and 1991 interviews with Phillip Baldwin, Lola Bonner, Frances Clark, Guy Clark, Susanna Clark, Dave Segler, and Townes Van Zandt. Journalist Bill DeYoung gave me his extended interview with Susanna Clark from May 1, 1996. Robert Earl Hardy, author of *A Deeper Blue: The Life and Music of Townes Van Zandt*, shared a lengthy interview he conducted with

Susanna Clark in 2000. Writer Joe Specht granted me access to his transcripts of interviews with Guy Clark (February 27, 2004 and May 30, 2006), Lola Bonner, (October 4, 2004), Caroline Clark Dugan (October 4, 2004), Mary Lucille Jackson (October 1, 2004), Carl Synder (March 17, 2006), and Jan Clark (July 8, 2006). Haley Howle from Austin radio station KUT's *Texas Music Matters* shared her transcript from an interview with Guy in September 2011.

What follows is a short outline listing sources used in each chapter.

## Chapter 1
*Interviews*
Caroline Clark, Guy Clark, Jan Clark

*Other Sources*
Ancestry.com, Clark family archives, *The Dust Bowl* (PBS film), History.com, Louise O'Connor interviews, Ward County Archives, *Wagon Tracks: Washita County* Heritage, vol. 1, 1892–1976

## Chapter 2
*Interviews*
Juliette Brown, Caroline Clark, Guy Clark, Jan Clark, Carl Snyder, Minor Wilson

*Other Sources*
Ancestry.com, Aransas County [Tex.] Historical Society, Clark family archives, History.com, O'Connor interviews, Specht interviews

## Chapter 3
*Interviews*
Juliette Brown, Guy Clark, Carl Snyder

*Other Sources*
Clark family archives

## Chapter 4
*Interviews*
Bill Bentley, Sandra Carrick, Guy Clark, Jan Clark, Crow Johnson, Fran Lohr,

K. T. Oslin, Susan Slocum, Carl Snyder, Jerry Jeff Walker, Gary White, Minor Wilson

*Other Sources*
Clark family archives, The Folk Music Revival (Dicaire), O'Connor interviews, *Texas Monthly*

## Chapter 5
*Interviews*
Guy Clark, Susanna Clark, Gary White, Minor Wilson

*Other Sources*
Allmusic.com, Billboard, Clark family archives, O'Connor interviews, Susanna Clark letters and diaries

## Chapter 6
*Interviews*
Rosanne Cash, Guy Clark, Susanna Clark, Rodney Crowell, Richard Dobson, Steve Earle, John Lomax III, Jim McGuire, Chips Moman, Keith Sykes, Jerry Jeff Walker

*Other Sources*
Allmusic.com, Billboard, Clark family archives, Guy Clark lyric books, Music Row archives, Susanna Clark letters and diaries

## Chapter 7
*Interviews*
Michael Brovsky, Guy Clark, Susanna Clark, Travis Clark, Rodney Crowell, Steve Earle, Joe Galante, Vince Gill, Mike Lipskin, John Lomax III, Jim McGuire

*Sources*
Allmusic.com, Austin Sun, Billboard, Charlotte Observer, Clark family archives, Dallas Morning News, Fort Worth News, Guy Clark lyric notebooks, Melody Maker, Old No. 1 audio and liner notes, Omaha Rainbow, Playboy, Playgirl, Record World, Rolling Stone, Soho Weekly News, Twin Cities Reader, Texas Cookin' audio and liner notes, unreleased first album audio

## Chapter 8
*Interviews*

Michael Brovsky, Rosanne Cash, Guy Clark, Caroline Clark, Jan Clark, Rodney Crowell, Emmylou Harris, Craig Leon, Lloyd Maines, Jim McGuire, Jerry Jeff Walker

*Other Sources*

Allmusic.com, *Better Days* audio and liner notes, *Billboard*, Clark family archives, *Guy Clark* audio and liner notes, Guy Clark lyric notebooks, *Rough Mix* (Bowen and Jerome), *South Coast of Texas* audio and liner notes, *Texas Monthly*, Warner Brothers Records archives

## Chapter 9
*Interviews*

Terry Allen, Rob Bleetstein, Keith Case, Guy Clark, Susanna Clark, Rodney Crowell, Richard Dobson, Joe Ely, Vince Gill, Emmylou Harris, Richard Leigh, Ken Levitan, Lyle Lovett, Kathy Mattea, Buddy Mondlock, Barry Poss, Verlon Thompson, Miles Wilkinson

*Other Sources*

Allmusic.com, *Billboard*, Clark family Archives, *Diamonds and Dirt* audio and packaging, Keith Case archives, Kerrville Folk Festival book and archives, *Keys to the Highway* audio and packaging, *Music Row*, *New York Times*, O'Connor interviews, *Old Friends* audio and packaging, *Street Language* audio and packaging, Susanna Clark letters and diaries

## Chapter 10
*Interviews*

Guy Clark, Susanna Clark, John Condon, Rodney Crowell, Joe Ely, Radney Foster, Ray Wylie Hubbard, Robert Earl Keen, Lyle Lovett, Gary Overton, Verlon Thompson, J. T. Van Zandt

*Other Sources*

Allmusic.com, *Austin City Limits*, *Billboard*, *Country Music*, Clark family archives, Keith Case archives, Grammy archives, Hardy interview with Susanna, O'Connor interviews, *Music Row*, Susanna Clark letters and diaries, *Village Voice*, *Washington Post*

## Chapter 11

*Interviews*

Rob Bleetstein, Guy Clark, Susanna Clark, Travis Clark, Dub Cornett, Rodney Crowell, Rosie Flores, Tom Gribbin, Jon Grimson, Cyndi Hoelzle, Kyle Lehning, Lyle Lovett, Wendy Pearl, Steven Sharp, Keith Sykes, Verlon Thompson, Miles Wilkinson, J. T. Van Zandt

*Other Sources*

Austin American Statesman, Boats to Build audio, video, and CD packaging, "Baton Rouge" video, Bloodshotrecords.com, Clark family archives, Country Music, Craftsman audio and CD packaging, Dublin Blues audio and CD packaging, Gavin, Guy Clark lyric books, Los Angeles Times, Music Row, No Depression, Pulse!, Susanna Clark letters and diaries

## Chapter 12

*Interviews*

Terry Allen, Guy Clark, Keith Case, Dub Cornett, Rodney Crowell, Steve Earle, Emmylou Harris, Jack Ingram, Kyle Lehning, Terry Lickona, Joyce Maynard, Barry Poss, Sherri Talley, Verlon Thompson, J. T. Van Zandt

*Other Sources*

Allmusic.com, Austin City Limits, Billboard, Clark family archives, The Essential Guy Clark CD and packaging, Guy Clark tour books and calendars, Keepers CD and packaging, Music Row, No Depression, Susanna Clark letters and diaries, Tennessean

## Chapter 13

*Interviews*

Shawn Camp, Guy Clark, Susanna Clark, Rodney Crowell, Vince Gill, Lyle Lovett, Buddy Mondlock, Lee Roy Parnell, Barry Poss, Keith Sykes, Sherri Talley

*Sources*

Allmusic.com, Americana Music Association, ASCAP Awards, Billboard, CBS Late Show with David Letterman, Clark family archives, Cold Dog Soup CD and packaging, Country Music, Grammy archives, Journal of Country Music, The Key CD and packaging, No Depression, Saviano diaries, Step Inside This House CD and packaging, Susanna Clark letters and diaries,

## Chapter 14

*Interviews*

Terry Allen, Keith Case, Hayes Carll, Guy Clark, Rodney Crowell, Joe Ely, Sharon Ely, Vince Gill, Robert Earl Keen, Noel McKay, Ashley Monroe, Gary Overton, J.T. Van Zandt

*Other Sources*

Allmusic.com, Americana Music Association, *Austin City Limits*, *Billboard*, Clark family archives, Country Music Hall of Fame archives, Gauthier road diary, Grammy archives, Guy Clark tour schedule and calendar, Leadership Music, Sirius XM Satellite Radio, Saviano diaries, *Somedays the Song Writes You* CD and packaging, Susanna Clark letters and diaries, *Tennessean*, *Workbench Songs* CD and packaging

## Chapter 15

*Interviews*

Terry Allen, Shawn Camp, Keith Case, Rosanne Cash, Caroline Clark, Guy Clark, Jan Clark, Susanna Clark, Rodney Crowell, Emmylou Harris, Jack Ingram, Brennen Leigh, Chris Maxwell, Noel McKay, Sherri Talley, Verlon Thompson, J.T. Van Zandt, Jerry Jeff Walker

*Other Sources*

Academy of Country Music, Allmusic.com, Americana Music Association, *Billboard*, Clark family archives, Grammy archives, *My Favorite Picture of You* CD and packaging, Saviano diaries, *Songs and Stories* CD and packaging, *This One's for Him: A Tribute to Guy Clark*

# SOURCES

## Personal interviews

Grant Alden—August 21, 2015

Terry Allen—October 18, 2010; November 6, 2014

Bill Bentley—April 23, 2015

Ryan Bingham—October 6, 2010

Peter Blackstock—August 21, 2015

Rob Bleetstein—March 23, 2015

Michael Brovsky—April 17, 2015

Juliette Brown—June 1, 2015

Shawn Camp—December 9, 2008; February 1, 2011; December 11, 2014

Hayes Carll—October 19, 2010

Sandra Carrick—October 26, 2013

Keith Case—May 31, 2012

Rosanne Cash—September 17, 2015

Caroline Clark Dugan—June 10–11, 2011; May 13, 2012; June 1, 2015

Guy Clark—April 1, 2000; May 2002; December 9, 2008; December 22 and
    29, 2010; January 28, 2011; February 1, 2011; March 29, 2011; June 7–13,
    2011; August 15 and 19, 2011; September 23, 2011; June 1, 7, and 14, 2012;
    February 27, 2013; July 26 and 27, 2014; November 6, 2014; December 11,
    2014; January 2, 2015; May 9, 2015; July 8, 2015; July 31, 2015; September
    14, 2015

Jan Clark—February 24, 2011; February 27, 2011; June 10–11, 2011; July 23,
    2011; May 13, 2012; June 1, 2015

Susanna Clark—April 1, 2000; February 1, 2011; August 19, 2011; December
    16, 2011; June 14, 2012

Travis Clark—July 17, 2013; April 20, 2015

John Condon—November 20, 2013

Dub Cornett—August 25, 2015

Rodney Crowell—January 27, 2010; June 2, 2011; May 23, 2012; November 6,
    2014; January 13, 2015

Richard Dobson—April 20, 2015

Steve Earle—February 1, 2011; November 6, 2014

Harold Eggers—April 13, 2015

Ramblin' Jack Elliott—November 6, 2014

Joe Ely—January 5, 2012; November 6, 2014; June 9, 2015

Sharon Ely—January 5, 2012
Joy Fletcher—September 21, 2011
Rosie Flores—August 26, 2015
Radney Foster—January 28, 2010; July 2, 2015
Joe Galante—July 15, 2015
Bonnie Garner—May 1, 2013
Vince Gill—May 21, 2012
Jimmie Dale Gilmore—June 9, 2015
Holly Gleason—November 30, 2011
Patti Griffin—January 6, 2011
Jon Grimson—March 30, 2015
Jeff Hanna—July 20, 2015
Emmylou Harris—May 21, 2012
William Hedgepeth—May 4, 2015
Terri Hendrix—January 4, 2011
Craig Hillis—October 25, 2013
Cyndi Hoelzle—July 2, 2015
Ray Wylie Hubbard—October 18, 2010; June 8, 2015
Kathleen Hudson—June 9, 2015
Jack Ingram—January 28, 2010; June 8, 2015
Crow Johnson—July 23, 2015
Robert Earl Keen—October 19, 2010; June 24, 2013; November 6, 2014
Hal Ketchum—May 29, 2015
Rick Lambert—May 20, 2015
Kyle Lehning—November 20, 2013
Brennen Leigh—June 9, 2015
Richard Leigh—April 2, 2015
Craig Leon—August 11, 2015
Ken Levitan—April 29, 2015
Terry Lickona—June 8, 2015
Mike Lipskin—July 30, 2015
Fran Lohr—June 30, 2015
John Lomax III—December 1, 2011
Lyle Lovett—January 6, 2011
Lloyd Maines—August 4, 2015
Dale Martin—October 22, 2014
Kathy Mattea—March 10, 2015
Chris Maxwell—May 13, 2013
Joyce Maynard—January 29, 2012; February 2, 2012
Jim McGuire—February 1, 2011; November 6, 2014; December 11, 2014
Noel McKay—June 9, 2015

James McMurtry—March 7, 2012

Paul Milosevich—July 23, 2015

Buddy Mondlock—May 6, 2015

Ashley Monroe—May 29, 2012

Elyse Moore—June 21, 2013

Gary Nicholson—January 31, 2012

Tim O'Brien—August 7, 2013

Louise O'Connor—January 3, 2012

K. T. Oslin—December 16, 2013

Gary Overton—January 12–13, 2012

Lee Roy Parnell—April 1, 2000

Wendy Pearl—June 27, 2013

Richard Pells—June 30, 2015

Gretchen Peters—April 27, 2015

John Porter, July 25, 2012

Barry Poss—April 16, 2015

Mickey Raphael—May 11, 2015

Glen Ratliff—September 21, 2011

Dave Rawlings—August 15, 2015

Kim Richey—October 1, 2013

Don Sanders—July 9, 2013

Darrell Scott—August 7, 2013

Steven Sharp—August 19, 2015

Susan Spaw Slocum—October 2, 2013

Carl Snyder—July 28, 2011; June 1, 2015

Jon Randall Stewart—July 12, 2012

Keith Sykes—July 14, 2015

Sherri Talley—July 8, 2013; August 26, 2013

Liz Thiels—January 20, 2012

Verlon Thompson—December 9, 2008; February 4, 2011; June 7–13, 2011;
    December 11, 2014

Victor Torres—July 15, 2014

John Townes Van Zandt II—June 22, 2013; June 9, 2015

Ben Vaughn—December 22, 2011

Jerry Jeff Walker—June 21, 2013; November 6, 2014

Gillian Welch—July 18, 2015

Kevin Welch—January 4, 2011

Gary White—April 13, 2015

Miles Wilkinson—November 25, 2013

Minor Wilson—September 24, 2011

Steve Young—January 30, 2012

## Essays, Profiles and Reviews

Adamson, Dale. "Guy Clark." *Houston Chronicle*, January 4, 1976.

———. "That Guy Has Talent." *Houston Chronicle*, July 21, 1974.

Alden, Grant. "Guy Clark *Cold Dog Soup* Review." *Country Music*, April/May 2000, 78.

Alexander, Alice. "Good Vibes, Hard Times." *Tennessean*, December 14–20, 1975.

Allen, Bob. "Guy Clark: Songwriter." *Country Music*, November/December 1989, 39–42.

"Americana Moves to Another Country." *Gavin*, January 20, 1995.

Andrews, Gregg. "It's the Music: Kent Finlay's Cheatham Street Warehouse in San Marcos, Texas." *Journal of Texas Music History* 5, no. 1 (Spring 2005): 8–24.

"Arts Official Is Dead, Wounds Self-Inflicted." *Oklahoman*, May 5, 1970.

Baird, Robert. "Recording of the Month: Guy Clark *Keepers*." *Stereophile*, June 1997, 221.

Bane, Michael. *Guy Clark* album review. *Country Music*, January/February 1979, 88.

Bisco, Jim. "Guy Clark Joins Country Music Outlaws." *Buffalo Evening News*, February 21, 1976.

Block, Billy. "Roots Revival Defines Genre Busting New Movement." *Western Beat Monthly*, January 1997, 1.

———. "Walkin' the Walk (or How to Make a Living in Alternative Country)." *Western Beat Monthly*, August 1997.

Bogard, Steve. "Death of a Cynic." *Music Row*, November 23, 1996.

Broyles, William. "My Montrose." *Texas Monthly*, February 2013.

Caligiuri, Jim. "No Lonesome Tune—Committing Guy Clark to the Air." *Austin Chronicle*, September 12, 2008.

Clark, Guy. "Hondo Crouch Remembered." *Luckenbach Monthly Moon*, 1978 (specific date unknown).

Claypool, Bob. "Respects Offered at 'Last Call' for Hopkins." *Houston Post*, February 3, 1982.

———. "Van Zandt Back at Last—Old Quarter Recordings Low-Keyed Gems of Style and Emotion." *Houston Post*, date unknown.

"Coleman Bonner Is Killed by Train near Texarkana." *Texarkana Gazette*, May 13, 1938.

Cooper, Peter. "Brian Ahern: Americana's Magic Maker." *Tennessean*, September 8, 2010.

———. "Guy Clark's craftsmanship shows no sign of withering." *Tennessean*, September 22, 2009.

———. "Verlon Thompson: I've Fallen but I Can Get Up." *No Depression*, May/
June 2003, 28.

Corcoran, Michael. "Fan Letters from Lyle." *Austin American Statesman*, September 22, 1998.

———. "Measure of a Songwriter—Guy Clark's Lyrical Authority Runs Deep
in Texan Hearts." *Austin American Statesman*, September 15, 2006.

"Critic's Voice: Q&As with Music Critics." *Music Row*, June 23, 1996, 8–12.

Cusic, Don. "Guy Clark Sings at the Exit/In: Poet Laureate of the Honky
Tonks." *Record World*, 1975 (specific date unknown).

Davis, John T. "Faster Is Not Better: Guy Clark Pays Attention to Details
When Crafting Songs." *Austin American Statesman*, April 13, 1995.

———. "Performer Sets Sail on a New Label: Clark Previews *Boats to Build* at
LaZona Rosa." *Austin American Statesman*, September 3, 1992.

DeLuca, Dan. "Country Changes Course." *Philadelphia Inquirer*, April 20, 1997.

DeYoung, Bill. "Talk, Talk, Guy Clark." *Goldmine*, March 28, 1997, 14–15.

"Doctor R. S. Bonner Buried Here Monday." *Texarkana Gazette*, May 17, 1928.

*Dublin Blues* review. *Modern Screen's Country Music*, 1995 (specific date unknown).

Eliscu, Lita. "Texas Bar-B-Q, Guy Clark, the Other End." *SoHo Weekly News*
(New York City), December 9, 1976, 37–38.

"Ellis Clarks Entertain in Honor of Son's Birthday." *Rockport Pilot*, November
11, 1954.

Escott, Colin. Liner notes, *The Late Great Townes Van Zandt*. Tomato Records,
1972.

Fallwell, Marshall. "Watch This Face: Guy Clark." *Country Music*, August 1974,
20.

Flippo, Chet. "Country Music's Drop in '96: Cause for Worry?" *Billboard*,
January 25, 1997.

———. "The Genre-Bustin' Rise of Insurgent Country—Movement Helps
Broaden the Music's Base." *Billboard*, December 28, 1996, 1, 111.

———. "Triple-A, Country Outlets Warm to Roots Music." *Billboard*, December 28, 1996, 81.

———. *Wanted! The Outlaws*, RCA Records liner notes, January 1976

Freeman, Doug. "We Were from Texas: Guy Clark and the High Price of
Inspiration." *Austin Chronicle*, July 19, 2013.

Friskics-Warren, Bill. "Guy Clark's Live Album Lends a New Vitality to His
Time-Worn Classics." *No Depression*, March/April 1997, 72–75.

Gaillard, Frye. "New from Nashville: Picker-Poet Guy Clark." *Charlotte Observer*, 1975 (specific date unknown).

Goodman, Frank. "A Conversation with Guy Clark." Puremusic.com, December 2002. www.puremusic.com/guy2.html.

Graham, Renee. "Good Ol' Country Music: Admit It. You Miss It." *Boston Globe*, May 8, 2001.

"Grandma Holds Court: Fort Towson Woman Made U.S. Commissioner by Judge Williams; She Hits Bootleggers Hard," *Daily Oklahoman*, June 6, 1926.

"Guy Clark's Debut a Country Classic." *Melody Maker*, June 5, 1976.

Hall, Douglas Kent. "Mr. Bojangles' Dance: The Odyssey and Oddities of Jerry Jeff Walker." *Rolling Stone*, December 19, 1974, 9.

Harrington, Richard. "Country Comes to Town." *Washington Post*, March 17, 2006.

Havighurst, Craig. "CMA Executive Works on How to Tune up Country Music's Image." *Tennessean*, September 30, 2000.

———. "Even Label Chiefs Don't Listen to Country, One Says." *Tennessean*, March 16, 2001.

———. "Reading Music: Is There Still a Market for Country Music Fan Magazines?" *Tennessean*, August 13, 2000.

———. "Record Execs Pose Solutions for Country Slump." *Tennessean*, April 19, 2001.

———. "Point of CMA Campaign's New Slogan Leaves Some Puzzled." *Tennessean*, May 13, 2001, Business section page 1E, 4E.

———. "Wit Happens—Surprise! Tart-Tongued Robbie Fulks Doesn't *Really* Hate Nashville." *Country Music*, April/May 2000, 20.

———. "With These Hands—Guy Clark Doesn't Just Play and Love Guitars; He Builds Them With as Much Care as He Writes His Celebrated Songs." *Tennessean*, January 2004.

Hedgepeth, William. "Kris Kristofferson, First Superstar of the New Country Music." *Look*, July 13, 1971.

———. "The Talk of the Townes." *New Yorker*, 1997.

———. "Townes Van Zandt—Messages from the Outside." *Hittin' the Note*, May 1977.

Helton, Lon. "Better Radio—Not Music—Key to Keep 'Sky from Falling.'" *Radio & Records*, September 20, 1996, 58.

———. "For Format Panelists, It's a Matter of Music." *Radio & Records*, November 1, 1996, 52.

Hilburn, Robert. *Boats to Build* review. *Los Angeles Times*, 1992 (specific date unknown).

"Hillbilly No More, Country Music Sweeps the U.S.A." *Look*, July 13, 1971.

Himes, Geoffrey. "Guy Clark—Built to Last." *No Depression*, August 31, 2002.

Hoffman, Jan. "Cookin' Texans." *Village Voice*, May 13, 1981.

Horvath, Elek. "Dreaming up a Kitchen—The *Journal of Country Music* Interview with Guy and Susanna Clark." *Journal of Country Music* 22, no. 2 (2002): 28–33.

Hudson, Kathleen. "Great Music Continues to Flow into the Hill Country." *Mountain Sun* (Kerrville, Tex.), February 25, 2004.

Hunter, James. "Striking the Right Chords—The Fine Art of A&R in Country." *New Country*, November 1996.

Hurt, Edd. "Guy Clark—Walkin' Man in a Digital World." *American Songwriter*, September/October 2006, 41–46.

Kael, Pauline. "Heartworn Highways." *New Yorker*, June 1, 1981.

Keel, Beverly. "Forbidden Themes—What Radio Won't Let You Hear." *Music Row*, November 8, 1996, 10–13.

———. "The Real Cost of High Dollar Deal." *Music Row*, November 23, 1996.

Kosser, Michael. "Everybody Wants to Know: What's Gonna Happen to Country?" *In Review*, April 21, 1997, 29.

———. "What You Don't Know about Music Row—With Mainstream Country Slumping, Nashville's Record Labels Diversify." *In Review*, March 1997, 22–23, 28–29.

Langer, Andy. "Waitin' 'Round to Live—'Poet,' the Little Tribute That Could." *Austin Chronicle*, February 8, 2002.

Lanham, Tom. "Guy Clark, Better Living through Incisive Songwriting." *Pulse!*, March 1995, 41.

Leichtling, Jerry. "Guy Clark Sings a Novella." *Village Voice*, 1975 (specific date unknown).

Leigh, Spencer. "What's up With the Walkin' Man?" *Country Music People*, August 2006, 12–16.

LeMay, Joseph. "The Next Great Diva: A Q&A with Grace Potter." *American Songwriter*, March 14, 2011. http://americansongwriter.com/2011/03/the-next-great-diva-a-qa-with-grace-potter.

Linder, Greg. "Guy Clark." *Twin Cities Reader*, 1978 (specific date unknown).

Littleton, Bill. "Susanna and Guy—Real Artists at Producing His-and-Her Hits." *Country Style*, June 1976, 6.

Lock, Cory. "Counterculture Cowboys: Progressive Texas Country of the 1970s and 1980s." *Journal of Texas Music History* 3, no. 1 (Spring 2003): 14–23.

Magee, Harvey. "Song Painter." *Hank: Tennessee's Original Music Magazine*, February 2, 1976, 16–19.

McCall, Michael. "Country Songwriters—A Top 10 Who's Who on Today's Music Row." *Pulse!*, June 1995, 85.

———. "Married to Multimedia—Guy and Susanna Clark Exhibit Their Mutual, Multifaceted Talents." *Country Music*, March 2002, 110.

———. "An Outlaw Comes Home—Steve Earle Talks about Sobriety, Settling Down and Seeking New Challenges." *Country Music*, June/July 2000, 44–45.

McLeese, Don. "Guy Clark's New Release Demands Notice." *Austin American Statesman*, November 3, 1992.

McVey, Dick. "The State of Country Music: Is Greed Hurting the Business?" *Performance*, June 13, 1997.

Miller, Ed. "Texas Music Notes: The Yin and the Yang, a Dallas Whore," *Fort Worth Star Telegram*, 1975 (specific date unknown).

Miller, Townsend. "Clark Gaining Fans as Singer." *Austin American Statesman*, September 2, 1976.

Monahan, Casey. "Writing Music and Performing 'Symbiotic' to Guy Clark." *Austin American Statesman*, October 21, 1988.

Moore, Lee. "Watermelon's Heinz Geissler, Growing Pains." *Austin Chronicle*, March 17, 1995.

Morris, Chris. "Clark Charts New Ground on Asylum," *Billboard*, January 9, 1993, 28.

Morris, Edward. "Can Country Survive?" *Country Music*, Winter 2000, 42–43.

———. "Hitting the Limits." *Music Row*, October 1983, 24.

Moss, Marissa. "Guy Clark: The High Price of Inspiration." *American Songwriter*, July 22, 2013. http://americansongwriter.com/2013/07/guy-clark-the-high-price-of-inspiration.

Nash, Alanna. "Country Reviews: Guy Clark *Keepers*." *Entertainment Weekly*, March 21, 1997, 74.

———. "Guy Clark Shapes Some Classics." *Stereo Review*, January 1993, 75.

Novak, Ralph. "Picks and Pans: *Boats to Build*, Guy Clark." *People*, April 19, 1993, 23–24.

Oermann, Robert K. "Disclaimer: Lyle Lovett, 'Private Conversation.'" *Music Row*, November 23, 1996.

*Old Friends* review. *Village Voice*, 1989 (specific date unknown).

*Old Friends* review. *Washington Post*, 1989 (specific date unknown).

*Old No. 1* review. *Playgirl*, 1975 (specific date unknown).

*Old No. 1* review. *Playboy*, March 1976.

Oppel, Pete. "Clark Gains New Polish after 9 Months on Circuit." *Dallas Morning News*, November 3, 1976.

———. "Clark Shows Why He's One of a Kind." *Dallas Morning News*, January 21, 1976.

———. "Guy Clark a Dream Chaser in Song." *Dallas Morning News*, February 1, 1977.

———. "Guy Clark Old No. 1 and Rising." *Dallas Morning News*, January 25, 1976.

O'Rear, Caine. "Role Models: Guy Clark." *American Songwriter*, November 11, 2011. http://americansongwriter.com/2011/11/role-models-guy-clark.

———. "Role Models: Emmylou Harris." *American Songwriter*, November 7, 2012. http://americansongwriter.com/2012/11/role-models-emmylou-harris.

Palmer, Robert. "Nashville: Sound: Country Music in Decline." *New York Times*, September 17, 1985.

Patoski, Joe Nick. "Guy Clark—Desperado Waiting for His Fame." *Austin Sun*, 1975 (specific date unknown).

Patterson, Rob. "Q&A with Rodney Crowell." *Texas Music*, no. 36 (Fall 2008), 24–29.

Petty, Celinda. "Monahans Native Guy Clark: A Texas Storyteller and Bona Fide Hero." *Monahans News*, February 9, 1995.

Phillips, Beau. "Improving the Record-Radio Relationship." *Radio & Records*, April 11, 1997, 16.

Powers, Ann. "Record Brief: Guy Clark, *Boats to Build*." *New York Times*, January 17, 1993.

Racine, Marty. "1,000 Mourners Pay Tribute to Musician Lightnin' Hopkins." *Houston Chronicle*, February 1, 1982.

Randall, Alice. "The Teachings of Guy Clark." *American Songwriter*, August 2, 2013. http://americansongwriter.com/2013/08/the-teachings-of-guy-clark.

Reed, Bobby. "Unfettered Angel: Shedding Management, Label and Status Quo, Emmylou Harris Is Soaring with a Prolific Burst of Creative Energy." *Country Music*, Holiday 1999, 30–34.

"Regular Guy." *Melody Maker*, August 21, 1976.

Rockwell, John. "Guy Clark Is Singing Progressive Country." *New York Times*, December 9, 1976.

Roland, Tom. "Country May Have Seen the Bottom." *Tennessean*, March 9, 1997.

———. "Industry Trying to Decide Its Direction for Future." *Tennessean*, 1994 (specific date unknown).

Russell, Rusty. "Edge of the Row—Jim Lauderdale Rules." *Music Row*, October 8, 1996, 19.

Saviano, Tamara. "Heart's Desire—Lee Roy Parnell's Passion for Music Is Equaled Only by His Love of the Land." *Country Music*, Holiday 1999, 36–39.

Scelsa, Vin. "Sounds—Guy Clark Is One of the Great American Musicians of the Past Two Decades; Writers Far More Famous Idolize This Man, Tremble at the Mention of His Name." *Penthouse*, date unknown.

"Science Foundation Director Named." *Oklahoman*, October 28, 1967.

Scoppa, Bud. "Grievous Angel." *Rolling Stone*, March 1, 1973.

Skanse, Richard. "For the Sake of the Song—These 20 Essential Singer-Guitarists Helped Write America's Story." *Acoustic Guitar*, March 2015, 34–35.

———. "Guy Clark." *Performing Songwriter*, December 1998, 20.

———. "Guy Clark cover story feature." *Texas Music*, Fall 2006.

———. "Guy Clark Q&A." *Lone Star Music*, September 2006.

————. "A Man Must Carry." *Texas Music*, Spring 2004, 58, 62–63.

Spong, John. "He Ain't Going Nowhere." *Texas Monthly*, January 2014. http://www.texasmonthly.com/articles/he-aint-going-nowhere.

————. "Urban Cowboy Turns 35." *Texas Monthly*, June 2015. http://www.texasmonthly.com/the-culture/urban-cowboy-turns-35.

Stark, Phyllis. "Country Debates Crossovers—Radio Split over Multiformat Exposure." *Billboard*, June 28, 1997, 1, 81, 88.

Stimeling, Travis. "Viva Terlingua! Jerry Jeff Walker, Live Recordings and the Authenticity of Progressive Country Music." *Journal of Texas Music History* 8 (2008): 21–32.

Sylvester, Bruce. "Country Junction—10 Questions for Guy Clark." *Goldmine*, April 4, 2003, 28.

Taggart, Patrick. *Texas Cookin'* review. *Austin American Statesman*, date unknown.

Terrell, Steve. "Guy Clark: On Writing, Life without Townes and *Cold Dog Soup*." *Thirsty Ear*, August/September 1999.

White, Timothy. "Creating Country's 'Far' Side." *Billboard*, 1997 (specific date unknown).

"W. N. Greene Passes Away in State Hospital," *Hugo (Okla.) Daily*, November 28, 1926.

Wonsiewicz, Steve. "Country's Old-New Balancing Act." *Radio & Records*, March 21, 1997, 29.

Wood, Gerry. "The Clarks—Man, Wife Duel in Chart Race. " *Billboard*, 1975 (specific date unknown).

Wooton, Richard. "Guy Clark, Interviewed at the Office of Travis Rivers in Nashville, Tennessee." *Omaha Rainbow*, no. 15 (December 1977).

Zepeda, Joe. "Legendary Performer Clark Comes to Hill Country Opry." *Mountain Sun* (Kerrville, Tex.), February 25, 2004.

## Books

Bowen, Jimmy, and Jim Jerome. *Rough Mix: An Unapologetic Look at the Music Business and How It Got That Way—A Lifetime in the World of Rock, Pop, and Country as Told by One of the Industry's Most Powerful Players*. New York: Simon & Schuster, 1997.

Dicaire, David. *The Folk Music Revival 1958–1970: Biographies of Fifty Performers and Other Influential People*. Jefferson, N.C.: McFarland, 2011

Evans, Nick, and Jeff Horne, *Song Builder: The Life and Music of Guy Clark*. [United Kingdom]: Amber Waves, Heartland Publishing, 1998.

Hardy, Robert Earl. *A Deeper Blue: The Life and Music of Townes Van Zandt*. Denton: University of North Texas Press, 2008.

Hudson, Kathleen. *Telling Stories, Writing Songs: An Album of Texas Songwriters*. Austin: University of Texas Press, 2001.

Jackson, John Porter. *Taking the Tide: My Family's Ebb and Flow in Rockport, Texas.* J. Jackson, 2011.

Jennings, Waylon, with Lenny Kaye. *Waylon: An Autobiography.* New York: Warner Books, 1996.

Kennedy, Rod. *Music from The Heart: Rod Kennedy, Kerrville Folk Festival Founder/Producer—The Fifty Year Chronicle of His Life in Music (With a Few Sidetrips!)* Kerrville, Tex.: Eakin Press, 1998.

Malone, Bill C. *Country Music U.S.A.* Rev. ed. Austin: University of Texas Press, 1985.

Reid, Jan. *The Improbable Rise of Redneck Rock.* Austin: University of Texas Press, 2004.

Whitburn, Joel. *Joel Whitburn's Hot Country Songs, 1944–2008.* Germantown, Wisc.: Record Research and Billboard, 2008.

*Wagon Tracks: Washita County Heritage*, vol. 1, 1892–1976. Oklahoma City: Washita County [Okla.] History Committee, 1976.

## Audio

Clark, Guy. *Better Days.* Warner Brothers, 1984.

———. *Boats to Build.* Asylum/Elektra, 1992.

———. *Cold Dog Soup.* Sugar Hill, 1999.

———. *The Dark.* Sugar Hill, 2002.

———. *Dublin Blues.* Asylum/Elektra, 1995.

———. *Keepers.* Sugar Hill, 1997.

———. *My Favorite Picture of You.* Dualtone Music, 2013.

———. *Old Friends.* Sugar Hill, 1989.

———. *Old No. 1.* RCA, 1975.

———. *Somedays the Song Writes You.* Dualtone Music, 2009.

———. *Songs and Stories.* Dualtone Music, 2011.

———. *The South Coast of Texas.* Warner Brothers, 1981.

———. *Texas Cookin'.* RCA, 1976.

———. Unreleased RCA album, produced by Mike Lipskin, 1974. Collection of Mike Lipskin.

———. *Workbench Songs.* Dualtone Music, 2006.

Clark, Guy, Steve Earle, and Townes Van Zandt. *Together at the Bluebird Café.* American Originals, 2001.

———. *Together at the Bluebird Café, Part 2.* Unreleased. Collection of Bluebird Café.

Crowell, Rodney. *Street Language.* Columbia Records, 1986.

*This One's For Him: A Tribute to Guy Clark.* Icehouse Music, 2011.

*Where Love Goes*, soundtrack to book by Joyce Maynard, 1994.

*Unreleased Tapes (Guy Clark Collection)*

The Bob Edwards Show & Live@XM, XM Satellite Radio, February 16, 2005.

The Bob Edwards Show, Music City Mondays, Sirius XM Radio, November 29, 2010.

Guy Clark and Townes Van Zandt live at McCabes, 1991.

Guy Clark and Townes Van Zandt live at University of Texas, 1991.

Guy Clark live at Cactus Ballroom, Austin, Texas, May 15, 2005.

Guy Clark live at Cactus Ballroom, Austin, Texas, June 25, 2007.

Guy Clark live at Cactus Ballroom, Austin, Texas, September 18, 2008.

Guy Clark live at Cactus Ballroom, Austin, Texas, February 26–27, 2009.

Guy Clark "Stuff That Works" commercial for NAPA Auto Parts, October 2000.

Guy Clark *The Dark* radio special, hosted by Rusty Miller, Americana Entertainment, LLC, 2002.

*60th Birthday Tribute to Guy Clark.*

## Video

*American Music Shop* #909307, *Old Friends*, with Guy Clark, James McMurtry, Nanci Griffith. Guy Clark collection.

ASCAP Lifetime Achievement Award. October 1998. ASCAP Collection, Nashville.

ASCAP Living Video Archive, interview with Guy Clark, circa 2006. ASCAP Collection, Nashville.

*Austin City Limits* #103, Townes Van Zandt, 1976. *Austin City Limits* archives, Rock and Roll Hall of Fame, Cleveland, Ohio.

*Austin City Limits* #802, West Texas Songwriter Special, 1983. *Austin City Limits* archives, Rock and Roll Hall of Fame, Cleveland, Ohio.

*Austin City Limits* #2309, Celebration of Townes Van Zandt, December 7, 1997. *Austin City Limits* archives, Rock and Roll Hall of Fame, Cleveland, Ohio.

*Austin City Limits* #3403, Songwriters Special: Lyle Lovett, John Hiatt, Guy Clark and Joe Ely, May 7, 2008. Austin City Limits archives, Rock and Roll Hall of Fame, Cleveland, Ohio.

*Austin Pickers*, Townes Van Zandt with special guest Blaze Foley, 1984. Guy Clark collection.

*Bobby Bare and Friends*. Bareworks, Inc., Nashville Network, 1983. Guy Clark collection.

Burns, Ken. *The Dust Bowl*. Arlington, Va.: PBS, 2012.

*CBS Late Show with David Letterman*, July 21, 1998.

Clark, Guy. "Boats to Build" music video, Asylum Records/Vector Management 1992. Guy Clark collection.

————. "Baton Rouge" music video, Asylum Records/Vector Management 1992. Guy Clark collection.

————. Guy Clark, and Verlon Thompson live, Hotel du Nord, Paris, France, July 23–24, 2002. Guy Clark collection.

————. *Live at Dixie's Bar and Bus Stop*, Austin, Texas, 1984. May6 Entertainment, released November 25, 2013, Austin, Texas.

————. *Live from Austin, TX*. Los Angeles: New West, 2007. Recorded live, November 10, 1989, *Austin City Limits*.

Country Music Hall of Fame Artist in Residence Series, Guy Clark, Demetria Kalodimos, Genuine Human Productions, September 2006. Genuine Human Productions Archives, Nashville.

Country Music Hall of Fame Medallion Ceremony, Emmylou Harris induction, April 27, 2008. Tamara Saviano collection.

David Elkins. *Back to the Basics*. Documentary about Luckenbach, Texas, 1994. Guy Clark collection.

*For the Sake of the Song: The Story of Anderson Fair*. DVD. Houston: Ghost Ranch Films and Fair Retail Films 2010.

Grassrootstv.org. Guy Clark and Verlon Thompson live, February 19, 2010. Guy Clark collection.

Guy Clark biography and EPK, Asylum Records/Vector Management 1992. Guy Clark collection.

*Live from the Bluebird Café #218*, Guy Clark, Hal Ketchum, Verlon Thompson, October 16, 2000. Guy Clark collection.

Luckenbach, Texas, footage with Hondo Crouch, Jerry Jeff Walker, Guy Clark, and Gary P. Nunn; Michael Brovsky, producer, 1976–77. Guy Clark collection.

*Mountain Stage #304*, Guy Clark. West Virginia Public Broadcasting, 2002.

*Music City Tonight*, Guy Clark. Nashville Network, May 31 1995.

*Nashville Now!*, Guy Clark. Nashville Network, circa 1983.

*Nashville Skyline*, Emmylou Harris with Special Guests: Angel Band, Guy Clark, Rodney Crowell, Vince Gill. Home Team, 1993.

*Old Friends* concert, Guy Clark, Rodney Crowell, Vince Gill, Nanci Griffith, Emmylou Harris. Ryman Auditorium, May 15, 1999; directed by Peter Kimball. Peter Kimball collection.

*Summer of Love*, PBS *American Experience*, March 2007.

Texas Heritage Songwriters Association Hall of Fame inductee interview, Guy Clark, 2009. Texas Heritage Songwriters Association Archives, Austin, Texas.

*Wish I Was In Austin: A 70th Birthday Tribute to Guy Clark*, Center for Texas Music History, November 2, 2011. Center for Texas Music History Archives, San Marcos, Texas.

## Archives and Other Resources

Academy of Country Music
Americana Radio Chart, Gavin and Americana Music Association, 1995–2015
Aransas County Historical Society, Rockport, Texas
Briscoe Center for American History, University of Texas, Austin
John Avery Lomax Family Papers 1842, 1853–1986
Rob Roy Rice Papers, 1925–66
Richard King IV Collection, 1985–88
Bloodshotrecords.com
Broadcast Data Systems
Clark family archives, Rockport, Texas
Compassrecords.com
Country Music Hall of Fame, Nashville
Del Mar College transcripts, Corpus Christi, Texas
Grammy Archives
Guy Clark personal archives, Nashville
History.com
Keith Case archives
Kirkpatrick family archives
Kirkpatrick Foundation
Leadership Music, Nashville
Mary Gauthier personal archives, Nashville
MusicRow archives, Nashville
Nielsen, Soundscan record sales reports 1991–2013
RCA Records archives, Nashville
Tamara Saviano journals 2000–2015, Nashville
Allen County Historical Society, Scottsville, Kentucky
Susanna Clark letters and diaries, 1960–2012, Nashville
Ward County (Tex.) Archives, Monahans, Texas
Warner Brothers Records archives, Los Angeles

# LYRIC CREDITS:
# USED WITH PERMISSION

## Prologue

"Expose"
(Guy Clark/Rodney Crowell/Hank DeVito)
EMI April Music Inc. and Sony/ATV Tunes LLC and Little Nemo Music.
Administered by Bug Music

## Chapter One
"Monahans"
(Guy Clark)
Sunbury/Dunbar

## Chapter Three
"Blowin' Like a Bandit"
(Guy Clark)
Warner/Chappell Music, Inc.

## Chapter Five
"A Nickel For The Fiddler"
(Guy Clark)
Warner Chappell Music, Inc.

"Black Haired Boy"
(Guy Clark/Susanna Clark)
Warner Chappell Music, Inc.

## Chapter Six
"L.A. Freeway"
(Guy Clark)
Warner Chappell Music, Inc.

"Luckenbach, Texas (Back To The Basics of Love)"
(Chips Moman/Bobby Emmons)
Universal Music Publishing Group

## Chapter Seven
"Desperados Waiting For A Train"
(Guy Clark)
Warner/Chappell Music, Inc.

"The Ballad of Laverne and Captain Flint"
(Guy Clark)
Warner/Chappell Music, Inc.

## Chapter Eight
"South Coast of Texas"
(Guy Clark)
Warner/Chappell Music, Inc.

"The Randall Knife"
(Guy Clark)
EMI April Music, Inc.

## Chapter Nine
"Indian Cowboy"
(Joe Ely)
Joe Ely DBA Eiffel Tower Music

"Come From the Heart"
(Susanna Wallis Clark/Richard C. Leigh)
EMI April Music, Inc, Lion Hearted Music, GSC Music

"Better Days"
(Guy Clark)
EMI April Music, Inc.

## Chapter Ten

"Easy From Now On."

(Susanna Clark/Carlene Carter)

Bug Music OBO Songs of Cash, Inc.

"Ramblin' Jack & Mahan"

(Guy Clark/Richard C. Leigh)

EMI April Music, Inc., Lion Hearted Music, GSC Music

## Chapter Eleven

"Dublin Blues"

(Guy Clark)

EMI April Music, Inc.

"Black Diamond Strings"

(Guy Clark)

EMI April Music, Inc.

"Stuff That Works"

(Guy Clark/Rodney Crowell)

EMI April Music, Inc., Sony/ATV Songs LLC

## Chapter Thirteen

"Red River"

(Guy Clark)

EMI April Music, Inc.

"The Key to Life"

(Vince Gill)

Kobalt Music Pub America OBO Vinnie Mae Music

## Chapter Fifteen

"My Favorite Picture of You"

(Guy Clark/Gordie Sampson)

EMI April Music, Inc., Music of Windswept OBO Bughouse,
   OBO Dash8 Music

# INDEX